This volume offers an account of English literary culture in one of its most volatile and politically engaged moments. From the work of Milton and Marvell in the 1650s and 1660s through the brilliant careers of Dryden, Rochester and Behn, Locke and Astell, Swift and Defoe, Pope and Montagu, the pressures and extremes of social, political, and sexual experience are everywhere reflected in literary texts: in the daring lyrics and intricate political allegories of this age, in the vitriol and bristling topicality of its satires as well as in the imaginative flight of its mock-epics, fictions, and heroic verse. The volume's chronologies and select bibliographies will guide the reader through texts and events, while the fourteen essays commissioned for this Companion will allow us to read the period anew.

THE CAMBRIDGE
COMPANION TO
ENGLISH
LITERATURE
1650–1740

CAMBRIDGE COMPANIONS TO LITERATURE

The Cambridge Companion to Old English Literature
edited by Malcolm Godden and Michael Lapidge

The Cambridge Companion to Dante
edited by Rachel Jacoff

The Cambridge Chaucer Companion
edited by Piero Boitani and Jill Mann

The Cambridge Companion to Medieval English Theatre
edited by Richard Beadle

The Cambridge Companion to Shakespeare Studies
edited by Stanley Wells

The Cambridge Companion to English Renaissance Drama
edited by A. R. Braunmuller and Michael Hattaway

The Cambridge Companion to English Poetry, Donne to Marvell
edited by Thomas N. Corns

The Cambridge Companion to Milton
edited by Dennis Danielson

The Cambridge Companion to British Romanticism
edited by Stuart Curran

The Cambridge Companion to James Joyce
edited by Derek Attridge

The Cambridge Companion to Ibsen
edited by James McFarlane

The Cambridge Companion to Brecht
edited by Peter Thomason and Glendyr Sacks

The Cambridge Companion to Beckett
edited by John Pilling

The Cambridge Companion to T. S. Eliot
edited by A. David Moody

The Cambridge Companion to Renaissance Humanism
edited by Jill Kraye

The Cambridge Companion to Joseph Conrad
edited by J. H. Stape

The Cambridge Companion to Faulkner
edited by Philip M. Weinstein

The Cambridge Companion to Thoreau
edited by Joel Myerson

The Cambridge Companion to Edith Wharton
edited by Millicent Bell

The Cambridge Companion to Realism and Naturalism
edited by Donald Pizer

The Cambridge Companion to Twain
edited by Forrest G. Robinson

The Cambridge Companion to Whitman
edited by Ezra Greenspan

The Cambridge Companion to Hemingway
edited by Scott Donaldson

The Cambridge Companion to the Eighteenth-Century Novel
edited by John Richetti

The Cambridge Companion to Jane Austen
edited by Edward Copeland and Juliet McMaster

The Cambridge Companion to Samuel Johnson
edited by Gregory Clingham

The Cambridge Companion to Oscar Wilde
edited by Peter Raby

The Cambridge Companion to Tennessee Williams
edited by Matthew C. Roudané

The Cambridge Companion to Arthur Miller
edited by Christopher Bigsby

The Cambridge Companion to the Modern French Novel
edited by Timothy Unwin

The Cambridge Companion to the Classic Russian Novel
edited by Malcolm V. Jones and Robin Feuer Miller

The Cambridge Companion to English Literature, 1650–1740
edited by Steven N. Zwicker

THE CAMBRIDGE
COMPANION TO
ENGLISH LITERATURE
1650–1740

EDITED BY
STEVEN N. ZWICKER
Washington University, St. Louis

CAMBRIDGE
UNIVERSITY PRESS

PUBLISHED BY THE PRESS SYNDICATE OF THE UNIVERSITY OF CAMBRIDGE
The Pitt Building, Trumpington Street, Cambridge, United Kingdom

CAMBRIDGE UNIVERSITY PRESS
The Edinburgh Building, Cambridge CB2 2RU, UK   http://www.cup.cam.ac.uk
40 West 20th Street, New York, NY 10011–4211, USA   http://www.cup.org
10 Stamford Road, Oakleigh, Melbourne 3166, Australia

First published 1998
Reprinted 1999

Printed in the United Kingdom at the University Press, Cambridge

Typeset in Sabon 10/13 pt. [CE]

A catalogue record for this book is available from the British Library

Library of Congress cataloging in publication data

The Cambridge companion to English literature, 1650–1740, / edited by Steven N. Zwicker
p.   cm. – (Cambridge companions to literature)
Includes bibliographical references and index.
ISBN 0 521 56379 8 (hardback). – ISBN 0 521 56488 3 (paperback)
1. English literature – Early modern, 1500–1700 – History and criticism.
2. English literature – 18th century – History and criticism.
I. Zwicker, Steven N.   II. Series.
PR437.C36   1998
820.9'004 – dc21   98–30165
CIP

ISBN 0 521 56379 8 hardback
ISBN 0 521 56488 3 paperback

CONTENTS

List of illustrations   *page* ix
List of contributors   x
Preface   xi
Chronologies   xiv

Part 1: Contexts and modes

1 England 1649–1750: differences contained?   3
   JOHN SPURR

2 Satire, lampoon, libel, slander   33
   MICHAEL SEIDEL

3 Gender, literature, and gendering literature in the Restoration   58
   MARGARET A. DOODY

4 Theatrical culture 1: politics and theatre   82
   JESSICA MUNNS

5 Theatrical culture 2: theatre and music   104
   JAMES A. WINN

6 Lyric forms   120
   JOSHUA SCODEL

7 Classical texts: translations and transformations   143
   PAUL HAMMOND

Part 2: Writers

8   "This Islands watchful Centinel": anti-Catholicism and proto-Whiggery
    in Milton and Marvell   165
    CEDRIC C. BROWN

9   John Dryden   185
    STEVEN N. ZWICKER

10 John Wilmot, Earl of Rochester   204
    ROS BALLASTER

11 The authorial ciphers of Aphra Behn   225
    MARGARET FERGUSON

12 Swift, Defoe, and narrative forms   250
    JOHN MULLAN

13 Mary Astell and John Locke   276
    PATRICIA SPRINGBORG

14 Alexander Pope, Lady Mary Wortley Montagu, and the literature of
    social comment   307
    DONNA LANDRY

    Index   330

ILLUSTRATIONS

2.1   *Contrivance*, from Jonathan Swift, *Gulliver's Travels* (1726),   *page* 54
      Book 3, chapter 5.

4.1. Dorset Garden Theatre *c.* 1671, design attributed to Sir   85
      Christopher Wren.

4.2   A scene from Elkanah Settle's *The Empress of Morocco* (1673).   86

4.3   London playbill, 1725.   98

4.4   The Queen's Theatre, the Haymarket (1707).   100

Figs. 4.1–4.4 are reproduced from the collections of the Theatre Museum by courtesy of the Trustees of the Victoria and Albert Museum, London.

CONTRIBUTORS

ROS BALLASTER, Mansfield College, Oxford

CEDRIC C. BROWN, University of Reading

MARGARET A. DOODY, Vanderbilt University, Nashville

MARGARET FERGUSON, Columbia University, New York

PAUL HAMMOND, University of Leeds

DONNA LANDRY, Wayne State University, Detroit

JOHN MULLAN, University College, London

JESSICA MUNNS, University of New Orleans

JOSHUA SCODEL, University of Chicago

MICHAEL SEIDEL, Columbia University, New York

PATRICIA SPRINGBORG, University of Sydney

JOHN SPURR, University of Wales, Swansea

JAMES A. WINN, University of Michigan, Ann Arbor

STEVEN N. ZWICKER, Washington University, St. Louis

PREFACE

The aim of this volume is to introduce students to English literary culture in one of its most volatile and politically engaged moments. The literature created between the years of Republican ferment in the 1650s and the coalescence of a Georgian state in the early eighteenth century reflects the instability and partisanship of rebellious and factious times. But literature in these years was more than a mirror of the age. Literary texts were central to the celebration of civic persons and institutions, to polemic and party formation, to the shaping of public opinion, indeed to the creation of political consciousness itself.

From the efforts of Marvell and Milton to forge a Republican idiom in the 1650s to the brilliant careers of Dryden, Rochester, and Behn, of Locke and Astell, of Swift and Defoe, and of Pope and Montagu, the world of letters was enmeshed with policy and faction. Writers created their texts and fashioned their careers amidst recurrent political crisis and intrigue. Poetry and theatre were encouraged by powerful aristocrats, but political grandees also bullied and intimidated writers in a world marked by libel and slander. Dryden's elegies on Anne Killigrew and Henry Purcell are delicate constructs, Congreve's drama reveals a subtle theatrical culture, Swift's allegories and Lord Hervey's memoirs, Pope's verse epistles and Montagu's letters orchestrate an incomparable range of satirical registers. But we should be mindful, even as we read their work, that theirs was an age distinguished less by fragility and refinement than by obscenity and brutality, by the hectoring of the press and the anger of parliamentary debate, and by the fierce competitive edge of poetry no less than partisanship.

Political and social theory were the province of strong intellects – Thomas Hobbes, James Harrington, Algernon Sidney, John Locke, Mary Astell, and Bernard Mandeville – but political programs were often effected by thugs, urban crowds, and political gangs. The extremes of social and political experience are everywhere reflected in the aesthetic of this literature: in its daring lyrics and intricate political allegories, in the vitriol and bristling topicality of its satires as well as the imaginative flight of its mock-epics, fictions, and heroic verse.

The literature written between the years of the Cromwellian Protectorate and the coalescence of the Georgian state makes high demands on our knowledge of historical particulars, but its topicality should not obscure the reach of literary imagination, the inventiveness of literary design, or the generic resourcefulness of an age that created theatre rivaling the Elizabethan stage, opera that went beyond the extravagance of the early Stuart masque, political theory unmatched in analytical maturity – and always a capacity for irony that quickens the most familiar literary forms. Pastoral and georgic were deepened by Milton and Marvell; such modes as allegory, romance, and travel narrative were transformed into that modern epic form, the novel; while women writers, emboldened by the upheavals that challenged hierarchies and overturned the social order in the 1650s, wrote beyond the earlier confines of devotion and lyric. From what might seem a paradoxical space – opened after 1660 by court culture and Tory, indeed patriarchal, ideology – Aphra Behn, Mary Astell, and Delarivier Manley embarked on bold careers in theatrical writing, philosophy, and the novel. They not only imitated and admired men's writing, they also mocked and challenged their male peers.

Indeed, mockery, scandal, and envy drove much of the satire we associate with this world; but Marvell's *Last Instructions*, Swift's *Modest Proposal*, and Pope's *Dunciad* continue to engage us by their moral authority and their verbal mastery. Pastoral and epic were inverted and mocked to brilliant effect, but in these same years Virgil, Juvenal, Horace, and Homer were rendered classics not of translation but of a self-conscious national literature. Dryden's Virgil and Pope's Horace are texts central to English literary culture, and it is partly in homage to their evocative power that the late seventeenth and early eighteenth centuries have often been thought of as an Augustan age. This was a time that embraced strong cultural experimentation but also enduring meditations on antiquity.

Once glossed over as an age of court corruption and social comedy, a mere pause in the progress of English liberty and English letters, the years between the Cromwellian Protectorate and the coalescence of the Georgian state are now valued for their political sophistication, their philosophical – even spiritual – strengths, and their daring experiments with social and sexual identities. Indeed, it is the pervasive sense of irony and contingency in this age, its subtleties and ambiguities, and its inflections of gender that remind critics and scholars of nothing so much as our own time. To disclose the role of gender in this world is also to demonstrate how critical were definitions of masculinity and femininity to conceptions of style, to the discourse of sociability and sentiment, and to the languages of politics and state.

The discourse of sociability was also articulated through the press, by commerce, and in the reconfiguration of public spaces. The press had become more than a vehicle for inflaming partisan tempers, it was central to the cultivation of manners and the institution of fashion. The daily newspaper and the weekly journal, clubs and coffee houses, the library, the spa, and the public park all participated in the refashioning of self and society. And a financial revolution that began as a way of funding William III's wars to contain France resulted in an expanded domestic economy, in the swelling of professions, the creation of empire, the importation of luxury, and the profusion of that commodity called taste. How different taste and empire must have seemed from the world of Ranters and Muggletonians, but even as we calculate the distance between eighteenth-century civility and the projects of spiritual reform and political innovation of the 1650s, we should remember that the Republican past was deeply implicated in the aspirations and aesthetics, even the anxieties, of Georgian England.

The essays in this volume extend an invitation to read the major texts, to think about the central intellectual practices, and to imagine the relations among the books, people, and politics of Restoration and early eighteenth-century England. These essays introduce the critical perspectives that shape our current work in literary criticism and cultural history even as they remind us of the aesthetic theories and literary practices of Augustan England, a world in which social relations and the life of the state were inextricably bound to the imagination of writers.

CHRONOLOGIES

EVENTS AND TEXTS

1642   Last Christmas entertainment at court (6 January); beginning of the Civil Wars (22 August); closing of the London theatres (2 September)
        Browne, *Religio Medici*; Hobbes, *De Cive* (in Paris)

1644   Milton, *Areopagitica*

1645   Milton, *Poems*

1648   Filmer, *Anarchy of a Limited or Mixed Monarchy*; Herrick, *Hesperides* and *Nobles Numbers*

1649   Execution of Charles I (30 January); An Act for abolishing the kingly office in England (17 March); Commonwealth proclaimed (19 May)
        Charles I, *Eikon Basilike*; Lovelace, *Lucasta*; Ogilby, *Works of Virgil*; Milton, *Eikonoklastes*

1650   Davenant, *Preface to Gondibert*; Vaughan, *Silex Scintillans*

1651   Hobbes, *Leviathan*; Marvell writes *Upon Appleton House*

1653   Protectorate established (16 December)
        Cavendish, *Poems and Fancies*; Walton, *Compleat Angler*

1655   Cavendish, *The Philosophical and Physical Opinions, The Worlds Olio*

1658   Death of Oliver Cromwell, Lord Protector of England (3 September)

1659   Collapse of the Protectorate
        Baxter, *Holy Commonwealth*; Davenant, *Siege of Rhodes*

1660	Charles Stuart enters London on his thirtieth birthday (29 May); Pepys begins his *Diary*, (1 January); first meeting of the Royal Society (28 November)
1661	Coronation of Charles II (23 April)
1662	Royal Society chartered
1663	Butler first publishes *Hudibras*
1664	The printer Twyn executed for sedition Dryden and Howard, *The Indian Queen*; Evelyn, *Sylva*; Philips, *Poems*
1665	Second Anglo-Dutch War formally proclaimed (4 March); Great Plague (April to December) Hooke, *Micrographia*
1666	Great Fire of London (2 September)
1667	Peace Treaty of Breda concluding Anglo-Dutch War (21 July) Dryden, *Annus Mirabilis*; Marvell, *Last Instructions*; Milton, *Paradise Lost*; Sprat, *History of the Royal Society*
1668	Dryden appointed Poet Laureate Dryden, *An Essay of Dramatic Poesy*; Etherege, *She Would If She Could*
1671	Buckingham, *The Rehearsal*; Dryden, *The Conquest of Granada*; Milton, *Paradise Regained . . . To which is added Samson Agonistes*
1672	Declaration of Indulgence proffering religious freedoms
1675	Founding of Royal Observatory at Greenwich Dryden, *Aureng-Zebe*; Rochester, *Satyr Against Mankind*; Wycherley, *The Country Wife*
1676	Charles II signs Secret Treaty with Louis XIV (16 February) Etherege, *The Man of Mode*; Wycherley, *The Plain-Dealer*
1677	Behn, *The Rover*
1678	Oates and Tonge give evidence of a Popish Plot to kill Charles II and crown the Duke of York, Charles's Roman Catholic brother Bunyan, *The Pilgrim's Progress*
1680	Second Bill of Exclusion, aimed at preventing the succession

of James, Duke of York to the throne, defeated in the Lords
(15 November)
Burnet, *The Life and Death of the Earl of Rochester*; Filmer,
Patriarcha; Rochester, *Poems*

1681   Shaftesbury acquitted on charges of treason (24 November)
Blow, *Venus and Adonis* (dating not certain); Dryden,
Absalom and Achitophel (17 November); Marvell,
Miscellaneous Poems; Oldham, *Satires upon the Jesuits*

1682   Dryden, *Religio Laici*; Otway, *Venice Preserv'd*

1683   Russell and Sydney executed for treason

1685   Death of Charles II (6 February); coronation of James II
(23 April); Duke of Monmouth executed after raising arms
in rebellion against James II (15 July)
Killigrew, *Poems*

1687   James issues a Declaration of Indulgence (4 April)
Dryden, *The Hind and the Panther*; Halifax, *Letter to a
Dissenter*; Newton, *Principia Mathematica*

1688   Birth of James Francis Edward Stuart, son of James II and
Mary of Modena (10 June); William of Orange lands at
Torbay (5 November); James II flees to France (24 December)

1689   The crown is offered to William of Orange and Mary
(13 February); Toleration Act (24 May); Battle of the Boyne
(1 July)
Dryden, *Don Sebastian*; Locke, *A Letter Concerning
Toleration*; Purcell and Tate, *Dido and Aeneas* (performed)

1690   Locke, *Two Treatises of Government*, *Essay Concerning
Human Understanding*

1691   Purcell and Dryden, *King Arthur*

1693   Congreve, *The Double Dealer*; Rymer, *A Short View of
Tragedy*

1694   Bank of England established; death of Queen Mary
(28 December)
Astell, *A Serious Proposal to Ladies*; Dryden, *Love
Triumphant*

1695   Congreve, *Love for Love*; Locke, *The Reasonableness of
Christianity*; Southerne, *Oroonoko*

1696	Toland, *Christianity Not Mysterious*; Vanbrugh, *The Relapse*
1697	Treaty of Ryswick concluding Nine Years War (10 September) Blackmore, *Prince Arthur*; Collier, *Short View of the English Stage*; Defoe, *An Essay Upon Projects*; Dryden, *The Works of Virgil*
1698	Sidney, *Discourses;* Milton, *Prose Works*, ed. Toland
1700	Astell, *Some Reflections Upon Marriage*; Congreve, *The Way of the World*; Defoe, *The Pacificator*; Dryden, *Fables*
1701	Act of Settlement establishing the Hanoverian succession (12 June) Defoe, *The True-Born Englishman*; Dennis, *Advancement of Modern Poetry*
1702	Death of William III (8 March); coronation of Queen Anne (23 April) Clarendon, *History of the Great Rebellion*; Defoe, *Shortest Way with Dissenters*; *The Daily Courant* begins publication and runs until 1735
1703	Chudleigh, *Poems on Several Occasions*
1704	Battle of Blenheim (2 August) Newton, *Optics*; Swift, *Tale of a Tub*, *Battle of the Books*
1705	Steele, *The Tender Husband*
1706	Farquhar, *The Recruiting Officer*
1707	Proclamation of Union with Scotland (1 May)
1709	The Copyright Act; Act for the Encouragement of Learning Berkeley, *New Theory of Vision*; Steele, *The Tatler* begins and runs until 1711
1710	Sacheverill Trial (27 February–23 March)
1711	Handel, *Rinaldo*; Pope, *Essay on Criticism*; *The Spectator*; Shaftesbury, *Characteristics*
1713	Treaty of Utrecht (31 March) Addison, *Cato*; Berkeley, *Three Dialogues of Hylas and Philonous*; Pope, *Windsor-Forest*
1714	Death of Queen Anne (1 August); coronation of George I (20 October)

Gay, *Shepherd's Week*; Mandeville, *Fable of the Bees*; Pope, *Rape of the Lock*

1715   Jacobite rising

1716   The Septennial Act extending the life of parliaments to seven years (26 April)
Montagu, *Town Eclogues, Court Poems*

1719   Defoe, *Robinson Crusoe*

1720   South Sea investment scheme (bubble) collapses (1 September–14 October)

1722   Defoe, *Moll Flanders*; Steele, *The Conscious Lovers*

1723   Waltham Black Act creating fifty new capital offences including poaching hares and fish (27 May)

1724   Burnet, *History of My Own Time*; Handel, *Giulio Cesare*; Oldmixon, *Critical History of England*

1725   Pope's edition, *The Works of Shakespeare*

1726   Swift, *Gulliver's Travels*

1727   Death of George I (11 June); coronation of George II (11 October)

1728   Gay, *Beggar's Opera*

1729   Pope, *Dunciad Variorum*; Swift, *Modest Proposal*

1730   Thomson, *The Seasons*

1731   *Gentleman's Magazine*; Lillo, *The London Merchant*

1732   Bentley, ed. *Paradise Lost*; Fielding, *Covent Garden Tragedy*; Hogarth, *A Harlot's Progress*; Mandeville, *Origin of Honour*

1733   Bolingbroke, *Dissertation Upon Parties*; Hogarth, *A Rake's Progress*; Wortley Montagu and Lord Hervey, *Verses Addressed to the Imitator of Horace*

1737   Stage Licensing Act (24 June)

1738   Wesley's 'conversion'
Bolingbroke, *Patriot King*; Johnson, *London*

1740   War of Austrian Succession
Richardson, *Pamela*

1741	Fielding, *Shamela*; Handel, *Messiah*; Hume, *Essays, Moral and Political*
1742	Walpole resigns as Prime Minister (11 February) Fielding, *Joseph Andrews*
1744	Formal declaration of war with France
1745	Death of Walpole (18 March); landing of the Young Pretender in Scotland (23 July) Hogarth, *Marriage-à-la-Mode*; Edward Young, *Night Thoughts*
1747	Richardson, *Clarissa*
1749	Fielding, *Tom Jones*; Johnson, *Vanity of Human Wishes*; Cleland, *Memoirs of a Woman of Pleasure*
1751	Gray, *Elegy Written in a Country Churchyard*
1752	Adoption of the Gregorian (New Style) calendar
1753	The Jewish Naturalization Bill (passed 22 May; royal assent 7 June; repealed 20 December); founding of the British Museum
1755	Johnson, *Dictionary of the English Language*
1758	Hume, *Enquiry Concerning Human Understanding*
1760	Death of George II (25 October); coronation of George III (22 September 1761) Sterne, *Tristram Shandy*
1763	Wortley Montagu, *Letters Written During her Travels* (published posthumously)
1765	Walpole, *The Castle of Otranto*
1766	Goldsmith, *The Vicar of Wakefield*
1768	Founding of the Royal Academy
1771	First edition of *The Encyclopedia Britannica*
1776	American Declaration of Independence

CONTEMPORARY LIVES

Thomas Hobbes	1588–1679
Izaak Walton	1593–1683
Oliver Cromwell	1599–1658
Charles I	1600–1649
Edmund Waller	1606–1687
Sir William Davenant	1606–1668
John Milton	1608–1674
Edward Hyde, Earl of Clarendon	1609–1674
Gerrard Winstanley	1609–1676
Queen Henrietta Maria	1610–1669
James Harrington	1611–1677
Samuel Butler	1612–1680
Thomas Killigrew	1612–1683
Richard Baxter	1615–1691
Sir John Denham	1615–1669
Sir Roger L'Estrange	1616–1704
Abraham Cowley	1618–1667
Sir Peter Lely	1618–1680
John Evelyn	1620–1706
Lucy Hutchinson	1620–?
Andrew Marvell	1621–1678
Roger Boyle, Earl of Orrery	1621–1679
Anthony Ashley Cooper, Earl of Shaftesbury	1621–1683
Henry Vaughan	1622–1695
Algernon Sidney	1622–1683
Margaret Cavendish, Duchess of Newcastle	1623–1673
John Aubrey	1626–1697
Sir Robert Howard	1626–1698
Robert Boyle	1627–1691
John Bunyan	1628–1688
William Temple	1628–1699
George Villiers, Duke of Buckingham	1628–1687
Charles II	1630–1685

John Tillotson	1630–1694
John Dryden	1631–1700
John Locke	1632–1704
Katherine Philips	1632–1664
Anthony à Wood	1632–1695
Sir Christopher Wren	1632–1723
James II	1633–1701
George Savile, Marquis of Halifax	1633–1695
Samuel Pepys	1633–1703
George Etherege	1634–1691
Robert Hooke	1635–1703
Thomas Betterton	1635(?)–1710
Thomas Sprat	1635–1713
Queen Catherine of Braganza	1638–1706
Charles Sackville, Earl of Dorset	1638–1703
Sir Charles Sedley	1639–1701
Aphra Behn	1640–1689
Thomas Rymer	1641–1713
William Wycherley	1641–1716
Thomas Shadwell	1642–1692
Sir Isaac Newton	1642–1727
Gilbert Burnet	1643–1715
Sir Godfrey Kneller	1646–1723
John Wilmot, Earl of Rochester	1647–1680
James Scott, Duke of Monmouth	1649–1685
William III	1650–1702
Jeremy Collier	1650–1726
John Churchill, Duke of Marlborough	1650–1722
Jane Barker	1652–1726
Thomas Otway	1652–1685
Sir Richard Blackmore	1652–1729
Nahum Tate	1652–1715
John Oldham	1655–1683
Mary, Lady Chudleigh	1656–1710
Jacob Tonson	1656(?)–1736

Edmond Halley	1656–1742
John Dennis	1657–1734
Queen Mary of Modena	1658–1718
Henry Purcell	1658–1695
Thomas Southerne	1659–1746
Daniel Defoe	1660–1731
George I	1660–1727
Anne Killigrew	1660–1685
Robert Harley, Earl of Oxford	1661–1724
Nicholas Hawksmoor	1661–1736
Richard Bentley	1662–1742
Queen Mary II	1662–1694
Matthew Prior	1664–1721
Sir John Vanbrugh	1664–1726
Queen Anne	1665–1714
Mary Astell	1666–1731
Jonathan Swift	1667–1745
William Congreve	1670–1729
Bernard Mandeville	1670–1733
Delarivier Manley	1670–1724
John Toland	1670–1722
Anthony Ashley Cooper, 3rd Earl of Shaftesbury	1671–1713
Joseph Addison	1672–1719
Richard Steele	1672–1729
Nicholas Rowe	1672–1718
Isaac Watts	1674–1748
Robert Walpole, Earl of Oxford	1676–1745
George Farquhar	1678–1707
Henry St. John, Viscount Bolingbroke	1678–1751
George II	1683–1760
Edward Young	1683–1765
John Gay	1685–1732
George Berkeley	1685–1753
George Frederick Handel	1685–1759
Alexander Pope	1688–1744

James Stuart, the Old Pretender	1688–1766
Samuel Richardson	1689–1761
Lady Mary Wortley Montagu	1689–1762
George Lillo	1693–1739
Philip Stanhope, Earl of Chesterfield	1694–1773
John, Lord Hervey	1696–1743
William Hogarth	1697–1764
James Thomson	1700–1748
John Wesley	1703–1791
Henry Fielding	1707–1754
Samuel Johnson	1709–1784
David Hume	1711–1776
Laurence Sterne	1713–1768
Lancelot "Capability" Brown	1716–1783
Thomas Gray	1716–1771
David Garrick	1717–1779
Horace Walpole	1717–1797
Tobias Smollett	1721–1771
Christopher Smart	1722–1771
Adam Smith	1723–1790
Sir Joshua Reynolds	1723–1792
Thomas Gainsborough	1727–1788
John Wilkes	1727–1797
Oliver Goldsmith	1728–1774
Edmund Burke	1729–1797
Thomas Percy	1729–1811
William Cowper	1731–1800
Charles Churchill	1731–1764
James Macpherson	1736–1796
Edward Gibbon	1737–1794
Thomas Paine	1737–1809
George III	1738–1820
James Boswell	1740–1795

Part 1

CONTEXTS AND MODES

I

JOHN SPURR

England 1649–1750: differences contained?

The century between the Civil War and the reign of George II saw the transformation of English political, social, and religious life. The scale of these changes may become apparent if we put our late twentieth-century selves into the picture for a moment. We would surely find mid seventeenth-century England strange and alien, violent, authoritarian, credulous, poverty-stricken; confident that virtue and responsibility were inherited by gentlemen and monarchs; cowering in the face of a hostile environment and universe; absorbed in a religious fundamentalism which included hair-raising beliefs about salvation, other denominations, and the cosmic purpose of history. Mid eighteenth-century England, on the other hand, although not "modern," would be full of familiar sights and institutions. For all its inexplicable addiction to the periwig, this was a world comfortingly like our own in many ways: with newspapers and tea-tables, concerts and public parks, insurance policies and sales taxes, a post office and bureaucrats; a world which held a place for "the ladies," "the consumer," "the citizen," and "the middle class." This society of shopkeepers and professional people valued diversity and regarded competition and social mobility as natural, yet it also respected politeness and restraint and feared "enthusiasm." Even to compare the England of Charles I and George II in this way is to reinforce the common perception that England progressed from chaos to stability, from traumatized victim of "intestine" civil wars to a self-confident trading and maritime power. Certainly Hanoverian England seemed a stable society: the political system weathered storms; trade boomed and the wealth it generated led to the sophisticated urban life whose architectural expression is still visible in the squares and terraces of cities like Bath, Cheltenham, Bristol, Edinburgh, and York. England was on the way to becoming Great Britain – a Union was achieved with Scotland in 1707 – and Great Britain was well on her way to imperial grandeur. In the seventeenth century England had been a weak and peripheral European state, but after 1688 she became a leading actor on the continental stage

3

and eventually, in 1713, rewrote the European balance of power. Sheltered by the wooden walls of her navy, confident in the prowess of her generals and armies, Britain was by the 1750s fighting France and Spain on four continents and on the high seas.

But success and refinement are not the whole story. Again and again we are brought up with a jolt when we encounter the animosities and bigotry, the bizarre beliefs and casual cruelties just beneath the surface of Augustan life. No century should be glibly summarized, but for all its glitter and its advance toward civility, this was also an ugly, violent age. Ugly in its systematic brutality toward the poor and the criminal – the eighteenth century saw a huge increase in the penalties for offenses against property – and ugly in its political uses of terror – from the executions during the Popish Plot to the massacre at Glencoe and the campaign after Culloden. The masses were easily stirred to violence against those who seemed alien – whether it was Catholics or Nonconformists, the Irish or the Jews, or evangelicals like John Wesley. In their portraits of Britain in the 1730s and 1740s, William Hogarth, John Gay, and Alexander Pope have left powerful images of a corrupt and vicious society.[1] Perhaps this is the dark underbelly of any age, and more historically significant are the deep political and religious animosities which ran through English life during this period. Every town and every city, almost every parish, was divided. The strife of Dissenter against churchman, Protestant against Catholic, and Whig against Tory suggests that English enmities ran deep. It is true, of course, that the English people had never been as one, but the sixteenth-century Reformation and its repercussions, followed by the crisis of Stuart kingship in the 1630s, engendered antagonisms which the ensuing civil war and military rule could only deepen and embitter. After the restoration of the monarchy each subsequent decade seemed to bring another confrontation or crisis which was incorporated into a complicated legacy of hatreds, confirming the old in their feuds and poisoning the next generation.

Augustan England seems then to have been divided, ill at ease with itself, and yet successful and stable. And it is this paradox which fascinates historians and sets them hunting for the process by which England tamed sectarian hatreds. How were these differences contained so that political and social life could continue? A variety of answers have been offered to this question by historians taking a variety of approaches. In 1967 J. H. Plumb traced the growth of political stability in England between 1675 and 1725; he defined this stability as government by a single party, the control of the legislature by the executive and the creation of a sense of common identity in those who wielded social, economic, and political power, in other words, the system of Sir Robert Walpole, the dominant minister of the 1720s and 1730s. The possibility of stability, and the raw materials of stability (such as jobs in the gift of the government), had all existed from the 1670s, according to Plumb; it was just that the political nous was lacking, a deficit supplied by the genius of Walpole. Plumb implies that the political instability of the later Stuart period had much the same causes as the political stability of Walpole's era: the contest for seats in parliament, for government sinecures, for spoils, was behind "the rage of party," but once these spoils were all dispensed by one consummate politician, they would contribute toward cohesion and political inertia. This picture was elaborated by Geoffrey Holmes, who took a wider social view and argued that the new professions were vehicles of social mobility. The expansion in the numbers of lawyers, doctors, teachers, clergymen, naval and army officers, and civil servants, and just as importantly the increase in their social status, meant that those excluded from political life could find avenues for advancement and outlets for their energies.[2] Jonathan Clark, on the other hand, plays down the pace of social and economic change, and indeed challenges the economic reductionism of accounts which suggest that political power inevitably flowed toward a new middle class. He stresses instead the persistence of pre-industrial forms and mentalities, a slavish loyalty to monarchy and the Church of England, a deeply aristo-cratic society and political system, and the retention of a confessional state, in which office and power were restricted to conforming Anglicans, until the 1830s. The main threats to the stability of this *ancien régime* were dynastic rivalry until the defeat of Jacobite hopes in the Forty-five and thereafter religious heterodoxy. In response, many historians have reas-serted that eighteenth-century men and women recognized elements of aristocratic government in the British system, but saw theirs as "a commer-cial society" and themselves in Blackstone's phrase as "a polite and commercial people."[3]

Among the many changes afoot in Augustan England two trends deserve special attention. One is the growth of the state. What under Charles I had been a classic multiple monarchy – a collection of territories united by nothing more than the person of their ruler – was becoming a state. Kingship would never be the same after 1649, and much of the next century was devoted to finding ways to curb a king and to weld two kingdoms and several provinces into a single Great Britain. The emergent state rested on sound finance: the royal debt was replaced by a national debt based on the state's credit not the king's; local government by amateurs was reinforced by a professional bureaucracy; and the state's fiscal demands soared. Entwined with the rising state was the emerging "public sphere." This term is shorthand for the world of newspapers, pamphlets, coffee-houses, and political and social clubs, in which the nation's affairs were discussed and public opinion was formed. The development of the state and the public sphere were accompanied by the growth of trade, science, and technology, the waning of religious zeal, the rise of reason and politeness, and the legitimation of political "party." And together they contributed to the formation of practices and institutions which made it possible for the English to live with their undeniable cultural, religious, and political diversity. Differences were managed: while contest was allowed in some arenas, partisanship was rigorously excluded from other areas of life. In practice, the same institution or process could embody both principles: "by a curious paradox that same transformation of the professions which was so vital a force for social change in England became almost by the same token, a powerful tranquillising and stabilising agent as well.'[4] The same can be said of the many associations which came into being in our period. This was a great age of joining and belonging: from leisure activities such as subscription concerts, musical societies, choirs, and bell-ringing, to discussion clubs and coffee-houses, from setting up almshouses and hospitals to building bridges and policing the community, men of property and good will came together because that was simply the most effective way of getting things done. Contradictory impulses were often at work simultaneously. Religious and political partisanship led to strife in existing institutions of church and local government; new clubs and societies, cultural and philanthropic bodies, were then created either as alternative institutions or as neutral meeting grounds.[5]

And what is true of the professions and voluntary associations, of polite society and political parties, is also true of works of the literary imagination. It is no function of this essay to survey the literary achievements of Augustan England, but it is impossible to disentangle literature and its makers from political and social life, or indeed the imagination from politics. It is not simply that so much of the literature was topical, partisan, and satirical. Nor that these writers were so deeply engaged – as politicians themselves, as self-appointed spokesmen of the age, or as Grub Street hacks making a profession of journalism and pamphleteering. It is rather that Augustan literature provided the language in which politics was conducted, it supplied the metaphors of monarchy and the discourses of civility and commerce: it did much to constitute the public sphere. And, naturally, it is implicated too in the paradoxical process of change and stability: it manages to thrive on ideological difference and yet simultaneously contain animosities.

6

Revolution to revolution, 1649–1689

Shortly after Charles I's execution on 30 January 1649, the office of king was abolished. While the new republic was ostensibly governed by a parliament, power lay with the New Model Army and its leader Oliver Cromwell. The New Model represented the "good old cause," and its complex, often contradictory, agenda of religious liberty, social reform, and messianic expectations, but it was out of step with the overwhelming majority of the country, and especially those who held property and influence. This was Cromwell's quandary: on the one hand, he was personally committed to the godly; on the other, settlement could only come from placating the gentry. Under Lord Protector Cromwell – as he became in 1653 – policy see-sawed between godly reform and traditional political institutions. Radicals often felt betrayed and conservatives were wary. But the general trend of the 1650s was toward ever more tried and trusted constitutional forms. Monarchy was a flawed system, especially if the monarch was, like Charles I, unable to temper his own concerns and accommodate the different currents of public feeling. But no better system, none which could contain and manage all these differences, was on offer. This point was rubbed home in the chaotic months after Cromwell's death in 1658. The godly cause disintegrated, and army units vied with each other and with civilian politicians, until with military backing an elected Convention met in April 1660. It was the Convention, from which ex-royalists had been excluded, that voted for the restoration of Charles II. On 29 May, his birthday, Charles arrived in London.

Charles was aware of his wide political debts and took care to conciliate wherever possible – reprisals were small-scale and many ex-Cromwellians found royal favor at the center and in the provinces. Religious policy, however, was at odds with the conciliatory political settlement. The restoration of the Church of England with most of its pre-1640 powers intact disappointed those who had been led to expect a wider national church and it denied the "liberty to tender consciences" which Charles had explicitly promised. Moreover the settlement created a new category, Dissent, which was an uneasy combination of all the dissident religious groups, ranging from the conservative Presbyterians to the sectarian Quakers and Baptists. The distinction between churchman and Dissenter was to spread like a stain, inevitably coloring all of Restoration life. The settlement confirmed a sense that Anglicanism was a sure sign of loyalty and political trustworthiness and that Dissent was synonymous with king-killing puritanism. This was underlined by a series of laws of the 1660s, known misleadingly as the "Clarendon Code" after

Lord Chancellor Clarendon, which persecuted Dissenters and restricted office-holding to communicant members of the Church of England. These measures failed to create a one-party state but succeeded in keeping the memories and issues of the 1640s and 1650s simmering away.

The first precarious decade of the restored monarchy was punctuated by risings and plots, plague and fire, and naval defeats, and culminated in Charles's attempt to solve his diplomatic, religious, and financial problems at a single audacious stroke in 1672. Charles declared war on the Dutch in alliance with Louis XIV of France; he issued a Declaration of Indulgence which suspended all the penalties against Protestant Dissenters; and he announced a suspension of the repayments on his debts. Unfortunately, the quick victory needed to clinch this bold bid eluded Charles. Parliament was recalled and the king was castigated for his arbitrary setting aside of the religion and church "as established by law." In no uncertain terms Charles was told that he had no power to suspend parliamentary statutes or to dispense individuals from the provisions of statutes. More opposition was probably generated by the declaration's unconstitutional character than by its attempt to improve the position of non-Anglicans. Grudgingly parliament offered war funds, but extorted in return a Test Act which was designed to exclude Roman Catholics from public office. In 1673 Members of Parliament gave voice to the emerging "Country" opposition which helped to give a new shape to politics. A drift toward a more arbitrary style of government was perceived in Charles's close links with France and in the attempts of the Earl of Danby, the king's chief minister from about 1675, to "manage" parliament through a system of placemen and bribery and in the interests of "the old Cavaliers and the Church party." The preference shown toward "the Church party" was suspect in itself. Many of the English believed that the bishops of the church were unnecessarily intolerant toward the Dissenters, and, even worse, that they encouraged Charles and his brother in grandiose ambitions of absolutist government. As Andrew Marvell put it in 1677, "there has now for diverse Years a Design been carried on, to change the lawful government of England into an Absolute Tyranny, and to Convert the Established Protestant Religion into down-right Popery."[6] The growing realization that Charles might not produce a legitimate heir, and the fact that James, Duke of York, a professed Catholic married to an Italian Catholic princess since 1673 was next in line to the throne, did much to fuel anxiety about the growth of popery and arbitrary government.

Then in the autumn and winter of 1678 the nation and parliament were convulsed, first by Titus Oates's fanciful revelations of a Popish Plot, involving the murder of the king, the burning of London, and the massacre of 100,000 Protestants, and then by the genuine disclosure of Danby's secret negotiations with France. The hysteria of political life over the next three years was, and still is, shocking; it can be explained in part by such factors as deep-rooted anti-popery, the coincidental expiry of press censorship, three general elections, and the deliberate politicization of the masses and of office-holding; but much of the story can only be explained by fear and rumor, denunciation and counter-allegation, and the sheer pressure of events. By the spring of 1679, with a second Test Act on the statute book and the trials of plotters underway, the central political issue was no longer the investigation of the plot, but the parliamentary exclusion of the Duke of York from the succession to the throne. Interference in the rights of royal succession was an explosive issue – it implied constitutional innovation, even rebellion, and it could by extension undermine all inherited property rights. The exclusionists claimed to be defending Protestantism, but to many they seemed to be promoting Dissent. Voters and MPs faced a choice of two evils, each of which was stigmatized by a pejorative nickname: those who supported the monarchy and the rights of James to succeed were dubbed "Tories" after Irish Catholic brigands of that name, and the exclusionists were slandered as "Whigs," a colloquial Scottish term for Presbyterian rebels.[7] As so often in this era, extremism bred extremism. Although the attempts of the Tory propagandists to turn the tables on their opponents by creating an alternative "Whig plot" were never successful, they certainly managed to tar the Earl of Shaftesbury, the Whig leader, his allies, and his witnesses with sedition, republicanism, and Dissent. The years after 1681 saw a "Tory revenge," an attempt to drive Whigs from public life and the century's worst wave of persecution of Dissenters.

In 1685 James II succeeded to the throne with the blessing of the Church of England, a well-disposed parliament, and some loyal and competent ministers (including Clarendon's sons). He also came to the throne with the overriding ambition to restore Roman Catholicism to England and to repeal the Tests. Historians tend to see him as the victim of an *idée fixe* rather than as an absolutist, but contemporaries can be excused if they found these distinctions more difficult to draw. James saw off the foolhardy rebellion of the Duke of Monmouth, Charles II's bastard, and the victory confirmed the king in his belief that God was on his side and that he was justified in increasing the army. James soon realized that his Tory supporters would not cooperate in the demolition of the Anglican political monopoly and he turned instead to an alliance of all those groups hitherto excluded – Catholics, Dissenters of many hues, including Quakers, and former Cromwellians, Parliamentarians, and Whigs. James displayed his authority by violating the Test Act, having the courts rubber-stamp his dispensing power, and in April 1687 exerting his suspending power in a Declaration of Indulgence which effectively granted religious toleration. His comprehensive attack on the Tory hold over government also included a purge of JPs and the militia, the intrusion of Catholics into the universities, the ejection of the fellows of Magdalen College, Oxford, and the trial of seven bishops for their part in the clergy's refusal to read the reissued Indulgence from the parish pulpits.

Across the North Sea, the Dutch prince William of Orange, James's son-in-law, was watching English affairs anxiously, and by the spring of 1688 was actively preparing to intervene in England. William prepared his ground carefully, ensuring both backing from James's opponents and the benign attitude of Tories. He deliberately courted bipartisan support – identifying himself with Tory causes, claiming to want only a free parliament and to protect the rights of his wife, James's daughter Mary, after the birth of a male heir to James in June. On 5 November William and his troops landed at Torbay in Devon. Through several tense weeks, William's and James's armies maneuvered while the real battle was fought out in print: James lost his propaganda war, he lost his generals – John Churchill changed sides – and he lost confidence, paralyzed by indecision and nosebleeds: after one botched attempt at flight, James left for France on 23 December.

The Glorious Revolution was a moment of political unity in late December and January. It was bipartisan action, and although the Whigs later misappropriated the credit, this was not a Whig revolution. In 1688–89 the general line was that God had intervened, that divine providence had altered the course of the succession. God had raised up the Prince of Orange like another Moses or David "to Deliver his People from the most Pitiful State and Condition."[8] On 28 January 1689 the Convention Parliament resolved that James had abdicated and the throne was vacant. The evasive language was deliberate. It threw the responsibility onto James and made no reference to any deposition. Like so much else about the Revolution, this resolution was to be reinterpreted in years to come as if James had been deposed for breaking an original contract between ruler and people. Such a Whig rereading of the Revolution, with all it implied about the nature of English monarchy, and all that it owed to the post-1688 popularity of John Locke's political philosophy, was only possible because of the huge changes brought about under William III.

The last of the Stuarts, 1689–1714

The opportunity to redefine the constitution was missed in 1660; the role of parliament, the precise limits of the royal prerogative, and the location of sovereignty were left undecided. Politically, Charles took the path of expedience and placated his erstwhile enemies rather than his long-suffering friends. He then spent twenty-five years squirming under his self-imposed restraints and trying to wriggle out of his dependence upon parliament; it is a measure of his and his brother's partial success in freeing themselves – in, for instance, keeping a standing army without parliamentary sanction, or suspending and dispensing with the operation of various laws – that the Convention Parliament of 1689 devoted itself to the task of tying William to various conditions "more strictly . . . than other princes had been before."[9] The resulting Declaration of Rights may have been "an implied contract" between William and his new subjects. That was certainly what radical Whigs in the Convention Parliament intended. The declaration spells out James II's misdeeds, asserts the nation's ancient liberties, declares William and Mary king and queen, and sets forth the immediate succession. But William did not promise to respect these liberties before he was crowned – they were simply read to him and his queen at a curious ceremony in the Banqueting Hall at Whitehall. Later, the declaration became a statute, the Bill of Rights, with the additional proviso that the monarch cannot be, nor be married to, a Roman Catholic. The royal assent may have been assumed to be a promise to respect these rights: yet the act had no provisions to ensure that these pious and rather airy principles were enforced.[10]

Many would also see the religious settlement of 1662 as a missed opportunity, but the "Toleration Act" of 1689 was at best a partial remedy for religious division. It extended no right of toleration, it simply "indulged" or exempted Protestant Dissenters from the penalties of a long list of statutes, all of which remained in force. Even to qualify for these exemptions, Nonconformists had to register and take a series of oaths. The country's estimated 60,000 Roman Catholics, of course, gained nothing from the Act. The civil disabilities borne by non-Anglicans such as exclusion from all public office and from the universities remained in place; and in 1711 and 1714 Tory parliaments enacted serious limitations on the toleration enjoyed by Protestant Dissenters. Nor can the Toleration Act of 1689 be said to have been popular. Many moderate Nonconformists had aspired to reunion with the Church of England. But moves for a reunion or "comprehension" failed, and so the Toleration Act applied to perhaps four times more Protestants than had originally been intended: in 1715–18 it was estimated that there were 338,000 Dissenters out of a national population of 5.4 million.

Another direct consequence of the Revolution of 1688–89 was England's involvement in the front line of major European wars for eighteen of the next twenty-three years. William of Orange had intervened in England because he needed to bring her into his war against Louis XIV, but once he had gained the English throne William was also forced to defend it against Stuart forces in Scotland and Ireland. William spent summer after summer – sixty-two months of his reign in total – campaigning abroad. The Nine Years War (1689–97) saw William bogged down in the Netherlands, staving off French advances, and rarely achieving any outright victory. So wasteful of men and money was this monotonous war that it convinced many at home of the virtues of a "blue water" strategy, a naval war against French trade, shipping, and colonies.

This unprecedented warfare was not cheap; the war of 1689–97 cost £5.5 million a year, the war of 1702–12, £8.5 million. And parliament in 1689 had deliberately kept William short of money. "If you settle such a revenue as that the king should have no need of a Parliament," said Paul Foley, Speaker of the House, "I think we do not do our duty to them that sent us hither."[11] William's ordinary revenue was less than £1 million a year, whereas James had £1.5 million. So parliament had to finance the war. The resulting Land Tax was fixed by an assessment of rental value and rated at two shillings in the pound in peace time and four shillings in wartime. Although accuracy of assessment varied, for most of William's and Anne's reigns the Land Tax was a 20 percent income tax on those who lived off rents: this is taxation on a twentieth-century scale. It represented 40 percent of the government's revenues and brought in £2 million each year. The efficiency of this tax helped to underpin the evolving public credit. The government was raising huge sums, some of them directly against parliamentary revenues such as the Land Tax, others against more long-term income, and others simply on public credit or, in other words, on confidence in the government's ability and intention to repay. That confidence was based not only on the fiscal system, but also on the Bank of England, which was established in 1694. The government borrowed from the Bank and from concerns such as the East India Companies and the South Sea Company, which was set up in 1711 as a device to convert the £9 million owed to government creditors into their stock in an independent financial enterprise. Investors who rushed to buy stocks in all of these institutions were generally rewarded with good returns on their money.

In 1689 William admitted that "whilst there was a war he should want a parliament."[12] In the long term, parliament's regular sessions and fiscal powers led to a new constitutional importance, but in the short term, parliament still needed day-to-day political management. After a flirtation with a mixed ministry of Tories and Whigs, William threw in his lot with a group of Whig aristocrats, Lords Somers, Halifax, Wharton, Oxford, and

Sunderland, known as the Junto. The opposition sniped from the back-benches at the Land Tax, the Bank, the influence of William's Dutch favorites, and led by Paul Foley and Edward Harley they scored some significant victories. In 1698 William was forced to accept a peace-time army of 7,000 English-born troops, rather than the 20,000 he wanted. In 1701 the Act of Settlement, which laid down the succession of the Hanoverians should Princess Anne die without children, included a great catalog of protest at William's perversion of the constitution. The Act imposed a series of statutory limitations on the monarch, who henceforth had to be a conforming Anglican; it stipulated that parliamentary consent was necessary for foreign wars; and it freed the judiciary from royal interference. The Act of Settlement was perhaps the most notable of the constitutional victories achieved over the crown during William's reign.

Queen Anne's reign coincided with England's second great bout against Louis XIV. While the Duke of Marlborough defeated the French, his ally the Earl of Godolphin took care of the home front. The two men served Anne as pragmatic political managers, working with politicians across the spectrum. However, their commitment to punitive peace terms became an obstacle to peace, and so by 1708 they had given way to Somers and Wharton, the great Whig ministers of the 1690s. War or peace became the great issue, not just in politics, but in social terms too. Contemporaries perceived English society as divided between the rival "monied" and "landed interests." Henry St. John claimed in 1709 that "the whole burden" of twenty years of war had fallen on "the landed interest," men who had "neither served in the fleets nor armies, not meddled in the public funds and management of treasure." Meanwhile the new monied interest had arisen on the back of "a sort of property which was not known twenty years ago." The monied interest was thought to "ruin those that have only land to depend on, to enrich Dutch, Jews, French and other foreigners, scoundrel stock-jobbers and tally-jobbers, who have been sucking our vitals for many years."[13] In part these interests were literary constructs: the landed interest gained a voice in Jonathan Swift's *Examiner* (1710–11), or less flatteringly in the figure of Sir Roger de Coverley, the archetypal squire who crossed swords with the merchant Sir Andrew Freeport in the pages of *The Spectator* and *Tatler*.[14] But in general the perception of social change was justified. Before 1688 the English were undertaxed and possibly under-governed by an amateur bureaucracy of gentlemen landowners; by the 1690s they paid a swingeing Land Tax, supported a huge National Debt, and found professional administrators interfering ceaselessly in their affairs. A society based on the ownership of land was giving way to a more complex society which included new professional and administrative classes, and the powerful "monied interest" that had no intention of giving up commerce and investment for a life of rural ease as convention had demanded.

The tensions naturally found political expression. The Tories were the party of the landed interest, constantly criticizing the Whigs for the war and their pandering to the whims of financiers, foreigners, and Dissenters. The Tory cry of "the church in danger" was particularly effective in mobilizing support: it rang from the lips of the rioters who in 1710 demonstrated their approval of Dr. Henry Sacheverell's vitriolic attacks on the Glorious Revolution by destroying Dissenters' chapels. The slogan seemed to find support too among the electorate, for the Tories generally succeeded at the polls whenever they invoked the dangers to the Church of England or the issue of foreign policy, just as the Whigs profited from their trump card, "the Protestant succession in danger." In 1710 the Tories captured power and offered a coherent vision of a paternalistic society and government which would retreat from deficit finance, foreign entanglements, and protection of dissident Protestants. Unfortunately their leadership did not match their platform: Harley and St. John (or the Earl of Oxford and Viscount Bolingbroke as they became) were personal rivals. And the Hanoverian succession issue loomed ominously: this was a problem for the Earl of Oxford, who had alienated Hanover by making a peace in 1713 which left Britain's allies in the lurch; and it exposed the variety of Tory attitudes to the succession – some Tories dreamt of a Stuart restoration, and a few, to whom Bolingbroke gave leadership, toyed with Jacobitism, the cause of James II and, after James's death in 1701, of his son, the so-called James III, the Pretender to the British throne. In the last months of Queen Anne, the Tory ministry was falling apart.

The Hanoverians, 1715–1745

God "has now saved us by a train of wonders," rejoiced the Whig bishop Gilbert Burnet on the accession of George I. "We were, God knows, upon the point of at least confusions, if not of utter ruin, and are now delivered and rendered as safe as any human constitution can be."[15] George himself – fifty-four years old, unable to speak English, honest but dull, preoccupied with the affairs of Hanover and of his dreary entourage – was hardly a wonder. The new king had made it plain that he had little time for Tories: a Whiggish ministry was formed under Earl Stanhope; Bolingbroke fled to the Pretender in France; and in the summer of 1715 the Highlands of Scotland rebelled in expectation of the Pretender and of a reciprocal English Jacobite rebellion. The Pretender arrived late, and the English rising not at all: the Fifteen was undermined by lack of unity and leadership. But the abortive rebellion led to the blanket proscription of the Tories from political life. The Whig ministry embarked upon a purge "down to the meanest" office-holder: in Middlesex alone, for instance, sixty-eight Tory JPs were dismissed. The way was being prepared for single-party government. In May 1716 the Septennial Act prolonged the existing Whig parliament for another four years and extended the maximum life of future parliaments to seven years; anti-Dissenter legislation was repealed; and an attempt was made to ensure a permanent Whig majority in the House of Lords. Like so many politicians before him, both Whig and Tory, Stanhope was attempting to ensure the permanence of his own party's grasp on power. It was in fact a junior minister and one-time dissident, Sir Robert Walpole, who came nearest to turning this dream into a reality.

The financial and political scandal caused by the boom and subsequent crash in the value of South Sea Company stock in 1720 destroyed Stanhope's ministry and gave Walpole his chance. He restored public credit, salvaged something for the stock-holders, and screened his ministerial colleagues from the worst of the accusations. Having established his ascendancy in the Commons, Walpole went on to enhance his standing with the king by exposing Bishop Atterbury's Jacobite plot in 1722. With similar adroitness, Walpole attached himself to the new king when George II succeeded his father in 1727. The late 1720s and early 1730s saw Walpole at his zenith, commanding majorities in the Commons, dominating the ministry, and secure at court – functioning, many believe, as the first Prime Minister. Walpole had no secret: he boasted that he was "no saint, no spartan, no reformer." He did not lead moral crusades: as Paul Langford observes, "Walpole stood for many things, fiscal economy, political prudence in defence of the Protestant succession, pragmatic wisdom in handling religious controversies, robust but unadventurous self-interest in dealing with foreign powers. Men of the world and political experience admired him."[16] Walpole's domination, the "robinocracy," was based on hard work and on force of personality: he was able to retain the confidence of both George I and George II and to convince them of the need to keep the Tories in the political outer darkness; he remained a member of the House of Commons so that he could overawe the backbenches. Of course, he was ensured of a solid phalanx of administration votes; the "corps" of government supporters comprised men in the pay of the crown or those returned for the many pocket boroughs controlled by the Dukes of Newcastle, Devonshire, and Argyll. But another explanation for his success was the absence of effective opposition.

There was little parliamentary opposition since those MPs not bought off were mainly Tory backbenchers stigmatized as Jacobites. Although the Tories were organized, they could hope for nothing from George I. Meanwhile, however, there was a growing list of Walpole's cast-off allies and friends, men like William Pulteney and Charles Townshend, who might be able to marshal more anti-government votes in parliament. Such opponents could make common cause with the extra-parliamentary opposition, now led by Bolingbroke, who had returned from exile, been pardoned, but barred from the House of Lords. He turned instead to the press and used his journal *The Craftsman* to mount his campaign against "the great man," Walpole, and his betrayal of all that 1688 had stood for. Bolingbroke and the "patriot" opposition decried the official corruption and the prevalence of "party"; they demanded the reduction of the standing army, a cutback in the number of placemen, the lifting of press restrictions, reduction of the national debt, and the revival of the Triennial Act. Direct comparisons were made between Walpole and earlier tyrants such as Sejanus and Cardinal Wolsey; Swift, Gay, and Pope enjoyed drawing parallels between the public robber Walpole and the notorious thief Jonathan Wild; the *Beggar's Opera* compared Westminster with Newgate Gaol; and when Gay got into trouble for his criticism, Swift ironically reminded him that "in this most refined Age, the Virtues of a Prime Minister are no more to be suspected than the Chastity of Caesar's Wife."[17]

Walpole suffered his first serious blow in 1733 when he proposed an unpopular excise tax. Business interests were hostile and the mob took to the streets chanting "no slavery, no excise, no wooden shoes." Losing support in the Commons, Walpole allowed the measure to drop, but then turned on his tormentors with such ferocity that Pulteney advised Bolingbroke to return to exile. Henceforth Walpole was on the defensive. He faced an increasingly talented array of enemies, including former friends like the Duke of Argyll, John Carteret, and Bishop Gibson, and by 1737 Frederick, Prince of Wales, had defected and taken up Bolingbroke's mantle. Protest greeted Walpole's agreement with Spain in 1739, which seemed to sacrifice British commercial and imperial ambitions to Hanoverian interests. When he was eventually forced into a war with Spain, Walpole so mismanaged it that he was defeated seven times in the lobbies in two months. In 1742 Sir Robert bowed out of office. George II continued to draw his ministers and majorities from the old corps of Whigs through the long years of the Pelham brothers' ascendancy, but in 1760 George III came to the throne, detesting the old corps and intent on annihilating the name of party. George III repudiated the very notions upon which Walpole and his heirs had based their oligarchy: the utter unacceptability of the Tories and the consequent necessity of one-party rule. The political pack-ice was at last breaking up.

Politics and party

The English are monarchists. Even at the height of the puritan revolution doctrinaire republicans were few in number. The early modern political nation believed in responsible, even balanced, monarchy and expected monarchs to respect the law, liberties, and property of their subjects. English laws "are our ancient title to our lives, liberties, and estates; and without which this world were a wilderness."[18] The ill-defined liberties protected by the law were essentially negative: the English propertied class saw itself as free from the encroachments of both the crown and those without property. Unfortunately Charles I and his two sons gave the English a distinct feeling that their law, liberties, and property were under threat. Although it is often asked whether the Stuarts aspired to an absolute monarchy on the model of that of their French Bourbon cousins, this is a misjudged question. Stuart intentions, or indeed abilities, were far less pertinent than the interpretation their subjects placed on their actions. The revolution of 1688 was essentially defensive. All who made the revolution, Whig or Tory, were convinced that the English enjoyed their liberty and property "as a right inherent in themselves, and never transferred, alienated or conveyed to any king."[19] In other words, the revolution was a reassertion that their rights were inalienable personal property, not the gift of a ruler. The people were supposed to have a "property" in their laws – laws, after all, made for the public good – and in their religion, and neither of these properties could be touched by a king acting without parliament. There is no doubt that the revolution located sovereignty in "the king-in-parliament," that is, in laws made by parliament and king together. The reality was plain to anyone who compared Henry VIII's or Edward VI's ability to impose a religion on their subjects with the fate of James II or the stipulation in 1701 that the monarch be an Anglican. In 1689 parliament became the guarantor of English rights. "We have had such violation of our liberties in the last reigns, that the Prince of Orange cannot take it ill, if we make conditions to secure ourselves for our future," asserted one MP in 1689.[20] But the constitutional conditions were nebulous and needed constant reassertion. Parliament's real power grew through the more gradual process of political and procedural maturation.

Despite, or perhaps because of, its successes in the 1640s, parliament did not see itself as part of the government of the country after 1660. John Miller has argued that parliament was emphatically not seizing the initiative during the 1660s and 1670s – which simply makes the developments after 1678 all the more novel.[21] The pressure for the statutory exclusion of James from the throne certainly was a seizing of the constitutional initiative; and after 1688, the European wars virtually guaranteed the permanence of parliament. For all the large number of placemen in the parliaments of the 1690s, repeated "tacks" of contentious issues to money bills ensured that the parliamentary opposition got its own way. And for all its overt flattery, there is the ring of truth in Walpole's admission to parliament in 1739 that he had lived long enough to know that his safety lay in the approbation of the House.

The growing political weight of parliament is largely explained by its purpose. Parliament was there to do the monarch's business and Augustan monarchs had plenty to put before it. The political pieties of the age were that parliament should be harmonious, that MPs came together to serve the common good and should be independent of both the government and the electorate; hence the detestation of "managers" or "undertakers," "faction," "party," or "formed oppositions," and either "placemen" or "instructions" to MPs from their constituents. But the realities were very different. Monarchs needed subsidies voted, alliances supported, and policies approved by parliament, and it was a prime duty of ministers such as Clarendon or Danby or Walpole to make sure this happened. But no single individual could deliver a majority for every proposal in both the Lords and Commons, especially as parliaments sat more often, were more frequently elected, and their taxes were more vital to the crown. In broad terms, monarchs increasingly saw that majorities could be delivered by several different political managers in several different combinations; the trick was to balance the managers' principles and pride in an effective cabinet council, and whenever possible to leave the monarch a degree of freedom of maneuver. The managers, some of them superlative in these dark arts, others mercurial figures of overweening ambition, were often rather distant from the supposed principle of "party" and prepared to work with men of any or all political persuasions: as one of the greatest of them, the Earl of Sunderland, summed it up, "what matter who serves his Majesty, so long as his Majesty is served."[22]

To the devotees of party, of course, it mattered intensely who served his majesty because careers, patronage, principles, and even policies depended upon it. Party was a deeply contentious issue, in part because it is a general notion rather than a concrete institution. Party referred not only to a group of individuals acting in concert; it was also a factious self-interested activity in the eyes of contemporaries. Party, it has been said, was like sin, universally condemned and widely indulged.[23] The taint of party was so feared that although they often discerned it in others, most people saw themselves as defending the constitution, promoting the common good, or advancing the cause of improvement. In parliament, the advent of party was vital to the legitimation of opposition. The modern notion that the executive needs to be kept in check by official and constant organs of opposition was not so obvious to the monarchical cast of mind. As late as 1757 it was a common view that "a form'd general Opposition" was one of "the most wicked combinations that men can enter into – worse and more corrupt than any administration."[24] Opposition, partisan opposition, conflicted with deep-rooted notions of duty, loyalty, law, and providence, it conflicted indeed with the posture of the main opposition group, the "Country" or "Country party."

The ideology of the Country was ostensibly a non-ideology. The Country had no principles nor programs beyond restraining the government: its most profound instinct was that that government governs best which governs least. Responsible government is prudent, low-taxing, and respectful of existing private, local, or parliamentary privileges. This was the view of landowners who saw their lands as entitling, even obliging, them to participate in local government and central decision-making. The Country wanted frequent parliaments full of independent men, and purged of placemen, so that they could properly scrutinize the executive; small armies and, better still, blue water policies; and an end to foreign entanglements. Country ideology could be seen as a set of immediate opposition slogans or as an instinctive substratum of the Tory party, but it also grew out of a notion of political virtue.

The Country outlook with its deferential, conservative values overlapped with a tradition of opposition which owed much to the republican Commonwealthmen of the 1650s. This tradition's central premise was that civic virtue was constantly in danger of corruption, that luxury or the human instinct to consume was a vice which politicians repeatedly exploited to deprive free people of their liberty. The moral health of the polity depended on a class of men possessing sufficient property to be able to play an independent part in government. What was dangerous was the growth of a class whose wealth flowed from investment in the government and upon whom the government was dependent for war funds. Such views were shared by a number of political leaders and political analysts who can be classified as Whigs of one kind or another; but by the time of Walpole the same ideas were being employed by figures like Swift, Bolingbroke, and Pope, who have to be seen as Tories. One helpful characterization of these disparate figures is that they spoke the political language of virtue rather than that of rights; in other words, they stressed the danger that voters, MPs, and parliament might become corrupt and abdicate their political responsibilities, whereas rights theorists laid more emphasis on the threat posed to individuals' rights by overmighty rulers or governments with standing armies and intrusive officials.

The Whig and Tory parties, however, were very different beasts from the Country; they represented "another level of political consciousness."[25] Whigs and Tories were competing for power and they stood for programs. If one party was in power, then for all the anti-party rhetoric the other was obliged to oppose the government. These were not modern political parties, but they often look like them. Whig and Tory positions first crystallized in the Exclusion Crisis. The Whigs were more of a coalition than a united party: some were moved by fear of James, others by a desire to help Nonconformists, yet others were part of the London radical tradition derived from the Levellers of the 1640s. In parliament the Exclusionist vote was precarious; by 1680 the backbenchers, whose fear of popery had led them at first to join in the Whig attack on Charles and James, began to identify the rabble-rousing methods and extreme rhetoric of the Whigs as a greater threat to their ordered world. MPs of this kind began to be convinced by the Tory cry that "1641 was here again." It was the controlling conservatism of these squires which ensured the failure of Exclusion as a parliamentary demand. The Exclusion battle helped give the Tories a sharper definition. The Tory position was based on real principles, the indefeasible divine right of monarchy, and non-residence. In Charles's last years, the Tories encouraged, and often invited, vigorous royal inter-ference in provincial government. The Commissions of the Peace were purged of all their opponents; and town charters were revised to give the Tories the electoral advantage. This was to give hostages to fortune: James II, and later George I, turned these weapons against the Tories themselves. For most of the 1680s, the existence of Whig and Tory parties can be attributed to mutual hostility and fear. Once the parties had cohered and men began to assume or be attributed the labels of Whig and Tory, once political and local offices began to be distributed according to party allegiance, a process of self-perpetuation had begun.

The Glorious Revolution, like the French Revolution, threw up enough dust to obscure its antecedents; and like 1789, it became a cause in itself: attitudes toward the Revolution and the settlement became the touchstones by which Whigs and Tories were identified. After 1689 the Whigs and Tories were clearly distinguished by their views on the Revolution and on the related issues of the succession, the defense of the Church of England, the conduct of "King William's war," and the abjuration of James II and his descendants. In particular, these clear party lines gave rise to party voting and discipline; thus it can be shown from division lists in Queen Anne's parliaments that the vast majority of MPs voted consistently on party issues. But the characters of the Whig and Tory parties were changing. The Whigs were becoming a party of government, an aristocratic, Court-inclined, set of managers; the sort of politicians who were deeply involved in the institutions and financing behind the wars: in short, the sort of men who propped up Walpole and his administration. The Tories were more ambiguous: many retained a residual loyalty to James II, the rightful king, and his heirs even while recognizing William as the *de facto* king; in parliament Tories accepted the leadership of Edward Harley and supported the Country protests against placemen and standing armies – it is often claimed that the 1690s saw the Tories being educated in the ways of party and opposition. Doubt over their loyalty to William was always a weak spot for the Tories. The Junto Whigs took advantage of the 1696 assassination plot against William to subscribe an Association affirming that William was "rightful and lawful king," and when 100 MPs and 26 Lords refused to sign they were tarred as Jacobites. Under James's daughter Queen Anne, the Tories seemed a coherent party, campaigning on "the church in danger" slogan, legislating against Occasional Conformity and dissenting academies, and lobbying for office and place: this was decidedly not Country party behavior.

Hanoverian party politics manage to be very clear cut and quite baffling. Since Tories had no chance of office, the labels of Whig and Tory could be almost meaningless, to the point that anyone who voted with the government after 1714 tended to be classified as a Whig. This convinces many scholars that Whig–Tory divisions had in reality given way to a Court–Country split. One view is that both parties had Court and Country wings under Anne, but after 1714 the Tories were solely a Country party. It then became the task of Court Whigs to prevent the Country wings of the Tory and Whig parties from forming an alliance, which was done by smearing the Tories as Jacobites. Yet, "despite such impediments, by 1760 Court and Country had effectively replaced tory and whig."[26] On the other hand, it is still worth asking what Hanoverian Whigs and Tories actually believed in. The Whigs had very little connection with the pro-Dissent, liberal principles of their predecessors: they were in cahoots with the Church of England and her bishops, and in 1711 had even backed the Occasional Conformity Bill to gain dissident Tory help against the peace policy; they were no friends to wide electorates, frequent elections, or even freedom of expression. Although the Tories still bore the stigma of Jacobitism, there was an organized Tory party in the constituencies and at Westminster led by astute politicians such as Sir John Cotton and Sir William Wyndham.[27] Yet it is doubtful whether they could realistically expect to be taken into government; Walpole had spent too long persuading himself and his royal masters of their untrustworthiness; and most Tories were vociferous in their support of the Church of England and their criticism of a Hanoverian bias to British foreign policy, neither of which endeared them to suspicious monarchs.

It was inevitable that the advent of political parties also saw a widening of political activity in society. Nothing helped to politicize the nation like the frequent and bitterly fought elections of the period: the three elections in 1679 and 1680 were a dress rehearsal for the eleven general elections held between 1689 and 1713 (that is, on average, one every two years). The electorate was probably 4.6 percent of the population in 1715 – which was the largest electorate before 1832 – but some seats were "popular" or open, with a wide franchise, while others were closed boroughs in the pocket of some magnate. Geoffrey Holmes concludes that the elections of this period tended to exaggerate, but not misrepresent, the will of the people.[28] If that is so, then the country was Tory on most issues, and the only Whig majorities were gained in 1708 and 1715 at the time of invasion scares. Of course, the electorate, like the franchise, was only hazily defined; at some stage, those who could vote merged with those who, despite being unenfranchised, formed the wider audience for politics. Memories were still fresh of the unprecedented political debate and activity of the 1640s and 1650s which had formed attitudes and expectations that were not to be denied. From 1695 until the Walpole years the press was free of government control, and those disseminators of news, rumor, and propaganda, the newspapers, periodicals, clubs, and coffee-houses, flourished. Both men and women became fiercely partisan: when the upper-class Ann Clavering was told by an acquaintance that her extreme Whig views would repel suitors, she retorted, "O madam . . . you mistake that matter. I despise all Tories, and were their estates never so large; and yet don't despair, for I am sure the Whigs like me better for being true to my party."[29]

The capital was an important forum for popular politics. During the Exclusion Crisis the London crowds were managed and manipulated by sophisticated propaganda.[30] The popular Whig platform asserted that parliament was the best defense of English liberties, and indeed the best defense of the king, against the threat of popery. This message was slanted toward the Nonconformists by the insinuation that the intolerant Church of England aided and abetted the growth of popery and arbitrary government. Meanwhile the Tory crowd was told that the Nonconformists and Whigs were to blame for dividing the Protestant cause and thus leaving the nation vulnerable to the common enemy of popery. After 1688 the Whig politicians of London shifted their ground, just as they did in parliamentary politics, and the London Tories came to represent the cause of "liberty" in city politics.[31] This Tory populism aimed at giving the freemen of the city a greater say in the election of aldermen and it drew much of its strength from the small traders and manufacturers who were being left behind in the Whig boom.

Popular politics of this sort was organized around clubs, meetings, and processions, and so it was not that surprising when these activities spilled over into disorder and riot. Yet this disorder never seems to have contained a real threat of rebellion or revolution. It is doubtful whether radical Whigs could have launched a rising in London after the Exclusion Crisis. Holmes thinks that the Sacheverell rioters of 1710 were "respectable," with clearly specified and ideologically informed aims (i.e., tearing down Nonconformist meeting houses): the Whig and Tory mobs, the Church and Jacobite mobs, even the "No Excise" crowds, all seem to have been mouthing the slogans of their social superiors, rather than any distinctive grievances of their own. Politicians and parliament were also prepared to give way to opinion "without doors," as happened in the Excise Crisis, over war fever in 1739, or the Jew Bill. The only rebellion of our period (excluding the invasions of 1688, 1715, and 1745) was Monmouth's rising of 1685, which drew upon the strength of the good old cause in the West Country. This puritan legacy was probably the reservoir of English political radicalism: former Cromwellians, ex-soldiers and sectaries, artisans and Nonconformists formed a shadowy underground which bred many abortive plots during the 1660s and 1670s. However, their potential leaders, men like Algernon Sidney or Edmund Ludlow, were in exile: it was the Popish Plot and Exclusion Crisis which brought these radicals once again to the fore in alliance with Shaftesbury and the Whigs. The ideology of this radical Whig party was complex: here there are hints of Leveller ideas, there evidence of die-hard republicanism; the radicals were convinced that Charles was subverting parliament and that civil rights were in jeopardy; but the most significant and pervasive strand of their thought was their hatred of religious intolerance and persecution. This mentality has been recently brought to life in Richard Ashcraft's study of John Locke's *Two Treatises*; here Locke's work appears as firmly democratic and as a clear justification for rebellion after the failure of Exclusion, and as a rationale behind the Whig plot to assassinate Charles II and his brother at Rye House in 1683. Ashcraft's Locke is firmly placed within the radical camp. Yet the Locke of the eighteenth century was a far more moderate figure: the fate of Locke, his later reputation, may stand as an example of the fate of English radicalism. The radical tradition was recuperated, it was claimed by the Whig aristocrats and oligarchs, and turned into one more prop of the social order. But it could equally be said that radical opposition had lost its purpose now that opposition was becoming institutionalized as party politics. The structure of English politics was partisan and people were beginning to see that this had benefits as well as costs. "In all free governments there ever were and will be parties," observed Edward Spellman in 1743; "parties are not only the effect, but the support of liberty."[32]

State and society

One measure of the strength of a state is the coercive force at its disposal. The naked power of military might, from Cromwell's bashaws to Louis XIV's dragoons, from James II's Catholic Irish troops to George II's Hessian mercenaries, was something with which people were familiar, and something which they feared. James II had built a formidable army by 1688, but his 20,000 men were as nothing compared to the huge armies under William and Anne: 70,000 men were in English pay in 1694 and over 100,000 a decade later. But these troops were paid by parliament and they were on the continent: the furore over William's attempt to maintain a standing army in peace time after the 1697 Peace of Ryswick illustrates that the nation had no time for royal armies at home.

Despite appearances the Augustan state was not a military state. It was principally a bureaucratic and tax-raising machine. By the 1720s, it employed 12,000 permanent administrators and had become the largest employer, borrower, and spender in the economy. The process probably began in the 1640s when parliament imposed an excise tax and a monthly assessment. Charles II's government took over the collection of its own taxes, while the Treasury established oversight of income and expenditure and organized efficient repayment of loans. The Land Tax sustained the government's credit during the wars against Louis XIV, but after 1714 its values dwindled in comparison with the excise, which by the 1720s was worth more to the government than all its other revenues put together. For all the importance of the Land Tax, in general terms this period saw a decisive switch from direct taxation of land and landed wealth to indirect taxation on consumption. Customs were paid on imported raw materials and basic foodstuffs; excise tax was payable on a range of domestically produced goods such as beer, spirits, cider, malt, hops, salt, leather, soap, candles, paper, and starch. Working people were now taxed on the necessities of life and the taxation was enforced by professional employees of the crown.

From the perspective of its predecessors the post-1640 state was intrusive and heavy-handed; but by comparison with other Western European states, the Augustan state was a ramshackle anomaly with some notable weaknesses. For instance, in 1660 crown and gentry recognized their need of one another; and in return for parliamentary support, the gentry were allowed a free hand in the shires. Thus the bargain at the very foundation of the restored monarchy made ideas of establishing a centralized administrative machine irrelevant. Eighteenth-century governmental policies, and the increasingly uniform, professional, and accountable government of the parishes and towns of Britain, were a result of JPs, constables, aldermen, and their communities making common cause with the state. When it came to the taxes which underpinned the war effort, we are reminded that the state was implementing and harnessing the energy of the propertied classes, those who thought a war was necessary, just, or even beneficial: "warfare on the English model was a triumph for an enterprising and acquisitive society, not an authoritarian state."[33] Although the increase in government tax receipts in this period has often been assumed to reflect economic growth, it now seems that the rise was due to increased taxation. The economy was certainly growing – at 0.69 percent per annum in real terms between 1700 and 1760 – but the spectacular increases were a nineteenth-century phenomenon. The most significant developments of the late seventeenth and early eighteenth centuries were rising agricultural productivity, an increase in the number of people living in towns, and an increase in the number of people engaged in non-agricultural production. By 1750 less than 50 percent of the population was working in agriculture. The rest were engaged in industry, commerce, services, or the professions.

As we have already seen, these economic and social changes had created new forms of property and new elites, which had a more intimate relationship with the government and the state than the landed gentry. The monied interest would have been unpopular in any context, as yuppies exploiting the mysteries of high finance, where money miraculously makes money, and the deeply suspicious stocks, shares, and securities allow speculators to accumulate without having contributed. But they were doubly damned because of their involvement with the government and with the war which the landed gentry believed they were subsidizing. The professions, too, were often associated with the state, which created all the opportunities for pen-pushers, tax-collectors, and career soldiers. These changes represented a tremendous growth in the leisured classes and of those with a little extra time and money to spend on themselves, whether it was by consulting a doctor, visiting Bath, or simply going shopping. In brief, life was improving for all. From about 1680, population, economic resources, and employment seem to have maintained a happy balance. Money wages were rising and prices of consumable goods remained steady and some, particularly luxuries, fell. English working people now ate wheat bread, rather than rye bread, and could afford and obtain small self-indulgences such as ribbons, laces, mirrors, toys, combs, and the like: a skilled worker in eighteenth-century London had the financial means to buy not only cheap print – ballads and chapbooks – but even substantial novels selling at six shillings a copy. Thanks to the growth of Britain's sea-borne trade, exotic luxuries such as fruit, coffee, tea, sugar, fabrics, and tobacco were arriving from the East and from the plantations of the New World. The stocks of provincial shopkeepers are testimony to the spread of gracious living, sophistication, and luxury to the country towns of Augustan England.

In what Peter Borsay dubs an "urban renaissance" the towns of England and Wales changed their style, ambience, even their functions, in this period. In short they became centers for leisure, civility, and consumption. Instead of being simply markets or industrial centers, towns became meeting places for the gentry and those who aspired to that status, for professionals, and for those who had made their money and now wished to enjoy it. Some of these towns such as Bath or Tunbridge Wells, made a speciality of leisure and became resorts, while others amalgamated functions. Whether the measure is the number of coffee-houses, daily and provincial newspapers, libraries or horse-race meetings, there is no denying the explosion of places to go and things to do and see in Augustan England. Towns became centers of polite living because there existed a leisured class, a majority of whom were female, who had the time to devote to tea-drinking, dancing, and cards, and the wealth to invest in the various purpose-built Assembly rooms and concert halls, parks, and civic amenities. And this leisured class deliberately chose to devote itself to civility as a means of creating a tolerant and tolerable, civilized and stable society.

A civil society

Civility is not just a product of superfluous wealth and leisure; it is created and sustained by cultural means, by practices which we might label as discursive or ideological. This is apparent, for instance, in the way in which Augustan England constructed notions of human nature. In this self-conscious "age of reason," human psychology was read against its irrational antithesis, "fanaticism" or "enthusiasm." Several different contemporary discourses – medical, scientific, religious, cultural, literary, and political – converged, and "in stressing the connection between enthusiasm, passions and melancholy, a clear psychological norm was offered as the basis for the social order: the sober, reasonable and self-controlled person."[34] Such human beings deserved freedom of intellectual inquiry and the right to believe and worship as they wished. The rational individual was also a benevolent and sympathetic being, a "man of feeling" or a "woman of sentiment" by the mid eighteenth century. For each of these readings of human nature, there were others which were suppressed or denied: that a human being might be inspired by the Holy Spirit, for instance; or that egotism is the well-spring of human motivation; or that female appetites might be safely met. And there were real human beings whose lives and aspirations refused to fit the model: Dissenters, Quakers, and Catholics; free-thinkers whose rational inquiry led to deism or atheism; readers of Thomas Hobbes and Bernard Mandeville; women like Aphra Behn or Mary Astell. So to argue that Augustan discourse privileges one set of assumptions about human nature is not to suggest that others were not present or unacknowledged. It is simply to propose that these assumptions were most conducive to the creation of a civilized and civilizing public sphere.

The point can be advanced by considering the power of conversation as a cultural trope of civility. In an *Essay on Conversation* Henry Fielding expands on "the art of good breeding," by which "I mean the art of pleasing, or contributing as much as possible to the ease and happiness of those with whom you converse."[35] This was a commonplace of the conduct books which taught "good breeding," but it was intended to do more than simply oil the wheels of social intercourse. Given the variety of religions amongst us, wrote John Constable, and the propensity of human beings to defend their religion with passion, they are a dangerous topic for discussion. "How to manage them right in Conversation, is the present Point . . . Commonly they are so handled, that one would almost hate to have them brought into Conversation. They are apt to end in Disgusts, if not in quarrels."[36] Note the underlying assumption that conversations among reasonable individuals should not be disrupted by contention, that religious differences need to be managed. We are close to a new social rule, that civilized, civil people keep politics and religion out of the conversation. The Spalding Society established in Lincolnshire in 1710 proudly announced that "we deal in all the arts and sciences, and exclude nothing from our conversation but politics, which would throw all into confusion and disorder."[37]

The civility of late seventeenth- and early eighteenth-century life is properly regarded as a key to the management of difference. Civility was an ideal, a vision of how the elite should conduct themselves, and it was put into practice in drawing rooms and assemblies, in political clubs and on boards and committees. Civility transformed an older vision of civic virtue as independence, frugality, and martial vigor into sociability, urbanity, and politeness. The philosopher, the third Earl of Shaftesbury, has been seen as crucial to this ideological transformation, and he defined precisely how liberty was linked to "politeness" and how both required social interaction: "All Politeness is owing to Liberty. We polish one another, and rub off our corners and rough sides by a sort of amicable *collision*."[38] Shaftesbury's diffuse essays were translated into a more approachable idiom by Joseph Addison and Sir Richard Steele, whose *Spectator* was aimed at readers "in Clubs and Assemblies, at Tea Tables and in Coffee Houses." Whether or not they were creating a bourgeois readership, they were certainly playing to a metropolitan and urban audience and turning their back on the court and its literary circles. It is even possible to see how literary discourses meshed with others in forming and informing tastes and aspirations. Dudley Ryder, a Dissenter and law student, "resolved to be very conversant with Mr Locke's works" to learn the secret of "that clear, close way of talking." He read the *Spectator* for the same purpose and was very taken with Archbishop Tillotson's prose style. Other diarists suggest a similar catholicity of influence. A Sussex shopkeeper, Thomas Turner, was another admirer of Tillotson, read John Milton through the lens of the *Spectator*, and also noted down "moral considerations" from the *Universal Magazine*.[39] There was a remarkable eclecticism in the cultural influences which were shaping the citizens of Hanoverian Britain. Essayists, dramatists, and novelists, as well as scientists, preachers, philosophers, and journalists, contributed to the construction of a civility based on tolerance, conversation, and intellectual commerce. The political role of literature was changing. The poets had toiled to transform the restored monarch Charles II into Augustus, but the spell was wearing even thinner by the eighteenth century, and when Pope addressed George II as Augustus in the 1730s this was no more than sarcasm.[40] The poets joined other writers in turning their attention away from princes and toward their fellow citizens, away from the celebration of heroism and majesty and toward the promotion of civility and sensibility.

The English could not resolve their political and religious differences between 1649 and 1750 – in fact they multiplied them. Yet simultaneously they were able to accommodate these differences, to prevent them from erupting as destructively as they had in the 1640s. The acceptance and limitation of party politics, the diversion of energy into accumulating wealth and enjoying leisure, and the formulation of cultural expectations about what it is to be rational and civilized and how social interactions should be conducted, all contributed to this containment, which was in itself one of the most striking achievements of the Augustan Age.

NOTES

1 On this theme see Ian Gilmour, *Riots, Risings and Revolution – Governance and Violence in Eighteenth-century England* (London, 1992).

2 J. H. Plumb, *The Growth of Political Stability in England 1675–1725* (London, 1967); G. Holmes, *Augustan England – Professions, State and Society 1680–1730* (London, 1982).

3 J. C. D. Clark, *English Society, 1688–1832: Ideology, Social Structure and Political Practice during the Ancien Regime* (Cambridge, 1985); J. Innes, "Jonathan Clark, Social History and England's 'Ancien Regime,'" *Past and Present*, 115 (1987), p. 181; P. Langford, *A Polite and Commercial People: England 1727–1783* (Oxford, 1989), pp. 690–91.

4 Holmes, *Augustan England*, p. 18.

5 See Jonathan Barry, "Bourgeois Collectivism? Urban Association and the Middling Sort," in J. Barry and C. Brooks (eds.), *The Middling Sort of People – Culture, Society and Politics in England 1550–1800* (London, 1994); see also P. Langford, *Public Life and the Propertied Englishman, 1689–1798* (Oxford, 1991).

6 [Andrew Marvell], *An Account of the Growth of Popery and Arbitrary Government* (1677), p. 3.

7 See R. Willman, "The Origins of 'Whig' and 'Tory' in English Political Language," *The Historical Journal*, 17 (1974).

8 Edmund Bohun, *Three Charges Delivered at the General Quarter Sessions, Holden at Ipswich, for the County of Suffolk, In the Years, 1691, 1692* (1693), p. 9.

9 *The Memoirs of Sir John Reresby*, ed. A. Browning (Glasgow, 1936; 2nd edn. 1991), p. 546.

10 The new Coronation Oath was at least an unequivocal promise to govern "according to the statutes in Parliament agreed on, and the laws and customs of the same" and to maintain "the protestant reformed religion established by law."

11 Quoted in J. Miller, *The Glorious Revolution* (London, 1983), p. 42.

12 H. Horwitz, *Parliament, Policy and Politics in the Reign of William III* (Manchester, 1977), p. 94.

13 G. Holmes and W. A. Speck (eds.), *The Divided Society: Party Conflict in England 1694–1716* (London, 1967), p. 135; W. A. Speck, "Conflict in Society," in G. Holmes (ed.), *Britain after the Glorious Revolution, 1689–1714* (London, 1969), p. 137.

14 A helpful introduction to this theme is W. A. Speck, *Society and Literature in England 1700–1760* (Dublin, 1983).

15 Holmes and Speck (eds.), *Divided Society*, p. 113.

16 Langford, *Polite and Commercial People*, pp. 723–24.

17 Jonathan Swift, *A Tale of a Tub and other Satires* (London, 1975), p. 242.

18 H. Nenner, "Liberty, Law and Property: The Constitution in Retrospect from 1689," in J. R. Jones (ed.), *Liberty Secured?: Britain Before and After 1688* (Stanford, 1992), p. 97.

19 *Ibid.*, p. 89.

20 William Garroway quoted in J. Brewer, *The Sinews of Power: War, Money and the English State, 1688–1789* (London, 1989), p. 114.

21 J. Miller, "Charles II and his Parliaments," *Transactions of the Royal Historical Society*, XXXII (London, 1982).

22 See G. Holmes, *British Politics in the Age of Anne* (London, 1966; rev. edn. 1987), p. 189 and chapter 6.

23 E. L. Ellis, "William III and the Politicians," in Holmes (ed.), *Britain after the Glorious Revolution*, p. 119; also see Speck's comments in J. Cannon (ed.), *The Whig Ascendancy: Colloquies on Hanoverian England* (London, 1981), p. 62.

24 Philip, second Earl Hardwicke, quoted in J. B. Owen, *The Eighteenth Century 1714–1815* (London, 1974), p. 109.

25 F. O'Gorman quoted in D. Hayton, "The 'Country' Interest and the Party System 1689–c.1720," in C. Jones (ed.), *Party and Management in Parliament 1660–1784* (Leicester, 1984), p. 65.

26 W. A. Speck, *Stability and Strife: England 1714–1760* (London, 1977), p. 7.

27 See L. Colley, *In Defiance of Oligarchy: The Tory Party 1714–60* (Cambridge, 1982).

28 G. Holmes, *The Electorate and the National Will in the First Age of Party* (Lancaster, 1976).

29 Quoted in Holmes and Speck (eds.), *Divided Society*, p. 87.

30 See T. Harris, *London Crowds in the Reign of Charles II: Propaganda and Politics from the Revolution until the Exclusion Crisis* (Cambridge, 1987).

31 See G. S. De Krey, *A Fractured Society: The Politics of London in the First Age of Party, 1688–1715* (Oxford, 1985).

32 Quoted in J. R. Jones, "The Revolution in Context," in Jones (ed.), *Liberty Secured?*, p. 36.

33 Langford, *Polite and Commercial People*, p. 697.

34 M. Heyd, "The Reaction to Enthusiasm in the Seventeenth-century: Towards an Integrative Approach," *The Journal of Modern History*, 53 (1981), p. 279.

35 Quoted in P. Rogers, *The Augustan Vision* (1974), p. 51.

36 [John Constable], *The Conversation of a Gentleman* (1738), pp. 218–19.

37 Langford, *Public Life*, p. 72.

38 L. E. Klein, "Liberty, Manners and Politeness in Early Eighteenth-century England," *The Historical Journal*, 32 (1989), p. 602.

39 *The Diary of Dudley Ryder 1715–1716*, ed. W. R. Matthews (London, 1939), p. 155; *The Diary of Thomas Turner 1754–1765*, ed. D. Vaisey (Oxford, 1985), pp. 3, 4.

40 See Pope's "First Epistle of the Second Book of Horace" (1737).

FURTHER READING

Ashcraft, Richard, *Revolutionary Politics and Locke's "Two Treatises of Government"* (Princeton, 1986).

Black, Jeremy (ed.), *Britain in the Age of Walpole* (London, 1984).

Borsay, Peter, *The English Urban Renaissance: Culture and Society in the Provincial Town 1660–1770* (Oxford, 1981).

Brewer, John, *The Sinews of Power: War, Money and the English State, 1688–1789* (London, 1989).

Cannon, John (ed.), *The Whig Ascendancy: Colloquies on Hanoverian England* (London, 1981).

Clark, J. C. D., *English Society, 1688–1832: Ideology, Social Structure and Political Practice during the Ancien Regime* (Cambridge, 1985).

Colley, Linda, *Britons: Forging the Nation 1707–1837* (Yale, 1992).

Dickinson, H. T., *Liberty and Property: Political Ideology in Eighteenth-century Britain* (London, 1977).

Dickson, P. G. M., *The Financial Revolution in England 1688–1756: A Study in the Development of Public Credit* (London, 1967).

Downie, J. A., *Robert Harley and the Press: Propaganda and Public Opinion in the Age of Swift and Defoe* (Cambridge, 1979).

Earle, Peter, *The Making of the English Middle Class: Business, Social and Family Life in London, 1660–1730* (London, 1989).

Gilmour, Ian, *Riots, Risings and Revolution: Governance and Violence in Eighteenth-century England* (London, 1992).

Glassey, L. K. J. (ed.), *The Reigns of Charles II and James VII and II* (London, 1997).

Gregg, Edward, *Queen Anne* (London, 1980).

Harris, Tim, *London Crowds in the Reign of Charles II: Propaganda and Politics from the Revolution until the Exclusion Crisis* (Cambridge, 1987).

Politics under the Later Stuarts: Party Conflict in a Divided Society 1660–1715 (London, 1993).

Haydon, Colin, *Anti-Catholicism in Eighteenth-century England – A Political and Social Study* (Manchester, 1993).

Hill, Brian, *The Growth of Parliamentary Parties, 1689–1752* (London, 1970).

Holmes, Geoffrey, *Augustan England – Professions, State and Society 1680–1730* (London, 1982).

British Politics in the Age of Anne (London, 1966; rev. edn. 1987).

(ed.), *Britain After the Glorious Revolution, 1689–1714* (London, 1969).

Holmes, Geoffrey and Speck, William (eds.), *The Divided Society: Party Conflict in England 1694–1716* (London, 1967).

Horwitz, H., *Parliament, Policy and Politics in the Reign of William III* (Manchester, 1977).

Hutton, Ronald, *Charles the Second – King of England, Scotland, and Ireland* (Oxford, 1989).

Jenkins, G. H., *The Foundations of Modern Wales 1642–1780* (Oxford, 1987).

Jones, Clyve, and Holmes, Geoffrey (eds.), *Britain in the First Age of Party 1680–1750* (London, 1987).

Jones, D. W., *War and Economy in the Age of William III and Marlborough* (Oxford, 1988).

Jones, James, *Country and Court: England 1658–1714* (London, 1978).

(ed.), *Liberty Secured?: Britain Before and After 1688* (Stanford, 1992).

Kenyon, John, *Revolution Principles: The Politics of Party 1689–1720* (Cambridge, 1977).

Klein, Lawrence E., *Shaftesbury and the Culture of Politeness: Moral Discourse and Cultural Politics in Early Eighteenth-century England* (Cambridge, 1991).

Langford, Paul, *A Polite and Commercial People: England 1727–1783* (Oxford, 1989).

Public Life and the Propertied Englishman, 1689–1798 (Oxford, 1991).

Miller, John, *Charles II* (London, 1991).

James II – A Study in Kingship (London, 1978).

Popery and Politics in England 1660–1688 (Cambridge, 1973).

Plumb, J. H., *The Growth of Political Stability in England 1675–1725* (London, 1967).

Pocock, John, *Virtue, Commerce and History: Essays on Political Thought and History, Chiefly in the Eighteenth Century* (Cambridge, 1985).

Rogers, Nicholas, *Whigs and Cities: Popular Politics in the Age of Walpole and Pitt* (Oxford, 1990).

Schwoerer, Lois, *The Declaration of Rights, 1689* (Baltimore, 1981).

Seaward, Paul, *The Restoration 1660–1688* (London, 1991).

Speck, William, *Reluctant Revolutionaries – Englishmen and the Revolution of 1688* (Oxford, 1988).

Stability and Strife: England 1714–1760 (London, 1977).

Walsh, John, Haydon, Colin M., and Taylor, Stephen (eds.), *The Church of England c.1689–c.1833. From Toleration to Tractarianism* (Cambridge, 1993).

Watts, Michael R., *The Dissenters: From the Reformation to the French Revolution* (Oxford, 1978).

Wilson, Kathleen, *The Sense of the People: Politics, Culture, and Imperialism in England, 1715–1785* (Cambridge, 1996).

2

MICHAEL SEIDEL

Satire, lampoon, libel, slander

According to Samuel Johnson's great eighteenth-century *Dictionary*, satire is a censorious poem, properly distinguished by the generality of its reflections but all too often confused with a lesser form, lampoon, distinguished by the particularity of its reflections. Libel is an actionable defamation, but the term was often used synonymously with lampoon. Slander is libel with a casual or callous disregard for truth.

In the Restoration and early eighteenth century, satire, libel, lampoon, and slander were inextricably mixed, whether the specific forms they took were poetic, dramatic, narrative, or expository. But when commentators wished to separate good vilification from bad the distinction was one of style. "Loose-writ" libels were never as effective as "shining satire," according to John Dryden and the Earl of Mulgrave in their joint effort, "An Essay Upon Satire" (1679). Perhaps "shining" does not take us very far conceptually in distinguishing satire from libel, lampoon, or slander as an embodiment of the literary spirit of opposition, but Dryden and Mulgrave have in mind the way effective satire always combines abuse with wit and imagination.

To say that a satiric work's expressive power is witty or imaginatively oppositional does not necessarily make the particular animus of that work any easier to define. Whereas certain attitudes and gestures of verbal opposition mark satire – tirade, derision, disdain, mockery, belittlement, sarcasm, irony – it is far from clear exactly what a subject must do to make him, her, or it qualify as a protagonist in a satiric action. Tragedy invites viewers to identify the key flaws in a character's nature that rationalize a reversal of fortune; in comedy audiences identify strains among lovers, families, generations, classes that temporarily unsettle the social order; and in epic readers quickly mark the national and the heroic. But in satire the object of an action is identified primarily by the stance taken against it. The satirist depicts things as absurd, disreputable, or hypocritical because he deems them so. "Indignation," as the Restoration satirist John Oldham puts it, "can create a muse."

Perhaps the best way to define what satire does is to recognize when it stops. Like pain, satire is either extensive or local, constant or intermittent, extreme or mild, sharp or dull, present or absent. There is a telling example in John Dryden's brilliant political poem, *Absalom and Achitophel*, when, after a scathing indictment of the first Earl of Shaftesbury (Achitophel) for everything from scandalous political ambitions to defective procreation – a son "Got, while his Soul did huddled Notions try; / And born a shapeless Lump, like Anarchy" – Dryden pauses in his satiric attack and praises Shaftesbury for his role years before as a judge in Israel's (read England's) courts.

> The Statesman we abhor, but praise the Judge.
> In *Israels* Courts ne'r sat an *Abbethdin*
> With more discerning Eyes, or hands more clean:
> Unbrib'd, unsought, the Wretched to redress;
> Swift of Dispatch, and easie of Access.
> Oh, had he been content to serve the Crown,
> With vertues only proper to the Gown . . .   (lines 187–93)

Dryden's aim is not necessarily to separate the deficient Shaftesbury from the sympathetic one, but to accommodate the actions of the statesman to the satirist's particular biases and prejudices. The very moment Dryden's attack abates – or *because* it abates – Shaftesbury emerges as human, measured, just, ethical. That is, Shaftesbury emerges from the world of opposition the satirist has created for him. Dryden was aware, at least in theory, that satire depends as much on the satirist's perspective as on the victim's nature: "In the character of an hero, as well as in an inferior figure, there is a better or worse likeness to be taken: the better is panegyric, if it be not false, and the worse is libel."[1] Bias extends to the very depths of language, satirical or polemical, and Dryden makes that point as well. He writes in *His Majesties Declaration Defended* (1681) of his outrage that enemies of King Charles manipulate phrases to blacken the reputation of the monarch's supporters for their supposed Catholic leanings: "*Popish* and *Arbitrary*, are words that sound high amongst the multitude; and all men are branded by those names, who are not for setting up Fanaticism and a Common-wealth."[2] Of course, Dryden plays the same game. Are we supposed to think that "*Popish*" is a foul and calumnious charge against the king, and "Fanaticism" a perfectly neutral word for Protestant dissent? Opposition is all about the spin of language, and the rhetoric of satire produces its victims as much as it identifies them.

Jonathan Swift comes to the same shrewd understanding when he comments in *A Tale of A Tub* that satiric opposition is always tactical:

"Thus, in the Choice of a *Devil*, it hath been the usual Method of Mankind, to single out some Being, either in Act, or in Vision, which was in most Antipathy to the God they had framed."[3] Swift's remark gets to the core of satire and its antipathetic essence, but from a very contrived vantage point. Tactical opposition is so much a part of the satirist's art that classical Roman verse satire included a restraining figure, an adversarius, to counter the satirist's expected – and sometimes even irrationally presented – bias against his subjects. An adversarius appears as a moderating device in the most famous Restoration adaptation of Roman satire, John Wilmot's (the Earl of Rochester's) *Satire Against Reason and Mankind*, when the satirist allows himself to be interrupted by a figure of civic authority who cannot believe the assault on reason is so relentless: "What Rage ferments in your degen'rate Mind, / To make you rail at Reason and Mankind?" (lines 58–59). The rage the satirist feels is part of the satiric rhetoric of the poem, and its writer, Rochester, inserts a stabilizing voice in the middle of the action to try to calm his satiric self down.

In an even more interesting variation of this rhetorical trope, Alexander Pope writes a satiric epistle to his physician, Dr. John Arbuthnot, and produces Arbuthnot himself in the role of restrainer or adversarius. While the satirist Pope is on a barely controlled riff against a figure named Sporus (representing the hated Lord Hervey), Arbuthnot tries to inject a note of moderation, or, at least, reason: "Satire or Sense alas! can *Sporus* feel? / Who breaks a Butterfly upon a Wheel?" (lines 307–08). Pope takes the point with the marker, "Yet," but his subsequent rant reveals satire as a kind of intractable revenger's history, a mode less interested in making things right than in getting even with those who, from the satirist's perspective, made them wrong: "Yet let me flap this Bug with gilded wings, / This painted Child of Dirt that stinks and stings" (lines 309–10).

For the satirist, everything is personal. Even what seems commonplace or conventional – civic programs, political faction, aesthetic theory – takes on the most personal dimensions for Dryden or Swift or Pope. Dryden identifies faction with civil disorder that could all too easily displace him from the position he occupies in the government he favors, the court of the reigning king, Charles II. Swift fears faction because of a conviction that even the faction he is in – the moderate Tory Anglican establishment – will find a way to displace him. Pope reviles faction because as a Catholic in a land of Protestants he thought it folly to call attention to affiliations – whatever they might be – that could call the wrong kind of attention to him.

The same personal dimension exists for other commonplace satiric subjects, say, greed or lust. Greed looks to Dryden like rivalry, to Swift like exclusion, to Pope like ostentation. Lust looks to Dryden like disorder, to Swift like madness, to Pope like folly. Satire always exists on a line of bias, and the more variegated, ingenious, and complex the nature of its presentation, the broader the invitation to readers to absorb satire's argument to their own biases and prejudices.

The bottom of the sublime

Prior to the Restoration and early eighteenth century in England, satire was a confused genre, not so much because confusing things happened in its spaces – though they did – but because no one was certain as to the origins of satire's abusive spirit. For a good while it was simply thought that the word *satire* derived from the Greek *satyr* or goat man of mythology who appeared in the satyr play interludes of Greek dramatic spectacles for the purpose of abusing prominent Athenians. The etymology was specious, but even long after scholars dispensed with it, satirists themselves kept the connection alive because they thought the rude, obscene, offensive satyrs represented the vehemence and brusqueness of their own craft. Satyrs, after all, emerged from nature to confront the local citizenry of Athens. Powerful creatures came to the civilized city to make fun of its citizens. Isn't that what satirists do?

Proponents for satire in the more urbane, the more self-consciously "modern" world of Restoration England argued that satire did much more. In the very midst of the deeply contentious world of Restoration life and politics, Dryden defended his own satiric efforts from the indignity of rudeness and barbarity to which satire had been reduced in previous eras. He claimed that satire could be – and his always were – a sub-category of heroic poetry.

The elevation of satire in the Restoration and early eighteenth century from its ruder origins assumed, of course, a Roman model for the kind of classical satire that really mattered to highly civilized states. Indeed, the etymology of satire was accurately presented as Latin *satura lanx*, meaning well-filled dish and signifying a medley or farrago of public literary styles. The satirist played the role of public poet, master of the feast, or civic host. Dryden argued with substantial energy and force (not to mention length) in his *Discourse Concerning the Original and Progress of Satire* (1693) that satire was an honored genre among the Romans, inviting the satirist to express a great range of attitudes and views, both negative and positive. In the hands of a writer such as Juvenal, satire could even be powerfully sublime in its themes, something Dryden emulated in his own heroic and panegyric works when he observed that "Satire will have room, where e're

I write" ("Epistle to Godfrey Kneller"). Swift later sensed something of this when he made fun of the pretensions of Dryden and other satirists in *A Tale of A Tub* for aspiring to reach the "bottom of the Sublime," at once a spatial joke and a very good description of the generic territory occupied by satire in the Restoration and early eighteenth century.

Dryden tried to make satire into an art so sublime that its local victims remained oblivious to the wounds it inflicted. He wrote of his own portrait of the Duke of Buckingham in *Absalom and Achitophel*: "a Man is secretly wounded, and though he be not sensible himself, yet the malicious World will find it for him: Yet there is still a vast difference betwixt the slovenly Butchering of a Man, and the fineness of a stroak that separates the Head from the Body, and leaves it standing in its place."[4] Here are a few of Dryden's fine strokes directed at Buckingham's neck:

> A man so various, that he seem'd to be
> Not one, but Mankinds epitome.
> Stiff in Opinions, always in the wrong;
> Was every thing by starts, and nothing long:
> But, in the course of the revolving Moon,
> Was Chymist, Fidler, States-man, and Buffoon. (lines 545–50)

The victim of satire is most effectively presented when least able to comprehend exactly what has happened to him. In the *Discourse*, Dryden takes the matter a step further. He points out that his favorite satirist, Juvenal, interpreted Roman law as requiring the poet to name none but the already dead. Such a reading of the law, reinforced by the ancient injunction from Roman legal tradition against evil utterance, comes close to the metaphoric center of satiric action. When the satirist has dispatched his victim properly – that is with wit and finality – that victim already belongs among the dead whether or not he breathes in the world he thinks he still inhabits.

A particularly rich and complex instance of a satirist at work in this vein comes a few years later with Jonathan Swift's attack on astrology in the *Bickerstaff Papers* (1708). Swift's Bickerstaff actually predicts the death of a rival astrologer named Partridge. When that astrologer protests he still lives, Bickerstaff pretends that an obvious imposter walks the streets as an "*uninformed* Carcass" masquerading as Partridge. *Uninformed* is without shape and without knowledge, and *carcass* is dead substance. The satiric image is even further complicated – and Swift is well aware of it – by the fact that Partridge had actually died many years before, though his name still appears on Partridge's *Almanac*. Partridge is made available for a fate perpetually in store for him, "like the General who was forced to kill his enemies twice over, whom a *Necromancer* had raised to life."[5]

For Swift, as for Dryden, wit is the murder weapon of choice in satire, a weapon that, at least on the face of it, disguises the messiness of satiric activity. Lack of wit is enough to cancel the effectiveness of satire. Dryden makes that point addressing his traditional political enemies in the prefatory remarks to *The Medal*; they fail at satire not because they fail at abuse but because they fail at wit: "Raile at me abundantly; and, not to break a Custome, doe it without wit . . ."[6] As he puts it of his enemies, in the *Discourse*, "I complain not of their Lampoons and Libels, though I have been the Publick Mark for many years. I am vindictive enough to have repell'd force by force, if I cou'd imagine that any of them had ever reach'd me; but they either shot at Rovers, and therefore miss'd, or their Powder was so weak, that I might safely stand them, at the nearest distance" (p. 8). For Dryden, very simply put, "There can be no pleasantry where there is no Wit" (p. 60).

Attack is something the satirist does; wit is something the audience understands. Dryden adds something very important to the spirit of satiric opposition. He allows the satirist – through the literary manipulation of style and tone – to make accomplices of his readers. Attack can even arrive in a package marked as praise, if readers are sensitive to all the ironies that language can provide. In *Mac Flecknoe*, a poem addressed to a rival poet, Tom Shadwell, Dryden praises a genius he does not value. The result is a special kind of abuse leavened by an almost calming wit that approximates the listlessness of failed poetry.

> Thy Genius calls thee not to purchase fame
> In keen Iambicks, but mild Anagram:
> Leave writing Plays, and chuse for thy command
> Some peacefull Province in Acrostick Land.   (lines 203–06)

An even more pointed example is Pope's imitation of an Horatian satiric epistle to the Roman emperor Augustus. In his *Epistle to Augustus* (1737), Pope changes the object of mock praise to King George II of England. He begins by noting the foreign king's prowess in foreign "arms," but the discerning reader – then as now – recognizes that Pope means George's ardor for his German mistress and not his lust for foreign combat. The satire here resides in the potential for misdirection, a witty pattern that Pope builds throughout the poem: "How shall the Muse, from such a Monarch, steal / An hour, and not defraud the Publick Weal?" (lines 5–6). The ironic answer is that any time stolen to praise George II is a felony. Pope even damns the poetic marketplace for the very enterprise that supposedly directs the effort at hand, "when straining with too weak a wing, / We needs will write Epistles to the King" (lines 368–69). Of course the satirist produces a blueprint for the poem in his very own mock befuddlement: "Besides, a fate attends on all I write, / That when I aim at praise, they say I bite" (lines 408–09).

When not insulting the reigning British king, Pope attempts to explain the history of the form in which the satirist conveys his attack. His understanding replicates Dryden's in elevating the original rude, rough-hewn status of satire to a higher level of poetic expression. Satire for our "rural Ancestors" consisted of jests and taunts in village feasts and celebrations, which, by the time Pope seems to identify with the Civil Wars in England, became craftier, wittier, more indirect, subtle, and elaborately designed to avoid the pitfalls of the law.

> But Times corrupt, and Nature, ill-inclin'd,
> Produced the point that left a sting behind;
> Till friend with friend, and families at strife,
> Triumphant Malice rag'd thro' private life.
> Who felt the wrong, or fear'd it, took th' alarm,
> Appeal'd to Law, and Justice lent her arm.
> At length, by wholesome dread of statutes bound,
> The Poets learn'd to please, and not to wound:
> Most warp'd to Flatt'ry's side; but some, more nice,
> Preserv'd the freedom, and forbore the vice.
> Hence Satire rose, that just the medium hit,
> And heals with Morals what it hurts with Wit.   (lines 251–62)

Moreover, the refinement of public art in the Restoration, at a time when the English court began to ape French culture, produced an almost heroic status for public forms like satire, embodied in the great works of Dryden, who, according to Pope, "taught to join / The varying verse, the full resounding line, / The long majestic march, and energy divine" (lines 267–69). Pope echoes Dryden's own observation that the best that could be done for satire was to release it from its sorry rank among the genres and provide it with a better set of literary *bona fides* than any age but imperial Rome had provided for it in the past.

"The Satyrical Itch"

The incursion into literary domains cordoned off by supposedly more honored and noble genres defines the history of satire in the Restoration and early eighteenth century. Many of the period's writers collapse, merge, and restyle traditional forms of literary representation into hybrids, all controlled by an expanding civic consciousness and a heightened sense of wit as an encompassing verbal strategy. These hybrid forms become the greatest original works of the Restoration period and after, from a host of famous stage comedies by Dryden, George Etherege, William Wycherley, and William Congreve, to Samuel Butler's *Hudibras* (1663), Andrew Marvell's *Last Instructions to a Painter* (1667), the Earl of Rochester's *Satire Against Reason and Mankind* (1679), Dryden's *Mac Flecknoe* (1681) and *Absalom and Achitophel* (1681), Swift's *A Tale of A Tub* (1704) and *Gulliver's Travels* (1726), Pope's *Rape of the Lock* (1714) and *Dunciad* (1729), John Gay's *Beggar's Opera* (1728), and Henry Fielding's stage farces of the 1730s and his novels of the 1740s, *Joseph Andrews, Jonathan Wild*, and *Tom Jones*.

Perhaps satire emerged from the ruins of the Civil War period in England at a time when words themselves were a form of just slightly suppressed warfare. More important – and harder to pin down exactly – the Wars evoked a general skepticism about human behavior that invited satiric speculation. In his *Discourse upon Satire*, Dryden suggested that faith itself had come to grief against modern skepticism, a skepticism that undermined the most compelling supernatural myths behind western, Christian culture. According to Dryden, the language of modernity, a language indebted to wit as a mode of historical and literary expression, tended to direct writers away from the vivid embellishing of material so necessary to the belief systems and heroic codes of the past. When in the interregnum, Abraham Cowley called the classical myths a heap of "antiquated *Dreams* of senseless *Fables* and *Metamorphoses*,"[7] he opened the door directly to their burlesque. Writers at first reacted in different ways to the discomfort of what they perceived as the detritus of empty myths, broken-down world systems, and the odds and ends of the heroic tradition. During the early years of the Restoration all sorts of satire and burlesque were published and widely distributed, from the infamous *Rump Ballads* about the radical politics of the Interregnum to the more obvious burlesques and travesties of Homer and Virgil written by Charles Cotton and others. The merit of any of these remains questionable, but they were trial runs for the later, more sophisticated, mock-epic satires of the age. This is surely the case for Pope's *Rape of the Lock* (1714) when he burlesques – or perhaps parodies is the kinder word – his own earlier serious translation of a famous passage on battle glory from the *Iliad*. Satiric burlesque serves as a substitute literary program, a way of rearticulating an important part of any culture's reassessment of its literary inheritance. For Pope, heroic glory becomes drawing-room sexual power:

But since, alas! frail Beauty must decay,
Curl'd or uncurl'd, since Locks will turn to grey;
Since painted, or not painted, all shall fade,
And she who scorns a Man, must die a Maid;
What then remains, but well our Pow'r to use,
And keep good-Humour still whate'er we lose
And trust me, Dear! good-humour can prevail,
When Airs, and Flights, and Screams, and Scolding fail.
Beauties in vain their pretty Eyes may roll;
Charms strike the Sight, but Merit wins the Soul.

(Canto 5, lines 25–34)

One of the Restoration's foremost satirists, Samuel Butler, was among the first to notice the disparity between heroic presumption and contemporary performance in the post-Civil War period: "No Age ever abounded more with Heroical Poetry than the present, and yet there was never any wherein fewer Heroicall Actions were perform'd."[8] His brilliant satire, *Hudibras*, a poem published over a fifteen-year period from 1663–78, stakes out an elaborate anti-heroic terrain. The action is set in war-ravished England, where an impoverished colonel travels the countryside in search of ever-so-small material victories. In a heroic–chivalric plot gone haywire, Sir Hudibras has his eyes on a widow's jointure, and the struggle for legal and psychological control of the courtship that would allow him to possess that jointure, which, in the larger satiric vista of the poem, is the mental, moral, and physical estate of England. Civil war, of course, divides the state, and that is the satiric metaphor that plays out in the poem. Martial relations, like marital ones (and ineptly named "jointures") wrench people apart.

A deep design in't, to divide
The well-affected that confide,
By setting Brother against Brother,
To claw and curry one another.

(Part 1, Canto 1, lines 737–40)

The opening lines of *Hudibras* place the scene in the middle of the Civil Wars; indeed, the lines reflect the contentious, divided plot of the poem as an image of those wars: "When *civil* Fury first grew high, / And men fell out they knew not why." Satire usually begins in crisis, and the most disturbing ones usually end right where they begin. Throughout Butler's poem there are supporting players – sectarians, renegades, military men, astrologers, thugs, casuists, and con men – who struggle to translate their obsessions, and the peculiar idioms in which they express these obsessions, into power.

For Butler's rebels and regicides, the Wars and Interregnum are the "good old cause," but for Butler himself, and for satirists after him, the Wars represented a national apostasy and a reversionary symbol, a nation and a people gone mad. When England seemed on the verge of revolution again in 1681, Dryden assumes in *Absalom and Achitophel* that "The Good old Cause reviv'd, a Plot requires" (line 82). Even a half-century later, Pope's son of Dulness in the *Dunciad* refers to his mighty mother's moment as a reversionary, invoking Butler's version of the Civil War period to do so: "Dulness! whose good old cause I yet defend, / With whom my Muse began, with whom shall end" (Book 1, lines 165–66).

In the early decades of the Restoration, *Hudibras* was King Charles II's favorite satire, partly because he thought it so effectively mocked the hypocritical bleakness and casuistry of the Wars and Interregnum. The return of the Stuart court at the Restoration brought with it a great deal of delight, glamor, wit, public display, and a vast literary energy directed at abusing the religious, political, and economic values of the previous period. Of course, the returned Stuart court soon fell victim to the very satiric energy it had released. Though the Crown kept tight control on potential seditious writing through the Licensing Act of 1662, satirists and lampoonists were ingenious in figuring ways to represent current state affairs indirectly: lampoons of court officials, pasquinades on current events, mock court-session poems, instruction poems to historical painters, mock pope-burning procession verses, dialogue poems, dream visions, pseudo-monologues, songs, odes, dramatic epilogues and prologues, verse essays, and formal verse satires were part of the abundant satiric literature of the Restoration. Every significant writer of the period contributed to that abundance.

Andrew Marvell is perhaps the most accomplished of the anti-court satirists in the period. He was also the most careful. As a Member of Parliament from Hull, he had no intention of running up against the authorities in King Charles's court; therefore he signed none of his satiric works, nor did he admit to writing them. Marvell's best anti-court satire is the extraordinary *Last Instructions to A Painter*, printed only after the Stuart kings were out of power but written and circulated at the time of Charles II's deteriorating position during the naval fiasco of 1667 after England's military and merchant fleet was attacked by the Dutch Admiral de Ruyter. De Ruyter advanced well into mouth of the Thames and the inland waters of the Medway river, an action that represented to Marvell the softness and rottenness of the realm and gave him the opportunity in his satire to indict both the policies and the ethos of the restored monarchy in England. Marvell's satiric attack began to do what the next generation of satirists – Swift, Pope and Gay – did so extensively and so well: present entire social and political systems as vast conspiracies of state corruption and ineptitude.

In *Last Instructions*, Marvell plays on the idea of a *petto* or secret crime while mocking the attempt on the part of Crown and court officials to avoid responsibility for the Dutch naval invasion. Charles's government tries to scapegoat the hapless Peter Pett, superintendent of the dockyard at Chatham. The satire's wit centers on the way Marvell uses the name and word, Pett, to indicate those who would escape from the action implied by it. *Pett* seems to suggest everything from slighted or piqued, to petty or insignificant, to concealed or undisclosed. The figure blamed becomes less real the more it is named, and part of the satire's power is the compression of all Marvell's ironic indignation into one word.

> After this loss, to rellish discontent,
> Some one must be accus'd by Punishment.
> All our miscarriages on *Pett* must fall:
> His Name alone seems fit to answer all.
> Whose Counsel first did this mad War beget?
> Who all Commands sold thro' the Navy? *Pett*
> Who would not follow when the *Dutch* were bet?
> Who treated out the time at *Bergen*? *Pett*
> Who the *Dutch* Fleet with Storms disable met,
> And rifling prizes, them neglected? *Pett*
> Who with false News prevented the *Gazette*?
> The Fleet divided? Write for *Rupert*? *Pett*
> Who all our Seamen cheated of their Debt?
> And all our Prizes who did swallow? *Pett*
> Who did advise no Navy out to set?
> And who the Forts left unrepair'd? *Pett*
> Who to supply with Powder, did forget
> *Languard, Sheerness, Gravesend*, and *Upnor*? *Pett*
> Who all our Ships expos'd in *Chathams* Net?
> Who should it be but the *Phanatick Pett*.   (lines 765–84)

As the political problems of Charles II magnified through the 1670s and early 1680s, the king became subject to increasingly bitter satiric attack. Charles had the machinery of state regulation at his disposal, and, at least until 1679 when he allowed the Licensing Act of 1662 to lapse, used it well. The Licensing Act had barred "abuses in printing seditious, treasonable, and unlicensed books and pamphlets." For years the king's primary propagandist, Sir Roger L'Estrange, served as "Sovereign of the Imprimery" or state licenser. Behind the Licensing Act was the Treason Act of 1660, offering the Crown the opportunity to prosecute "all printing, writing, preaching, or malicious and advised speaking calculated to compass or devise the death, destruction, injury, or restraint of the Sovereign, or to deprive him of his style, honor, or kingly name."

Anti-court satirists saw it as their greatest challenge in the Restoration to deprive the king of his style and not suffer the consequences of imprisonment, or the legally dictated loss of an ear or a nose, in the process. Charles II, after all, had a good deal of style of which to be deprived. Many thought him nothing but style, and attacked him precisely because they perceived him as wasting real power in licentiousness and luxury. Here, for example, is what Charles would expect in regard to his well-known liaisons with ladies of the court, stage, and streets. Of his most famous mistress, Nell Gwynne, we learn:

> Hard by Pall Mall lives a wench call'd Nell.
>> King Charles the Second he kept her.
> She hath got a trick to handle his p_____,
>> But never lays hands on sceptre.
> All matters of state from her soul she does hate,
>> And leave to the politic bitches.
> The whore's in the right, for 'tis her delight
>> To be scratching just where it itches.   (Anonymous, 1669)

Lampoons and libels directed at the king had grown so rampant by the late 1670s that a supporter of the Stuart monarchy, the dramatist Thomas Otway, wrote a poem, *The Poet's Complaint of His Muse; or, a Satyr Against Libells* (1679), cataloguing the volume of scurrilous verses and pamphlets. Not only Charles but his courtiers and ministers were subject to merciless treatment. When the Earl of Danby resigned as treasurer to be replaced by commissioners led by Henry Guy, here is what the town heard in a pasquinade.

> Take a turd
> Upon my word
> And into five parts cut it,
>> And put it
>> Into a pie,
>> To convince
>> Our good prince
>> What it can be
>> To mince
> Thomas Earl of Danby
> Into five commissioners and a Guy.   (1679)

Charles paradoxically eased up on strict censorship policies during the Popish Plot and Exclusion Crisis because he hoped that literary satire could help release some of the more dangerous pressure that had been building against his rule. Forbearance may have been his shrewdest recourse, though attacks such as John Oldham's four *Satires upon the Jesuits* (1678–81), secretly printed, were particularly trying for the king because in a round-about way they got very close to the core of Stuart policy, an over-cozy relationship with Catholic Europe at the expense of England's Protestant succession. The scenes depicted in Oldham's poems read as though Shakespeare's Iago and Molière's Tartuffe were planning to sell out the English Crown to the Catholic See in Rome.

Oldham's poems not only point directly at Catholic conspiracy in the context of the Popish Plot of 1678 and after; they also point to a conviction in seventeenth-century England that religion is always a deeper form of politics. For Oldham, to speak of religion is to speak of infiltration and state terror. The ghost of one of the conspirators in the Catholic Gunpowder Plot of Jacobean times berates a cadre of living Jesuit conspirators in the court of Charles II for failing to bring the English realm back to the Roman fold in the name of the order's founder, Loyola.

> Are you then Jesuits? are you so for nought?
> In all the Catholick depths of Treason taught?
> In orthodox and solid pois'ning read?
> In each profounder art of killing bred?
> And can you fail, or bungle in your trade?
> Shall one poor life your cowardice upbraid?
> Tame dastard slaves! Who your profession shame,
> And fix disgrace on our great Founder's name.
>
> (Satire 1, lines 23–30)

Oldham's poems reveal qualities central to political satire of the period. No category of action is exempt from contamination by another. Politics arrive disguised as religion. Religious principles mask aesthetic ones. Aesthetics are aligned with class loyalties. For example, if Catholicism is a code for state conspiracy in Oldham's satires, radical Protestantism is a code for vulgar art in Dryden's. In *Mac Flecknoe* (1681), Dryden works with a set of charged analogies that allow him to name a poet, Tom Shadwell, as mock son of the awful Interregnum poet, Richard Flecknoe, and then in the subtitle of the poem call Shadwell a "True-Blew Protestant Poet." Religious dissent makes the overweight and overblown Shadwell even worse than Dryden nominally presents him. As a writer, Shadwell is badly inspired by religious principles inimical to monarchy, which, from Dryden's perspective, are also principles inimical to wit.

Dryden begins Lear-like, with the old wretched poet, Richard Flecknoe, about to give over his reign to a figure who has become almost a substance, a waste product. The issue of succession is one that troubled the Crown at the time of the poem, and Dryden knows it. By association, the realm of art has its usurpers just as does the world of politics, and the inclination of revolutionaries and regicides, whether in art or politics, is true-blue.

> This *Flecknoe* found, who, like *Augustus*, young
> Was call'd to Empire, and had govern'd long:
> In Prose and Verse, was own'd, without dispute
> Through all the realms of *Non-sense*, absolute.
> This aged prince now flourishing in Peace,
> And blest with issue of a large increase,
> Worn out with business, did at length debate
> To settle the Succession of the State:
> And pond'ring which of all his Sons was fit
> To Reign, and wage immortal War with Wit,
> Cry'd, 'tis resolv'd; for Nature pleads that He
> Should onely rule, who most resembles me:
> *Sh*—— alone my perfect image bears,
> Mature in dullness from his tender years;
> *Sh*—— alone, of all my Sons, is he
> Who stands confirm'd in full stupidity.
> The rest to some faint meaning make pretense,
> But *Sh*—— never deviates into sense.
> Some Beams of Wit on other souls may fall
> Strike through and make a lucid intervall;
> But *Sh*——'s genuine night admits no ray,
> His rising fogs prevail upon the Day:
> Besides, his goodly Fabrick fills the eye
> And seems design'd for thoughtless Majesty:
> Thoughtless as the Monarch Oakes, that shade the plain,
> And, spread in solemn state, supinely reign.   (lines 3–28)

Mac Flecknoe gains its greatest strength as satire by insisting that bad art is bad succession. The bad successor poet, Shadwell, is not only a rival poet – competing with Dryden as a playwright – but one who represents a particularly broad and farcical style of humor comedy that Dryden had long attacked as primitive in implicit opposition to the higher style, taste, and wit of the Stuart court in the Restoration. That Shadwell's very name is represented in the poem as an unfortunately partitive "Sh——," only suggests that the reader is correct to imagine what the poet is capable of producing in Dryden's eyes.

It does not take long to realize that Dryden's very witty build-up of charges and abuses against the poet Shadwell in *Mac Flecknoe* is essentially the same bill of attainder Dryden would draw against those who would replace the current reign of the Stuarts in England with a tyranny of mass, of number, of mixture, of usurpation. The plot of *Mac Flecknoe*, buried so casually under a heap of insults about the life and art of a fat rival dramatist, is the same plot as Dryden's deeply thoughtful and powerful political satire, *Absalom and Achitophel*. The unworthy son is on the alert to take over from the father. At the end of the poem, Richard Flecknoe is on stage delaying succession by speaking too long and too pompously. He is king of dulness because he does what dulness does: goes on *beyond* his time. As he proclaims his son's wit, actors from one of Shadwell's plays release a trap door on stage underneath him, thereby replicating in the poem the kind of absurd stage action that, from Dryden's perspective, ruined Shadwell's comedies in the first place. Shadwell is ready to take the throne of witlessness before his poetic father, the first Flecknoe, is fully ready to relinquish it. As Richard Flecknoe praises the son-poet about to depose him, the action ends.

> For *Bruce* and *Longvil* had a *Trap* prepar'd,
> And down they sent the yet declaiming Bard.
> Sinking he left his Drugget robe behind,
> Born upwards by a subterranean wind.
> The Mantle fell to the young Prophet's part,
> With double portion of his Father's Art. (lines 212–17)

The subterranean wind recalls the same satiric trope suggested by Shadwell's truncated name: Father Flecknoe's artistic throne is the jakes, a notion that is reinforced when the alliterative "prophet's part" demands the ghost rhyme that does not quite exist, "father's fart." In *Mac Flecknoe*, the termination of a king is a burlesque; in a more serious political poem it could be a regicide.

Mac Flecknoe circulated in manuscript until Dryden chose to print it close to the time he published a much more serious poem on succession *Absalom and Achitophel* (1681). In that work, only intermittently satiric, Dryden's task was not to represent a king who gave up power, but who held onto it by choosing to exercise it sparingly and tactically. It is no coincidence that at the very time Dryden depicts King Charles as King David resuming control of the realm in *Absalom and Achitophel*, Charles also began reimposing measures against seditious libels and satires. That is one of the things a strong king feels licensed to do when he has his style back.

> Thus long have I, by native mercy sway'd,
> My wrongs dissembl'd, my revenge delay'd:
> So willing to forgive th' Offending Age,
> So much the Father did the King assuage.
> But now so far my Clemency they slight,
> Th' Offenders question my Forgiving Right.
> That one was made for many, they contend;
> But 'tis to Rule, for that's a Monarch's End.
> They call my tenderness of Blood my Fear,
> Though Manly tempers can the longest bear.
> Yet, since they will divert my Native course,
> 'Tis time to shew I am not Good by Force.
>
> (lines 939–50)

When Charles had fully secured his throne after the crisis that marked the early 1680s he officially reinstituted the Licensing Act that had lapsed in 1679. And the Act remained on the books for the benefit of William III, at least in the first few years after the 1688 Revolution. It is ironic that Dryden, no friend to William III, slyly castigated him in the figure of the Roman Augustus for doing what Charles II had done just a few years earlier: "conscious to himself of so many Crimes which he had committed, [he] thought in the first place to provide for his own Reputation, by making an Edict against Lampoons and Satires" (*Discourse*, pp. 66–67). For this reason, among others, the last years of Charles II and the early years of William III were lean ones for the satiric arts developed so assiduously in the earlier Restoration. It would take the energies of Swift and Pope in the next decade to reinvigorate them.

Modern times

In 1695, the Licensing Act lapsed again, but at a time when satire no longer focused exclusively on the remnants of factions from Civil War and Restoration politics. Instead, satire of the post-Revolutionary period centered on matters involving the burgeoning professional and entrepreneurial classes in England – the very classes whose interests, obsessions, desires, and styles would absorb the new literary empires of print journalism and prose fiction that increasingly characterized the new age. Two important satires of the post-Revolutionary period, Samuel Garth's *Dispensary* (1699) and Defoe's *True-Born Englishman* (1701), reflect the changing interests of the period. Garth sought and found his subject in the emerging professions and monopolies of the expanding economic marketplace of the 1690s. His mock-epic on the drug-dispensing practices of physicians and apothecaries illustrates the shift in satire from a predominantly political focus to a more broadly based social one. Individuals in the *Dispensary* are recessed into social policy, which is essentially anonymous. Garth understood as much when he depicted his chief physician in the poem, one Mirmillo, as desiring to run everything behind the scenes without subjecting himself to any kind of public scrutiny: "Then shall so useful a *Machin* as I / Engage in civil Broyls, I know not why?" (Canto v, lines 23–24).

In his *True-Born Englishman*, Defoe offers a different insight into the post-Revolutionary dispensation of England. His satire attacks the notion that purity of bloodline and innate or inherent rights based upon descent determine nationhood. Behind this attack, of course, is a revulsion at the general idea of privilege as the basis for political dominance, a theme that Defoe elaborates in his huge twelve-book satire, *Jure Divino* (1706). *The True-Born Englishman* was one of the most popular satiric poems of the era. For Defoe, the virulent xenophobia broadly directed at the reigning king, William III, was particularly offensive in light of the "vain ill-natur'd" claims that the native English made to power based on the purity of race.

> These are the Heroes that despise the *Dutch*,
> And rail at new-come Foreigners so much;
> Forgetting that themselves are all deriv'd
> From the most Scoundrel Race that ever liv'd.
> A horrid Medley of Thieves and Drones,
> Who ransack'd Kingdoms, and dispeopl'd Towns.
> The *Pict* and Painted *Britain*, Treach'rous *Scot*,
> By Hunger, Theft, and Rapine, hither brought.
> *Norwegian* Pirates, Buccaneering *Danes*,
> Whose Red-hair'd Off-spring ev'ry where remains.
> Who join'd with *Norman-French*, compound the Breed
> From whence your *True-Born Englishmen* proceed.
>
> (lines 233–44)

Defoe employs many of the terms associated with satire in the period – lampoon, irony, banter, ridicule – against the claims of rank or race.

> The Wonder which remains is at our Pride,
> To value that which all wise men deride.
> For *Englishmen* to boast of Generation,
> Cancels their Knowledge, and lampoons the Nation.
> A *True-Born Englishman*'s a Contradiction,
> In Speech an Irony, in Fact a Fiction.
> A Banter made to be a Test of Fools,

Which those that use it justly ridicules.
A Metaphor invented to express
A Man *a-kin* to all the Universe.   (lines 368–77)

The universal sweep of such satires as the *Dispensary* and *The True-Born Englishman* connects the enterprise of these poems to what can be called the great "systems" satires of a few years later, Swift's *Gulliver's Travels*, John Gay's *Beggar's Opera*, Pope's *Dunciad*, and Fielding's *Jonathan Wild*. Though earlier Restoration satirists such as Butler, Marvell, and Dryden began the long and elaborate process of turning a heavily localized and virtriolic brand of satire based mainly on verbal tirade, pointed lampoon, and libel into a more general attack on systems of related behaviors that encompass politics, aesthetics, religion, commerce, and knowledge, that process was greatly expanded in the next generation of satirists. Satire drew for its resources on the immensely various world of print that evolved in the early decades of the eighteenth century. Print was big business, and its productions a kind of compendium for modern living. Business was, by its nature, a subject that intrigued – and sometimes horrified – satirists. John Arbuthnot of Pope's circle of friends conjured up the new entrepreneurial spirit of England by inventing a satiric figure to represent it – "John Bull." The name has stuck through the ages. The image of a single-minded, bull-headed, trade-oriented, on-the-make, commercially spirited John Bull reflects not only the political dispensation that encouraged him but the new print world that supported him, including that of the mercurial journalist John Duntun and the dauntless Daniel Defoe, author of every kind of review, manual, conduct book, memoir, and modern adventure imaginable.

Traditional forms of satire – burlesque, mock-epic, verse satire – still thrived in the post-1688 Revolution period in England, but satirists were more and more eager to mimic the newer forms of print culture that they saw as particularly commercial or particularly daft. The most powerful group of satirists centered around Pope and Swift called themselves the Scriblerian Club. The name is well chosen to mark the print world that at once so intrigued and appalled them. One of the massive joint projects of the Scriblerians – the sketchy *Memoirs of Martinus Scriblerus* – was an attempt to insinuate their own work into modern memory. The *Memoirs* touched on everything from commercial autobiography to travel literature and served as a mock template for all brands of modern writing and modern sensibility.

The early dealings and discussions of the Scriblerian satirists around 1712 and 1713 produced their plan satirically to refashion all of modern culture, though most of the Scriblerian memoirs were never written exactly in the form conceived for them. Instead, the club shared ideas that ended up as the great individual satires of the period, including Gay's *Beggar's Opera* (1728), an idea given to Gay by Swift, Swift's *Gulliver's Travels* (1726), an idea given to Swift by Pope, and Pope's *Dunciad* (1729), an idea given to Pope by Swift. Each of these, to a degree, evokes worlds of truly vulgar magnificence and each satirizes, to a degree, a new kind of commercial and material order in England. A key subject of the Scriblerians is the figure of Robert Walpole, the Treasurer and then first Prime Minister of the realm, as the entrepreneur of a huge spoils system that dominated English cultural, political, and aesthetic life. Walpole shows up in one form or another everywhere, as Reldresal and Flimnap in Swift's Lilliputian court in *Gulliver's Travels*, as the thief MacHeath in Gay's *Beggar's Opera*, as the slimy manipulator in many of Fielding's domestic stage farces, as the head of an underworld network in Fielding's *Jonathan Wild*, and as the corrupt force of history in Bolingbroke's often satiric periodical, *The Craftsman*. In Pope's *Dunciad*, where one of the controlling ideas of the satire holds that government, like everything else, reflects the chaos of modernity, Walpole steps forward at the very end of the satire and names himself as first minister of Chaos and Tyrant of all Dunces.

> Perhaps more high some daring son may soar,
> Proud to my list to add one Monarch more;
> And nobly conscious, Princes are but things
> Born for First Ministers, as Slaves for Kings,
> Tyrant supreme! shall three Estates command,
> And MAKE ONE MIGHTY DUNCIAD OF THE LAND!
>
> (Book 4, lines 599–604)

The Dunciad is a monumental instance of how the scope of satire expands in the early eighteenth century to absorb virtually everything modern society can display and produce. Pope's poem offers the same spectacle of cultural rot that Dryden portrayed in *Mac Flecknoe*, but Dryden had confined that rot to a carefully delineated neighborhood of London. Pope's subject is a full migration, "*one, great* and *remarkable action*," described in the prefatory material to the poem as "the Removal of the Imperial seat of Dulness from the City to the polite world." That movement enacts the worst revolutionary nightmares of the previous century, and Pope well knew it. His satire cuts across all classes, professions, and orders in the world of London, from the shops on Watling Street, to the West End theatres, to the palace drawing rooms at Whitehall. The sons of Dulness gather their mother's forces.

And now the Queen, to glad her sons, proclaims
By herald Hawkers, high heroic Games.
They summon all her Race: An endless band
Pours forth, and leaves unpeopled half the land.
A motley mixture! in long wigs, in bags,
In silks, in crapes, in Garters, and in rags,
From drawing rooms, from colleges, from garrets,
On horse, on foot, in hacks, and gilded chariots:
All who true Dunces in her cause appear'd,
And all who knew those Dunces to reward.

(Book 2, lines 17–26)

Metaphors of abundance and multiplication rule in the *Dunciad* as hacks, hawkers, tractarians, orators, pantomimists, patrons, entrepreneurs, and virtuosi coagulate on the streets. From Pope's perspective as satirist, London is stuffed with the bodies of dunces and awash in printer's ink. Writers on the scene write too much and end up simply producing oblivion in their readers: "While pensive Poets painful vigils keep, / Sleepless themselves, to give their readers sleep" (Book 1, lines 93–94). The implicit story of the poem is a Virgilian dispensation of mindlessness, a dispensation that also suggests the worst kind of second coming.

"O! when shall rise a Monarch all our own,
And I, a Nursing-mother, rock the throne,
'Twixt Prince and People close the Curtain draw,
Shade him from Light, and cover him from Law . . ."

(Book 1, lines 311–14)

Dulness annihilates so much sense and sensibility that the concluding lines of the poem are a magnificent redaction of the creation of the world in *Genesis*. The world is sucked back into a state of its own pre-origins. Pope knows that the properties of dulness let loose will convert form and matter to gas, and that the yawn at poem's end, a word etymologically connected to the Greek chaos or gas, is the ultimate satiric spectacle, a reverse creation. By time Pope is done with Dulness, there really is literally no other subject left, and the end of the poem returns to an image presented near the beginning where "things destroy'd are swept to things unborn" (Book 1, line 241).

Thus at her felt approach, and secret might,
Art after *Art* goes out, and all is Night.
See skulking *Truth* to her old Cavern fled,
Mountains of Casuistry heap'd o'er her head!
Philosophy, that lean'd on Heav'n before,

Shrinks to her second cause, and is no more.
Physic of Metaphysic begs defence,
And *Metaphysic* calls for Aid on *Sense*!
See *Mystery* to *Mathematics* fly!
In vain! they gaze, turn giddy, rave, and die.
Religion blushing veils her sacred fires,
And unawares *Morality* expires.
Not *public* Flame, nor *private*, dares to shine;
Nor *human* Spark is left, nor Glimpse *divine*.
Lo! Thy dread Empire, CHAOS! is restor'd;
Light dies before thy uncreating word;
Thy hand, great Anarch! lets the curtain fall;
And Universal Darkness buries All.   (Book 4, lines 639–56)

The *Dunciad* is the closest satire gets in the eighteenth century to the full project envisioned by the Scriblerian Club of writing up England as a parody of its own worst literary productions. Always at issue in the Scriblerian world is the impulse to invade the design of other literary forms and subvert their premises. In a concentrated way, that same impulse is at the heart of Jonathan Swift's great satires as well. For example, his famous tract advocating an unusual solution for Ireland's economic problems, *A Modest Proposal* (1729), works by foisting itself off as an economic pamphlet consonant in tone with other schemes and projects of its time. Swift knew that the form in which he conveyed his proposal would look and sound familiar even while he imagined an outlandish scheme in which an oppressed nation butchers, trades, and fricassees its own progeny.

From his first efforts at satire decades earlier, Swift identified his talent as almost ventriloquial. In *A Tale of A Tub*, conceived in the early 1690s and printed in 1704, he speaks of his own technique "where the Author personates the Style and Manner of other Writers, whom he has a mind to expose" (p. 3). Even the look of the printed page in *A Tale* suggests the objects of Swift's parodies, the fits and starts of modern writing where everything is a prospectus and a promise. In *Gulliver's Travels*, he actually includes a diagram in the narrative representing a contrivance by which writers could produce texts without the time-consuming effort of actually writing them: "Every one knew how laborious the usual Method is of attaining to Arts and Sciences; whereas by his Contrivance, the most ignorant Person at a reasonable Charge, and with a little bodily Labour, may write Books in Philosophy, Poetry, Politicks, Law, Mathematicks and Theology, without the least Assistance from Genius or Study" (Book 3, ch. 5). The mechanism simply takes in letters and spews out random syllables and, with luck, random phrases (see fig. 2.1).

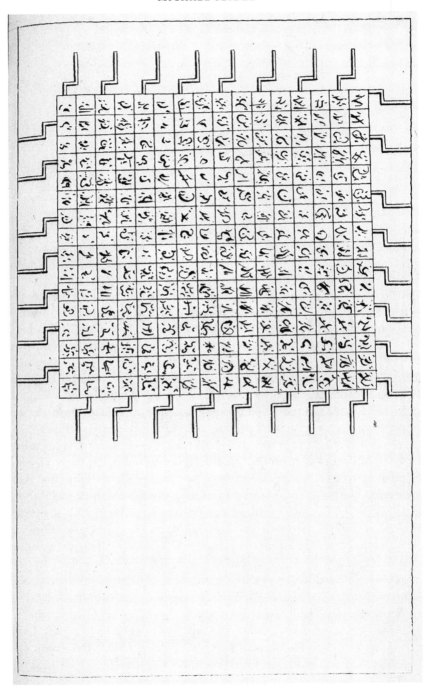

2.1 *Contrivance*, from Jonathan Swift, *Gulliver's Travels* (1726), Book 3, chapter 5

In *Gulliver's Travels*, Swift bevels along the edges of the most important evolving forms of contemporary writing: the personal memoir, the true history, the life and adventure – forms contributing to what is now loosely called the novel. His narrative seems at first to possess all the attributes of the novel form – a detailed contemporary setting, a wealth of circumstantiating information, a concentration on contingencies and necessities of modern living, a narrative focus on an adventurer of middling or professional class status. But to mark *Gulliver's Travels* as a novel fails to grasp that the style of novels such as Defoe's *Robinson Crusoe* (1719) is precisely what Swift satirizes. Gulliver, for example, sinks into Crusoe's skin when he notes late in his adventures, "My Design was, if possible to discover some small Island uninhabited, yet sufficient by my Labour to furnish me with Necessaries of Life, which I would have thought a greater Happiness than to be first Minister in the politest Court of *Europe*" (Book 4, ch. 11). But instead of on his own island, Gulliver ends up in his own barn, deluded into thinking he can talk to horses.

By getting so close to his subjects, that is, by taking over the very forms in which they present themselves, Swift's work exacerbates a condition that has always troubled satire. The relationship between satirist and subject becomes not one of simple opposition but one of uneasy proximity or sharing. In his fascinating short essay, *Meditation Upon a Broomstick*, Swift imagines how that object which is supposed to do the job of cleaning ends up making itself dirty. The result is not unlike the ending of *Gulliver's Travels*. Swift's broom is "by a capricious Kind of Fate, destined to make other Things clean, and be nasty it self." Swift goes on to point out that the "universal Reformer and Corrector of Abuses; a Remover of Grievances; rakes into every Slut's Corner of Nature, bringing hidden Corruption to the Light, and raiseth a mighty Dust where there was none before; sharing deeply all the while in the very same Pollutions he pretends to sweep away."[9]

Swift is the last person who would want to be blamed for polluting the literary environment, and, for this reason, above all others, he invents a series of surrogates, sacrificial satiric brooms, to do his dirty work for him, whether the modern hack in *A Tale of A Tub*, the economic projector in *A Modest Proposal*, the astrologer in the *Bickerstaff Papers*, the cloth merchant in the *Drapier's Letters*. Similarly, Swift sends Gulliver out at the end of his travels to both absorb and perform all the dirty work the species has to offer. As an English yahoo, Gulliver is left sputtering at the end about what has plagued him as a character from the beginning, the absurd vice of pride in his being, his bearing, his nation, and his times.

I dwell the longer upon this Subject from the Desire I have to make the Society of an *English Yahoo* by any Means not insupportable; and therefore I here intreat those who have any Tincture of this absurd Vice, that they will not presume to appear in my Sight. (Book 4, ch. 12)

Whose presumption is at issue here? The conclusion of the *Travels* brings us back to the nature of satiric action. Most literary actions end with the reader feeling a sense of closure or satisfaction. Satire tends to end in the same state of disrepair in which it begins. Classical literary criticism calls the process of resolving an action a denouement, meaning an unraveling of the complicating knots within the plot. But satire knows no denouement unless, of course, it stops being satire. More likely its action ends up another kind of knot, a *snafu*, in which the reader comprehends in the acronym the action satire represents: SITUATION NORMAL, ALL FOULED (or a variant thereof) UP.

NOTES

1 *A Parallel of Poetry and Painting*, in *The Prose Works of John Dryden*, ed. W. P. Ker, 2 vols. (Oxford: Clarendon Press, 1900), vol. II, p. 146.

2 In *The Works of John Dryden*, ed. E. N. Hooker and H. T. Swedenberg, Jr., 20 vols. (Berkeley and Los Angeles: University of California Press, 1956–), vol. XVII, *Of Dramatic Poesy* (1971), ed. Samuel Holt Monk, pp. 196–97.

3 *A Tale of a Tub*, ed. Herbert Davis (Oxford: Blackwell, 1965), p. 100.

4 *The Works of John Dryden*, vol. IV, *Poems 1693–1696* (1974), ed. A. B. Chambers and William Frost, p. 71. Further citations to the *Discourse* will be to this edition with page number given in parenthesis in the text.

5 *Bickerstaff Papers and Pamphlets on the Church*, ed. Herbert Davis (Oxford: Blackwell, 1966), p. 164.

6 "Epistle to the Whigs" of *The Medal, The Works of John Dryden*, vol. II (1972), ed. H. T. Swedenberg, Jr., p. 41.

7 "Preface to the Poems (1656)," in J. E. Spingarn (ed.), *Critical Essays of the Seventeenth Century* (Bloomington: University of Indiana Press, 1957), vol. II, p. 88.

8 *Characters and Passages From Note-Books*, ed. A. R. Waller (Cambridge: Cambridge University Press, 1908), p. 442.

9 *Meditation Upon a Broomstick*, in *A Tale of a Tub, with Other Early Works 1696–1707*, ed. Herbert Davis (Oxford: Oxford University Press, 1965), pp. 239–40. The same notion seems to have carried into the twentieth century. George Bernard Shaw, an Irish compatriot of Swift's two hundred years removed, told an interviewer, "You cannot carry out moral sanitation, any more than physical sanitation, without indecent exposures."

FURTHER READING

Elliot, Robert C., *The Power of Satire: Magic, Ritual, Art* (Princeton, NJ: Princeton University Press, 1960).

Gill, James (ed.), *Cutting Edges: Postmodern Critical Essays on Eighteenth-Century Satire* (Knoxville: University of Tennessee Press, 1995).

Griffin, Dustin, *Satire: A Critical Reintroduction* (Lexington: University of Kentucky Press, 1994).

Lord, George deForest (ed.), *Poems on Affairs of State: Augustan Satirical Verse, 1660–1714*, 7 vols. (New Haven: Yale University Press, 1963–75).

Paulson, Ronald (ed.), *Modern Essays in Criticism: Satire* (Englewood Cliffs, NJ: Prentice Hall, 1971).

Rawson, Claude, *Satire and Sentiment, 1669–1830* (Cambridge: Cambridge University Press, 1993).

Seidel, Michael, *Satiric Inheritance, Rabelais to Sterne* (Princeton, NJ: Princeton University Press, 1979).

3

MARGARET A. DOODY

Gender, literature, and gendering literature in the Restoration

At least until very recent times no literary era has been as conscious of what we call "gender" as the period we call "the Restoration." It is impossible to deal with literature of this period (not excluding Milton) without encountering observations upon masculinity and femininity, statements about the male and the female and the androgyne.[1] These elements or attributes, if often represented in terms of opposition and conflict, are also represented as essential. Yet if these attributes are essences, they lack Aristotelian fixity. They are not fixed but mutable, iridescent and flickering like Pope's airy sylphs in *The Rape of the Lock*.

Why was the Restoration so peculiarly gender-conscious? There may be no absolute answer, but some important factors should be considered. The Civil War was an event of the utmost importance to the English, an instance of very open and certainly not imaginary conflict raging over questions of power and authority (including the authority of interpretation). The king and Court were associated with Continental rather than English beliefs and fashion. The idea of the "foreign" is always "feminine" rather than "masculine." That Charles had married a French queen seemed only a kind of proof of the association of Royalists with dangerous, alien – and wickedly alluring – femininity.

I have said elsewhere "The Civil War was a war of *styles*" (*The Daring Muse*, p. 45). Style was both accident and essence. It is not only in the modern popular view that the Cavaliers are associated with long locks, lace, and licentiousness, or the Roundheads with short ugly haircuts and dark plain clothing. Both the parties concerned and their enemies thought so too. Royalists wore their hair long and in curls, a courtly style associated with the reign of Charles I. Such a style was inveighed against as unnatural, unChristian, and unmanly. One pamphlet attack was called *The Unloveliness of Lovelocks*. According to John Aubrey (1626–97), an undergraduate at Oxford in the early 1640s, the head of Trinity College in that era was "irreconcileable to long haire." He went about with a pair of scissors for the benefit of any Trinity Scholars whose hair had grown too long," and "woe be to them that sate on the outside of the Table."[2]

Hair remained an issue. In that anti-Restoration Restoration epic *Paradise Lost* (1667), John Milton is at pains to deal with Adam's hair. Adam is living in the natural state in Paradise, and the natural state of course includes nakedness. That is less problematic, in a way, than the fact that Adam's hair must grow, as he knows no tools nor barber. Milton must not, however, allow his Adam to look like a Cavalier. Adam's hair is shorter than Eve's, as Milton explains it should be:

> His fair large Front and Eye sublime declar'd
> Absolute rule; and Hyacinthin Locks
> Round from his parted forelock manly hung
> Clustring, but not beneath his shoulders broad:
> Shee as a vail down to the slender waste
> Her unadorned golden tresses wore
> Dissheveld, but in wanton ringlets wav'd
> As the Vine curls her tendrils, which impli'd
> Subjection, but requir'd with gentle sway
>
> (Book IV, lines 300–08)

Long hair, long curls, signify wantonness and subjection, feminine imperfection. Unfallen Nature is strangely careful not to let Adam's hair grow, since Adam can take no technological means to curtail it. What can be more "natural" than letting hair grow? And hair on a young male head, when allowed to grow uncut, does not necessarily remain shorter than a woman's – as young people in the 1960s satisfactorily demonstrated. In Milton's later Restoration work, *Samson Agonistes* (1671), the Biblical hero is suffering from the effects of barbering. He was "Effeminatly vanquish'd" (line 562). Paradoxically, Samson "effeminated," seduced by Dalila, stopped looking like a Cavalier. Samson became an inadvertent Roundhead who needs to recover. He has recovered when he refers to the hair he has regrown: "these redundant locks / Robustious to no purpose, clustring down" (lines 568–69). Samson now is in tune with the Restoration fashion, which went in for redundancy of hair (supplemented by the wide wig); Samson with his restored and full "robustious" hair now may even look a little like Charles II.

The hirsute contrast of Milton's heroes exhibits some of the tensions and paradoxes within all such signs of gender and power. Hair seems an essential part of the natural body, a visible and tangible portion of identity, and yet it is easily parted, parted with, and altered. It is almost too carnal to be comfortable, a redundancy of mere matter, subject to constant transformation. To have another person (more especially of the opposite sex) disarrange or remove one's hair is a sign that the stable self is a fiction. Hair is ever readily subject to drastic change, even at the very spur of the moment, as Belinda will find in *The Rape of the Lock* (1712). Hair, grown or cut (and in youth equally growable or cuttable), is a good indicator and sign of various other kinds of cultural instability and changefulness. It is noticeable that whenever the English arrive at times of stress and national tension they mess about with their hair, as the punks did in the 1980s; such representations of hair enact rebellion and instability, and point out the unfixedness of conventional signs, including marks of gender and thus gender itself.

The Cavaliers' style was in the eyes of some an offense to traditional masculinity. It expressed the decorative idea of the Renaissance in a mannerist way, favoring the thin figure (like the real body of King Charles I). It favored elegant decoration and appurtenances (lace and plumed hats) and valued airy grace over what was stocky and muscular. We have to wait for the era of Aubrey Beardsley and the aesthetes of the late Victorian age to find another group of English males defining itself in a manner so little in the bulldog style. The king's own (fatal) representation of himself, the Royal Patriarch, as feminine or "effeminate" forced a conceptual disjunction. This is not a question of what we call "sexual orientation." It was Charles's father who indulged himself with male favorites; this may have added to a sense of offense in some quarters, but it was not different from the practices of many other kings. Sexual preference did not in itself accentuate the "feminine." King Charles I was considered both feminine and uxorious. Indeed, to be too fond of a woman, or of women, traditionally (if curiously) makes a man "effeminate." Opponents of King Charles I and his heirs ridicule them in phrases indicating they are small and soft, as Marchamont Needham did in perpetually referring to Charles II as "Baby Charles." These people are not competent, they are not real grown-up males.

Cromwell presented himself as a grown-up male, a stout and stout-hearted warrior and a no-nonsense gentleman of the bulldog kind. But the advent of this masculinity was associated with a sense of loss:

> Though for a time we see White-hall
> With cobweb-hanging on the wall,
> Instead of gold and silver brave,
> Which formerly, 'twas wont to have
> > With rich perfume
> > In every room,
> > Delightful to that princely train . . .
> (Anon., ballad, "When the King Enjoys His Own Again")

According to this Cavalier view, a superflux of masculinity has adversely affected the beautiful space. The palace is rendered barren, without ornament, denuded not only of visual and tactile pleasures but lacking its other sensualities, its "rich perfume." The feminine, the luxurious and pleasurable, has not been displaced by strong male accoutrements and signifiers. Rather, there is a gap, emptiness. Nothing replaces the sensuous tapestries – save the feebly sensuous, unintelligent, and unsignifying cobweb, more fragile than the fabric whose place it usurps.

If the major political events that constitute the Civil War and the Interregnum involved complex senses of gender, gender roles, and displacements, it can be no wonder that the culture of the next two or three generations, of those who came of age or were born after the settlement of 1660, was imbued with ideas of gender – and of gender as problematic. As we can see, it is quite possible to talk in gender terms and about gendered conflicts even when all the human subjects involved are males. Class terms readily become gender terms. If monarchy is "feminine," if aristocracy also becomes feminized, then the merchant classes should, in contrast, be "masculine." Hence, government and all proper patriarchy might really belong to them, a view enforced by Protestant Puritan emphasis on the head of the household's role as priest of his household, responsible for saying prayers before his assembled subjects and looking well into all their ways. The claim of the merchant class, its appropriation of the patriarchal role, was again acted out in the so-called "Bloodless Revolution" of 1688 and the settlement of 1689.

Such gendered class warfare runs straight into a paradox. If the real "male heir" to social power is the masculine merchant class, that class can succeed only by persuading people to import and buy and use "feminine" luxuries like silk and porcelain. This group's new money rests on feminine and feminizing sources. Pope's Belinda, ambiguous heroine of *The Rape of the Lock*, as Louis Landa points out, is an archetypal consumer.[3] She thus may represent the wastefulness of the female aristocrat, but she equally represents the eligible image of England's desirable trade, productivity and consumption. There is not really felt to be an alternative to this sort of civilization. Thomas Hobbes had already pointed out that the truly simple and individualistic life resting on male individual power is unlivable and uncivilized – in the famous phrase of Hobbes's *Leviathan* (1651), in the "naturall condition" of humanity, which is "a warre . . . of every man, against every man," we find that "the life of man [is] solitary, poore, nasty, brutish, and short" (*Leviathan*, ch. 13, pp. 88–89). This sounds like a parodic account of manliness. Such brutishness is the logical conclusion of an (imaginary) entirely non-effeminate masculinity.

Civilization always looks somewhat "feminine," and "masculinity," if it is projected too far along one trajectory, ends in the Hobbesian state of Nature. Very few of the new patriarchs wanted to be painted warts and all; an endeavor to appropriate the stuff of the old "feminine" monarchic aristocracy is noticeable in all trends, including manners and furnishings. The concept of "sensibility," a major philosophical idea which was to furnish a partial answer to the conceptual and philosophical–social problems of the new colonial and mercantile era, was not arrived at in a hurry. The soothing mediation of "sensibility," as the eighteenth century developed it, ascribed previously "feminine" qualities to normal male psychology and behavior, and assured us of a smoother social interaction during a time of great economic and social disruption. This concept also smoothed the progress to a complex capitalist society and the new industrial age. As G. J. Barker-Benfield points out, part of the program of the new "sensibility" is "The Reformation of Male Manners." Sensibility, Barker-Benfield emphasizes, is connected with consumerism; although others have argued that the period saw a new separation of the sexes in public and private spheres, Barker-Benfield points out that the development of capitalism meant that men and women now often shared, to a greater degree than before, the same spaces in work and leisure. The new code of decency was to question certain traditional male pastimes, including heavy drinking, practical jokes, and wife-beating.[4] To put it simply, shopkeepers had to learn to treat customers with a new "civility," and not to offend them by acts like spitting on the floor, as well as not to mock or curse or grumble at them. The processes which bring such change were at work in the Restoration, but without the new definitions and styles of resolution. "Sensibility," which brings a new self-consciousness with it, made it possible to grasp these inevitable alterations in what had seemed like "nature." The relation between strangers and sensibility has perhaps been insufficiently taken into account. As we can see clearly in a work like Samuel Richardson's *Sir Charles Grandison* (1753–54), with its universalist optimism, the idea of "sensibility" furnished all classes not only with a concept of "manners" but also with a belief in the inner responsiveness of all mankind. It thus made less terrifying the unavoidable encounter with strangers in this new, more mobile, and constantly exchanging society. Despite Jean Hagstrum's claim that the "Age of Sensibility" begins with Milton and Dryden, we can see that the Restoration was largely without the reassuring mediation of the concept of "sensibility." Without this emollient and intellectual resource, the Restoration played out its uncertainties, its estrangements, its (often irate) apprehensions of social conflict, and its understanding of conflicts within individual psychology, in terms of what *we*, following theorists such as Judith Butler (see her *Gender Trouble*), prefer to call "Gender" rather than "Sex." We should remember that this is our terminology, though the concept is arguably already present. "Gender" imbues everything, and nothing is to be discussed without it.

If this was so, it was partly at least because after the Restoration of King Charles I's son, Charles II, which represented a kind of triumph of the "feminine," there was a sudden lack of clarity about the significance of the gendrification of sociopolitical life. No gender was quite victorious. At this point in English history, and at this point alone, the culture in general demonstrated that it was possible to play with both gender and politics. The situation almost meets the specifications of instability and interrogation implicit in Judith Butler's prescription: "the task is . . . to repeat . . . and through a radical proliferation of gender, to *displace* the very gender norms that enable the repetition itself." Butler alleges that "there is no ontology of gender on which we might construct a politics"(*Gender Trouble*, p. 148). She wants us to recognize this *now*, when there is a resistance to accepting such a lack, but in England just after 1660 (and through the Revolution of 1688–89), the ontologies of both gender and politics were radically fragmented. What we see in the literature is "a radical proliferation of gender" and a displacement of gender norms. Much of the "wit" for which the era is so often (if often vaguely) celebrated arises from the recognition of the need constantly to repeat gender norms – and constantly to break, reverse, dismiss, or otherwise abuse them.

From the point of view of women, the prevalent distrust of both gender norms and political truths, and the consequent lack of simple wholesome clarity, presented certain welcome opportunities. Writing, which permitted access to public media, including even the very public medium of the stage, was not only economically tempting to women writers, but also psychologically inviting. For the first time it was really possible for a woman to enter this public realm of the kingdom – or republic – of letters, and to do so effectively. The printing press, however, was not grand; it had been thoroughly deconstructed. It had produced not only books and poems but also small pamphlets and squibs of all kinds. The press had got down and dirty and spewed out many different kinds of propaganda during the Civil War (and even in the highly censored Interregnum); it was visibly not masculine master but feminine servant. If the press was, as its enemies so frequently proclaimed, a prostitute, and not only a whore but a fecund womb of error (as it is already in Spenser's *The Faerie Queene*), it was not and could not be a patriarch.

Milton, in his 1644 defense of the liberty of the press and of its readers, turns to a story of the feminine, an Egyptian myth about a goddess. Readers and writers in search of truth are "imitating the carefull search that *Isis* made for the mangl'd body of *Osiris* . . . gathering up limb by limb still as they could find them" (*Prose Works*, vol. ii, p. 549). What Milton is too polite to say in *Areopagitica* is that the part of Osiris' mangled body Isis had trouble finding (according to Egyptian myth) is the virile member.[5] We may read all the books and pamphlets that tumble out of a printing press uncensored (as Milton wishes it to be), and never come to an end, a final phallic say. Despite Derrida's well-known complaint about the "phallogocentric culture," in this flow of emission coming from the printing press it is hard – nay, impossible – to find the phallus. If the pen is masculine, the press where the products of the pen come to birth is an unruly feminine reproductive organ. So it is for Pope in the *Dunciad* (1728–43) – the goddess Dulness is the new despicable dirty Power, the teeming womb of the press.

In the Restoration, writing becomes a gender-indeterminate activity, if yet an activity incessantly about gender. The Restoration's terms of stylistic criticism are also terms of gender classification. But any classification is followed by questioning, by revisions of unstable reclassification. We can see this, for example, in Aphra Behn's "To the Unknown Daphnis on his Excellent Translation of Lucretius":

> Methinks I should some wonderous thing Reherse
> Worthy *Divine Lucretius*, and *Diviner You*!
> . . .
> In Gentle Numbers all my Songs are drest:
>   And when I would Thy Glories sing,
>   What in Strong Manly Verse should be exprest
>   Turns all to Womanish Tenderness within;
>   Whilst that which Admiration does Inspire,
>   In other Souls, kindles in Mine a Fire.
> Let them admire thee on – whilst I this newer way
>   Pay thee yet more than They,
>   For more I ow, since thou hast taught Me more
>   Than all the Mighty *Bards* that went before;
>   Others long since have pauld the vast Delight,
>   In Duller *Greek* and *Latine* satisfi'd the Appetite:
>   But I unlearn'd in Schools disdain that Mine
>   Should treated be at any feast but Thine.   (lines 5–24)

Behn goes on to say that until now she has "curst my *Sex* and *Education* / And more the scanted Customs of the Nation" for forbidding "the Female Sex to tread / The Mighty Paths of Learned *Heroes* Dead" (lines 25–28).

Women have hitherto been kept from Latin and Greek poetry, but Thomas Creech's translation of Lucretius represents a progress of civilization; Creech is the "Daphnis" of a literary love affair based on the old novel *Daphnis and Chloe*, but he combines the role of pastoral lover with that of a true caregiving pastor. Just as the bards once taught men to leave off savage manners and ranging the woods,

> So Thou by this *Translation* dost advance
> Our Knowledge from the State of Ignorance
> And Equallst us to Man!   (lines 41–43)

Behn's poem of 1683 implicitly takes issue with the account of the world given in the first chapters of Genesis and in Milton's *Paradise Lost*. Woman did not lose the world in falling from her own original "State of Innocence," but was left behind in a primitive "State of Ignorance" until language came to the rescue, personified by heroic Creech who bridges the gap between civilized knowledge and woman's language. Despite Behn's proclamation that she, as Woman, knew no classical literature before, we may catch echoes of Horace and of the kind of Epicurean history offered in, for instance, the third Satire of the first book, where Horace paints a picture of a rough and brutal mankind until life changed when man acquired speech – "until they discovered words and names by which to describe voiced cries and feelings" (lines 99–104). Behn's praise of Creech may not be orthodox from a Christian point of view, and is not as straightforward as it seems. There are further complexities.

At the outset the speaker of this poem is already a writer, and already thoroughly female. She is not capable of "Strong Manly Verse," but finds that her poetry emerges in "Gentle Numbers" and "Womanish Tenderness." This might seem a thoroughly hierarchical arrangement, an orthodox expression of humble inferiority. But the next lines express the ability of the mind that owns gentleness and tenderness to seize on the (male) writer's work not with cold admiration (like a male reader), but with "Fire." The fire of passion, of sexual approval and desire, and the fire of literary imagination kindled are all combined. Male readers and the other male writers get the worst of it. They will not, or cannot, appreciate Creech's accomplishment, as they have already dulled their appetites by plodding (at school presumably) through Greek and Latin. The "vast Delight" is not to be theirs. Poor souls, they have used up the supply of delightful incandescence in the wrong way; they have taken in the source of inspiration at dogged intervals and by rote. The leading metaphor at the end of the opening verse paragraph is "Appetite" – and the woman reader has it. She is ready for the feast, as male readers are not. Dulness and a lack of sexual energy become the properties of males as readers (and implicitly of many male writers). A doubt is cast on the ability of poets other than Creech to rise to any occasion. Creech, in being thus singular among men, loses some of the dull ordinariness of implied masculinity and acquires a kind of androgynous allure, the power of the exceptional. The compliments to Wadham College and its progeny in the second half of Behn's tribute to Creech make it clear that there *are* wonderful male writers. But such male writers themselves share "feminine" qualities:

> No sooner was fam'd *Strephons* Glory set,
> *Strephon* the soft, the Lovely, Gay and Great;
> But *Daphnis* rises like the Morning Star
> That guides the wandring Traveller from afar
> *Daphnis*, whom every Grace, and Muse inspires
> Scarce *Strephons* Ravishing Poetick Fires
> So kindly warm, or so Divinely Cheer   (lines 107–13)

Daphnis–Creech is like Lucifer and like Venus, the morning star. "Strephon" perhaps should resemble the sun, as he has set. But "Strephon" – a name for John Wilmot, Lord Rochester, one of his comic-poetic names for himself – is also both masculine and feminine. He shares with the speaker the leading quality of "Fire." His ardor, passion, sexuality – his "Fires" – are to be found in his poetry, which is "Ravishing," not in the sense of committing rape but in the feminine sense of being charming and seductive. Strephon is "the soft, the Lovely, Gay and Great." Only one of these substantial adjectives is masculine. Strephon–Rochester's "greatness" would seem to be compounded of his softness, loveliness, and gaiety. That he is "the Gay" suggests several qualities of airiness, wit, and sexual gayness, or freedom to engage in a variety of adventures. The poet pastoralized (or mock-pastoralized as "Strephon") is a perfect androgyne, a sun king as gay lady. Indeed, the poem indicates that the very qualities that make Rochester great as a poet are these astounding mixtures of gendered qualities. Writing is an experience of mixing the genders. It is truly promiscuous.

Such a view accords very well with Rochester's own literary practice, and with the theories one can identify behind that practice. No poet of renown in English literary history is more unstable than Rochester, or more in favor of instability. This labile quality contributes largely to making his poems ever fresh and ever shocking. It is possible, after all, to be both pornographic and offensive and yet to be dull, as in, say, the works of the satirist Charles Churchill later in the eighteenth century. Rochester is always intellect at play – an intellect that is willing to discountenance itself.

In "To a Lady in a Letter," for example, the speaker addresses his Chloris in terms totally opposed to Richard Lovelace's Cavalier who could not love his lady so much did he not love Honor more. In Rochester's poem, nobody loves Honor, and everyone is unfaithful. We might anticipate the pose of a male speaker reprehending an unfaithful female – a traditional stance. Complaints against female inconstancy and wickedness traditionally abound in what are (as Rochester makes us realize) very male poems. There is a customary presumption, behind such plaints, that the female has a duty to be constant. Unchastity, according to dominant social morality, is hardly a vice in a man but a dreadful vice in a woman, a terrible fall that makes her totally unsuitable for the male, no matter how many sexual partners he may have. As a male possession she has the absolute duty of not getting stolen. Rochester deals very differently with the subject of the inconstant female. The speaker in Rochester's poem defies all conventions of any ownership by denying any right to jealousy:

> Such perfect Blisse, faire *Chloris*, wee
> In our Enjoyment prove
> 'Tis pity restless Jealousy
> Should Mingle with our Love.
> (lines 1–4; *Poems*, ed. Walker, p. 41)

Rather than a plea to the lady not to wrinkle her brow and ruin her composure by being jealous of him, as we might expect after such a start, the piece develops into an unexpected outline of what might make their "perfection":

> Lett us (since witt has taught us how)
> Raise pleasure to the Topp:
> You Rival Bottle must allow
> I'le suffer Rivall Fopp.   (lines 9–12)

The Gentleman-speaker's drinking and the Lady's promiscuity are treated in parallel. The appetites of both, gargantuan and unstoppable, must be respected. The matter is treated in regular meters and cadences resembling those of love-elegies of an idealistic cast. This deceptive smooth manner allows for the new tone – a tone itself part of the subject, and defended implicitly as an expression of frankness. A new and open honesty is to replace old poetic and social conventions. The free-ranging woman is paradoxically desired, while a subordinated woman, far from being desirable, could not be a good partner at all:

> All this you freely may Confesse,
> Yett wee nere disagree

> For did you love your pleasure lesse,
> You were noe Match for mee.
>
> Whilst I my pleasure to pursue
> Whole nights am takeing in,
> The Lusty juice of Grapes, take you
> The Juice of Lusty Men.   (lines 25–32)

It is not difficult to see why the bawdy Rochester was a favorite with women writers, praised not only by the dissolute Aphra Behn but also by the virtuous Anne Wharton, who sees in him an educative force: "He civiliz'd the rude and taught the young, / Made Fools grow wise" ("Elegy on the Earl of Rochester," lines 20–21).[6] Rochester may have been a terrible husband in real life, but as a poet he rejects the power role. He is perfectly conscious that convention governs our ideas as to appropriate behavior. He will not even play the conventional rake. In other works he writes about impotence (a topic affording a kind of sub-genre of poetry of the late seventeenth century), and he raises ideas of sexual pleasure by disconcertingly moving from homosexual to heterosexual experience and back again.

Rochester certainly does want to shock – there is a punk rocker quality about him, as about the Ovid of the *Amores*. Or perhaps Ovid's *Amores* is to rock video what Rochester's work is to punk rock – but in Rochester the punk rock quality is raised to the very highest style. His poetry is almost always aggressive, but it is aggressively questioning.

Aggressiveness is a dominant tone or manner of the Restoration, and aggressive questioning one of its norms. Sexuality is explored in its connection with power constructs and power relations. Power relations of any kind can hardly be talked of without recourse to sexual language and very conscious gendered imagery.

> Not that your Father's Mildness I condemn;
> But Manly Force becomes the Diadem.
>   . . .
> Perhaps his fear, his kindness may Controul.
>   . . .
> If so, by Force he wishes to be gain'd,
> Like womens Leachery, to seem Constrain'd:
> Doubt not, but when he most affects the Frown,
> Commit a pleasing Rape upon the Crown.
>   (John Dryden, *Absalom and Achitophel*, lines 381–474)

So says the villainous Achitophel in a great male–male seduction scene where, like Satan with Eve, he tries to urge his unequal interlocutor on to a bad deed. Achitophel uses Absalom (or Shaftesbury uses the illegitimate Monmouth) for his own purposes, but Achitophel can arousingly delude his puppet in the very act of seducing him by playing on his idea of "manliness." The rhetorical scene plays with the parallel between Achitophel's seduction of Absalom–Monmouth and Absalom–Monmouth's fantasized rape – or rather he would prefer to think, seduction – of his father, the now-feminized King David–Charles. A number of gender clichés are ironically implied and employed in Achitophel's speech: we're all men together, we know that women really want it, that there's no such thing as unwanted rape, manliness means getting on with what you want, force is allowed both in sex and in war . . . Absalom–Monmouth, however, exhibits his stupidity not only in his obtuseness to irony in general, but also in his desire to believe that gender terms and ideologies of gender are stable, and thus can serve as stable analogies to a politics still in the making.

All questions of war and politics seem here, as elsewhere in Restoration writing, thoroughly sexualized. The word "Manly" is scarcely used in this period without irony, though the irony was rarely carried so far as in William Wycherley's presentation of his tormented and brutal hero Manly in *The Plain Dealer* (1674). Wycherley's *The Country Wife* (1672) had already dealt very fully with the ironies of sexual identity. Only by losing the reputation for "manliness" can Horner be free to have all the women he wants, and thus to cuckold all the husbands. The extreme of masculine power has to become an apparently helpless feminized androgyny. The more aggressive Horner is, the more asexual he has to look. In a society which prefers reputation to realities, this is commonly thought too big a price to pay. But the joke is that the males who think they are and look very "manly" are as ridiculous as Horner appears. That Horner would or could bring himself to pay the price of forfeiting the name of masculinity shows that he is really, as others say he is, the figure of a man and not a recognizable male. But that is only because the recognizable males dwell in what we can clearly see are merely imbecilic if soothing communal fictions about masculinity.

Paradoxically, in an era that dealt in paradoxes, the aggressiveness of male writers in discussing sex and gender gave some freedom to women writers to tackle gender matters from new points of view, and to deal with their own anger, desire, and questioning. The very idea of writing is gendered, but any gendering as soon as announced is ripe for question. "A Female Pen" may be a contradiction in terms, but the Restoration lived by and with contradictions. Aphra Behn complains in her preface to *Sir Patient Fancy* (1678) that women did not support her but found fault with the play because it was bawdy, although this is no fault in other theatrical productions. Behn's preface picks up the gender game and uses it in Behn's own way, working up an anger (if partly in jest) against her own sex for not acknowledging what they do like.

Behn uses aggression very wittily and effectively, and she is not alone. Most of the leading Restoration writings sound like attacks on someone or something. We should never make the mistake of thinking the women writers are somehow "nicer." Pious Jane Barker in some unpublished satires sends her (political) enemies, the supporters of William, to Hell (Magdalen MS. 343), and the Duchess of Newcastle in *The Blazing World* imagines a new kind of superweapon that confounds the Roundheads and subjugates the world to the Stuart monarch. *Absalom and Achitophel* arguably goes further than usual as the author, when he published it, was seeking the real-life death of the model for the poem's anti-hero. Moreover, Dryden can complain in *The Medal* (1682) that this man, this Shaftesbury, is not alive to begin with – he is a fake, an image, a counterfeit, like the medal in his honor, with its false writing. Lethal wishes are thus justifiable. Dryden, who drew a famous comparison between the satirist and the skilled executioner, uses writing to annihilate. Restoration writing sometimes gleams with the weird luster of imaginary murder. Well into the next century, this quality is still perceptible in Jonathan Swift, especially in his poems:

> Like the ever-laughing Sage,
> In a Jest I spend my Rage:
> (Tho' it must be understood,
> I would hang them if I cou'd:)
>
> ("An Epistle to a Lady," lines 171–74)

Aggression in Restoration writing is intimately related to gender – it is aggression sexualized, enacted between entities with a sexual dynamic that exists even when the conflicted entities are both imaged as of the same sex: for example, Hudibras and Ralpho in *Hudibras* (both male); Satan and Christ in *Paradise Regained* (both male); the Hind and the Panther in Dryden's poem of 1687 (both female); Aphra Behn and the females in her audience in the case of *Sir Patient Fancy* (all female).

There is plenty of aggression in women's writings, and it emerges in relation to all sorts of topics. The point is to be able to keep anger under control, to make power-moves while looking cool. It helps that everything is on the table for question, that new definitions can constantly be introduced. The "virgin" is one of the figures refigured. The idea of the "virgin" in much traditional male writing means centrally a young ripe woman, not yet sexually branded as the possession of anyone other than her father; she is to be disposed of to the most qualified male. The virgin is attractive as a transitional figure, nubile, on the edge of initiation. Otherwise, the virgin is an antiquated spinster and a figure of fun. But women writers of the Restoration (especially but not only those of Catholic backgrounds) speak in defense of the "virgin" as a representative of the most desirable state for a woman. The virgin in the new definitions is not a sentimental reflection of the Virgin Mary but a human being with a sense of her own identity. She is free to think for herself, and to engage in good works and sensible conversation:

> Whose equal mind, does alwaies move,
> Neither a foe, nor slave to Love;
> And whose Religion's strong and plain,
> Not superstitious, nor profane.
> (Katherine Philips, "The Virgin," lines 19–22)

That Philips herself (not a virgin, but subject to the rules governing married women) may not have wanted to hide her work from the public press, even if she had to look as if she resented getting her poems published, has been convincingly argued.[7] Jane Barker amplifies Philips's defense of the virgin, in "A Virgin life":

> Since, gracious Heven, you have bestow'd on me
> So great a kindness for verginity,
> Suffer me not, to fall into the power,
> Of Mens, allmost omnipotent Amours.
> But let me in this happy state remain,
> And in chast verse, my chaster thoughts explain.
> Fearless of twenty-five and all its train,
> Of slights, or scorns, or being call'd Old Maid,
> Those Goblings, which so many have betray'd:
> . . .
> Ah! lovely state how strange it is to see,
> What mad conceptions, some have made of thee.
> (lines 1–16)[8]

We can see that the poet steadily amplifies both her scorn for the "goblins" (a Rossetti-ish touch) that scare ladies away from this desirable state, and her love for the occupations of the unmarried woman, including reading and religious meditation:

> Her Closet, where she do's much time bestow,
> Is both her Library and Chappel too,
> Where she enjoys Society alone,

I' th' Great Three-One –
She drives her whole Lives business to these Ends,
To serve her God, enjoy her Books and Friends.[9]

Barker included a version of this poem in her collection *Poetical Recreations* (1688) and another, heavily revised, in her novel of 1723, *A Patch-Work Screen for the Ladies*. In this late publication she softened the impact of the last line of 1688, changing it to "To serve her God, her Neighbours and her Friends." One feels the loss of the powerful Restoration sex-word "enjoy." In 1688, however, Barker was willing to risk explaining that the unmarried woman has great resources of enjoyment – if not sexual enjoyment. She needs no patriarch, no priest, no male center of family prayers. The virgin's self-containment does not exclude relation to "Books and Friends," a relation which is positive, pleasurable – even, some might think, self-indulgent. The aggressiveness of Barker's attack on the social bugbears and the women who are foolishly scared by them is matched by the exhibition of available self-confidence. Far from wearing out a fretful existence of lapdogs and maladies, any woman who tried this mode of existence would find whole new dimensions to her life. The author is willing to take on large sets of cultural stereotyping and produces a new gender-type which doesn't quite fit traditional views. This "virgin" is neither waiting for somebody else to give her a life, or lamenting that no one has done so. Instead she makes a life. We find, here as so often elsewhere in literature of the Restoration, an ambition to remake gender-types, and to break the conventional mold.

This is of course not done easily – in fact in works by both men and women a certain amount of wreckage may be expected. Anne Finch, Countess of Winchilsea, complains of spleen and expresses some very testy views – although neither so testy or so sexy as those of the saintly Anne Killigrew identifying herself as one of Diana's nymphs in a poem entitled "On a Picture Painted by her self, representing two Nimphs [*sic*] of *DIANA*'s, one in a Posture to Hunt, the other Batheing [*sic*]":

> In Swiftness we out-strip the Wind,
> An Eye and Thought we leave behind;
> We *Fawns* and Shaggy *Satyrs* awe;
> To *Sylvan Pow'rs* we give the Law:
> Whatever does provoke our Hate,
> Our Javelins strike, as sure as *Fate*.   (lines 9–14)

These maidens are free to move, free to hate and strike. But their aggressiveness as male-resembling hunters and strikers has not canceled out their femininity:

> We Bathe in Springs, to cleanse the Soil,
> Contracted by our eager Toil;
> In which we shine like glittering Beams,
> Or Christal in the Christal Streams;
> Though *Venus* we transcend in Form,
> No wanton Flames our Bosomes warm!   (lines 15–20)

This well-known topos (nymphs bathing) is frequently employed as a means of enjoying female beauty as object in the works of Renaissance painters; we can also find it in the works of Renaissance poetic writers, such as Sidney's *Arcadia*. It is amazing how different the topos seems once the figures become "we." Here, the pleasure of being crystalline and Venus-like is subjectively experienced or indulged, like the pleasure of bathing. Killigrew's "nimph" is regendered, or, rather, a new species of gender-representative emerges, like a new discovery in natural philosophy. This new strange entity is, as Killigrew knows, impossible to locate on the socio-political map:

> If you ask where such Wights do dwell,
> In what Bless't Clime, that so excel?
> The Poets onely that can tell.   (lines 21–23)

Referring to or admitting the absence of these "nymphs" does not dismiss them, but betrays a gap, a lack, in the nature of things as we are supposed to accept them. Once we have subjectively imagined Killigrew's nymphs, they participate in the proliferation of genders, displacing norms.

In identifying herself with the classical "nymphs," Killigrew arguably stays within the conventions – she is a female representing herself as a female. But, we ought to note, she escapes into being another kind of female, not a well-bred Anglican gentlewoman in delicate health, but a wild free aggressive goddess-led virgin. She reclaims a (non-existent) gender identity which becomes increasingly confusing. Who is the speaker, where does this voice come from? How can the speaker announce her own unreality and remain so aggressive? In claiming a (male) pagan mythology as her own, Killigrew frees it from one-sidedness, as she frees the feminine from a decorous or obedient definition. She fantasticates her landscape and relocates herself.

Writing, after all, is a fantastication, based on acts of imagination. Writing takes liberties. Even non-fictional prose discourse in its speculative-ness, its egotism, and its imaging of alternatives can be accused (nearly as much as fiction) of juggling with the truth. We ought, so Puritans tell us, strictly to contemplate only reality, and some complaints against "Romance" or fiction in general are based on the dislike of humans contriving an escape from the reality God gave us to deal with. (For Puritans and other religious people, of course, reality includes divine reality.) Fictions clutter up the psyche, displacing what ought to be there: "they leave the Memory so full of fantasticall Images of things which are not, that they cannot easily dismisse them."[10] It is, however, hard to find pure material for the furnishing of the mind. When writers (even historians or philosophers) offer to bring us "reality," they, like the Romancers, are offering us mere representations. The Renaissance had already felt the difficulties arising from the proliferation of mere language. Words were supposedly merely feminine, after all, and only deeds masculine. Language may be seen as the Word, the sacred word, the Logos, the authority of the Father, the way of reality – which is how many editors, translators, and interpreters of the Bible genuinely wanted to see it. But so much editing, translating, and commenting had made people uneasily aware that the Bible itself can dissolve into a multiple set of texts and possible texts, a pattern of words upon words.[11] Contemplated that way, it is no longer the clear voice from Horeb, Sinai, or Olivet. All written words, even those in the Bible, are subjected to new forms of historical and stylistic criticism, like Father Simon's *Critical History of the Old Testament*, which, as Dryden said in *Religio Laici* (1682), showed us "what Errours have been made / Both in the *Copiers* and *Translaters Trade*," and ironically pointed out "where *Infallibility* has fail'd" (lines 248–51). Written words are no defense against error, no bulwark against time. The Bible is a human and erroneous text, even under "*God's own people*" and their devoted scholarly or priestly Christian clerics who followed:

> And who did neither *Time*, nor *Study* spare
> To keep this Book *untainted, unperplext*;
> Let in gross *Errours* to corrupt the *Text*:
> Omitted *paragraphs*, embroyl'd the *Sense*;
> With vain *Traditions* stopt the gaping Fence,
> Which every common hand pull'd up with ease:
> What Safety from such *brushwood-helps* as these?
>
> (lines 260–66)

This is a succinct account of the first onslaught of what later came to be called the Higher Criticism of the Bible, in Father Simon's attempt to refute the Protestant's naive dependence on the Bible as a solid foundation-stone. The Bible stops sounding like "itself" if we begin to talk of "text" and "paragraphs." Moreover, in this version of Simon's account, the Bible itself (and the Protestant and Catholic traditions alike) begins to seem curiously feminine. Dryden's claim that oral tradition is as likely to err as the written one makes everything a story of fallibility and confusion: "if *one* Mouth has fail'd, / *Immortal Lyes* on Ages are intail'd" (*Religio Laici*, lines 269–70). Verbal religion and the inspired word become identified with what is weak, wrought upon, full of gross errors, embroiled, gaping, touched by common hands, lying . . . like a drab, in short. Neither written text nor male transmitted tradition are dependable. Words – including the words of the greatest written text of all – are a bricolage and confusion, subject to the weaknesses conventionally associated with womankind.

The status and stability of written language is constantly queried in Restoration texts. These texts themselves may be great and witty out-pourings of words, but they are customarily distrustful about words, and witty upon (as well as in) the written language. We have just seen how *Religio Laici* questions the written religious words. *The Hind and the Panther* is all talk but no action. No solution can be reached within argument; we still have to wait for a divine revelation. In Samuel Butler's *Hudibras*, the masculine interest in written language is everywhere registered as ridiculous; the eponymous anti-hero may pride himself on his knowledge of language and discourse, but his "*Hebrew* Roots" prove only that he is "barren ground" (Part 1, Canto 1, lines 59–60). Hudibras's pompous disquisitions and eagerness to take the text as his own property are at one with his desire to take the Widow as his property – as he attempts to do in his ridiculous love-letter, "An Heroical Epistle of Hudibras to his Lady" at the end of Canto III. Her retort, "The Ladies Answer to the Knight," clearly demonstrates that the male writer is not the best writer. Hudibras might think her stupid enough to be caught by "Poetique Rapture," but "Shee that with Poetry is won, / Is but a Desk to write upon." Not a subject or a means of more bombastic text, the Lady turns on Hudibras in a gender-crossing jeer: Hudibras, she says, may think her stupid or subservient enough to be terrified into awe by men, and (by implication) there may be some women silly enough to "Let Men usurp th'unjust Dominion / As if they were the *Better Women*" ("The Ladies Answer," lines 381–82). This complex jeer, the last lines of Butler's poem, reverses common stereotypes of the bossy woman setting herself out to prove "the better man" (in vulgar proverb the grey mare proving "the better horse"). This gibe also makes fun of any appearance of the phrase "better man," reminding us that social and political life is run by males as if the world were only theirs, an assumption depending on the idea that their superiority needs no proof. If Puritans fight against the "unjust Dominion" of monarchs, they have in logic no reason to assent to male dominion. All they have given us is the soapsuds of their texts. And if there is superiority anywhere, why should not the victorious character be declared the "Better

Woman" as well as the "Better Man"? All this and more may be drawn from the Widow's remark, and still we are left with the residue, the conjuring-up both of the male–female which is not androgyne but in conflict, and a public or republic of plural entities who are all primarily definable as "women." The shock entailed in understanding these lines provides part of the effect of Butler's mockery of the truly phallogocentric Puritan males who are his butts and anti-heroes.

The Widow in *Hudibras* thinks little of the men's written language, and she is not singular in the Restoration. Males are, very commonly, textual persons, but the kind of written language that may be expected from males is repeatedly cast into doubt. In William Congreve's *The Way of the World* (1700), the bluff country squire Sir Wilfull Witwoud comes from Shropshire to London to look up his half-brother, Witwoud, the would-be wit and man about town. After Witwoud tells "Brother *Wilfull* of Salop" that " 'tis not modish to know Relations in Town," the country gentleman diagnoses the state of affairs:

> The Fashion's a Fool; and you're a Fop, dear Brother. 'Sheart – I've suspected this. By'r Lady I conjectured you were a Fop, since you began to change the Stile of your Letters, and write in a scrap of Paper gilt round the Edges, no broader than a *Subpoena*. I might expect this when you left off Honour'd Brother; and hoping you are in good Health, and so forth – To begin with a Rat me, Knight, I'm so sick of a last Nights debauch – Od's heart, and then tell a familiar Tale of a Cock and a Bull, and a Whore and a Bottle, and so conclude. You cou'd write News before you were out of your Time, when you liv'd with honest *Pumple Nose*, the Attorney of *Furnival*'s Inn. (Act III, scene i)

Witwoud has changed his style, and exchanged one kind of letter for another. But the old-fashioned epistle that Sir Wilfull prefers will strike the audience as ludicrous and tiresome, while the new rakish style is clichéd, as well as egotistical and unsociable. Witwoud the younger has moved from one standard male style to another, an affectedly and self-consciously "masculine" style of writing – the manner of the rake who is living it up. The rake is more "feminine" if less modest than the Shropshire clerk. Here, in a characteristic trope of the Restoration, we see gendrification within gendrification. Witwoud wants to be another kind of man, and his style is a representation of himself as that other (fancied) kind of man, which is practically a different gender within his gender. For Sir Wilfull, the ideal sort of man writes like a country attorney – or a country attorney's apprentice. But lawyerly writing is exactly the kind that has long been considered verbose and inane, the opposite of nervous "manly" prose. Witwoud's foppish kind of letter has some literary pretensions which the first does not, but both kinds of masculine writing are rendered ridiculous. No wonder the beautiful and intelligent Millamant, heroine of Congreve's play and at times his most important voice, judges masculine writing as of little worth, using the best of it – the verse – to pin up her hair, but finding male prose hopelessly unfit for that or any other task.[12] If, like the Widow in *Hudibras*, she will not be a desk to write upon, Millamant mischievously turns their writing into a matter for the toilette table. Once again, gender troubles are associated and entangled with the hair.

To neither male nor female authors, evidently, is it clear that males excel at writing, or that writing is an essentially masculine activity – even if it is never an essentially feminine activity. The cosmetic work of Millamant and her maid Mincing indicates that writing is a form of cosmetic. It is likewise but a consumable commodity – even male writing done with the male pen, uncontaminated by the promiscuous press.

For Millamant the power of the pen and the cosmetic powers are interchangeable. From that point of view, the "*Cosmetic* Pow'rs" adored by Pope's Belinda and Pope's own poem are the same thing, as I think Pope knows (see *The Rape of the Lock*, Canto 1, line 124). In Margaret Cavendish's *Blazing World* (1666), writing offers the power of cosmic creation – even if that creation is only of that which is not. As she says, her world cannot be termed a poor world "for there is more gold in it than all the chemists ever did and (as I verily believe) will ever be able to make" (Salzman [ed.], *Anthology of Seventeenth-Century Fiction*, p. 252). If the reader can enjoy it, she will be "a Happy Creatoress" (as the phrase is printed in the seventeenth-century printings). Her new word "Creatoress" creates a feminine form of a word thought of usually only as a masculine monad: the Creator. Writing offers a way out of all binary systems and all depositions of reality; it mimics authority, but only on a basis of equality. The author can claim "I endeavour to be Margaret the First" and admit her own ambition: "rather than not to be mistress of one, since fortune and the fates would give me none, I have made a world of my own." But making such "a world of one's own" only acknowledges the right of all others to do the same, as she says at the end of her preface, "for which nobody, I hope, will blame me, since it is in everyone's power to do the like" (p. 253). Writing is power but only in the terms which allow others access to the same power. Hierarchy is destroyed and obedience rendered naught by the power of a woman to make up her own world – a world that can be innocent of any tales of Adam and his rib or Eve and the serpent.

Language playfully and not anxiously used allows gender to recreate itself – as it does in *The Blazing World* where the Empress and her friend Margaret the Duchess of Newcastle both go and inhabit the body of the latter's husband, the Duke of Newcastle, making a new trinity in unity. We could scarcely say "what sex" this new entity is, or who is the "Better Woman." In the examination of gender in language, boundaries melt and definitions shift. They shift, indeed – as Cavendish wittily shows – into new categories impossible to define by old terms. To use language is to set gender drifting. The eighteenth century had to cope with this insight of the late seventeenth century, and to try to battle with and contain it. Some early eighteenth-century works have the old Restoration ginger; Pope's *Rape of the Lock*, particularly with the addition of the sylphs, is still in touch with the aggressive wit and unsettling transmutations of the Restoration. But as the eighteenth century proceeds we can see the process of laying out new terms, fresh reassurances about stable gender boundaries and relations. The new dictates which stabilized gender arose from a new ideology, a blending of sensibility with the Whiggish politico-economic ideology of the free market and the autonomous economic individual. Not all elements of sensibility as a philosophic concept inevitably lead in this Whiggish direction. I believe we can see in writers like Samuel Richardson – at least, the Richardson of *Pamela* (1740–41) and *Clarissa* (1747–48) – the possibility of using the terms of sensibility to fashion a radical respect for human rights which would include a recognition of the need to share. (Arguably this shadow side of an ideological alternative accompanied later movements, especially in England, such as Chartism and women's suffrage.) The Whiggish individualized ideology and the new picture of gender stability were, however, to be most fully defined in the powerfully influential work of Jean-Jacques Rousseau, whose *Emile* (1762) notably arrives at a firm settlement of gender questions. The new ideology of gender entailed the exchange of the old aggressive tone for a milder, more melancholy one. Gender became the creature of an internalized sensibility rather than the topic of wit's transformative powers.

NOTES

1 There are some parallel developments in France, especially during the period of the wars of La Fronde (1648–52) and the minority of Louis XIV. For an excellent discussion of the treatment of gender in French literature of this period, see Joan DeJean, *Tender Geographies: Women and the Origin of the Novel in France* (New York: Columbia University Press, 1991).

2 John Aubrey, *Brief Lives*, ed. Oliver Lawson Dick (London: Secker and Warburg, 1950), p. 183. This scissors-wielding college head was Ralph Kettell, president of Trinity College from 1599 until his death in 1643.

3 See Louis A. Landa's essay, "Pope's Belinda, the General Emporie of the World, and the Wondrous Worm," first published in *South Atlantic Quarterly*, 70 (1971).

4 See G. J. Barker-Benfield, *The Culture of Sensibility: Sex and Society in Eighteenth-Century Britain* (Chicago: University of Chicago Press, 1992), ch. ii, pp. 37–103. Barker-Benfield draws on Pocock's insights in *Virtue, Commerce and History* (Cambridge: Cambridge University Press, 1985) regarding the demand of the new world of commerce for new behavior and a new kind of persona.

5 Milton's *Areopagitica* connects the reader with the goddess: "the sad friends of Truth, such as durst appear, imitating the carefull search that *Isis* made for the mangl'd body of *Osiris* . . . gathering up limb by limb still as they could find them. We have not yet found them all, Lords and commons, nor ever shall doe, till her Masters second comming; he shall bring together every joynt and member, and shall mould them into an immortall feature of livelines [*sic*] and perfection" (Milton, *Complete Prose Works*, ed. D. M. Wolfe et al. [New Haven: Yale University Press, 1953–82], vol. ii (1959), ed. Ernest Sirluck, p. 549).

Readers, writers and all seekers after truth gather together under a female sign to carry out a work that (like all woman's work) is never done; it cannot come to a climax and cannot be complete. Milton makes a fascinating original use of the myth of Isis and Osiris as he probably knew it from Plutarch. (See Plutarch, *De Iside et Osiride*, 365B, ed. John Gwyn Griffiths (Swansea: University of Wales Press, 1970). That the phallus is only an image, a piece of conceptual cobbling or bricolage, seems recognized by, for example, Butler in *Hudibras*, in the ridiculous procession of the Skimmington and elsewhere. We make a parade of what does not exist.

Unlike other types of the dying god, the reanimated Osiris never returns to the upper world but becomes a god of the underworld. Even in his revivified state, Osiris is a suitable emblem for what is hidden, incomplete. He is also not easily classified as to gender in his posthumous state, and Milton's own rhetoric soon changes Truth's representative from mangled god to beautiful woman. If we follow Milton's rhetorical figures, we see a surprising gender-cross or gender transformation, as torn-up Osiris becomes – hey presto! – a lovely lady.

6 Anne Wharton, like Aphra Behn, wrote an elegy on the death of Rochester (who was her uncle). This presumably circulated in manuscript, and was soon published, if only, apparently, after its author's own death; the quotation is from the version in Nahum Tate's *Poems by Several Hands* (1685), reprinted in Germaine Greer et al. (eds.), *Kissing the Rod: An Anthology of Seventeenth-Century Women's Verse* (London: Virago, 1988; New York: Farrar Straus Giroux, 1989), pp. 287–88.

7 The case for Katherine Philips's intention to publish has been presented by Germaine Greer, in public lectures and in *Slip-Shod Sibyls: Recognition, Rejection, and the Woman Poet* (London: Viking, 1995), ch. 5, pp. 147–72.

8 *Kissing the Rod*, pp. 360–62.

9 Magdalen College MS version reproduced in *Kissing the Rod*, pp. 360–61.

10 The quotation is from Nathaniel Ingelo, who argues the case against fictions (including Homeric epics as well as novels) in the preface to his Puritan allegory of 1660, *Bentivolio and Urania* (C1v–C2r). (See my discussion of this work and of seventeenth-century attitudes to fiction in *The True Story of the Novel* [New Brunswick, NJ: Rutgers University Press, 1996], ch. 11, pp. 251–73.)

Ingelo had reason to feel particularly sour in 1660, when his side had lost; in the entire period (from the beginnings of the Civil War through the Restoration) aesthetic issues are inseparable from political issues. They are perhaps never truly separable from religious, or at least ontological, issues.

11 For an excellent discussion of anxieties over truth and the word in the seventeenth century, see Richard Kroll, *The Material Word: Literate Critics in the Restoration and Early Eighteenth Century* (Baltimore: Johns Hopkins University Press, 1991). His essay of 1986, "*Mise-en-Page*: Biblical Criticism and Inference during the Restoration," in O. M. Brack Jr. (ed.), *Studies in Eighteenth-Century Culture* (Madison: University of Wisconsin Press, 1986), vol. xvi, is a valuable account of the perception of the multiplicity of biblical texts and uncertainties about textuality in the period.

12 What Millamant actually says is "I am persecuted with Letters – I hate Letters – No Body knows how to write Letters; and yet one has'em, one does not know why – They serve to pin up one's Hair . . . Only with those in Verse, Mr. *Witwoud*. I never pin up my Hair with Prose. I fancy ones Hair wou'd not curl if it were pinn'd up with Prose" (Act II, scene i).

Millamant's speech is obviously an impish boast about her attractiveness; her pronominal "one" is upper-class mock-modest generalizing, meaning "I." Other women are not necessarily beleaguered with daily epistles and verses. Millamant's speech, however, is not uttered mainly in rivalry to other women, but in mockery of the males who see their verbal and especially their textual utterances as inevitably significant. "No Body knows how to write Letters" – that is males don't, but ignorant males (really nobodies), perpetrate epistles, believing in the power of masculine written language. Instead of receiving the publicity they really crave, the would-be poets are condemned to a hopelessly private station, which could be only symbolically erotically gratifying.

For a discussion of Congreve's own anxious endeavors to ensure himself status as a man of letters, producing not ephemeral entertainments but books that mattered, see Julie Stone Peters, *Congreve, the Drama, and the Printed Word* (Stanford, CA: Stanford University Press, 1990).

FURTHER READING

Aubrey, John, *Brief Lives*, ed. Oliver Lawson Dick (London: Secker and Warburg, 1950).

Barker, Jane, *Poetical Recreations Consisting of Original Poems, Songs, Odes, &c.* (London: Benjamin Crayle, 1688).

Barker-Benfield, G. J., *The Culture of Sensibility: Sex and Society in Eighteenth-Century Britain* (Chicago: University of Chicago Press, 1992).

Behn, Aphra, *The Works of Aphra Behn*, vol. I, *Poetry*, ed. Janet Todd (London: Pickering, 1992).

Butler, Judith, *Gender Trouble: Feminism and the Subversion of Identity* (New York: Routledge, Chapman & Hall, 1990).

Butler, Samuel, *Hudibras*, ed. John Wilder (Oxford: Clarendon Press, 1967).

Cavendish, Margaret, Duchess of Newcastle, *The Blazing World*, as reproduced in Paul Salzman (ed.), *An Anthology of Seventeenth-Century Fiction* (Oxford: Oxford University Press, 1991).

Congreve, William, *The Complete Plays of William Congreve*, ed. Herbert Davis (Chicago: Chicago University Press, 1967).

DeJean, Joan, *Tender Geographies: Women and the Origin of the Novel in France* (New York: Columbia University Press, 1991).

Doody, Margaret A., *The Daring Muse: Augustan Poetry Reconsidered* (Cambridge: Cambridge University Press, 1985).

The True Story of the Novel (New Brunswick, NJ: Rutgers University Press, 1996).

Dryden, John, *Works of John Dryden*, vol. II, ed. H. T. Swedenberg, Jr. (Berkeley and Los Angeles: University of California Press, 1972).

Greer, Germaine, *Slip-Shod Sibyls: Recognition, Rejection, and the Woman Poet* (London: Viking, 1995).

et al. (eds.), *Kissing the Rod: An Anthology of Seventeenth-Century Women's Verse* (London: Virago Press, 1988; New York: Farrar Strauss Giroux, 1989).

Hagstrum, Jean, *Sex and Sensibility: Ideal and Erotic Love from Milton to Mozart* (Chicago: University of Chicago Press, 1980).

Hobbes, Thomas, *Leviathan*, ed. Richard Tuck (Cambridge: Cambridge University Press, 1991).

Ingelo, Nathaniel, *Bentivolio and Urania, in Four Bookes* (London: Richard Marriot, 1660).

Killigrew, Anne, *Poems. By Mrs. Anne Killigrew* (London: Samuel Lowndes, 1686).

Kroll, Richard, *The Material Word: Literate Culture in the Restoration and Early Eighteenth Century* (Baltimore: Johns Hopkins University Press, 1991).

"*Mise-en-Page*, Biblical Criticism and Inference during the Restoration," in O. M. Brack Jr. (ed.), *Studies in Eighteenth-Century Culture* (Madison: University of Wisconsin Press, 1986), vol. XVI, pp. 3–40.

Landa, Louis A., "Pope's Belinda, the General Emporie of the World, and the Wondrous Worm," first printed in *South Atlantic Quarterly*, 70 (1971), pp. 215–35; rpt. in *Essays in Eighteenth-Century English Literature* (Princeton: Princeton University Press, 1980).

Milton, John, *Areopagitica*, in *The Complete Prose Works of John Milton*, ed. D M. Wolfe et al. 8 vols. (New Haven: Yale University Press, 1953–82) vol. II, ed. Ernest Sirluck (1959).

Paradise Lost, in *The Complete Poetry of John Milton*, rev. edn., ed. John T. Shawcross (New York: Doubleday & Co., 1971).

Peters, Julie Stone, *Congreve, the Drama, and the Printed Word* (Stanford, CA: Stanford University Press, 1990).

Philips, Katherine, *Poems By the most deservedly Admired Mrs. Katherine Philips The Matchless Orinda* (London: J. M. for H. Herringman, 1667).

Plutarch, *Peri Isidos kai Osiridos*, ed. and trans. John Gwyn Griffiths as *De Iside et Osiride* (Swansea: University of Wales Press, 1970).

Pope, Alexander, *The Rape of the Lock and Other Poems*, ed. Geoffrey Tillotson (London: Methuen & Co; New Haven: Yale University Press, 1962).

Swift, Jonathan, *Poetical Works*, ed. Herbert Davis (London and New York: Oxford University Press, 1967).

Wilmot, John, Earl of Rochester, *The Poems of John Wilmot, Earl of Rochester*, ed. Keith Walker (London: Basil Blackwell, 1984).

4

JESSICA MUNNS

Theatrical culture 1: politics and theatre

Parliament's first ordinance against stage plays in 1642 did not entirely suspend theatrical activity in England during the Civil War and Interregnum. Companies played before the Cavalier court at Oxford, and in London illicit performances continued to be staged at the Fortune, the Red Bull, and other locations, including the great London fairs. The reissuing of ordinances against stage playing and the frequency with which Parliamentary soldiers were sent to close down performances indicate that though often harassed, theatre was not dead. Masques were performed for state occasions at Cromwell's court and Sir William Davenant (1606–68) played a major role in the revival of professional theatre during the last years of the Protectorate.[1] The influence of Davenant's dramas with their use of moveable scenery, dance, and music cannot be doubted, least of all given that Davenant was one of the two men subsequently granted royal permission to run theatre companies in London. However, this was not a period during which many new plays were written: older plays were recycled, often as popular episodes stitched together. Lack of regular employment led many actors to work abroad, and the hand-to-mouth existence of the surviving theatrical troupes inhibited the recruiting and training of new actors. Although the degree to which theatre had been quashed can be exaggerated, overall theatrical performance during the period 1642–60 was occasional, often illicit, and was not an integral part of the life of the capital. Nevertheless, the performances staged toward the end of this period were already developing in directions that would be consolidated after 1660.

Theatres, stages, audiences

Charles II landed at Dover in May 1660, and by August he had granted a monopoly to run two theatre companies to William Davenant and to Thomas Killigrew (1612–83), their heirs and assignees. The speed with

which these grants ensuring governmental control of theatrical performance were issued is indicative of the extent to which the "restoration" of
theatre was a significant part of the Stuart resumption of control in the
capital. The new patentees went rapidly into action, quashing all rivals,
dividing up the existing stock of plays, recruiting actors, and staging
dramas. During the reign of Charles II the relationship between court and
theatre was very close: legally, in terms of the status and privileges of the
actors as royal servants; financially, in terms of gifts of cash and clothing;
politically, in terms of censorship; and more generally in terms of the need
for noble patrons. The close relationship between theatre and state was
replicated in Ireland where in 1662 a Theatre Royal, established at Smock
Alley, Dublin, under the direct patronage of Lord Ormonde, the Lord
Lieutenant, was very much an extension of the viceregal court.[2]

The patents of 1660, formally issued in 1662, did not restore theatre as it
had existed in London during the pre-Civil War era. Instead of a number of
theatres only two were licensed: Killigrew managed the King's Company
and Davenant the Duke's Company, named for the king's brother, James,
Duke of York. A very significant innovation was permission to employ
women to act female roles. Killigrew's 1662 grant explains that this was to
produce "harmless delight ... useful and instructive":

> for as much as many plays formerly acted doe conteine severall prophane,
> obscene, and scurrulous passages, and the women's parts therein have byn
> acted by men in the habit of women, at which some have taken offence, for
> the preventing of these abuses for the future ... wee doe likewise permit and
> give leave, that all the woemen's part ... may be performed by woemen soe
> long as their recreacones, which by reason of the abuses aforesaid were
> scandalous and offensive, may by such reformation be esteemed not onely
> harmless delight, but also useful and instructive.[3]

The hope that this innovation would produce modest theatre and avoid
transvestism was not fulfilled and was not, perhaps, the paramount reason
for introducing women onto the stage.

There was a shortage of boy actors trained to portray women: Edward
Kynaston whom Samuel Pepys saw acting in *The Loyall Subject* in August
1660 – "the loveliest lady that ever I saw in my life" – was a notable
exception. However, the decision to allow women on stage represents
more than necessity: actresses helped in the creation of a new style and
type of performance which aimed to attract the court and its adherents
and did not seek to conciliate Puritan sensibilities – which indeed would
have been vexed to decide whether boys dressed as women were more or
less deplorable than women flaunting their bodies publicly.[4] The exiled

courtiers, including Davenant and Killigrew, would have seen women performing female roles at the theatres in Paris and there was a Stuart tradition supporting female performance. The king's mother, Henrietta Maria, for instance, had acted in theatricals at court, and been rather hysterically denounced for so doing by the Puritan lawyer William Prynne (to his cost – he lost his ears). The introduction of actresses in 1660 was one of the many innovations that created a theatrical culture reflective of the court's interests and tastes.

Killigrew was the first to present plays commercially, opening at Gibbon's Tennis Court in Vere Street in November 1660. Davenant spent longer converting his premises and opened at Lisle's Tennis Court in Portugal Street, Lincoln's Inn Fields in June 1661, where the company stayed for the next ten years. Tennis courts provided a viable theatrical space since they were enclosed spaces with galleries and boxes for viewing. Killigrew's King's Company took the lead in the race to construct custom-built theatres, taking over an old riding school in Bridges Street near Drury Lane and converting it into the first London Theatre Royal which opened in May 1663. This structure burnt down in January 1672, forcing the company to take over the theatre in Lincoln's Inn Fields, now abandoned by the Duke's Company. However, by March 1674 a new Theatre Royal had risen in Drury Lane. The Duke's Company, still under the management of the Davenant family, built the Dorset Garden Theatre fronting the river Thames, according to tradition designed by Sir Christopher Wren, which opened in November 1671.

All these new theatres were fully enclosed structures using artificial lighting, and incorporating aspects of the private playhouses and court theatres of the pre-Civil War era. In terms of staging techniques Davenant was consistently more innovative than Killigrew. Even when performing in Lincoln's Inn Fields, his was the first company to use the moveable and changeable scenery typical of performances at court in a professional theatre.[5] These innovations have been described as productive of a "stable, transcendent unity" that enabled "clarity of expression, elegance of plot and the resolution of moral issues" in dramas where there are "no unanswerable questions."[6] However, the Restoration stage did not have the physical capacity to represent a "stable, transcendent unity" through the presentation of illusions sealed off from the spectators and is better seen as transitional, neither as reliant on the audience's cultural senses of place, space, and status as the Elizabethan stage, nor as distanced and illusionistic as later eighteenth- and nineteenth-century stages. Clarity of expression was achieved only by some dramatists, plots range from the elegant to the chaotic, and moral issues and questions are debated rather than resolved.

4.1   Dorset Garden Theatre *c.* 1671, design attributed to Sir Christopher Wren

Restoration theatres had a proscenium arch, equipped with entrance doors for the players, and the part of the stage on which most of the acting took place thrust out into the auditorium. The stage recessed behind the arch to provide the "scenic stage," whose floor was grooved to allow for sliding scenery, "shuts," for changes of scene and "discoveries." A curtain hung from the proscenium arch was raised after the prologue and not dropped until the epilogue, so all scene changes, usually accompanied by music to muffle the creaks, were carried out before the spectators. As well as providing an area for scene changes, including aerial descents, the space behind the proscenium arch allowed for perspective scenery creating illusions of depth, as can be seen in the engravings of Elkanah Settle's *The Empress of Morocco*, performed at Dorset Gardens in 1673. There is debate over how much acting, as opposed to static tableaux effects, took place on the scenic stage; however, stage directions such as "*Scene opening discovers a Scaffold and a Wheel*" for the climactic execution of Pierre and suicide of Jaffeir in Thomas Otway's *Venice Preserv'd* (Dorset Garden, hereafter abbreviated DG, 1681) indicate that important and powerful episodes were acted in this area.[7] What was created was a stage whose physical shape allowed for the articulation

4.2   A scene from Elkanah Settle's *The Empress of Morocco* (1673)

of alternative representational modes – worlds of intimacy and complicity and worlds of spectacle and wonder – and in this bifurcation the stage was suited to the dramas performed on it. These ranged from dual plot plays, especially popular during the first decade of the Restoration, which combined heroic romance with situational and character comedy, as well as serious dramas shot through with ironic humor and comedies seamed by bitter cynicism.

The seating pattern established at these theatres was arranged in boxes, galleries, and the pit, which was now a highly desirable and fashionable part of the theatre. Audience capacity was around 650, and admission prices varied somewhat according to the nature of the performance, but were always relatively high. The size of the theatres, the seating arrangements and their pricing all indicate that the new theatres of the Restoration were not aiming to provide mass entertainment for a wide cross-section of the London population – as theatres such as the Globe or Fortune had done. From the first, tradesmen and merchants and their families went to the theatres; indeed, prologues and epilogues frequently complain at the absence of a more noble audience, and we know from Samuel Pepys's *Diary* that minor bureaucrats also attended. Nevertheless, although the audience was somewhat mixed, these were coterie theatres under direct royal control and patronage, and the court and those who followed the court made up a significant part of their spectators.

From the many anecdotes about members of the audience interrupting performances to express knowing witticisms, from complaints in plays, prologues, and epilogues about the audience chatting to each other or making assignations, it seems clear that people came to socialize as much as they came to see plays. Due to the repertory system of the companies' organization, the audience rapidly knew the players well and would react to performances in terms of their knowledge of their off-stage reputations as well as their expected casting. Sometimes such knowledge was exploited to produce ironic effects, as with the casting of Nell Gwynne, known both for her comedy roles and for her affair with the king, as a virtuous Roman princess in John Dryden's serious drama, *Tyrannick Love* (Theatre Royal, Bridges Street, 1669).[8] Dryden gave her an epilogue in which she rises from her bier and mocks the conventions of theatrical death ("Hold are you mad? You damn'd confounded Dog, / I am to rise, and speak the Epilogue"), subverting the high seriousness of the preceding drama, and drawing attention to her equivocal sexual status, *"Here Nelly lies, who, though she live'd a Slater'n, / yet died a Princess, acting in S. Cathar'n."*[9] Cross-casting was not always intentionally ironic nor was it always successful. Colley Cibber describes a performance in the 1690s when Samuel Sandford, renowned for acting villains, was cast against type. The pit, he informs us, sat quietly for three of four acts in the expectation of seeing him revealed as a villain, but when it turned out that "Sandford was really an honest Man to the end of the Play, they fairly damn'd it, as if the Author had impos'd upon them the most frontless or incredible Absurdity."[10] *Roscius Anglicanus, Or An Historical Review of the Stage* (1708), by John Downes, book-keeper to the Duke's Company, is an important source of information about how plays were cast, performed, and received and his brief descriptions often reveal the intimacy and irreverence of this period's theatre.

Downes's comments frequently show that a full house could not be relied upon: elite patronage fluctuated with the exodus of country gentry at the end of the Parliamentary and legal sessions and army officers at the beginning of wars. With the theatres competing for a limited audience, which had other possible forms of entertainment – from gambling to concerts – it is not surprising to find that they were obliged to change their repertory rapidly. Four or five days represents a usual run – with the author getting the house-takings on the third day – and ten days' consecutive performance indicates a smash hit. A play that succeeded had to be a play that people were prepared to see again and a play that was ridiculed on its first performance by the all-powerful wits who sat in the pit meant a terrible financial loss in sets and costumes for the company.

Popular theatre, that is theatre watched by the working people of London as well as the middling and upper sections of society, took place outside the two patent theatres, during the civic pageants of the Lord Mayor's ceremonials and the annual London Bartholomew and Southwark Fairs when drolls – short, often farcical, plays – and puppet shows were performed.[11] The Stuarts, however, did not favor the public processions, entries, and civic ceremonials of the Tudor era. These were reinvented during the time of the Popish Plot and Exclusion Crisis (1678–82), when public dramatic enactments such as *London's Drollery; or, The Love and Kindness between the Pope and the Devil* (1680), and the Pope Burning Processions, were the expression of oppositional politics. Ironically, in a manner similar to the royal and aristocratic custom of passing on their fine robes to the theatres, the Whig magistrate Sir William Waller provided confiscated Catholic vestments for display in the processions.

Comedy, spectacle, and serious drama

R. D. Hume, in *The Development of English Drama in the Late Seventeenth Century*, presents us with a box-office driven theatre. He dismisses the modern critical debates of those he terms "profundity-zealots" over plays' modes and meanings to insist that "seldom do they probe character deeply or present ideas which are essentially more than commonplaces." Their aim was to "entertain" providing "casual entertainment, the equivalent of everyday television fare" in a sharply competitive world in which a success at either theatre had to be swiftly replicated, with embellishments, by its rival.[12] However, the theatrical culture of the Restoration was formed by the opportunities and constraints of operating between royal and aristocratic patronage, which was not especially generous, and a wider market-place for theatre which as yet barely existed.[13] The degree to which the theatres were dependent on royal and court patronage was in the nature of a double-edged benefit. While court patronage was vital, satisfying the tastes of the court required expensive sets, costumes, stage machines, and musicians, which could be ruinously expensive. Not so much profit, but survival was frequently the issue. There are also problems with the assumption that profit-driven dramas circulate "essentially . . . commonplace" ideas or that such circulation does not require much analysis. The ideas that plays articulated about love and marriage, subjects and sovereigns, liberty and license, law, status, property and wealth, language and meaning are sometimes clichés, sometimes profound, and either way they are of interest as we try to understand the dramatic modes which emerged. And while it is true that dramas used stereotypical characters and formulaic plots, one might argue that it is only via the manipulation of known terms and structures that meaningful critiques get articulated.

Hume's description of vogues and fashions for varieties of tragedies and comedies following hard on each other's heels is, however, more flexible and useful than the traditional divisions of drama into Comedies of Manners and Heroic Dramas. These are highly problematic categories that can be interpreted either so generously that they include virtually all the dramas written during this period, since most serious dramas consider honor and most comedies at all times deal with manners and morals, or so narrowly that only a few plays fit the categories. The comedies of this period generally follow the mode of Caroline social comedy rather than that of Shakespearean pastoral romance. With a few exceptions, such as Thomas Shadwell's *The Lancashire Witches* (DG, 1681), not until the turn of the century with plays like Sir John Vanbrugh's *The Relapse* (Drury Lane, hereafter abbreviated DL, 1696) and the plays of George Farquhar does comedy move to rural settings. Many Restoration and later seventeenth-century comedies are set in London locations familiar to the audience – Pall Mall, Covent Garden Piazza – and generally the characters in Restoration comedies are neither aristocrats nor rogues, but are the younger sons of the landed gentry, wealthy heiresses, rich city merchants, and town gentlemen of leisure and pleasure. There are, of course, exceptions such as dual-plot plays – Sir George Etherege's *Love in a Tub; or, The Comical Revenge* (Lincoln's Inn Fields, hereafter abbreviated LIF, 1664), or Dryden's *Marriage à la Mode* (LIF, 1672) – whose "high" plot characters are noble and tend to speak verse. However, the "low" comedy plot characters who are less socially elevated, more lively, and prose-speaking, came to dominate the form.

Comic form ranged from almost plotless plays such as Etherege's *The Man of Mode* (DG, 1676) to densely plotted intrigue comedies often, as in Samuel Tuke's *The Adventure of Five Hours* (LIF, 1663), taken from Spanish sources, and set in exotic locations. Aphra Behn, in particular, had a great aptitude for intrigue, brilliantly controlling large casts of characters falling in and out of beds, balconies, and sewers. Edward Ravenscroft's experimental play *Scaramouch a Philosopher, Harlequin a Schoolboy* (DL, 1677), which drew on the Italian *commedia dell'arte* tradition (which was based on the "stock" characters of Harlequin, Scaramouch, Columbine, and Punchinello and used mime and improvisation) and the burlesques of Thomas Duffet are indicative of the wide range of comic modes.

During the first decade of the Restoration, many comedies refought the past war on a comic and domestic scale. Etherege's *She Wou'd if She Cou'd* (LIF, 1668) shows Lady Cockwood attempting vainly to confine her husband, Sir Oliver, to a Puritanical lifestyle and clothing, while Sir Jolly Joslin, a cheery Cavalier, teaches him defiance and pleasure. Puritans are frequently depicted as sexual hypocrites, like Snarl in Shadwell's *The Virtuoso* (DG, 1676) who berates his family for their license but sneaks away to be birched by his mistress. Cavaliers, on the other hand, are depicted as fun-loving and open-hearted. However, Cavaliers were rapidly becoming old-fashioned, and the dismissal of Edward Hyde, Earl of Clarendon from the Chancellorship in 1667 signaled a diminution of the influence on the king of those who had shared his exile. A thread of political realism that increasingly runs through many plays associates Cavaliers with outmoded – and unrewarded – concepts of honor. As Beaugard remarks in Otway's *The Souldiers Fortune* (DG, 1680), "Loyalty and Starving are all one" and the Cavaliers "got such a trick of it at the Kings Exile, that their posterity could never thrive since" (Act 1, lines 15–17). By the late sixties and seventies, many comic heroes express a libertine skepticism with regard to matters social and, above all, matters sexual. Indeed, sexual idiom and innuendo often shaped the social and political discourse of loyalty, liberty, rights, and obligations, expressed in terms of family life, personal inclination, potency, and impotence.[14]

The combination of a politically correct rejection of Puritan morality, a court-endorsed sexual license, and the erotic potential of actresses enabled drama, comic and serious, to speak and enact sexual situations more frankly than would again be the case until the later twentieth century. However, the extent to which Restoration comedies were subversively exploring a new sexual morality can be exaggerated. On the whole, virgins remain virgin and their goal, marriage, comes to be shared by the young men who pursue them. Usually the double-standard reigns and women who enact a sexual appetite equal to men are comic figures, such as Mrs. Loveit in *The Man of Mode*. What is frequently acknowledged by playwrights, however, is the very fact of the sexual double-standard as writers examine its operations and consequences. Few do so more than Aphra Behn whose Hellena in *The Rover* (DG, 1677), if attracted to a free and open sexual contract, points out its disadvantages for women: "what shall I get? a cradle full of noise and mischief, with a pack of repentance at my back?" (Act 5, scene 1, lines 439–40).[15]

Male characters are allowed a large degree of sexual license, although it is not until the mid-seventies when the trend for sex comedies sets in that they are regularly to be found seducing women before settling down in the fifth act with the virgin. The rampant sexuality of the predatory male, often articulated via a fashionable Hobbesian discourse of nature and artifice, has philosophic and political resonances; however, the unlimited freedom of sexual choice the libertine hero longs for is usually shown to be illusory.[16] The possibility of operating outside the bounds of man-made and, hence corruptible, law is shown as an unworkable option: although society may limit freedom it also offers protection from anarchy – a real consideration for a society recovering from civil war. As Rhodophil and Palamede in Dryden's *Marriage à la Mode* conclude, although wife-swapping is an attractive idea it raises too many problems and they "make a firm league not to invade each other's propriety" (Act 5, scene 1, lines 319–21). The "Extravagant Rake," such as Nathaniel Lee's Duke of Nemours in *The Princess of Cleves* (DG, 1680), or Willmore in Behn's *The Rover* is an ambiguous figure and, despite his wit, as much an object as a source of humor.[17] Overall, the longevity of the bold and amorous young male on the English stage is an indication of the extent to which this character is not intrinsically subversive but represents conventional views with regard to male sexual appetites and rights while also indicating that sowing wild oats should not be a lifestyle. In the "cleaner" comedies of the eighteenth century, the rake reappears as a wild but good-hearted character, such as Charles Surface in Sheridan's *School for Scandal* (DL, 1777).

Arranged marriages for the wealthy were the norm, and in suggesting that marriage should be based on love rather than money or property, and in presenting strict fathers as blocking devices, playwrights were challenging parental authority. In William Wycherley's *The Gentleman Dancing-Master* (DG, 1672), for instance, the heroine, Hyppolita, concludes the play by blessing her father, rather than the other way around, and announces, "When Children marry, Parents shou'd obey, / Since Love claims more Obedience far than they."[18] However, there are limits to the young people's subversions, for although they seek to select their own partners, these partners are within their status group. Gerrard in *The Gentleman Dancing-Master* is a gentleman disguised as a dancing-master in order to court his mistress: marriage across social groups is a punishment reserved for fools who find themselves wedded to other men's whores.

It was the Puritans who had put love and sexual compatibility in marriage on the agenda and if these plays did not express these ideas in their terms they were certainly not refuting them. Few comedies suggest that the institution of marriage is itself at fault: it is materialistic criteria that are attacked with a connection frequently made between arranged marriages and prostitution. Female characters object to being sold in marriage by parents or guardians and male characters are usually initially reluctant to marry. Misogyny is a feature of both the comic and serious dramas with heterosexual desire seen as enslaving the male to the lesser gender. However, marriage to women of intelligence and vivacity frequently provides the formulaic structural conclusion and may also be seen to articulate the cultural trend toward what we know as the companionate marriage.[19]

The comedies that explore unhappy marriages are more subversive and provide an ironic counterpoint to the pursuit of matrimony by other characters in the plays. This trend has antecedents in the late 1670s with such harsh comedies as Wycherley's *The Country Wife* (DL, 1676) and Otway's *Friendship in Fashion* (DG, 1678) but comes into its own in the nineties with plays such as Vanbrugh's *The Provoked Wife* (LIF, 1697), Thomas Southerne's *The Wives' Excuse; or, Cuckolds Make Themselves* (DL, 1691), and even Cibber's *Love's Last Shift* (DL, 1696). The divorce solution provided in some unhappy marriage comedies, such as Farquhar's *The Beaux' Stratagem* (Queen's Theatre, Haymarket, 1707), was at that time no solution but an expression of authorial idealism satisfying audience fantasies. Heroic dramas have often been characterized in terms of their idealism and escapism and comedies, seen as a reverse form, praised for their cynicism and realism. However, just as it is misleading to read heroic drama's exotic locations in terms of a distance from contemporary events, the comedies' social realism and fashionable libertinism can obscure the idealism with which they propounded unlikely liberties of choice for their protagonists. Nevertheless, comedies work within the culturally agreed designations of power: women may be witty but their liberty rarely extends beyond the right to love the hero: men rule and socially appropriate marriages are the goal.[20]

Charles II's enthusiasm for the theatre, including its actresses, helped to make theatre fashionable and his direct interventions were significant. According to Charles Morrice, secretary to Roger Boyle, Earl of Orrery, it was the king who suggested that Orrery write a heroic-couplet drama:

> King Charles was the first, who put my lord upon writing plays, which his
> majesty did upon occasion of a dispute, that arose in his royal presence about
> writing plays in rhyme: some affirmed it was not to be done; others said it
> would spoil the fancy to be so confined, but Lord Orrery was of another
> opinion; and his majesty being willing a trial should be made, commanded his
> lordship to employ some of his leisure that way, which my lord readily did.[21]

Orrery's play *Henry the Fifth* (LIF, 1664) had ten consecutive performances, and its success, due in part to clear signs of royal approval, helped
establish a trend for largely heroic-couplet verse dramas. These follow the
plots and patterns of French romance literature, are usually set in locations
distant in time and place, and present the major characters with dilemmas
based on conflicts between public duty and personal desire. The language is
elevated – characters do not simply fall in love, they feel love's flames – and
the action is exaggerated – Dryden's Almanzor in *The Conquest of
Granada*, Parts 1 and 2 (Theatre Royal, Bridges Street, 1670) conquers
entire armies. The hero usually concludes the play happily triumphant in
both love and war with his honor tested yet intact.

These dramas have often been regarded as unreal and escapist, but
recently critics have stressed their contemporary relevance to the events and
politics of the 1660s.[22] Usurpation and exile are major themes in many of
these plays, with the hero frequently revealed as the true heir and
triumphantly enthroned, as in Sir Robert Howard's and Dryden's *The
Indian Queen* (Theatre Royal, Bridges Street, 1664). The plays can be seen
to delineate in elevated terms the dilemmas of a dangerous loyalty to an
exiled monarch or a comfortable life under an efficient usurper that many
of the audience had experienced.

Orrery's popular *Henry the Fifth* had topicality, given Charles II's
reputation, in its depiction of a prince renowned for debauchery maturing
into a highly competent king, regaining lands usurped by the French and
restoring order to the realm.[23] The triangulated love-plot between Henry,
the Princess Katherine, and Owen Tudor has been dismissed by William
Smith Clark, Orrery's twentieth-century editor, as a "sentimental conflict
between love and honor attendant upon an appropriate, pseudo-historical
situation" (*Works*, vol. 1, p. 166). However, in Orrery's play, as, indeed, in
Shakespeare's, there is more than sentimentality in the submission of the
princess, who represents the land of France, to the rhetorically encoded
power of the legitimate monarch. Honor, as Richard Braverman argues,
"defines the relationship of sovereign and subject and lends political
resonance to the play insofar as it mediates the moral economy that binds
them. The *sine qua non* of honour, service, is expressed in the language of
debt."[24] Love, loyalty, submission is an expression of that debt owed by the

subject to the sovereign and, figured as wedlock, also establishes the legitimacy and naturalness of political relationships in power and domination. Love and honor, in fact, are not really conflictual elements in many of these plays, but parts of a whole that has been disrupted through usurpation and exile.

These plays articulated what have been called the "fictions of authority," and their monarchical biases were part and parcel of the ideological apparatus of the restoration of the monarchy to England.[25] Despite their royalism, however, depictions of usurpations, the schemes of treacherous statesmen, as well as a careless habit of mislaying royal babies, could suggest the fragility, as much as the legitimacy of monarchical rule. Even during the height of Charles II's popularity in the sixties, many heroic-couplet plays can be seen to explore, as much as to affirm, issues of legitimate authority. Indeed, both serious and comic dramas look at how authority is constituted and how it is challenged – in the state and in the family.

In the prologue to *Aureng-Zebe* (1675) Dryden announced he had "grown weary of his long-loved Mistress, Rhyme," and although rhymed dramas continued to be written they no longer represented the norm. By the mid-1660s a new generation of writers emerged – Thomas Otway, Nathaniel Lee, Aphra Behn, Elkanah Settle, and Henry Nevil Payne – for whom, as for the audience, the recycling of the previous generation's past of exile and restoration was increasingly irrelevant. Explaining the past was less important than dramatizing a present marked by disillusionment over the character of Charles II, disappointment over a series of naval and military fiascos, and anxiety over the succession with the king's wife (if not his mistresses) barren, and his brother and heir, the Duke of York, a declared Roman Catholic following the Test Act of 1673. Issues of succession loom large in many plays, and unlike the earlier dramas' "lost-heir" motif, the later dramas do not provide an easy solution. For instance, Aureng-Zebe, the victor in the Indian throne succession dispute, is not the eldest son and has also been described as "strikingly akin in mentality and achievement to his villainous counterparts."[26] In Otway's dramas of this period the throne is either inherited by someone who does not want it, *Alcibiades* (DG, 1675), left in the possession of a demented monarch who has just murdered his heir, *Don Carlos* (DG, 1676), or inherited by a ruler bent on tyranny, *Titus and Berenice* (DG, 1677).

The new dramas of the 1670s turned away from courteous heroes and military prowess toward blood and thunder with a large infusion of lust, as in Settle's *Empress of Morocco*, and Behn's *Abdelazar* (DG, 1676).[27] In this, parallels can be drawn with the sex-comedies of the mid-1670s. The focus of serious drama changes, as does its depiction of heroes who tend to be morally ambiguous, to be superseded in energy and emotion by charismatic villains of either gender, and to be faced by dilemmas whose resolutions remain uncertain.[28] Plots are set in motion not by conflicts between competing rights but by lustful queens pursuing the hero, or lascivious kings competing for their son's mistress – trends set by *Aureng-Zebe* (DL, 1675) and followed in Otway's *Don Carlos* (DG, 1676), Charles Davenant's *Circe* (DG, 1677), and Lee's *Mithridates* (DL, 1678). The new dramatic fictions present regal authority as fractured and uncertain. Rulers may be magnificent like Hannibal in Lee's *Sophonisba; or Hannibal's Overthrow* (DL, 1675) or Alexander in his play *The Rival Queens* (DL, 1677), but, as with Antony in Dryden's *All for Love* and Sir Charles Sedley's *Antony and Cleopatra* (staged in 1676 at Drury Lane and Dorset Garden respectively), what is dramatized is their decline. Monarchs are also depicted as entirely mad and tyrannical as in Dryden's *Tyrannick Love* (1669), or Lee's *Nero* (DL, 1674). Undoubtedly profit motives encouraged the rival theatres to produce spectacular horror-shockers drawing on Elizabethan and Jacobean models rather than French romance novels for their plots and incidents. However, anxieties felt over the uncertain political situation were also significant.

Spectacle was often an important feature of Restoration serious drama, and there was a distinct fashion for elaborate productions that involved changeable scenery, sung episodes, and dance in the 1670s.[29] Scenes requiring such changes usually involved magic, as well as seduction, activities whose mood was heightened by orchestral music, song, and dance.[30] The Duke's Company's move to their new theatre in Dorset Garden enabled them to present musical spectaculars such as *Psyche* in 1675, which included a fifth act descent from the clouds by thirty-two musicians. Undoubtedly, the machinery was expensive and the managers wanted to see it used, and during the early and mid-seventies plays which were not operatic dramas made heavy use of aerial descents and scene changes, music and dance. However such utilization involved further outlays and, despite successes, the costs involved in staging operatic productions were not adequately rewarded. Spectacle and music remained a feature of serious drama, but the vogue for operatic dramas ebbed to reappear in the 1690s and, by the eighteenth century, the popularity of the Italian opera made it a rival to English operatic dramas, indeed, to drama in general.

Dryden's adaptation of *Antony and Cleopatra* as *All for Love; or, the World Well Lost* helped to make Shakespeare fashionable and, during the years of the Popish Plot and Exclusion Crisis (1679–82), his Roman and history plays provided models for the dramatization of political conflict. John Crowne adapted parts of *Henry VI* as *The Misery of Civil War* (DG, 1680) and *Henry the Sixth* (DG, 1681), and Nahum Tate produced adaptations of *Richard II*, as well as *Coriolanus*, and his *History of King Lear* (DG, 1681) – now notorious for giving the tragedy a happy ending. Ravenscroft in *Titus Andronicus; or, The Rape of Lavinia* (DL, 1678–79) and Otway in *Caius Marius* (DG, 1680) used Shakespearean sources to give horrific depictions of civil conflict. In the process of using Shakespeare's plays as models, the dramatists were also participating in the elevation of Shakespeare to the status of national Bard.[31]

Most plays expressed royalist sentiments, though Dryden's *The Spanish Fryar* (DL, 1680) while loyally replaying the theme of the true king restored also satirizes Roman Catholics.[32] Indeed, by 1680 the strength of the Whig faction in London enabled the performance of plays such as Settle's virulently anti-Roman Catholic *The Female Prelate: Being the History, Life and Death of Pope Joan* (DL, 1680). There are also plays where it is unclear which faction, if any, is being endorsed or satirized, for example, Lee's *Lucius Junius Brutus* (DG, 1680), or Otway's *Venice Preserv'd* (DG, 1682). There is no doubt that the violent, corrupt, and disruptive civic politics both plays depict are inspired by contemporary events. Comedies also responded to the times with political satires such as Behn's *The Roundheads; or the Good Old Cause* (DG, 1681), and John Crowne's *City Politiques* (DL, 1683), and the Whig author Shadwell wrote explicitly political comedies.[33]

The Popish Plot and Exclusion Crisis produced some magnificent plays but not equally magnificent profits and in 1682 Dorset Garden and Drury Lane united, pooling their actors, plays, and material resources. This event was catastrophic for writers since the United Company was now well stocked with plays and commissioned few new works. Thomas Otway and Aphra Behn died in poverty, Otway in 1685, Behn in 1689, and during their last years they eked out a living with non-dramatic writing, and by 1692 Nathaniel Lee, one of the most talented writers of the age, died insolvent and insane. Few playwrights enjoyed as did Dryden and Shadwell consistent and generous noble patronage and when elite support waned the theatre went into decline. Royal patronage declined during the brief and troubled reign (1685–88) of James II and subsequently William of Orange (1688–1702), and Mary (1688–92), and Queen Anne (1702–14) had little interest in theatre. By 1695 Thomas Betterton led a "revolt" from the hard-pressed United Company, taking its oldest and best actors to the now rather dingy premises at Lincoln's Inn Fields where the company performed for the next decade.

Betterton had pioneered actor-management, but by the eighteenth century this became usual and is symptomatic of the shift from an elite theatre run by and for courtiers to a more commercial theatre orienting itself toward a wider audience. Increased newspaper advertising is indicative of the search for audiences whose varied tastes were appealed to by a range of *entr'acte* song and dance routines. A 1704 Drury Lane advertisement for Shadwell's *The Miser*, for instance, promises

> Entertainments of Danceing by Monsieur du Ruell. And Mr. Clinch will perform these several Performances, first an Organ with three Voices, then the Double Curtel, the Flute, the Bells, the Huntsman, the Horn, and Pack of Dogs, all with his Mouth; and an old Woman of Fourscore Years of Age nursing her Grand-Child; all which he does open on the Stage. Next a Gentleman will perform several Mimick Entertainments on the Ladder.[34]

Ballet, popular for *entr'actes*, gradually moved toward independent status with the rise of the *ballet d'action* (an entirely danced narrative), the first of which was John Weaver's *The Loves of Mars and Venus* (DL, 1717).

By the 1690s the theatre lacked royal patronage and there is strong evidence that the "ladies" had campaigned consistently for a reformation of stage morals; in such a context, the effectiveness of Jeremy Collier's attack on the sexual laxity of the theatre – *A Short View of the Immorality, and Profaneness of the English Stage* (1698) – is scarcely surprising.[35] The theatre had to find new plays more in tune with the altered moral codes of representation. Unfortunately, two of the most brilliant new dramatic talents, George Farquhar and William Congreve, did not last long: Farquhar died after the premiere of *The Beaux' Stratagem* in 1707 and Congreve did not write any plays after *The Way of the World* (DL, 1700).

From the late seventeenth and early eighteenth centuries onwards, there was an influx of professional female dramatists – Susannah Centlivre, Mary Pix, Catherine Trotter, Jane Wiseman, and Delarivier Manley. This was in part due to the fact that playwriting was not sufficiently profitable to produce intense male competition. These women writers' works, still underrepresented in publications, are not necessarily "feminist" – any more than were Aphra Behn's – however, they are female-oriented in terms of characters and plots. Centlivre's plays, as she frequently points out, adhere to Collier's prescriptions: they also treat the business of making and keeping money as serious and laudable, as when Mrs. Lovely in *A Bold Stroke for a Wife* (LIF, 1718), informs the hero that "Love makes but a slovenly figure in that house where poverty keeps the door" (Act 1, scene 2, lines 29–31).[36] In these respects, Centlivre's plays follow a trend toward a more decent – and less aristocratic – drama.

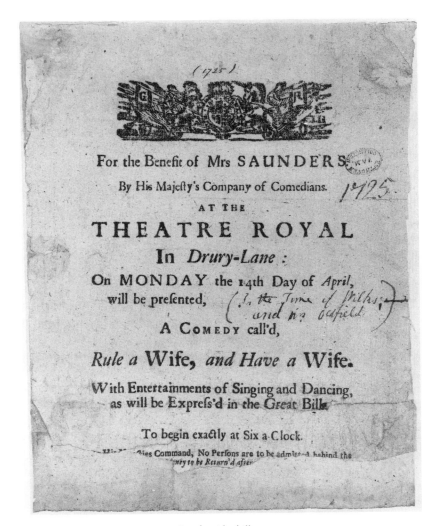

(1725)

For the Benefit of Mrs SAUNDERS

By His Majefty's Company of Comedians. 1725

AT THE

THEATRE ROYAL

In *Drury-Lane* :

On MONDAY the 14th Day of *April*,
will be prefented, *(In the Time of Mills and Mrs Oldfield)*

A COMEDY call'd,

Rule a Wife, and Have a Wife.

With Entertainments of Singing and Dancing,
as will be Exprefs'd in the Great Bill.

To begin exactly at Six a Clock.

... *...ies* Command, No Perfons are to be admitted behind the
...ry to be Return'd after

4.3 London playbill, 1725

Courtly insults to the merchant class were replaced by judicious estimations of their benefit to the nation. Merchants, Joseph Addison wrote in *The Spectator*, no. 69 (1711), "knit Mankind together in a mutual Intercourse of good Offices, distribute Gifts of Nature, find Work for the Poor, add Wealth to the Rich, and Magnificence to the Great." These sentiments, alien to the earlier theatrical culture, are echoed in Richard Steele's *The Conscious Lovers* (DL, 1730) when Mr. Sealand asserts "we merchants are a Species of gentry, that have grown into the World this last

Century, and are as honourable, and almost as useful, as you landed Folks" (Act 4, scene 2, lines 58–61).[37] The merchant, Thoroughgood, in George Lillo's *The London Merchant* (DL, 1731) has even more to say in their praise.

Eighteenth-century drama is often regarded as a decline from that of the late seventeenth century insofar as it expresses bourgeois values of comfort rather than glory, and esteems trade rather than war. The emergent dramatic mode has been characterized as "genteel" with "sentimental" comedies, and "pathetic" domestic tragedies. However, the traditions of the stage were powerful, older plays continued in repertory, and many of the trends on the eighteenth-century stage had earlier antecedents. For instance, Nicholas Rowe, first editor of Shakespeare as well as a successful tragic dramatist, acknowledged the influence of Otway, genuinely reforming heroes can be found in dramas of the earlier period, and spectacular musical presentations on the professional stage can be traced back to the 1650s.

Seemly and exemplary dramas with improving moral agendas were not the only new dramatic fare. Anti-government satirical ballad operas such as John Gay's *The Beggar's Opera* (LIF, 1728) and Henry Fielding's *The Grub-Street Opera* (Hay, 1731), played at much the same time as George Lillo's didactic *London Merchant* (DL, 1731), or *Sophonisba* (DL, 1730), James Thomson's Whig exploration of civic rights and individual liberties. Meanwhile, John Rich and John Lun were enormously popular as Harlequin, and Hester Santlow enchanted all with her dancing. Lacking the unifying patronage of the court, competing rather than dominant trends emerged in the early decades of the eighteenth century as theatre engaged with a more varied audience than before. The changes that took place were not necessarily generic nor uniformly signaled by the emergence of an affective sensibility. It is more profitable to look at the drama of this period, as J. Douglas Canfield has, in terms of "shifting tropes of ideology" as a new political and cultural orientation was working itself out through the patterns of the stage.[38]

Theatre finances remained perilous, and during the early decades of the eighteenth century companies rose, fell, regrouped, and rose and fell again. Nevertheless, the licensed companies survived, unlicensed companies proliferated, and new theatres were built. By the 1720s Londoners could choose between the Queen's (later King's) Theatre in the Haymarket, The Theatre Royal, Drury Lane, a renovated Lincoln's Inn Fields, two theatres in outer London at Greenwich and Richmond, and two new inner London theatres – the Little Theatre in the Haymarket, so called to distinguish it from the nearby grander theatre, as well as one at Goodman's Fields.

4.4 The Queen's Theatre, the Haymarket (1707)

This proliferation was not welcomed by the government which had long been seeking to reassert control over the theatres. Walpole had attended a performance of *The Beggar's Opera* and pretended to be amused – but Gay's follow-up, *Polly*, was swiftly banned. In 1737 the Little Theatre in the Haymarket, whose company had come under Henry Fielding's management, attempted to stage *The Golden Rump* (Anon., 1737), a skit on Walpole and the king, which provided the precipitate occasion for the Licensing Act of 1737. This reduced the London theatres to the two licensed companies and provided that all new plays, prologues, epilogues, and altered old plays must be submitted for approval to the Lord Chamberlain's office. Although there was no lack of theatrical talent, least of all in acting, by 1737 England's fictions of wealth, sexuality, and authority would, as Henry Fielding found when he lost his job, be equally or more effectively expressed in the novel.

NOTES

1 See Leslie Hotson, *The Commonwealth and Restoration Stage* (Cambridge, MA: Harvard University Press, 1928).

2 See William Smith Clark's *The Early Irish Stage* (Oxford: Clarendon Press, 1955).

3 *The London Stage, 1600–1800*, Part 1, *1660–1700*, ed. William Van Lennep with a critical introduction by Emmett L. Avery and Arthur H. Scouten (Carbondale: Southern Illinois University Press, 1965), p. xxiv.

4 For Puritan views on acting see Jonas Barish, *The Antitheatrical Prejudice* (Berkeley: University of California Press, 1982).

5 See Eleanore Boswell, *The Restoration Court Stage (1660–1702), With a Particular Account of the Production of Calisto* (London: Allen and Unwin, 1952), and Richard Southern, *Changeable Scenery: Its Origin and Development in English Theatre* (London: Faber and Faber, 1952).

6 See Catherine Belsey, *The Subject of Tragedy: Identity and Difference in Renaissance Drama* (London: Methuen, 1985), pp. 26, 92.

7 *The Works of Thomas Otway: Plays, Poems, and Love-Letters*, ed. J. C. Ghosh, 2 vols. (Oxford: Clarendon Press, 1932; reprinted 1968); all citations are taken from this edition. On the scenic stage, see Jocelyn Powell, *Restoration Theatrical Production* (London: Routledge and Kegan Paul, 1984), pp. 54–55; Peter Holland, *The Ornament of Action: Text and Performance in Restoration Comedy* (Cambridge: Cambridge University Press, 1979), p. 36.

8 All performance dates are as in *The London Stage, 1660–1800*, Part 1, *1660–1700*.

9 All citations from Dryden's works are taken from *The Works of John Dryden*, ed. E. N. Hooker and H. T. Swedenberg, Jr., 20 vols. (Berkeley and Los Angeles: University of California Press, 1956–   ). Text's emphasis.

10 Colley Cibber, *An Apology for the Life of Mr. Colley Cibber*, ed. B. R. S. Fone (Ann Arbor: University of Michigan Press, 1968), pp. 77–78. See also Peter Holland, *The Ornament of Action*, on patterns of casting, pp. 54–98, 79.

11 See Sybil Rosenfeld, *The Theatre of the London Fairs in the 18th Century* (Cambridge: Cambridge University Press, 1960), and Paula R. Backscheider, *Spectacular Politics: Theatrical Power and Mass Culture in Early Modern England* (Baltimore: Johns Hopkins University Press, 1993).

12 Robert D. Hume, *The Development of English Drama in the Late Seventeenth Century* (Oxford: Clarendon Press, 1976), pp. 30–31.

13 See Deborah Payne's forthcoming book *Patronage, Print, Professionalism and the Marketplace of Restoration Theatre, 1660–1685*.

14 See Giles Slade, "The Two Backed Beast: Eunuchs and Priapus in *The Country Wife*," *Restoration and Eighteenth-Century Theatre Research*, second series, 7, 1 (1992), pp. 23–43.

15 Aphra Behn, *The Rover*, ed. Anne Russell (Ontario: Broadview Press, 1994).

16 See Dale Underwood's *Etherege and the Seventeenth-Century Comedy of Manners* (New Haven: Yale University Press, 1957), and Robert Markley's *Two-Edg'd Weapons: Style and Ideology in the Comedies of Etherege, Wycherley, and Congreve* (Oxford, New York: Clarendon Press, 1988).

17 On the rake figure see Robert Jordan, "The Extravagant Rake in Restoration Comedy," in Harold Love (ed.), *Restoration Literature: Critical Approaches* (London: Methuen, 1972), and Harold M. Weber, *The Restoration Rake Hero: Transformation in Sexual Understanding in Seventeenth-Century England* (Madison: Wisconsin University Press, 1986).

18 William Wycherley, *The Complete Plays*, ed. Gerald Weales (New York: Anchor Books, 1966).

19 See Lawrence Stone, *The Family, Sex, and Marriage in England, 1500–1800* (London: Weidenfeld and Nicholson, 1977). Stone's work on this topic has, however, been vigorously challenged: see reviews by E. P. Thompson in *New Society*, 8 September 1977, pp. 499–501, and Alan Macfarlane in *History and Theory*, 18 (1979), pp. 104–25. Works such as Linda A. Pollock's *Forgotten Children, Parent–Child Relations from 1500–1900* (Cambridge: Cambridge University Press, 1983) and Ralph Houlbrooke's *The English Family, 1450–1700* (Harlow: Longman, 1984) and *English Family Life, 1576–1716* (Oxford: Basil Blackwell, 1988), offer significant modifications of Stone's thesis.

20 See Christopher Wheatley's "Romantic Love and Social Necessities: Reconsidering Justifications for Marriage in Restoration Comedy," *Restoration*, 14, 2 (1990), pp. 58–69.

21 *The Dramatic Works of Roger Boyle, Earl of Orrery*, ed. William Smith Clark II, 2 vols. (Cambridge, MA: Harvard University Press, 1937), vol. I, p. 23.

22 See Nicholas Jose, *Ideas of the Restoration in English Literature, 1660–1671* Cambridge, MA: Harvard University Press, 1984), p. 141.

23 Richard Braverman, *Plots and Counterplots: Sexual Politics and the Body Politic in English Literature, 1660–1730* (Cambridge: Cambridge University Press, 1987), p. 38.

24 *Ibid.*, p. 41.

25 See Susan Staves, *Players' Scepters: Fictions of Authority in the Restoration* (Lincoln: University of Nebraska Press, 1979).

26 See Derek Hughes, *Dryden's Heroic Plays* (London: Macmillan, 1981), p. 149.

27 See Paul D. Cannan, "New Directions in Serious Drama on the London Stage," *Philological Quarterly*, 73, 2 (1994), pp. 219–42.

28 See Derek Hughes's discussion of the decline of heroic idealism, *English Drama 1660–1700* (Oxford: Clarendon Press, 1996), p. 140.

29 Hume, *Development*, pp. 205–09, 280–83.

30 James A. Winn, *"When Beauty Fires the Blood": Love and the Arts in the Age of Dryden* (Ann Arbor: University of Michigan Press, 1992), chapters 4 and 5.

31 See Michael Dobson, *The Making of the National Poet: Shakespeare, Adaptation and Authorship, 1660–1769* (Oxford: Clarendon Press, 1992).

32 See J. Douglas Canfield, "Royalism's Last Dramatic Stand: English Political Tragedy, 1679–89," *Studies in Philology*, 82, 2 (1985), pp. 234–63.

33 See Jean Marsden, "Ideology, Sex, and Satire: The Case of Thomas Shadwell," and Jessica Munns, "'The Golden Days of Queen Elizabeth': Thomas Shadwell's *The Lancashire-Witches* and the Politics of Nostalgia," in James E. Gill (ed.), *Cutting Edges: Postmodern Critical Essays on Eighteenth-Century Satire* (Knoxville: University of Tennessee Press, 1995), pp. 43–58, and pp. 59–75.

34 Cited by Judith Milhous, *Thomas Betterton and the Management of Lincoln's Inn Fields 1695–1708* (Carbondale: Southern Illinois University Press, 1979), p. 175.

35 David Roberts, *The Ladies: Female Patronage of Restoration Drama 1660–1700* (Oxford: Clarendon Press, 1989).

36 Susannah Centlivre, *A Bold Stroke for a Wife*, ed. Nancy Copeland (Ontario: Broadview Press, 1995).

37 Richard Steele, *The Conscious Lovers*, in W. D. Taylor (ed.), *Eighteenth-Century Comedy* (London: Oxford University Press, 1961).

38 See J. Douglas Canfield, "Shifting Tropes of Ideology in English Serious Drama, Late Stuart to Early Georgian," in J. Douglas Canfield and Deborah Payne (eds.), *Cultural Readings of Restoration and Eighteenth-Century Theatre* (Athens: University of Georgia Press, 1995), pp. 195–227.

FURTHER READING

Brown, Laura, *English Dramatic Form, 1660–1760* (New Haven: Yale University Press, 1981).

Corman, Brian, *Genre and Generic Change in English Comedy 1660–1710* (Toronto: University of Toronto Press, 1993).

Howe, Elizabeth, *The First English Actresses* (Cambridge: Cambridge University Press, 1992).

Hume, R. D., *The Rakish Stage: Studies in English Drama 1660–1800* (Carbondale and Edwardsville: Southern Illinois University Press, 1983).

Leacroft, Richard, *The Development of the English Playhouse* (London: Eyre Methuen, 1973).

Loftis, John, *The Politics of Drama in Augustan England* (Oxford: Oxford University Press, 1963).

Milhous, Judith, and Hume, Robert D. (eds.), *A Register of English Theatrical Documents 1600–1737* (Carbondale: Southern Illinois University Press, 1991).

Owen, Susan J., *Restoration Theatre and Crisis* (Oxford: Clarendon Press, 1996).

Quinsey, Katherine M. (ed.), *Broken Boundaries: Women and Feminism in Restoration Drama* (Lexington: University of Kentucky Press, 1996).

Randall, Dale B. J., *Winter Fruit: Engish Drama 1642–1660* (Lexington: University of Kentucky Press, 1995).

Rothstein, Eric, *Restoration Tragedy: Form and the Process of Change* (Madison: University of Wisconsin Press, 1967).

Schofield, Mary Anne, and Macheski, Cecilia (eds.), *Curtain Calls: British and American Women and the Theatre, 1660–1820* (Athens: Ohio University Press, 1991).

Winton, Calhoun, *John Gay and the London Theatre* (Lexington: University of Kentucky Press, 1993).

5

JAMES A. WINN

Theatrical culture 2: theatre and music

The political turmoil that drove English theatre underground between 1641 and 1660 had a similarly devastating effect on English music. Puritan reformers disbanded cathedral choirs; Parliamentary soldiers smashed priceless organs; foreign court musicians, fearful of reprisals against Roman Catholics, returned to the Continent. But music was not utterly silenced. Oliver Cromwell's court, mindful of the need for pomp, maintained a reduced version of the royal band; at the wedding of Frances Cromwell on 11 November 1657, forty-eight violins accompanied "mixt dancing (a thing heretofore accounted profane) till 5 of the clock."[1] There was even one occasion involving musical theatre: the Protector presented *Cupid and Death*, a masque by James Shirley, as an entertainment for the Portuguese ambassador in 1653.[2] Matthew Locke, who may have written the music for that performance and certainly wrote the music for a second performance in Leicester Fields in 1659, lost his position as a boy chorister at Exeter Cathedral in 1641, but managed to continue his musical development during the Interregnum, traveling abroad and seizing what limited opportunities were available in England; he became one of the most important theatre composers of the Restoration period.

On the literary side, the central figure in the development of musical drama was Sir William Davenant (1606–68), author of the last masque presented at the court of Charles I (*Salmacida Spolia*, 1640), author and presenter of the first opera in English (*The Siege of Rhodes*, 1656), and after the Restoration, manager of the Duke's Company, which was responsible for most of the innovations leading to the mixed form later called semiopera. As Davenant knew from personal experience, the Stuart court masques incorporated episodes of music and dance within a largely spoken poetic text and employed impressive scenic effects. One early masque may even have been a kind of opera: in the headnote to *Lovers Made Men* (1617), Ben Jonson informs us that "the whole Maske was sung (after the Italian manner) *Stylo recitativo*, by Master *Nicholas Lanier*; who ordered and made both the Scene, and the Musicke."[3] The masques might be regarded as forerunners of the popular semioperas of the later seventeenth century, which also mixed music with spoken dialogue and dazzled their audiences with spectacular visions, but there are significant differences. The Stuart masques, performed on Twelfth Night at prodigious expense, were seen only by invited guests of the court; their texts were brief and abstract, presenting allegories splendidly realized by the visual illusions of Inigo Jones.[4] Restoration semioperas, by contrast, had to attract paying customers: their texts were fully plotted plays with interpolated musical episodes; their "flyings" and transformations were more frankly entertaining than the scenic miracles of Jones.

Despite Davenant's experience as a masque-writer, the development of Restoration musical theatre had less to do with the Stuart masque than with attempts to imitate Italian opera. Many Royalists who traveled abroad during the Interregnum were impressed by opera; John Evelyn's description of an evening in Venice is typical:

> This night ... we went to the opera, which are comedies & other plays represented in Recitative Music by the most excellent Musitians vocal and Instrumental, together with variety of Seanes painted & contrived with no lesse art of Perspective, and Machines, for flying in the aire, & other wonderful motions. So taken together it is doubtlesse one of the most magnificent and expensfull diversions the Wit of Men can invent: The historie was *Hercules* in Lydia, the Seanes chang'd 13 times.[5]

Davenant also admired Continental operas. As early as 1639, he had secured a patent from Charles I, licensing him to build a playhouse in which to "exercise Musick, musical Presentments, Scenes, Dancing, or other the like,"[6] and though we cannot know whether his plans for "musical Presentments" before the Civil War included operas with recitatives, he had embraced that plan by 1656, as he explains in his epistle "To the Reader," printed in the first edition of *The Siege of Rhodes*: "The Musick was compos'd, and both the Vocal and Instrumental is exercis'd, by the most transcendent of *England* in that Art, and perhaps not unequal to the best Masters abroad; but being *Recitative*, and therefore unpractis'd here; though of great reputation amongst other Nations, the very attempt of it is an obligation to our own."[7] The music, unfortunately all lost, was composed by Matthew Locke, Henry Lawes, Henry Cooke, George Hudson, and Edward Coleman; Locke and Cooke also sang in the production. Davenant's insistence on the "reputation" recitative enjoyed abroad reveals his interest in making that foreign form acceptable to potentially resistive English audiences, but he was not the only producer of musical dramas in the waning years of the Interregnum: Shirley and Locke must have expected an audience for the revival of *Cupid and Death* in 1659, and there is an extant record of *An Eclogue; or, Representation in Four Parts, to be Habited, Sung, and Acted ... before the Lord Mayor ... by the City Musick* later in the same year.[8]

Most French and Italian operas of this period have supernatural or mythological characters, but the singing characters in *The Siege of Rhodes* are soldiers, admirals, and a noblewoman – the faithful Ianthe, sung by Mrs. Coleman, who was presumably the first actress to appear on the English public stage. This kind of plot, featuring noble characters in an exotic setting, forced to choose between love and honor, became the norm for the rhymed heroic plays of the early Restoration; John Dryden's essay "Of Heroick Plays" (1672), printed with *The Conquest of Granada*, points to *The Siege of Rhodes* as the original model for heroic drama, and correctly identifies Davenant's sources: "For Heroick Plays ... the first light we had of them on the English Theatre was from the late Sir William D'Avenant ... The Original of this musick and of the Scenes which adorn'd his work, he had from the Italian Opera's; but he heighten'd his Characters ... from the example of Corneille and some French poets."[9] More debatable, however, is Dryden's influential assertion that *The Siege of Rhodes* was simply a play in disguise, an attempt to smuggle the banned drama back into London during the last years of the Protectorate:

> It being forbidden him in the Rebellious times to act Tragedies and Comedies, because they contain'd some matter of Scandal to those good people, who could more easily dispossess their lawful Sovereign than endure a wanton jest; he was forc'd to turn his thoughts another way: and to introduce the examples of moral vertue, writ in verse, and perform'd in Recitative Musique ... In this condition did this part of Poetry remain at his Majesties return: When growing bolder, as being now own'd by a publick Authority, he review'd his *Siege of Rhodes*, and caus'd it be acted as a just Drama. (*Works*, vol. XI, p. 9)

This version of Davenant's preferences and motives has been accepted by most modern scholars, who have usually believed that he first wrote *The Siege of Rhodes* as a play, and only had it set to music for political reasons.[10] Yet there are reasons to treat this part of Dryden's testimony with skepticism. Some parts of the text of *The Siege of Rhodes* appear to be designed quite carefully for various kinds of music – recitative, aria, chorus.[11] Davenant produced three more dramas in recitative before the Restoration: *The Cruelty of the Spaniards in Peru* (1658), *Sir Francis Drake* (1659), and Part II of *The Siege of Rhodes* (1659), continuing the story and adding a second female character.[12] Moreover, he continued to stage musical dramas after the Restoration, doubtless aware that Charles II, whom Dryden represents as the enabling patron of spoken drama, was a lifelong opera fan. In 1661, having secured one of the two precious patents for theatre companies available from the restored monarchy, Davenant opened the new theatre at Lincoln's Inn Fields with a revised and expanded version of *The Siege of Rhodes*, probably offering both parts on alternating days. Contemporary testimony records the success of this show, but the evidence about the music is incomplete and contradictory. Evelyn describes a performance of Part II in 1662 as "in *Recitativa* Musique," and the prologue to Dryden's *The Wild Gallant* (1663) appears to confirm that description, but some of the actors taking part in the Duke's Company production were not singers, and may have spoken their lines.[13] Both parts of the play remained in repertory for years, and performance practice probably moved slowly toward the conventions of the form later called semiopera, with episodes of song and dance alternating with scenes of spoken dialogue. In a piece called *The Playhouse to be Let*, first performed in the late summer of 1663, Davenant revived *The Cruelty of the Spaniards in Peru* and *Sir Francis Drake*, but framed them ironically, thus economically recycling his own materials while indicating his awareness of the tastes of the Restoration audience. The final act is a vulgar parody of a scene with a singing ghost in Katherine Philips's *Pompey*, which had probably been performed a few months earlier.[14] Although Davenant was engaging in parody and even self-parody with this strange production, his company continued to offer musical dramas with a straight face: Robert Stapylton's *The Step-Mother*, probably staged in the autumn of 1663, included "Instrumental, Vocal and Recitative Musick . . . compos'd by Mr. Lock."

Although Charles II was not prepared to revive the masque tradition, he was keenly interested in a plan to open a third theatre in Moorfields, which was to be devoted to opera. A group of Italian singers actually came to England hoping to start such a venture, but Charles lacked the funds to underwrite their company, and through-sung opera, as Davenant was discovering, had a limited commercial appeal.[15] On a more modest financial scale, Charles helped both his theatres stage musical shows: an extant warrant of 1664 orders "the Master of the Great Wardrobe to prouide and deliuer to Thomas Killigrew Esqr [patentee of the King's Theatre] to the value of forty pounds in silke for to cloath the Musick for the play called the Indian Queen"; later in the same year, the twenty-four string players of "the King's Musick" were split into two bands of twelve to play at the theatres.[16] Dryden and Sir Robert Howard, who collaborated on *The Indian Queen*, were helping Killigrew's company compete with Davenant's in lavish costumes, frequent changes of scenery, exotic settings, and effective music. Both *The Indian Queen* (1664) and Dryden's sequel, *The Indian Emperour* (1665), couplet dramas closely modeled on *The Siege of Rhodes* and *The Cruelty of the Spaniards*, have important musical episodes: each play features a musical scene of prophecy and incantation (using a set depicting a sorcerer's cave); *The Indian Emperour* also has a scene of seduction, in which a lyric song performed by an Indian woman lulls some Spanish soldiers into letting down their guard and being captured by Indian warriors.[17] As in most subsequent plays of the period, the major characters do not sing. In both companies, the leading actors were not singers, though several prominent actresses were able to sing; the standard solution was to have songs performed by servants, spirits, angels, and other peripheral figures.

Heroic plays with musical scenes enjoyed not only the patronage of the court but its imitation. In January of 1668, the diarist Samuel Pepys heard about a court performance staged by noble amateurs: "the ladies and the Duke of Monmouth and others acted *The Indian Emperour* – wherein they told me these things most remarkable: that not any woman but Duchesse of Monmouth and Mrs. Cornwallis did anything like, but like fools and sticks; but that these two did do most extraordinary well."[18] A month later both these ladies were in the cast of a similar court performance of Katherine Philips's translation of Corneille's *Horace*, with added music.[19]

While these court theatricals were in progress, the current commercial hit was a substantially altered version of *The Tempest*, the most overtly musical of Shakespeare's plays, which opened in November of 1667. Although nominally a comedy, *The Tempest* engages issues not unlike those featured in the rhymed heroic play – revenge, succession, conjuring, and courtship – but the drunken sailors so effectively parody the noble characters that there is no danger of our taking anything too seriously; the revised version, a collaborative effort by Davenant and Dryden, also undermines the purity of the Ferdinand–Miranda plot by adding new characters: Miranda's sister Dorinda, who has also never seen a young man before, and a young man named Hippolito, kept in a cage by Prospero, who has never seen a woman. Dryden and Davenant retained most of Shakespeare's songs and added a number of additional musical episodes, of which the most memorable was an "Echo Song" composed by John Banister, sung by Ferdinand and Ariel.[20] The success of this play encouraged more musical performances, despite Davenant's death in April of 1668. A revival of Fletcher's *The Faithful Shepherdess* in October of 1668 seems to have been chiefly memorable for the singing of a *castrato*,[21] and Dryden's *Tyrannick Love*, staged at great expense in June of 1669, has an extended operatic episode calling for a fast duet sung by flying spirits, a slow recitative, a strophic song, and a dance.[22] *The Rehearsal* (1671), the Duke of Buck-ingham's devastating parody of the heroic plays, includes a comic version of the duet, probably set to the same music.

Competition between the theatre companies was fierce: the Duke's Company gained the upper hand late in 1671, when they opened their splendid new house at Dorset Garden, equipped with all the latest machinery; their victory became complete when the rival theatre at Bridges Street burned to the ground on 25 January 1672, destroying all the scenes and machines owned by the King's Company. Although the King's men eventually completed a new theatre of their own at Drury Lane, it was, in Dryden's words, a "Plain Built House," not comparable to Dorset Garden when it came to operatic shows. Multimedia spectaculars at Dorset Garden included an operatic revival of Davenant's version of *Macbeth* (February 1673), an elaborate production of Elkanah Settle's *The Empress of Morocco* (July 1673),[23] and a refurbished, operatic version of *The Tempest* (March [?] 1674), with further adjustments to the text, probably by Thomas Shadwell.[24] All three had music by Matthew Locke, who was under contract to the Duke's Company; Pelham Humfrey and Pietro Reggio also contributed music to the operatic *Tempest*. The detailed stage directions for the opening of that show may suggest its musical and visual complexity:

> The Front of the Stage is open'd, and the Band of 24 Violins, with the Harpsicals and Theorbo's which accompany the Voices, are plac'd between the Pit and the Stage. While the Overture is playing, the Curtain rises, and discovers a new Frontispiece, joyn'd to the great Pylasters, on each side of the Stage. This Frontispiece is a noble Arch, supported by large wreathed Columns of the Corinthian Order ... Behind this is the Scene, which represents a thick Cloudy Sky, a very Rocky Coast, and a Tempestuous Sea in perpetual Agitation. This Tempest (suppos'd to be rais'd by Magick) has many dreadful Objects in it, as several Spirits in horrid shapes flying in the Air. And when the Ship is sinking, the whole House is darken'd, and a shower of Fire falls upon 'em. This is accompanied with Lightning, and several Claps of Thunder, to the end of the Storm.[25]

Locke's "Overture," played by a group twice the size of the usual theatre orchestra, is an effective piece of program music, with unusual chromatic harmonies and rapid scales (marked *"violent"* in the score) vividly repre-senting the storm.

Still under contract to the King's Company, which had inferior compo-sers and limited scenic resources, Dryden responded by writing a rhyming semiopera based on *Paradise Lost, The State of Innocence and the Fall of Man*, but his colleagues chose not to present it; a French opera, *Ariane, ou le mariage de Bacchus* (1674), was performed instead. For the London performances, the French musicians devised a new prologue in which three nymphs in a seashell sing the parts of the rivers Thames, Seine, and Tiber.[26] Masking intractable problems in vague halos of music and fond affection, the nymphs declare England the isle of love, praise Charles for bringing peace to his nation, and compliment the recent marriage of the Duke of York. Evidently impressed by the capacity of opera for political allegory, some members of the court, possibly led by York's new bride, Mary of Modena, began planning a musical show of their own. In February of 1675, after many public rehearsals, John Crowne's *Calisto* was acted at court by Princess Mary, Princess Anne, and their ladies-in-waiting.[27] This mythological masque (frequently referred to as "the opera" in surviving documents) includes five musical scenes performed by professional singers, the first of which is a fully sung, transparently political prologue with Peace, Plenty, and the four continents among its characters. Like the prologue to *Ariane*, it features the river Thames and compliments members of the court; Crowne also takes note of the political resistance long centered in the City of London, here called "Augusta."

Many of the same musicians, domestic and imported, also appeared in *Psyche*, a Dorset Garden production with French dancers, music by Locke, and a rhyming text by Shadwell, which opened a few days later.[28] Although the plot is another piece of mythological fluff, Shadwell and Locke did produce a more unified work than any earlier musical drama; Curtis Price has argued that "the synthesis of music and drama in *Psyche* is remarkably good, certainly unmatched in any later semi-opera, even *King Arthur*."[29] Significantly, this increased operatic activity during the early 1670s coincided with the waning popularity of the rhymed heroic play. If playgoers were willing to laugh with Buckingham at the absurdities of the rhymed heroic play, including its use of music, they continued to relish some aspects of those productions, including epic plots, magic, elaborate scenery, formal language (including rhyme), and music. Following the model provided by *The Tempest*, the semioperas of the early 1670s satisfied those needs without asking audiences to take their plots seriously; the frequent recourse to mythological plots is a symptom of that escapist impulse. But mounting such elaborate productions proved costly: the prologue to *Aureng-Zebe* (November 1675), Dryden's last rhymed play, and his only one without a musical episode, closes by comparing the theatre companies to "Monarchs, ruin'd with expensive War" (line 38). The King's Company, whose financial and managerial troubles soon led Dryden to break his contract, produced no more plays with elaborate music. The Duke's Company produced only one more full-scale semiopera, Charles Davenant's *Circe* (1677); three other productions – Dryden and Nathaniel Lee's

Oedipus (1678), Lee's *Theodosius* (1680), and Shadwell's *The Lancashire Witches* (1681) – had operatic elements.

When the King's Company finally collapsed in 1682, its assets and actors were absorbed into the so-called United Company. The resulting monopoly reduced the incentive to produce expensive semioperas, and there was clearly now pressure from the court to move toward through-sung opera. Two short, private "masques" on classical subjects – *Venus and Adonis* (music by John Blow, libretto anonymous) and *Dido and Aeneas* (music by Henry Purcell, libretto by Nahum Tate) – were staged at court during the 1680s, though exact dates are uncertain.[30] Also unclear is whether these works were intended or interpreted as political allegories.[31] Both were through-sung, catering to the king's taste for opera with recitative; neither had elaborate scenes or machines. Happily, the music for both works survives, and may remind us of how effectively the best English composers of the period could write for voices; the closing choruses of both works are especially impressive.[32]

In 1683, Charles dispatched the actor-manager Thomas Betterton to France to "fetch ye designe"[33] for a full-scale opera in the French style; Betterton brought back Louis Grabu, a Spaniard with a French name and compositional style who had written music for *Ariane* and *Oedipus*, but had returned to France during the anti-Catholic hysteria connected with the Popish Plot. Dryden, who was recruited to provide a libretto, planned to produce a mixed entertainment, with a semiopera based on the story of King Arthur serving as the main plot. He also wrote a fully sung prologue on the model of those for *Ariane* and *Calisto*, a transparent political allegory presenting the troubled relations between city and court as the unstable marriage of Augusta (London) and Albion (Charles). The king, whose taste in music ran strongly to French conventions, approved of a rehearsal of the prologue, whereupon the collaborators decided to abandon the Arthurian semiopera and expand the prologue into a work in its own right. Postponed by Charles's sudden death in February of 1685, *Albion and Albanius* finally opened on 3 June 1685; ten days and six performances later, news reached London that the Duke of Monmouth had landed in the West with an army. The resulting turmoil spoiled the run of the only publicly staged through-sung English opera of the period, but even without that misfortune, *Albion and Albanius* was not a promising model. A completely obvious allegory of political events from 1660 until 1683, with the title characters representing Charles and James, it departed radically from the conventions of earlier English operas. Grabu's ignorance of English meter and accent led to distortions of Dryden's carefully varied poetic text, and the music is generally undistinguished. The production lost over £2,000 for the United Company.[34]

Remarkably enough, the company nonetheless returned to semiopera just five years later: *Dioclesian, or The Prophetess* (1690), adapted by Betterton from an old play by Massinger and Fletcher, is a semiopera in the tradition of *The Tempest*, with wonderful music by Purcell. The success of *The Prophetess* probably led Dryden to revise his abandoned *King Arthur*, which Purcell set for performance in 1691. As audiences in Paris and London discovered from the full-scale revival presented in 1995, *King Arthur* is a rich and complex work, by far the best of the English semioperas. Not only is it a collaboration between the leading poet and the leading composer of the period, both operating at the height of their powers, but it picks up and extends many of the motifs we have noticed in our survey of musical dramas: heroic rant, conjuring and magical illusions, singing spirits, music as sexual temptation, political allegory,[35] and interpolated masques showing alternate worlds of ice and ocean. The next year saw an equally lavish production of *The Fairy-Queen*, again with music by Purcell; the "author," who constructed a libretto from *A Midsummer Night's Dream*, remains anonymous.[36] These performances initiated a decade in which no less than fourteen semioperas were performed, including a revival of *The Indian Queen* with new music by Purcell and a restaging of Nathaniel Lee's *The Rival Queens* as a semiopera entitled *Alexander*. Neither the death of Purcell in 1695 nor the secession of Betterton and some other leading actors from the United Company in the same year interrupted this string of dialogue operas; not only were new semioperas staged in almost every year from 1690 until 1701, but those from previous years, especially *King Arthur*, stayed in repertory, with frequent revivals.[37]

During the first decade of the eighteenth century, there were several attempts to stage Italian operas – some sung in Italian, some translated into English (in whole or in part), some in the form called *pasticcio*, in which favorite arias were strung together without much pretense of connected plot. The most successful of these was *Camilla* (1706), with music by Giovanni Bononcini and a text sung entirely in English.[38] During this period of experimentation and ferment, English semiopera held its own. As late as 1706, Betterton produced George Granville's *The British Enchanters*, a semiopera written and set aside during the 1680s, to considerable applause. The venue was the new theatre at the Haymarket, designed by John Vanbrugh and designated by the Lord Chamberlain in 1707 as the only theatre allowed to produce operas. As Robert D. Hume points out, "We can only wonder what demon of perversity had seized Vanbrugh that he should imagine a separate opera company to be financially viable."[39] Although there was clearly some interest in opera, imported singers demanded huge salaries, which led in turn to high ticket prices, frequent changes of management, bankruptcies, and vain appeals for payment by the performers.

Even George Frederick Handel, whose *Rinaldo* was a considerable success in 1711, staged only three more operas between that first production and the founding of the Royal Academy of Music in 1720. Moreover, despite the simplifications of common operatic histories, *Rinaldo* did not constitute a sharp break with the English theatrical past. As Curtis Price has shown, Aaron Hill, who wrote the scenario for *Rinaldo*, constructed it as a logical next step in the development of English musical theatre; there are many resemblances between episodes in *Rinaldo* and *King Arthur*.[40] Although *Rinaldo* was far more coherent musically than the various kinds of "opera" that preceded it, London audiences experienced Handel's work as an improvement over earlier operas, not as something wholly different in kind. To be sure, there were differences between *Rinaldo* and the English semioperas, not least the conventions of the *da capo* aria, which require a character to repeat the music and text of the "A" section after singing the contrasting "B" section, thus more or less paralyzing the action. The responses of English audiences to those conventions – acceptance in the theatre, humorous criticism in the press – resemble the earlier debates about the conventions of rhymed heroic drama.

We owe many of Handel's operas – including such masterworks as *Giulio Cesare* and *Tamerlano* – to the patronage of the Royal Academy, which opened in 1720 with a substantial capital base raised from the nobility and high hopes. As Hume laconically notes, "it bankrupted itself in fewer than nine seasons – capital, royal subsidy, high attendance, and astronomical prices notwithstanding."[41] When the artistic reaction came, in a powerfully original work by John Gay, who had served as Aaron Hill's secretary when Hill was working with Handel, it involved a return to a mixture of spoken dialogue and singing. The melodies in *The Beggar's Opera* (1728), which includes no less than sixty-nine musical numbers, are largely drawn from the familiar repertoire of British ballads, though Gay also borrows tunes from Purcell and Handel. Much of the irony that delighted the original audiences came from the disjunctions between the well-known words to these ballads and the new words written by Gay: Polly's sad, cynical Air VI ("Virgins are like the fair flower in its lustre"), for example, uses a tune originally associated with a male singer's boasting of his heroic feats as a lover. Framed by witty spoken dialogue and neatly incorporated into an effective plot, the songs appear without elaborate instrumental introductions and without the conventional repetitions of the *da capo* aria.[42] Gay's brilliant satire has many targets, including the excesses of Italian opera, but it is misleading to suppose that his main purpose was to poke fun at Handel, with whom he remained on cordial terms.[43] Nor should we give *The Beggar's Opera* blame (or credit) for the failure of the Royal Academy, which was doomed by its own financial structure. Gay was more interested in lampooning the corruptions of the Walpole administration and gaining his own audience than in damaging the Italian opera; the success of *The Beggar's Opera*, which ran for an unprecedented sixty-two performances in its first season, is largely the result of his genius, but may also indicate the stubborn survival of the British preference for forms of musical theatre combining the spoken and sung word. There were numerous imitations, and songs based on ballad tunes were incorporated into many theatrical productions during the rest of the eighteenth century.

The revival of Handel operas in major houses and recordings during the last thirty years has allowed audiences to experience the stunning power of his operatic music; recent productions more faithful to the performance practice of the eighteenth century have revealed the dramatic and even psychological subtlety of his work. But the fact that the libretti are in Italian means that these works are and were inevitably separate from the main line of English theatre and musical theatre. Although Handel wrote nearly twenty more Italian operas after the failure of the Royal Academy, he devoted a large part of his compositional energy during his later career to composing oratorios with English texts, including such familiar works as *Messiah*, *Israel in Egypt*, and *Solomon*. Although invariably performed in concert (and therefore not properly dramatic), these works apply the musical conventions of *opera seria* to biblical stories; they have remained in the choral repertoire since their premieres. If Handel, who set English texts in the oratorios with considerable skill, had composed English operas, the later history of British musical theatre would doubtless have been very different.

NOTES

1 See Roy Sherwood, *The Court of Oliver Cromwell* (London: Croom Helm, 1977), pp. 84, 135–38, and the letter from William Dugdale to John Langley, printed by Percy Scholes in *The Puritans and Music in England and New England* (London: Oxford University Press, 1934), p. 144.

2 For a complete text, see *Cupid and Death* in *Dramatic Works and Poems ...*, ed. William Gifford and Alexander Dyce, 6 vols. (London, 1833; reprinted New York: Russell and Russell, 1966), vol. VI, pp. 343–67. For a score, see *Cupid*

and Death, ed. Edward J. Dent, *Musica Britannica*, vol. II (London: Stainer and Bell, 1951). There is no recording. See also Murray Lefkowitz, "Matthew Locke," in Stanley Sadie (ed.), *The New Grove Dictionary of Music* (London: Macmillan, 1980).

3 See *Ben Jonson*, ed. C. H. Herford, Percy Simpson, and Evelyn Simpson, 11 vols. (Oxford: Clarendon Press, 1925–52), vol. VII, p. 454. The music is lost.

4 The best account remains Stephen Orgel and Roy Strong, *Inigo Jones: The Theatre of the Stuart Court* (Berkeley and Los Angeles: University of California Press, 1973).

5 *The Diary of John Evelyn*, ed. E. S. De Beer, 6 vols. (Oxford: Clarendon Press, 1955), vol. II, pp. 449–50 (June 1645).

6 Thomas Rymer, *Foedera, conventiones, literae, et cujuscunque generis acta publica . . .*, 20 vols. (London: A. & J. Churchill, 1705–35), vol. XX, pp. 377–78.

7 *The Siege of Rhodes*, ed. Ann-Mari Hedback (Uppsala: Acta Universitatis Upsaliensis. Studia Anglistica Upsaliensia, 1973), vol. XIV, p. 4.

8 *The London Stage, Part 1, 1660–1700*, ed. William Van Lennep, with a critical introduction by Emmett L. Avery and Arthur H. Scouten (Carbondale: Southern Illinois University Press, 1965), p. 9.

9 *The Works of John Dryden*, ed. E. N. Hooker and H. T. Swedenberg, Jr. (Berkeley and Los Angeles: University of California Press, 1956–), vol. XI, p. 9.

10 Edward J. Dent argues that "D'Avenant originally wrote the work as a drama in rhymed heroic couplets, and that it was only when he found it impossible to produce it as a play, that he decided to turn it into an opera by cutting it down, altering the lengths of the lines here and there, inserting songs and choruses, and finally getting the whole set to music." See his *Foundations of English Opera* (1928; reprinted New York: Da Capo Press, 1965), p. 66. Dent supports his argument by conjecturally rewriting some of the short lines as pentameters.

11 For a detailed argument, which I compress here, see my essay, "Heroic Song: A Proposal for a Revised History of English Theatre and Opera, 1656–1711," *Eighteenth-Century Studies*, 30 (1997), pp. 113–37.

12 All the vocal music for these works is lost. In *Music in the Restoration Theatre* (Ann Arbor: UMI Research Press, 1979), p. 158, Curtis Price identifies a surviving piece of instrumental music as the "sarabande with castanets" specified to be danced in *The Cruelty of the Spaniards*.

13 See *The Diary of John Evelyn*, vol. III, p. 309 (9 January 1662); John Downes, *Roscius Anglicanus* (1708), ed. Judith Milhous and Robert D. Hume (London: Society for Theatre Research, 1987), p. 51; and Mary Edmond, *Rare Sir William Davenant* (Manchester: Manchester University Press, 1987), p. 160. Samuel Pepys, who greatly admired *The Siege of Rhodes*, composed an alternate setting for one of the songs, "Beauty Retire," which may be heard in a recording by Richard Wistreich and Robert Jeffrey, *The Musical Life of Samuel Pepys* (Saydisc CD-SCL 385).

14 This translation of Corneille's *Pompée*, produced in Dublin in February 1663, was probably performed in London a few months later; see *The London Stage*, Part 1, pp. 64, 67. On the music, much of which is extant, see Price, *Music in the Restoration Theatre*, pp. 62–64.

15 For details about this troupe, see Margaret Mabbett, "Italian Musicians in Restoration England (1660–90)," *Music and Letters*, 67 (1986), pp. 237–47.

16 Public Record Office, Lord Chamberlain's Papers, 5/138, f. 15, printed in *The London Stage*, Part 1, p. 74. "The Musick" was the term for the instrumentalists who played between the acts and accompanied the songs. See also Andrew Ashbee, *Records of English Court Music*, vol. 1 (1660–1685) (Snodland, Kent: Andrew Ashbee, 1986), pp. 59–61, and Peter Holman, *Four and Twenty Fiddlers: The Violin at the English Court, 1540–1690* (Oxford: Oxford University Press, 1993).

17 There is an extant setting by Pelham Humfrey, more likely to have been used in a revival than in the original production. The music was first printed in Playford's *Choice Ayres, Songs, & Dialogues, The Second Edition* (1675). All five books of this important series are now available as *Choice Ayres, Songs, and Dialogues*, ed. Ian Spink, 2 vols. (London: Stainer and Bell, 1989), each of the five original volumes separately paginated. For a good facsimile of Humfrey's song, see vol. 1, pp. 66–67.

18 *The Diary of Samuel Pepys: A New and Complete Transcription*, ed. Robert Latham and William Matthews, 11 vols. (London: Bell, 1970–83), vol. IX, pp. 23–24 (14 January 1668). The entry also notes the presence in the audience of "the players of the Duke's house," including the singer and dancer Moll Davis, who had recently become the king's mistress, and who had important parts in *The Tempest*, *Calisto*, and *Venus and Adonis*.

19 See *The London Stage*, Part 1, pp. 128–29; Evelyn, *Diary*, vol. III, p. 505: "twixt each act a Masque & *Antique*: daunced."

20 Pepys calls this "a curious piece of Musique in an Echo of half-sentences, the Echo repeating the former half while the man goes on to the latter, which is mighty pretty" (*Diary*, vol. VIII, p. 522 [7 November 1667]).

21 Pepys, *Diary*, vol. IX, p. 329 (14 October 1668).

22 There is an early setting of the duet in BL Add. MS 19759, fols. 29v–30r, reproduced in facsimile in *The Songs of John Dryden*, ed. Cyrus L. Day (Cambridge, MA: Harvard University Press, 1932), pp. 19–20. This has sometimes been thought to be the original, but Curtis Price has argued shrewdly that the minor changes in the text make it more likely that this anonymous music was used for a revival. See *Henry Purcell and the London Stage* (Cambridge: Cambridge University Press, 1984), pp. 46–53. No contemporary music survives for the other songs in this play.

23 This play also had a court performance by amateurs, this time previous to its commercial staging; see James A. Winn, *John Dryden and his World* (New Haven and London: Yale University Press, 1987), p. 245.

24 On the "authorship" of this adaptation, see George R. Guffey (ed.), *After The Tempest* (Los Angeles: Clark Library, 1969), especially p. xxi, n. 20.

25 For an edited score, see *Matthew Locke, Dramatic Music, with the Music by Humfrey, Banister, Reggio and Hart for "The Tempest,"* transcribed and edited by Michael Tilmouth, *Musica Britannica*, vol. LI (London: Stainer and Bell, 1986). There is now a recording of all the extant music by Christopher Hogwood and the Academy of Ancient Music (L'Oiseau Lyre, DSLO 507). The incidental music has also been recorded by Peter Holman and the Parley of Instruments, on their disc entitled *Four and Twenty Fiddlers: Music for the Restoration Court Violin Band* (Hyperion, CDA66667).

26 For a comparison of the two versions of the opera, see Pierre Danchin, "The

Foundation of the Royal Academy of Music in 1674 and Pierre Perrin's *Ariane*," *Theatre Studies*, 25 (1984), pp. 55–67, especially pp. 58–60. For a much fuller account of the sources, see C. Basford, "Perrin and Cambert's 'Ariane, ou le mariage de Bacchus' Re-examined," *Music and Letters*, 72 (1991), pp. 1–26, especially pp. 3–14.

27 For a detailed account, with many new facts and interpretations, including a revised date for the first performance, see Andrew R. Walkling, "Masque and Politics at the Restoration Court: John Crowne's *Calisto*," *Early Music*, 24 (1996), pp. 27–62. The music, by Nicholas Staggins, survives in fragmentary form. There are seven melodies for the songs; Walkling prints one of these with a conjectural bass-line, p. 31. Peter Holman has found what may be some of the dance music; see *Four and Twenty Fiddlers*, pp. 366–73.

28 For a modern edition of the score, see *Musica Britannica*, vol. LI. There was a concert performance of Locke's music for *Psyche* by the Early English Opera Society in 1990, but no recording is yet available.

29 *Henry Purcell and the London Stage*, p. 297.

30 *Venus and Adonis* is usually dated 1681 or 1682. It received a second production in 1684 at Josias Priest's boarding school for girls in Chelsea; see Richard Luckett, "A New Source for 'Venus and Adonis,'" *Musical Times*, 130 (1989), pp. 76–79. We have long known that *Dido and Aeneas* was produced by the same school in 1689; recent scholarship suggests that it was produced earlier at court, though there is considerable disagreement as to the possible date. See Bruce Wood and Andrew Pinnock, "'Unscarr'd by turning times'? The Dating of Purcell's *Dido and Aeneas*," *Early Music*, 20 (1992), pp. 372–90; Mark Goldie, "The Earliest Notice of Purcell's *Dido and Aeneas*," *Early Music*, 20 (1992), pp. 392–400; Curtis Price, "*Dido and Aeneas*: Questions of Style and Evidence," *Early Music*, 22 (1994), pp. 115–25; Andrew R. Walkling, "'The Dating of Purcell's *Dido and Aeneas*'?: A Reply to Bruce Wood and Andrew Pinnock," *Early Music*, 22 (1994), pp. 469–81; and subsequent replies.

31 For a specific argument in favor of such interpretation, see Andrew R. Walkling, "Political Allegory in Purcell's "'Dido and Aeneas,'" *Music and Letters*, 76 (1995), pp. 540–71. For more general speculations on politics and opera in the entire period, see Curtis Price, "Political Allegory in Late Seventeenth-century English Opera," in Nigel Fortune (ed.), *Music and Theatre: Essays in Honour of Winton Dean* (Cambridge: Cambridge University Press, 1987), pp. 1–30; James A. Winn, *"When Beauty Fires the Blood": Love and the Arts in the Age of Dryden* (Ann Arbor: University of Michigan Press, 1992), especially chapters 3–5; and Robert D. Hume, "The Politics of Opera in Late Seventeenth-Century London," forthcoming in Derek Hirst and Richard Strier (eds.), *Destinies and Choices: Politics and Literature in Seventeenth-Century England* (Durham: Duke University Press).

32 Among the many recordings of *Dido and Aeneas*, three especially fine performances are those conducted by Andrew Parrott (Chandos ABRD 1034), Christopher Hogwood (L'Oiseau-Lyre 436 992–2) and William Christie (Erato 4509–98477–2). There is an excellent recording of *Venus and Adonis* conducted by Charles Medlam (Harmonia Mundi HMC 901276).

33 The quoted phrase is from correspondence that passed between Richard Grahame, Viscount Preston, Ambassador to France, and Robert Spencer, Earl of

Sutherland. See *Reports of the Commission on Historical Manuscripts*, VII, i, 288, 290.

34 Judith Milhous, "United Company Finances, 1682–1692," *Theatre Research International*, 7 (1981–82), pp. 37–53. The score, printed in folio at the time of the performance, is extant. There is no recording, though there was a concert performance of Act II by the Early English Opera Society in 1990. One short instrumental piece appears on *Four and Twenty Fiddlers* (cited above, n. 25).

35 The problem of political allegory in *King Arthur* takes on additional complexity because of the lost original version of 1683 and Dryden's claims to have revised it. I have argued that the revised play "walks a political tightrope, offering Williamites a vaguely patriotic vision of British glory while giving clever Jacobites frequent opportunities to detect Dryden's cynicism and irony." See *"When Beauty Fires the Blood,"* pp. 273–302.

36 Some of the music from *Dioclesian* may be heard on a recording conducted by Alfred Deller (Bach Guild BG 682); all of the music from *The Fairy-Queen* appears on a three-record set conducted by John Eliot Gardner (Archiv Produktion 2566 103, 104, 105); there are now numerous recordings of *King Arthur*, including one conducted by Alfred Deller (Harmonia Mundi HMC 252–HMC 253), and one conducted by Trevor Pinnock (Archiv Produktion 435 490-2, 491-2, 493-2).

37 I summarize here material much more fully described in Robert D. Hume, "Opera in London, 1695–1706," in Shirley Strum Kenny (ed.), *British Theatre and the Other Arts, 1660–1800* (Washington: Folger Shakespeare Library, 1984), pp. 67–91.

38 See Curtis Price, "The Critical Decade for English Music Drama, 1700–1710," *Harvard Library Bulletin*, 26 (1978), pp. 38–76. For details about the shifting financial arrangements during this period, see Robert D. Hume, "The Sponsorship of Opera in London, 1704–1720," *Modern Philology*, 85 (1988), pp. 420–32.

39 "Sponsorship of Opera," p. 424.

40 "English Traditions in Handel's *Rinaldo*," in Stanley Sadie and Anthony Hicks (eds.), *Handel Tercentenary Collection* (London: Royal Musical Association, 1987), pp. 120–35. See also some further development of this argument in my essay, "Heroic Song."

41 "Sponsorship of Opera," p. 431.

42 The only source for the music is the third edition (1729), which prints the full score of the overture (by Pepusch) and gives the airs as melodies with unfigured bass lines. Most scholars have assumed that the orchestra on hand for the overture (strings and two oboes) accompanied the singing. Of modern recordings, the least offensive is conducted by Denis Stevens (Musical Heritage Society, MHS 4011/12).

43 See William A. McIntosh, "Handel, Walpole, and Gay: The Aims of *The Beggar's Opera*," *Eighteenth-Century Studies*, 7 (1974), pp. 415–33.

FURTHER READING

Alssid, Michael W., "The Impossible Form of Art: Dryden, Purcell, and *King Arthur*," *Studies in the Literary Imagination*, 10 (1977), pp. 125–44.

Charlton, David, "'King Arthur': Dramatick Opera," *Music and Letters*, 64 (1983), pp. 183–92.

Dean, Winton, and Knapp, John Merrill, *Handel's Operas, 1704–1726* (Oxford: Oxford University Press, 1987; rev. edn., 1995).

Hammond, Paul, "Dryden's *Albion and Albanius*: The Apotheosis of Charles II," in David Lindley (ed.), *The Court Masque* (Manchester: Manchester University Press, 1984), pp. 169–83.

Haun, Eugene, *But Hark! More Harmony: The Libretti of Restoration Opera in English* (Ypsilanti: Eastern Michigan University Press, 1971).

Highfill, Philip H., Jr., Burnim, Kalman A., and Langhans, Edward A., *A Biographical Dictionary of Actors, Actresses, Musicians, Dancers, Managers and Other Stage Personnel in London, 1660–1800* (Carbondale: Southern Illinois University Press, 1973–90).

Luckett, Richard, "Music," in *The Diary of Samuel Pepys*, ed. Robert Latham and William Matthews, 11 vols. (London: Bell, 1970–83), vol. x, pp. 258–82.

Milhous, Judith, "The Multimedia Spectacular on the Restoration Stage," in Shirley Strum Kenny (ed.), *British Theatre and Other Arts, 1660–1800* (Washington, DC: Folger Shakespeare Library, 1983), pp. 41–66.

Milhous, Judith, and Hume, Robert D. (eds.), *Vice Chamberlain Coke's Theatrical Papers, 1706–1715* (Carbondale: Southern Illinois University Press, 1982).

Parsons, Philip, "Restoration Tragedy as Total Theatre," in Harold Love (ed.), *Restoration Literature, Critical Approaches* (London: Methuen, 1972), pp. 27–68.

Pinnock, Andrew, "Play into Opera: Purcell's *The Indian Queen*," *Early Music*, 18 (1990), pp. 3–21.

Powell, Jocelyn, *Restoration Theatre Production* (London: Routledge and Kegan Paul, 1984).

Roberts, David, *The Ladies: Female Patronage of Restoration Drama 1660–1700* (Oxford: Clarendon Press, 1989).

White, Eric Walter, *A History of English Opera* (London: Faber, 1983).

6

JOSHUA SCODEL

Lyric forms

The personal lyric, conceived as the expression of a highly individualized voice and subjective feeling, was not a major form between the early seventeenth-century flowering of the "metaphysical" lyric and the lyric resurgence of the late eighteenth century and Romanticism. From 1650 to 1740, England witnessed great social and political change, from the successive upheavals and reactions of the Interregnum, Restoration, and Glorious Revolution to the stabilizing consolidation of Whig constitutionalism, oligarchy, and bureaucracy. Profound economic and cultural transformations also occurred: a financial revolution, a growing commercial empire, and the increasing hegemony of a middle-class culture commercial in background and "polite" in aspiration. Traditional martial values (still crucial for England's foreign relations but tarnished by associations with civil war) clashed with aristocratic libertinism and middle-class ideals of civility. Men and women renegotiated their relations within the context of an increasingly prosperous, pacific, "feminized" domestic culture. Aggressively modern scientific and philosophical trends challenged the classics' still potent authority. After the Puritans' failure to transform the nation and its church, the English church's internal struggle between liberal and conservative factions and its external confrontation with diverse heterodoxies and secular currents kept religious life in ferment. Major talents cultivated discursive and didactic forms such as satire, epistle, and georgic in which public poetic voices participated directly in debates over politics, religion, and manners. Epigram, which could wittily attack social deviations or deftly install domestic life in its small place within a larger scheme, rivaled lyric as the dominant short form. While poets wrote notable poems considered lyric both then and now, their particular interest often lies in their relative "impurity," their incorporation of the public attitudes and themes characteristic of the period.

Andrew Marvell's "An Horatian Ode upon Cromwell's Return from Ireland" (1650) is unique in its complex response to epochal change but typical in exploiting a classic lyric genre to make a rhetorically weighty intervention in public events.[1] Awed at Oliver Cromwell's destruction of "the great work of time" (the English monarchy) (line 34), the poet speaks with a communal "we" that presumes, but actually seeks to forge, a post-monarchical consensus. Cromwell figures both as a Providentialist saint who heeded his calling as "heaven's angry flame" (line 26) and "urged" (line 12) his divine destiny, and as a Machiavellian "Fortune's Son" (line 113) whose military valor accrued power to be maintained with untiring force. Horace's political odes, written by a former supporter of the Roman republic, praise Augustus for bringing internal peace and external power. While English Royalists had written Horatian odes celebrating monarchy, Marvell adopts Horace's acknowledgment of new realities. In Marvell's principal model, the ode honoring Augustus's victory over Antony and Cleopatra at Actium, Horace declares that Romans must celebrate "now," while before this would have been criminal. Marvell begins his poem declaring, not without regret, " 'Tis time" (line 5) to abandon books and "languishing" (line 4) verse for armor – that is, to quit the life and poetry of retirement (which Marvell embraces in other lyrics) to defend the new order. Cromwell's victim, Charles I, appears dignified in dethronement, but his refusal to protest execution – he "bowed his comely head, / Down as upon a bed" (lines 63–64) – authorizes the new regime. Classical imitation underscores the point through differences: Charles recalls Horace's Cleopatra, who commits suicide to elude participating in a Roman triumphal ceremony (Ode 1.37.30–32), while Charles dies a "royal actor" in a "memorable scene" (lines 53, 58) scripted by Cromwell.

While Marvell's Horatian ode has no generic heirs, the "Pindaric" ode, fashioned by Abraham Cowley in the late 1650s, became the period's most popular lyric innovation and was widely considered the highest, quintessential lyric form. Transforming a classical genre, Cowley, an uneven but fascinating poet, created an instrument for treating themes particularly suited to so intensely political a period – the diverse sources of power. The odes of the archaic Greek poet Pindar, composed for public performance, celebrate the athletic victories of a ruler or aristocrat and his community as heroic achievements. Written for various occasions (marriages, funerals, military victories, book publications), English Pindaric panegyrics honor the accomplishments of monarchs, aristocrats, generals, scientists, and poets, often presented as both powerful individuals and icons of national strength. For ancient and English critics alike, Pindar's brilliant but obscure images, mythological digressions, and puzzling transitions encode a forceful "sublimity" that befits his great subjects by transcending decorous rules. Displaying less imagistic daring and clearer argumentative structures,

Cowley and his heirs pursue sublimity through stock images of power, some from Pindar himself, such as volcanoes or predatory animals. Despite Pindar's strict metrics, in a famous ode loosely translated by Cowley (*Ode* 4.2), Horace associates Pindar's poetic power, figured as an uncontrollable flood, with prosodic freedom. English poets follow Cowley and compose Pindaric odes that freely vary the number of stanzas, number and length of lines within stanzas, and rhyme patterns. Critics both then and now have complained that such formal freedom made the Pindaric easy to carry out but difficult to carry off, and numerous poets cranked out lengthy Pindarics that flatly flattered the powers-that-be. The best Pindaric panegyrics, however, particularly those by Cowley himself and John Dryden, convey genuine enthusiasm for or fascinated ambivalence toward power.

Cowley's *Pindaric Odes*, published in 1656 after Cowley's arrest by the Interregnum regime as a Royalist spy, includes political poems that imply the poet's hedged acceptance of the Royalists' defeat. Pindar mingled praise of his various patrons' victories with reminders of fortune's vagaries and the dangers of excessive pride; he also used myth for oblique warnings. Cowley's "Brutus" adapts Pindar's ambivalence about greatness and strategic obliquity to respond to current history.[2] Brutus's killing of Julius Caesar is defended, first, as "Th'*Heroick Exaltations of Good*" (stanza 2, line 5) misunderstood as "*Vice*" (stanza 2, line 7) but then Christ's passive suffering is represented as superseding Brutus's heroic tyrannicide. Providing an historical example with an ambiguous contemporary application, Cowley (like Marvell) acquiesces but prudently obscures whom he respects more, the Puritan victors or the defeated Royalists. If Caesar represents Charles I and Brutus represents Cromwell, Cowley praises Cromwell's heroic virtue while implying that the Puritan revolution was too extreme for Christians, who should passively suffer like Christ. If Caesar represents Cromwell (excoriated by Royalists as a tyrant), then Brutus represents Royalists who, in Cowley's view, nobly but vainly wished to continue battling the Interregnum regime instead of humbly accepting Providence.

Cowley's 1660 ode upon Charles II's Restoration is farther from Pindar and correspondingly more typical of many later English political Pindarics in its unambiguous praise of ruling powers.[3] With repeated images of destructive and beneficent greatness contrasting Cromwell's and Charles II's power, Cowley glorifies the latter as a Christic figure, whose trials recall the Savior's "*suffering Humanity*" (stanza 12, line 18) and justify a victorious return as the "*Image*" of Christ's "*Power Divine*" (stanza 12, line 20). Participating in the widespread identification of the Restoration with England's recovery of "Liberty" (stanza 4, line 2), pleasure, and bounty, Cowley's nineteen-stanza poem, the longest of his Pindarics, associates both its metrical freedom and formal expansiveness with "*Poetick* rage" (stanza 16, line 21), a transport of inspiration that befits a nation "flow[ing]" with celebratory wine and a "*wild fit*" (stanza 16, line 26) of joy.

Pindar often compares athletic to military prowess; in two Pindaric translations that open his 1656 volume, Cowley obliquely laments English civil war by elaborating Pindaric glorifications of peaceful competition. In a much imitated Pindaric ode lauding eminences in arts and letters composed during both the Interregnum and Restoration, Cowley glorifies English intellectual prowess with traditional heroic and martial imagery even while decrying "barb'rous Wars unlearned Rage" ("Upon Dr. Harvey," stanza 5, line 3). The physician Charles Scarburgh has won a "*Crown*" for medical "*Conquests*" ("*To Dr.* Scarborough," stanza 5, lines 1, 13), Thomas Hobbes's reason resembles Aeneas's shield ("*To Mr.* Hobs," stanza 5), the Royal Society contains "great Champions" in the "glorious Fight" for knowledge ("*To the* Royal Society," stanza 6, line 1, stanza 7, line 1). Cowley partially aggrandizes his subjects at the expense of his own poetic mode, praising in Pindaric high style Hobbes and the Royal Society's anti-rhetorical subordination of verbal expression to plain truth. Yet just as Pindar often analogizes the athletic victories he celebrates to his own poetic superiority, so Cowley's odes on modern English achievements highlight his own role as modernity's bard. Praising the Royal Society for freeing "Captiv'd Philosophy" ("*To the* Royal Society," stanza 2, line 16) from bondage to ancient thinkers, Cowley draws an implicit link to his own espousal of Pindaric "Liberty." Yet Cowley's aggressive self-placement among the moderns also pits him against Pindar: the description of Hobbes as a Columbus who discovers a "vast *Ocean*" of knowledge beyond the "slender-limb'ed" Mediterranean ("*To Mr. Hobs*," stanza 4, lines 2–5) reverses Pindar's warnings against hubris, often couched in claims that one should not dare sail beyond that sea's bounds – the "pillars of Hercules" (*Olympian* 3.42–45, *Nemean* 3.19–21, *Isthmian* 4.9–13).[4]

Cowley also writes odes on his Muse, on poetic wit, and on the poet Katherine Philips, whose posthumous *Poems* (1664) made her the first major female secular poet in English, very widely celebrated for her accomplishment, and an authorizing figure for later English women poets. Representing Philips as a woman without Greek or Roman rivals, Cowley treats her as the embodiment of modern English achievement. He also extends his praise of bloodless but glorious struggles to gender rivalry. Philips's "bold sally" ("*On Orinda's* Poems," stanza 1, line 14) against male dominance in "wits milde Empire" (stanza 5, line 5) reveals her victorious, androgynous combination of (manly) strength and (female) sweetness.

Cowley associates Philips's blend of traditionally male and female virtues with a widely shared cultural agenda of the Restoration – the recivilizing of England after a time of barbaric radicalism and violence: she can teach "rude" English men "Arts, and Civility" (stanza 4, lines 16–17).[5]

Pindaric odes after Cowley continue to construct an English line of powerful poets who rival the ancients. They also celebrate or advocate women's role within modern culture. "The Emulation, A Pindaric Ode" (1683), for example, protests that men have deprived women's "rational unbounded Mind" (line 16) of the learning with which they could challenge male "Empire" (line 37).[6] The title glorifies female emulation of male achievement by associating it with the Pindaric ode's traditional praise of competition, and the poem harnesses the Pindaric ode's formal associations with liberty to espouse female freedom from tyrannical male constraints.

The greatest writer of Pindaric encomia, John Dryden, celebrates monarchs, aristocrats, other artists, and the power of music (including the music of poetry). "To the Pious Memory of . . . Anne Killigrew," prefaced to Killigrew's posthumous book of poetry (1686), associates her with Philips and expands Cowley's theme of the androgynous female poet.[7] Dryden praises the deceased for her feminine beauty; a virtuous innocence that contrasts sharply with the immorality of contemporaneous male writers (including Dryden himself); and her poetic power, figured in masculine terms. Luxuriantly hyperbolic in associating Killigrew with the divine, the poem evokes an ideal of poetic excellence more than it memorializes a real woman. Yet echoes of Killigrew's own verse particularize the praise and intimate that her respectable (if minor) poetry has inspired Dryden's celebration of the ideal. Noting Dryden's own commitment to "art" (poetic craft and learning) as well as "nature" (natural talent), some critics have concluded that Dryden disparages when he praises Killigrew's sole reliance on "nature": "Art she had none, yet wanted none; / For Nature did that Want supply / So rich in Treasures of her Own, / She might our boasted Stores defy; / Such Noble Vigor did her Verse adorn" (lines 71–75). Yet Dryden, who throughout his career counterposes "nature" and "art," consistently notes the greater importance of natural power even when claiming the need for tempering art. Figuring Killigrew's untutored "nature" as a conventionally masculine "vigor," Dryden turns female cultural disadvantage – Killigrew's lack of the classical education deemed necessary for full access to "art" – into a "natural" male asset. His Pindaric praise of Killigrew decorously relies, moreover, upon Pindaric values espoused by Killigrew herself. Pindar often proclaims his dependence upon nature rather than art, and in her Pindaric ode "The Discontent" Killigrew bids her Muse no "Art or Labour use."[8]

Dryden further emphasizes Killigrew's "male" energy when character-izing her decision to paint as well as write verse: "But what can young ambitious Souls confine?" (line 91). Dryden's playful, hyperbolic analo-gizing of Killigrew to a conquering monarch who could not be "content" with a "Spacious Empire" (lines 88–90), which recalls Cowley's praise of intellectual achievements in martial terms while glancing satirically at Louis XIV, invites readers to weigh Killigrew's artistic successes against male violence. Killigrew herself contrasted masculine violence with female accomplishments: her volume opens with a fragmentary "Alexendreis" praising Alexander the Great's discontent after conquering the "spacious World" (line 3), but then proceeds in "To the Queen" to reject such "Frantick Might" (line 33) as far "inferiour" (line 22) to the "sublime" (line 17) virtue of Mary of Modena.[9] Dryden's analogy implies that Killigrew the innocent but forceful androgyne did not simply reject, but rather transmuted, masculinist ambitions.

"Alexander's Feast, or the Power of Music" (1698), the last and perhaps greatest of Dryden's Pindarics, is both joyous and disillusioned about masculinist power.[10] Written for St. Cecilia's Day, honoring music's patron saint, the poem celebrates poetry's power by depicting how the shifting melodies of the bardic Timotheus, a "Mighty Master" (line 93), aroused a gamut of passions in a helpless Alexander the Great before lauding, in a final stanza, St. Cecilia's Christian music. In this *tour de force* of metrical mimetics, Dryden applies the formal variety of the Cowleyan Pindaric ode to demonstrate metrical effects and the passions they arouse. In his mocking portrait of Alexander as vain, drunken, lecherous, and violent, Dryden, a Jacobite loyal to the deposed James II, satirizes the new king William III, who was praised as another Alexander by Dryden's poetic contemporaries, while the portrait of Timotheus encodes Dryden's fantasy of conquering England's despised conquerer. Yet Dryden also mocks Timotheus, who self-servingly flatters Alexander into believing himself a god; here the satiric target extends past Dryden's contemporaries to the Pindaric panegyrist as such, whose greatness depended upon celebrating the powerful, including perhaps Dryden himself, the erstwhile Pindaric encomiast of the Stuarts.

Eighteenth-century Pindaric panegyrics gradually became more restrained in praise, more metrically regular, but less interesting. Edward Young's series of odes in "Pindar's spirit," "*Imperium Pelagi* [Empire of the Sea] A Naval Lyric" (1729) employs varying numbers of a single six-line stanza to develop an aggressively modern theme, British trade as opposed both to bloody war and Pindaric athletes' "glory vain." Young's attempt to rescue trade from "the shore of Prose" fails, however, to reach sublime crests.[11]

Among his Pindaric odes Cowley had included meditative poems that mixed autobiographical with philosophical reflections on abstract forces like "Destinie." Pindaric expansiveness served numerous poets in treating such subjects by grandly surveying their diverse effects. Perhaps the greatest example, Anne Finch, Countess of Winchilsea's "Spleen" (1701) exploits the Pindaric's metrical variety to treat, in tonalities ranging from wistful to comic to bitter, melancholy's protean forms.[12] The poem includes wonderful lines on smells' psychological effects; comic and satiric observations on how melancholy provokes conflict between husbands' "Imperial Sway" and wives "arm'd with *Spleen*" (lines 61–63); and the poet's lament over her own melancholy as she anticipates criticism for writing poetry on "unusual Things" (line 83) (such as spleen!) rather than practicing the amateur visual arts deemed suitable for ladies. A Jacobite, Winchilsea also ventures a witty, guarded swipe at William III by declining to paint "The *Sov'reign's* blurr'd and undistinguish'd Face" (line 88). Though context suggests this portrait would be as inept as an "ill-drawn *Bird*" (line 87), readers could infer that it would be all too verisimilar.

The gender struggles often addressed in Pindaric odes are central to the period's lyrics of love and friendship. Philips, whose originality as a female poet was extolled by Cowley, proves most innovative and influential in celebrating friendship between women. Writing most of her poems during the Interregnum when she was the wife of a Parliamentarian but the member of a circle composed of Royalist sympathizers, Philips finds in such friendship an alternative to the "angry world" ("Friendship's Mystery, To my dearest Lucasia," line 4). Protesting the usual confines of ideal friendship (the mutual admiration of virtuous persons celebrated by so many classical and early modern writers) to "rational" men, her poem "A Friend" exclaims "If Souls no Sexes have, for Men t'exclude / Women from Friendship's vast capacity, / Is a Design injurious or rude, / Only maintain'd by partial [i.e., biased] tyranny" (lines 19–22). Philips asserts that such same-sex friendship is superior to marriage because more spiritual and free. She also, however, often adapts male love poetry's passionate adoration of women, infusing with erotic intensity a relationship treated as purer than physical desire.[13]

In constructing her ideal, Philips exploits John Donne's love poetry, taking up his treatment of heterosexual love as a religious mystery and mixing of souls: "There's a Religion in our Love," she declares ("Friendship's Mystery, to my dearest Lucasia," line 5), for "our twin-Souls in one shall grow, / And teach the World new Love" ("To Mrs. M.A. at Parting," lines 49–50). Adapting the conceit of twin compasses in "A Valediction, Forbidding Mourning" to signify the bond between separated female friends, Philips substitutes for Donne's stay-at-home foot that "leans, and hearkens after" (line 31) the traveling other, which encodes a conventional gender hierarchy of active male and responsive female, an image of mirroring equality: "Each follows where the other leans" ("Friendship in Embleme," line 27). In "An Answer to another perswading a Lady to Marriage," Philips claims that the single woman is a "public Deity" who by marrying would reduce herself to "A petty Household God" (lines 5, 8). In "The Sun Rising," Donne, with macho bravado, bade the sun confine itself to shining on himself and his beloved: "Shine here to us, and thou art everywhere" (line 29). Deflating both the suitor addressed and the masculine pride of Donnean love poetry, Philips equates the suitor's desire to marry with a presumptuous desire to monopolize the sun: "First make the Sun in private shine, / And bid the World adieu, / That so he may his beams confine / In complement to you" (lines 9–12).[14]

Philips inspired several late seventeenth- and early eighteenth-century female poets – including Winchilsea, Jane Barker, Elizabeth Rowe, Mary Masters, Mary Chandler, and Mary Barber – to celebrate female friendship; they often echo her conceits. Concurrently, however, the libertine erotic poetry of the late 1660s to early 1680s – coterie verse written by aristocratic amateurs at a hedonistic court – celebrates the male aristocrat's roving sexual appetite. In traditional metrical forms, many of them fit for song, these writers puncture conventional poetic conceits with conversational and obscene idioms and images. They not only treat longstanding erotic situations like persuading a lady to grant her favors and cursing one who refuses but also proclaim male inconstancy and deplore the sensual life's disappointments – impotence, premature ejaculation, post-coital satiety, and boredom. They frequently appeal to "nature," understood as the natural appetites described by hedonists from Ovid to Thomas Hobbes, to justify their rakish pursuits and satirize those foolish enough to accept traditional sexual mores.

In demystifying conventions in the light of "nature," the libertines resemble Cowley's lauded philosophers and scientists who attacked obfuscating verbiage in the name of truth. In "The Advice," the most stylistically distinctive and intellectually serious of the libertines, John Wilmot, Earl of Rochester, curses a chaste woman by exhorting "Live upon modesty and empty fame, / Forgoing sense [i.e., physical sensation] for a fantastic name" (lines 49–50). Rochester casually juxtaposes euphemistic poetic diction and brutal obscenity, beginning a "Song" by grandly but vaguely evoking love as a powerful yet rule-governed force before concluding the quatrain with graphic references to bodily realities: "By all loves soft, yet mighty powers, / It is a thing unfit / That men should fuck in time of flowers, [during menstruation] / Or when the smock's beshit" (lines 1–4). Charles Sackville, Earl of Dorset's "A Song to Chloris ..." partially revivifies the hoary *carpe diem* form by linking a woman's well-timed yielding with the enlightened disenchantment of the period: "We live in an age that's more civil and wise / Than to follow the rules of romances" (lines 3–4). His reference to the woman's inevitable aging, a conventional feature of the form, is untraditional in its slangy crudity: "When once your round bubbies begin but to pout / They'll allow you no long time for courting" (lines 5–6). Dorset's jaunty "A Song on Black Bess," which celebrates a whore for her beauty and erotic playfulness, contrasts "The truth that I know of bonny Black Bess" with the illusions of "fools" who complain, with the stock names and diction of pastoral lament and neopetrarchan adoration, that "Phyllis and Chloris" are "cruel and fair" (lines 1–6). Mocking pastoral conventions with more shocking originality, in another "Song" Rochester replaces the idealized shepherdess in her pretty pastoral setting with a pigkeeper in her sty – "Fair Chloris in a pigsty lay; / Her tender herd lay by her" (lines 1–2) – and recounts the girl's masturbatory fantasy of being raped, which keeps her both "innocent and pleased" (line 40).[15]

The libertines reject not only erotic illusions but also traditional heroism. Yet like Cowley in his Pindarics, they seek substitutes for the martial values that once undergirded male aristocratic claims to superiority. Dorset associates libertinism with "noble pride" ("The Advice," line 9), Rochester with the "pride" of those who "in love excel" ("Against Constancy," lines 14–15). Rocheter's libertinism is identified with an aristocratic greatness disdainful of constraint: in "Upon his Leaving his Mistress" he rationalizes his inconstancy by claiming that he thereby frees the mistress from being "confined" like "meaner spirits" to one man; instead she must live up to her (that is, his!) "mighty mind" (lines 8, 19–20).[16] "Sardanapaulus," a mock Pindaric of the 1670s by John Oldham, the satirist and ambivalent member of Rochester's circle, treats an infamously debauched ancient monarch who resembles both Charles II and his libertine courtiers. Obtaining a "vast Dominion" (line 54) of mistresses, Sardanapaulus made "C—t the only Field" in which to be "Great" (line 14) believing there was no crucial difference between having "Fought, or F—k'd for Universal Monarchy" (line 35). He is immolated along with a "Hecatomb" of virgins whom he rapes.[17] The poem simultaneously satirizes libertines and aggrandizes them as pornographic heroes of Pindaric disproportions.

Celebrations of another male pleasure, convivial drinking, dominate other lyric sub-genres of Restoration libertines, symposiastic (drinking-party) poems and drinking songs. The Greek poet Anacreon and the Anacreontic verse ascribed to him in our period advocate drunkenness as an escape from anxiety over one's place in the social world (riches, high station) as well as over aging and inevitable death. In the 1650s Anacreontic poetry appealed to Royalist Cavalier poets deprived of political power who were eager simultaneously to make a virtue of necessity and to mock Puritan sermons and Interregnum legislation against alehouses and drunkenness. Thomas Stanley's translations of Anacreon appeared in 1651, Cowley's in 1656 with an elegy celebrating Anacreon's inebriated rejection of "Bus'iness, Honor, Title, State."[18] Alexander Brome, dubbed the "English Anacreon," writes songs defying the killjoy Parliamentary–Puritan regime with "freedome of drinking" ("The Murmurer," line 4).[19] Charles Cotton similarly associates drinking with Royalist freedom; his "Ode: Come, let us drink away the time" concludes by impudently proposing that Cromwell sanction Cotton's modest sensual pleasures: "Let me have sack, tobacco store, / A drunken friend, a little wh–re, / *Protector*, I will ask no more" (lines 40–42).[20]

In two Interregnum sonnets of the mid-1650s, "Lawrence, of virtuous father ..." and "Cyriack, whose grandsire ...," John Milton captures a distinctively Horatian note in portraying companionable eating or drinking as what one "interpose[s]" between one's duties ("Lawrence," line 14). Horace diverges from Anacreon (and his English Royalist imitators) by treating symposiastic pleasure as a temporary, revivifying respite from social responsibilities. With numerous Horatian echoes, Milton contests the Cavaliers' appropriation of convivial poetry, pointedly celebrating a moderate Parliamentary–Puritan pleasure – a "light and choice" meal ("Lawrence," line 9), wine, restrained "mirth, that after no repenting draws" ("Cyriack," line 6) (and no Cavalier drunkenness or whores!). These recreational moments are set within a larger historical, Providential order evoked by scriptural echoes and by Milton's Horatian-style addressing of his young invitees in terms of their ancestry, the public-spirited lineage whose values they must uphold.[21]

With the Restoration, Royalists took up a different Horatian theme – celebration as a decorous response to joyous political events. Cotton's "To Alexander Brome" opens by echoing the first lines of Horace's Actium ode (used so differently by Marvell!): "Now let us drink ... / Never so fit a time for harmless mirth" (lines 1, 3). Cotton celebrates a loyal, free-spirited unanimity he missed in Interregnum England: "One Harmony, one Mirth, one Voice, / One Love, one Loyalty, one Noise / Of Wit, and Joy, one Mind, and that as free / As if we all one Man could be" (lines 49–52).[22] While ancient lyrics praise wine for loosening men's spirits, Cotton provides the most resonant lyric description of wine's dissolving of ego boundaries, bringing the possibility (at last!) of a unified body politic.

Tory drinking songs during the political struggles between Charles II and his Whig opponents in the late 1670s and early 1680s oppose conviviality to rebellious sullenness. In Thomas D'Urfey's "The King's Health" (1681), still a popular tune in the early eighteenth century, loyal toasts – "Joy to great *Caesar*, / Long Life, Love and Pleasure; / 'Tis a Health that Divine is, / Fill the Bowl high as mine is" (lines 1–4) – counter rebellious "Faction and Folly, / And State Melancholy" (lines 40–41).[23] The libertine poet Alexander Radcliffe's drinking songs of 1682 note that whoever drinks all day and "all night hugs a Whore" has no time for rebellion.[24]

Libertine drinking songs also celebrate drunkenness, more subversively, as expressions of transgressive personal hedonism. In a poem based upon Anacreontic models, Rochester requests a drinking cup carved with scenes of drunkenness and sex rather than battles, for with "war I've nought to do." The final quatrain moves from the geniality of Anacreontic verse, in which mythological bric-à-brac decorates the sensuality, to a simultaneously cruder and darker vein: "Cupid and Bacchus my saints are: / May drink and love still reign. / With wine I wash away my cares, / And then to cunt again" ("Upon his Drinking a Bowl," lines 10, 21–24).[25] Rochester complicates carefree Anacreontic joy by implying that eroticism itself brings cares – unless properly distanced by drink and thereby reducible to casual wenching.

Libertinism was not, however, the male poet's exclusive property. Aphra Behn, the most important Restoration female writer and, besides Philips, the most celebrated woman poet, sometimes adopts the voice of male speakers with typical libertine views. Other poems argue that women should be allowed the same erotic freedom as men. Reversing conventions, Behn dwells on men's physical attractions to women. More than her male libertine contemporaries, however, Behn celebrates happy lovers' mutual sexual ecstasy rather than male erotic "conquest" as the *ne plus ultra* – "Raptures unconfin'd; / Vast and Luxuriant" ('On a Juniper Tree, cut down to make Busks," lines 57–58).[26]

Behn also deplores the gender inequities of libertinism. Her best-known poem, "Love Arm'd" (1677), which like many lyrics of the period originally appeared as a playsong, details in pageant-like fashion the "Tyranic power" of "Fantastique" love over a woman whose heart is "harm'd" while her beloved "Victor is, and free" (lines 1, 4, 15–16). Behn's female speaker cannot master the libertine's professed strength, detachment from erotic delusions.[27]

Behn's frank expressions of female desire shocked but also fascinated contemporaries and successors. Other female poets followed Behn in both espousing and protesting libertinism. In "Maidenhead ..." the pseudonymous Ephelia, for example, mocks virginity. Yet her poetic volume, published circa 1679, reveals in an effectively straightforward style her unhappiness with a faithless lover. Occasionally she attacks rather than laments, as when she reverses a Roman and seventeenth-century topos that the male poet-lover's fancy created his beloved's charms and can strip them away. "To my Rival" claims her "Fancy," which "rais'd" her lover to his "Glorious State," "can as easily Annihilate" him (lines 18–20); the following poem, "Neglect Returned," extends the theme, noting that her amorous looks can "create" new lovers (line 14). Yet numerous poems that profess enduring passion concede Ephelia's inability to escape female victimization.[28]

Just as Pindaric panegyric became more restrained in the early eighteenth century, the celebration of sensual pleasure became more compatible with middle-class notions of politeness. The drinking song gradually gave way to depictions of more sober pleasures, as in the neoclassical invitation-to-dinner poem, which adopted the measured, conversational tone of Horace's epistles and Martial's epigrams. Even when celebrating promiscuity, erotic poetry similarly lost its shocking crudity. Matthew Prior, a master of light verse, leavens libertinism with polite epigrammatic wit that warns against taking either him or his arguments too seriously. In "A Better Answer" (1718), Prior defends himself in tripping meter against his mistress's complaints that he has praised in verse (and presumably enjoyed) other women by invoking the crucial period distinction between poetic fancies and real life: "What I speak, my fair CHLOE, and what I write, shews / The Diff'rence there is betwixt Nature and Art: / I court others in Verse; but I love Thee in Prose: / And they have my Whimsies; but Thou has my Heart" (lines 13–16). Prior writes verse that claims to be prose, whimsies that claim to be sincere, to a pastoral "Cloe" whom he treats as his "real" mistress. In another poem of uncertain date, "Chloe Beauty has and Wit," Prior good-naturedly praises his mistress's "good Nature" (line 8), i.e., promiscuity. He plays with Christian morality – Chloe charitably "keeps poor Mortals from [the sin of] despairing" (line 12) – and with poetic clichés – Chloe rightly brings a "Bucket" to "quench" the otherwise unbearable "Fire" she arouses in men (lines 19–20). "Bucket," earthy but euphemistic, is designed to amuse rather than shock. Eschewing the heroic posturing of the aristocratic Restoration rake, Prior pursues pleasure with awareness that it is not everything. His "Written in the Year 1696," also in a lighthearted rhythm, presents a sexual liaison as the weekend reward of a hard-working diplomat: "While with Labour Assiduous due pleasure I mix / And in one day attone for the Busyness of Six / ... / This Night and the next shal be Hers shal be Mine / To good or ill Fortune the Third we resign" (lines 1–2, 9–10). In so circumscribed a context, great claims for sexual liaisons are perforce mock-heroic: "Thus Scorning the world and superior to Fate / I drive on my Car in processional State" (lines 11–12).[29]

Poems devoted to the delights of the simple country life, a form of pleasure often contrasted with heterosexual relations, also became ubiquitous in the late seventeenth and early eighteenth century in reaction against London's ever increasing prominence as commercial metropolis and site of state power. Often nostalgically echoing classical retirement poetry, such poems celebrate contented ease far from the strife or pomp of city and/or court. During the Interregnum, retirement was praised by Royalist gentlemen sequestered on their estates as well as those unhappy for diverse reasons with Interregnum politics and policies. In "The Garden," probably written during this period, Marvell, tutor to the daughter of the disaffected ex-commander of the Parliamentary army Thomas Fairfax, celebrates what his (closely contemporaneous?) "Horatian Ode" rejects.[30] With unique wit, "The Garden" depicts retirement's sensual, intellectual, and spiritual pleasures in an ascending scale. The sensual pleasures of superabundant fruits surround the speaker and make him "fall on grass" (line 40) with a cheerful innocence implicitly contrasted with Adam and Eve; intellectual pleasures compress the outside world to the mind's dimensions, making, in a joyous phrase that eludes full explication, "a green thought in a green shade" (line 48); and the soul delights in its own beauty while preparing for a "longer flight" (line 55) to heaven. For such pleasures Marvell dismisses both public life and erotic desire. Wittily positing that the ambitious seek not public honor but only its tokens, laurels and bays, and that the pagan gods analogously pursued not nubile nymphs but the plants into which they metamorphosed to escape, Marvell playfully presents his garden with its "garlands of repose" (line 8) as the most inclusive object of everyone's desire. This outrageous reduction *ad absurdum* of incompatible goals bespeaks Marvell's awareness that choosing a way of life demands simplifying the alternatives. Katherine Philips's praise of retirement is more traditionally solemn. Closely associating retirement with same-sex friendship, she celebrates a detachment from society's troubles particularly resonant during the turbulent 1650s: "Here is no quarrelling for Crowns / Nor fear of changes in our Fate" she enthuses of the retired life in "A retir'd Friendship, To Ardelia" (lines 5–6).[31]

Marvell, Philips, and other retirement writers of the 1650s deploy strict stanzaic forms in short, tightly argued lyrics. In his posthumously published *Essays, in Verse and Prose* (1668), Cowley celebrates the joys of country life in a variety of genres, including – most influentially – Pindaric odes. Cowley's use of the form brings a new tonal complexity to retirement verse, adding the sense of both carefree and heroic activity to the conventional praise of restful ease. The Pindaric's formal freedom can convey the impromptu delights of a comfortable country gentleman following his whims rather than an imposed routine. The changing line lengths in Cowley's "Upon Liberty," for example, mime the unscheduled life with conversational ease: "Now will I sleep, now eat, now sit, now walk, / Now meditate alone, now with Acquaintance talk. / This I will do, here I will stay, / Or if my fancy call me away, / My Man and I presently go ride" (stanza 4). But Cowley also exploits Pindaric grandeur. While taking up the traditional theme of being contented with little by limiting one's desires, in an expansive countermovement Cowley compares his freedom to the "soaring boldly" of "Heroic" birds (stanza 3). Adapting Pindar's sublime self-representation as eagle (*Nemean* 3.80–82, 5.20–21), Cowley concludes by comparing the retired man's roving spirit to the "Imperial Eagle" always seeking "fresh game" (stanza 6).[32]

Celebrating the country gentleman's freedom with Cowleyan conversational informality, Cotton's Pindaric ode "The Retirement" enriches the portrait by evoking Cotton's own estate and natural environs.[33] Other Restoration Pindarics exalt genteel country pleasures. Wentworth Dillon, the Earl of Roscommon's well-known "Ode upon Solitude" grandly declaims of "Pleasures which ... exalt the mind" (line 40), though the poem's dual claim of "constant quiet" (line 22) and "nobler Vigour" (line 20) for the country life betrays strain.[34] By contrast, Dryden's Pindaric imitation (1685) of Horace's ode 3.29 uses the genre's expansiveness both to convey the uncontrollable power of fortune, figured as a powerful river, over those immersed in the active life and to suggest the supreme self-mastery of the retired person: "Happy the Man, and happy he alone, / He, who can call to day his own: / He, who secure within, can say / Tomorrow do thy worst, for I have liv'd to day. / Be fair, or foul, or rain, or shine, / The joys I have possest, in spight of fate are mine. / Not Heav'n it self upon the past has pow'r; / But what has been has been, and I have had my hour" (lines 65–72).[35] Celebrating the ownership of one's own life, Dryden intensifies with Pindaric amplitude Horace's praise of retired self-mastery by contrasting it with the limited power of "Heav'n it self." The varied cadence conveys the ease, while the three ringing alexandrines (twelve-syllable lines) convey the grandeur, of self-possession.

Partly inspired by men of science such as Isaac Newton and Robert Boyle, retirement poetry of the early to mid eighteenth century often celebrates nature as the manifestation of God. Poets praise the country life not only for its freedom but also for the tranquil survey of God's creation that they, as members of the leisured elite, could experience in joyful piety. Extended description of the landscape, whose beauty and usefulness revealed God's beneficence, and straightforward didacticism become more pronounced. Pindaric odes and longish poems in couplets accommodate open-ended, meditative expansiveness (often with allusions to the fuller vision one acquires after death). Thomas Parnell's seventy-eight line, octosyllabic couplet "A Hymn on Contentment" (1714) for example, finds "*Peace* of *Mind*" (line 1) in "sweet Retreat" (line 50) and ends with a vow to sing both of natural beauty and the "great SOURCE OF NATURE" God (line 63).[36] Winchilsea's 293-line "Petition for an Absolute Retreat" (1713) in octosyllabic couplets wishes for the "Unaffected Carelessness" (line 71) of retired life, for the "Windings and Shade" with which she closes each verse paragraph and which will provide the complementary pleasures of unconstrained movement through a bountiful landscape – with strawberries "Springing wheresoe'er I stray'd" (lines 45–46) – and escape from the sociopolitical world. She concludes, typically, wishing for the "extensive Joy, / When all Heaven shall be survey'd" (lines 291–92). In "A Nocturnal Reverie" (1713), Winchilsea's heroic couplets evoke solitary contemplation's "sedate Content." Descriptions of nocturnal sights, sounds, and smells emphasize the non-human world's serenity, inspiring the poet with a mystic sense of "Something, too high for Syllables to speak" (line 42).[37]

The accomplished octosyllabic couplets of Parnell's much-admired ninety line "A Night-Piece on Death" (1722) express the period's interest in "natural" piety by rejecting Scholastic theology and bookish ethics for a "readier Path" to moral wisdom "*below*" (lines 7–8). Literalizing the Christian spiritual journey and ideal of being "lowly wise," the poet describes his path to a churchyard in which he contemplates the buried dead and hears a voice promising immortality. Description of nightfall and the sky's reflection in a still lake "below" (line 16) allows somber meditation to emerge gradually from the natural scene. The didactic graveyard voice presents death as the final "Path" to God (line 67) and beatitude as access to a limitless view of "the glad Scene unfolding" (line 88).[38]

John Dyer's "Gongar Hill" combines the description of a specific landscape with the moralizing strains of natural religion.[39] The poem had begun as a sublime Pindaric in praise of an "aweful" hill but was reworked into a lengthy but modest octosyllabic poem celebrating the hill's "humble shade" (line 131). Dyer's poem mingles the cheerful and meditative tones of Milton's companion poems on outdoor wandering and reverie, "L'Allegro" and "Il Penseroso," which became popular models in the eighteenth century. Dyer celebrates "stray[ing]" (line 23) through a landscape that embodies life's delightfully "various journey" (line 97) but also inspires intimations of mortality. Ruins, for example, elicit didactic reflections on power's transcience: "A little rule, a little sway, / A sun beam in a winter's day" (lines 89–90).

The prominence of God as source of nature in retirement poetry is one culmination of a gradual process whereby religious verse lost its doctrinal focus upon the salvation of an individual "I" by a personal God conspicuous in the powerful meditative lyrics of such early seventeenth-century poets as Donne and George Herbert. The process began with the Puritan dismantling of the established church and the proliferation of religious sects and attitudes during the Interregnum, which loosened dogmatic underpinnings and poetic structures alike. While often echoing his acknowledged model Herbert, Henry Vaughan in *Silex Scintillans* (1650; 1655) replaces Herbert's carefully structured, Calvinist, liturgically attuned lyric devotions with poems memorable for their new range of tonality and thematics. These include high moments of Platonic rapture (conveyed in such famous lines as "I saw Eternity the other night," which opens "The World"); celebrations of a divinized nature that draw on occult Hermetic philosophy and voice such anti-Calvinist views as the belief that *all* creatures (not only the Calvinist "elect") will be "made new" on the Last Day ("The Book," line 27); evocations of a (nonCalvinist) innocence in which a child perceives the "shadows of eternity" in nature ("The Retreat," line 14); and elegiac laments in which the blissful state of the dead highlights the poet's isolation in a world out of joint ("They are all gone into the world of light! / And I alone sit ling'ring here" begins a famous poem).[40]

Thomas Traherne, whose poems went unpublished until the twentieth century, has an even more heterodox vision. Like Vaughan, he produces great passages rather than wholes, subordinating development to rapturous expostulation. Influenced like Vaughan by Hermeticism and Platonism, Traherne is additionally fascinated by contemporaneous scientific speculations on the universe's infinitude. His poems are most typical of their age when they celebrate the "boundless" – a "boundless" human spirit that can recover childhood wonder and grasp an infinite (rather than personal) God. As contemporaneous Pindaric odes were doing, Traherne celebrates a sublimely heroic mind that "Rove[s] ore the World with Libertie" ("Thoughts 1," line 66). The "vast, enquiring Soul" that "Brooks no Controul" in its search for God's "infinit Variety" transcends (like a spiritualized Alexander the Great) the "mean Ambition to desire / A single World" ("Insatiableness," part II, lines 1–8). Traherne's poems recall his childhood intuition that he possessed the "Various and Innumerable" "Treasures" of the world – "Fields, Mountains, Valleys, Woods, / Floods, Cities, Churches, Men" ("Speed," lines 17–18, 20, 22). His joyously heterogeneous lists suggest the innocent mind's unmediated grasp of God's superabundant bounty. Appropriating to mystic ends the diverse socio-political theories of his times, Traherne compares his felicity both to an absolutist monarch's ownership of his realm and to the Levellers' communitarian world without "Cursd ... Proprieties" (i.e., private properties) and their "Bounds" ("Wonder," lines 49, 53).[41]

Late seventeenth- and early eighteenth-century religious poetry also used the Pindaric ode's high style to praise God's infinite power. Writing Pindaric odes based upon scriptural descriptions of God as cosmic creator and destroyer, Cowley provides a popular form for the self-consciously "sublime" religious lyric, replacing not only the early seventeenth-century focus on personal salvation but also the individual "I" still present in Vaughan and Traherne with a public poet's awe before a "boundless" God.

The Nonconformist poet Isaac Watts writes a number of religious Pindarics such as "The Adventurous Muse" (1706), which imagines an "unconfined" (line 27) survey of the "boundless" (line 20).[42] The early eighteenth-century Pindaric odes of Mary, Lady Chudleigh have the particular resonance of a woman's piety. Chudleigh prefaces her first published poem, "The Ladies Defence" (1701), with an exhortation that fellow women resist being confined by ignorance, their passions, or misogynist preconceptions. Displaying wide reading as well as religious fervor, her 1703 Pindarics passionately resist constraint. "The Observation," for example, praises "the'active Mind" (line 16) that will not be "confin'd" (line 10) in the body. Her Pindaric paraphrase of the Hymn of the Three Children, an apocryphal addition to Daniel, runs to ninety stanzas. The headnote explains that Chudleigh chose the Pindaric form for its "Liberty" of "Fancy," while the poem praises contemplation that "will not be to any Place confin'd" (line 776) and provides pious "Delights" by surveying "boundless" nature, cosmic history from primeval chaos to apocalypse, and God's infinitude.[43]

The hymn is the other typical form of early eighteenth-century religious lyric. Like the ode it de-emphasizes the personal "I" but, in place of the Pindaric poet's rapturous and rambling adoration of a boundless God, the hymn features clear, concise expressions of devotion suitable for singing by a community of believers. Religious Nonconformists were major hymn writers. Watts wrote many; in contrast to his Pindarics, his popular hymns eschew (he notes) "bolder Figures" and "unconfin'd" "Variety" in order to remain understandable when sung. Closely echoing Scripture, their major license consists in Christianizing Old Testament passages (for which they were attacked). They present boundedness positively as a defense of the Nonconformist church, as in "The Church the Garden of Christ" (1707):

"We are a Garden wall'd around, / Chosen and made peculiar Ground; / A little Spot inclos'd by Grace / Out of the World's wide wilderness."[44]

Other poets, by contrast, adopted the hymn's clarity and succinctness in order to proclaim (with a note of spiritual imperialism) the universality of natural religion. Joseph Addison's "The spacious firmament on high" (1712) announces in three compact stanzas the universe's proclamation of God "to every land" (line 7) when attended to by "reason's ear" (line 21). Echoing Psalm 19, Addison joins Scripture to an explicitly rational, enlightened theology appropriate to his urbane middle-class audience but (potentially) accessible to all.[45] Adopting the metrical form of many hymns, "The Universal Prayer" (written 1715, published 1738) by Alexander Pope (a Catholic in a Protestant England that subjected Catholics to legal penalties) begins and ends by celebrating the universality of devotion and implicitly promoting religious toleration: "Father of All! in every Age, / In every Clime ador'd, / By Saint, by Savage, and by Sage, / Jehovah, Jove, or Lord!"; "To Thee, whose Temple is all Space, / Whose Altar, Earth, Sea, Skies; / One Chorus let all Being raise! / All Nature's Incense Rise" (lines 1–4, 49–52).[46] Despite his ethnocentric contrast between "Saint" and "Savage," Pope claims distinctive terms, dogmas, and places do not matter; God's true temple is the universe, as the four elements of earth, water, air, and fire combine in the altar and burning incense of praise.

While religious poetry treated death as the road to immortality, funerary poetry increasingly responded to secular trends. As in numerous Pindaric funerary poems, poetry commemorating the dead throughout the period often consists of public panegyric that recounts their enduring fame and heavenly blessings. Such panegyrics often serve a political function, as in the numerous Civil War poems commemorating fallen Royalists; as befits an age of satire and public polemic, elegies also often mixed praise of the dead with attacks on the living. Over the course of the late seventeenth and early eighteenth century, however, more personal modes of funerary poetry emerge as poets focus increasingly on personal attachments to the dead rather than upon their public significance and ignore religious strictures against extreme grief for the deceased.

Dryden's greatest elegiac poem, "To the Memory of Mr. Oldham" (1684), differs strikingly from his other major funerary poems in registering a personal sense of profound loss as well as joy in glorious achievement.[47] Virgilian allusions generalize and claim public importance for Dryden's feelings as he pays tribute to a younger fellow satirist and kindred spirit, comparing himself and Oldham to the well-known tragic Virgilian companions Nisus and Euryalus. The two final couplets – "Once more, hail and farewel; farewel thou young, / But ah too short, *Marcellus* of our Tongue; /

Thy Brows with Ivy, and with Laurels bound; / But Fate and gloomy Night encompass thee around" (lines 22–25) – evoke Roman mourning rituals and allude to the early death, lamented in the *Aeneid*, of Augustus's heir Marcellus, whom gloomy night surrounds in Hades (*Aeneid* 6.866). The Virgilian ambience registers the feeling of loss by ignoring Christian consolation for pagan pessimism about the dead. Yet Dryden's allusions also provide their own secular consolation by implying that both Oldham and Dryden glorify England's achievement by rivaling Roman achievement; Dryden plays the role of both grieving Augustus and commemorating Virgil.

To convey Oldham's public achievement, Dryden relies upon classical critical norms, simultaneously praising and criticizing Oldham as a satirist of vigorous "Wit" whose rough metrics betray the "noble Error" of youth, "too much force" (lines 15, 17–18). Dryden deploys Pindaric values to glorify Oldham. Oldham's winning of the "Race" (line 10) in satire and his "early ripe" (line 11) dying before "maturing time" could mellow his writing to "the dull sweets of Rime" (lines 20–21) recall Cowley's praise in his rendition of Pindar's *Nemean* 1 of an athletic victor who "early" won his race and of the victor's mythological analogue Hercules, who "ripe at first ... did disdain / The slow advance of *dull Humanitie*."[48] But Dryden's tempering of praise with blame adapts Horatian values to assess Oldham. Horace praises Pindar's overpowering natural force but also criticizes harsh meter and lack of artful restraint (*Satire* 1.4.6–8, 1.10.64–71). Dryden compliments the deceased by assessing him in terms of Oldham's own highest (Horatian) artistic standards: Dryden's question – "to thy abundant store / What could advancing Age have added more?" (lines 11–12) – as well as its answer, metrical art, echo Oldham's own Horatian values as expressed in his ode "Upon ... Ben. Jonson." Oldham's poem claims not only that to Jonson's "unbounded store / Exhausted Nature could vouchsafe no more" (lines 171–72) but also that Jonson, the supreme poet, combined "Nature and Art" (line 76) as well as "vig'orous youth" and "temp'erate age" (line 62).[49]

In contrast to Dryden's elegy, which appeals to public norms despite its personal grief, Pope's "Elegy to the Memory of an Unfortunate Lady" expresses more personal lament. The poet passionately defends an unnamed woman whose love suicide under obscure circumstances left her an outcast deprived of a public ritual and memorial. Like the opening of Cowley's "Brutus," Pope's "Elegy" celebrates a heroism mistaken for vice, defending a woman "Above the vulgar flight" who "love[d] too well," who was "too tender" in her feelings and "too firm" in her Roman resolve (lines 6–7, 11–12). Pope's unknown heroine is not, however, a public figure like

Brutus, and instead of promising to immortalize her, Pope ends by stressing their personal bond. He imagines his own eventual death and oblivion and the woman's consequent loss of her (one?) admirer: "The Muse forgot, and thou belov'd no more!" (line 82).[50]

While still a much-practiced form through the mid eighteenth century, poetic epitaphs, which had traditionally been epigrammatic, impersonal verse encomia, became more expansive and elegiac, expressing the particularized grief of the poet and/or relatives of the deceased. In influential epitaphs of the 1720s and 1730s, Pope moves from impersonal panegyric to more elegiac compositions that prevent the reader from separating the commemoration from the poet's own personal mourning process. While the first stanzas of his epitaphs on Simon Harcourt and on Robert and Mary Digby provide conventional panegyric, the second stanzas conjure the moment when the mourning poet inscribes his composition on the monument or implores its acceptance by the deceased: "Oh let thy once-lov'd Friend inscribe thy Stone, / And with a Father's Sorrows mix his own!" (lines 7–8); "Yet take these tears, Mortality's relief, / And till we share your joys, forgive our grief; / These little rites, a Stone, a Verse, receive, / 'Tis all a Father, all a Friend can give!" (lines 17–20).[51]

Elegies became a popular vehicle for widows and widowers to fervently articulate ideals of conjugal love, as if such personal feelings earned their full right to public treatment only in tragic retrospect. Elizabeth Rowe, for example, composed a much-admired elegy for her husband (published in 1719) that first proclaims a "grief" that can have "no excess" because of his "merit" (lines 9–10) but later describes her conjugal love as both fitting and excessive: "Whate'er to such superior worth was due, / Whate'er excess the fondest passion knew, / I felt for thee, dear youth" (lines 23–25).[52]

Non-satiric funerary poetry traditionally ignored the faults of the dead as a matter of decorum, but the growing importance of personal feeling, even at the expense of traditional morality, appears in elegies that forgive the dead. Lady Mary Wortley Montagu's elegy of the mid-1730s upon an adulteress, for example, claims the poet's right to "pay a pitying tear" (line 19) and "To draw a vail o'er faults she can't commend" (line 17).[53] Yet Montagu provides social critique as well as pathos: her determination to protect the deceased from "envious rage" and "prudes" (lines 16, 18) leads on to a final, mordant claim that gossips will soon find new victims and forget the deceased.

Montagu's elegy reveals both change and continuity in lyric forms during the period we have considered. The contrast between her concern with clashing social mores and Marvell's with military and political conflict in the "Horatian Ode," with which we began, registers a major shift in lyric focus from the mid seventeenth to the mid eighteenth century. Like Pope's and Rowe's, Montagu's appeal to personal feeling points forward to late eighteenth-century lyrics associated with the cults of sentiment and sympathy. Yet her satiric attack upon "th'illnatured crowd" (line 21) exemplifies the attentiveness to public norms and resultant tonal complexity that enrich the diversely "impure" lyrics of 1650–1740.

NOTES

1 *Andrew Marvell: Oxford Authors*, ed. Frank Kermode and Keith Walker (Oxford: Oxford University Press, 1990), pp. 82–85.
2 Abraham Cowley, *Poems*, ed. A. R. Waller (Cambridge: Cambridge University Press, 1905), pp. 195–97.
3 *Ibid.*, pp. 420–32.
4 *Ibid.*, pp. 157–78, 188–92, 197–201, 416–18, 448–53.
5 *Ibid.*, pp. 404–06.
6 Germaine Greer et al. (eds.), *Kissing the Rod: An Anthology of Seventeenth Century Women's Verse* (London: Virago, 1988), pp. 309–14.
7 *The Poems of John Dryden*, ed. James Kinsley, 4 vols. (Oxford: Clarendon Press, 1958), vol. I, pp. 459–65.
8 Anne Killigrew, "The Discontent," lines 1–2 in *Poems* (1685), ed. Richard Morton (Gainesville, Florida: Scholars' Facsimiles & Reprints, 1967), p. 51.
9 Killigrew, *Poems*, pp. 1, 6–7.
10 Dryden, *Poems*, vol. III, pp. 1428–33.
11 *The Poetical Works of Edward Young*, ed. John Mitford (London, 1896), vol. II, pp. 335–93 (quotations from p. 372).
12 *The Poems of Anne, Countess of Winchilsea*, ed. Myra Reynolds (Chicago: University of Chicago Press, 1903), pp. 248–52.
13 Katherine Philips, *Poems* (1667), intro. Travis Dupriest (Delmar, New York: Scholars' Facsimiles & Reprints, 1992), pp. 21, 95.
14 Philips, *Poems*, pp. 21, 76, 38, 155; John Donne, *The Complete English Poems*, ed. A. J. Smith (Penguin: Harmondsworth, 1971), pp. 85, 81.
15 *The Complete Poems of John Wilmot, Earl of Rochester*, ed. David M. Vieth (New Haven and London: Yale University Press, 1968), pp. 19, 139, 27–28; *The Poems of Charles Sackville, Sixth Earl of Dorset*, ed. Brice Harris (New York and London: Garland, 1979), pp. 76, 91.
16 Dorset, *Poems*, p. 77; Rochester, *Poems*, pp. 82, 81.
17 *The Poems of John Oldham*, ed. Harold F. Brooks and Raman Selden (Oxford: Clarendon Press, 1987), pp. 344–51.
18 Cowley, *Poems*, p. 60.
19 Alexander Brome, *Poems*, ed. Roman R. Dubinski, 2 vols. (Toronto: University of Toronto Press, 1982), vol. I, pp. 109–10; cf. vol. I, pp. 96–97, 117–18, 121–26, 129–30, 135–36, 137–41, 150–51, 153–56, 158–62, 209–11.
20 Charles Cotton, *Poems, 1630–1687*, ed. John Beresford (London: Richard Cobden-Sanderson, 1923), p. 359.
21 John Milton, *Complete Poems and Major Prose*, ed. Merritt Y. Hughes (New York: Odyssey Press, 1957), pp. 168–69.

22 Cotton, *Poems*, pp. 361–63.
23 *The Songs of Thomas D'Urfey*, ed. Cyrus Lawrence Day (Cambridge, MA: Harvard University Press, 1933), pp. 47–55.
24 Alexander Radcliffe, "Now at last the Riddle is expounded" (1682), line 14 in *The Ramble: An Anti-Heroick Poem* (London, 1682), rpt. in *The Works of Alexander Radcliffe* (1696), intro. Ken Robinson (Delmar, New York: Scholars' Facsimiles & Reprints, 1981), pp. 33–34; cf. pp. 15–19, 27–28, 34–35.
25 Rochester, *Poems*, pp. 52–53.
26 *The Works of Aphra Behn*, vol. 1, *Poetry*, ed. Janet Todd (Columbus: Ohio University Press, 1992), p. 40.
27 *Ibid.*, p. 53.
28 *Poems by Ephelia (c. 1679): The Premier Facsimile Edition*, ed. with intro. Maureen E. Mulvihill (Delmar, New York: Scholars' Facsimiles & Reprints, 1992), pp. 138–40, 158–61, 168–74.
29 *The Literary Works of Matthew Prior*, ed. H. Bunker Wright and Monroe K. Spears, 2 vols. (1959; 2nd edn. Oxford: Clarendon Press, 1971), vol. 1, pp. 451, 715, 158.
30 *Marvell*, pp. 47–49.
31 Philips, *Poems*, p. 28.
32 Abraham Cowley, *Essays, Plays, and Sundry Verses*, ed. A. R. Waller (Cambridge: Cambridge University Press, 1906), pp. 389–91.
33 Cotton, *Poems*, pp. 45–48.
34 *The Works of the English Poets*, ed. Alexander Chalmers, 21 vols. (London, 1810), vol. VIII, pp. 267–68.
35 Dryden, *Poems*, vol. 1, p. 436.
36 *Collected Poems of Thomas Parnell*, ed. Claude Rawson and F. P. Lock (Newark: University of Delaware Press/London and Toronto: Associated University Presses, 1989), pp. 111–13.
37 Winchilsea, *Poems*, pp. 68–77, 268–70.
38 Parnell, *Poems*, pp. 168–71.
39 John Dyer, *Gongar Hill*, ed. Richard C. Boys (Baltimore: Johns Hopkins University Press, 1941).
40 Henry Vaughan, *The Complete Poems*, ed. Alan Rudrum (New Haven and London: Yale University Press, 1976), pp. 227, 309–10, 172–73, 246.
41 Thomas Traherne, *Poems, Centuries and Three Thanksgivings*, ed. Anne Ridler (London: Oxford University Press, 1966), pp. 63, 134, 36–37, 8.
42 Isaac Watts, *Horae Lyricae* (1706; London, 1779), p. 186.
43 *The Poems and Prose of Mary, Lady Chudleigh*, ed. Margaret J. M. Ezell (New York and London: Oxford University Press, 1993), pp. 3–10, 124–25, 169, 201.
44 Isaac Watts, *Hymns and Spiritual Songs, 1707–1748*, ed. Selma L. Bishop (London: Faith Press, 1962), pp. liv, 71.
45 Roger Lonsdale (ed.), *The New Oxford Book of Eighteenth-Century Verse* (Oxford and New York: Oxford University Press, 1984), p. 45.
46 *The Poems of Alexander Pope*, ed. John Butt (New Haven: Yale University Press, 1963), pp. 247–48.
47 Dryden, *Poems*, vol. 1, p. 389.
48 Cowley, "The First Nemean Ode of Pindar," stanza 6 in Cowley, *Poems*, p. 173.
49 Oldham, *Poems*, pp. 196, 199.

50 Pope, *Poems*, pp. 262–64.

51 *Ibid.*, pp. 473, 498.

52 Elizabeth Rowe, *Miscellaneous Works in Prose and Verse*, 2 vols. (1739; 3rd edn. London: 1750), vol. I, p. 112.

53 Lady Mary Wortley Montagu, *Essays and Poems and Simplicity, A Comedy*, ed. Robert Halsband and Isobel Grundy (Oxford: Clarendon Press, 1977), p. 278.

FURTHER READING

Barash, Carol, *English Women's Poetry, 1649–1714: Politics, Community, and Linguistic Authority* (Oxford: Clarendon Press, 1996).

Cohen, Ralph, "On the Interrelations of Eighteenth-Century Literary Forms," in Phillip Harth (ed.), *New Approaches to Eighteenth-Century Literature* (New York and London: Columbia University Press, 1974), pp. 33–78.

Davie, Donald, *The Eighteenth-Century Hymn in England* (Cambridge: Cambridge University Press, 1993).

Hobby, Elaine, *Virtue of Necessity: English Women's Writing, 1649–1688* (London: Virago Press, 1988).

Miner, Earl, *Dryden's Poetry* (Bloomington and London: Indiana University Press, 1971).

  The Restoration Mode from Milton to Dryden (Princeton, NJ: Princeton University Press, 1974).

Morris, David B., *The Religious Sublime: Christian Poetry and Critical Tradition in 18th-Century England* (Lexington: University of Kentucky Press, 1972).

Røstvig, Maren-Sofie, *The Happy Man: Studies in the Metamorphoses of a Classical Ideal, 1600–1700*, 2 vols. (Oslo: Oslo University Press, 1954–58).

Scodel, Joshua, *The English Poetic Epitaph: Conflict and Commemoration from Jonson to Wordsworth* (Ithaca, NY: Cornell University Press, 1991).

Smith, Nigel, *Literature and Revolution in England, 1640–1660* (New Haven and London: Yale University Press, 1994).

Weinbrot, Howard D., *Britannia's Issue: The Rise of British Literature from Dryden to Ossian* (Cambridge: Cambridge University Press, 1993).

Williams, Anne, *Prophetic Strain: The Greater Lyric in the Eighteenth Century* (Chicago: University of Chicago Press, 1984).

Williams, Marilyn L., *Raising their Voices; British Women Writers, 1650–1750* (Detroit: Wayne State University Press, 1990).

Zwicker, Steven N., *Lines of Authority: Politics and English Literary Culture, 1649–1689* (Ithaca, NY: Cornell University Press, 1993).

7

PAUL HAMMOND

Classical texts: translations and transformations

In what respects is Andrew Marvell's "Horatian Ode" an Horatian ode? Marvell and his contemporaries gathered their ideas of Horace and of Horatian odes from a variety of sources. They would have read the Latin text of Horace's poetry in editions which surrounded it with glosses, notes, parallel passages, and perhaps a prose paraphrase; they would have practiced translating and imitating Horace's poetry at school; they would have read English translations and imitations of Horace by writers such as Jonson or Milton. Horace, therefore, was already a complex text for readers of Marvell's poem, a text which they fashioned for themselves out of all these interpretative materials. Horace's odes spoke of private and domestic experiences – love and desire, both homosexual and heterosexual; friendship and the pleasures of conviviality; the passage of time and the poignant delight which may attend an awareness of life's passing. The poetry also spoke of the great public events which were shaping Rome under Augustus, though often addressing such matters at a tangent, cautious about how a private citizen might speak to power or understand history, and jealous of the poet's precarious independence. It was perhaps with a teasingly deliberate naivety that Horace wrote:

> Vertue, Dear Friend, needs no defence,
> The surest Guard is innocence;
> None knew till Guilt created Fear
> What Darts or poyson'd Arrows were.[1]

For many seventeenth-century poets and readers, virtue was to be sought in innocent pastoral retirement, and this ideal was often imagined through material taken from Horace, notably his *Epode* II on the delights of country life.[2] But virtue does need defense in a period of civil upheaval such as both Horace and Marvell experienced; and much as Horace might praise the delights of the retired life on his Sabine farm, there might be times when retirement itself was no longer a virtue. And so,

The forward Youth that would appear
Must now forsake his *Muses* dear,
   Nor in the Shadows sing
   His Numbers languishing.
'Tis time to leave the Books in dust,
And oyl th'unused Armours rust:
   Removing from the Wall
   The Corslet of the Hall.

(Marvell, "An Horatian Ode upon Cromwell's return from Ireland", lines 1–8)

As readers pondered the significance of Marvell's invocation of Horace, they would recognize certain features of the ode as approximating to Horace's methods. The verse form mirrors one of Horace's meters, and there is a comparably adroit management of tone and voice through teasing shifts in subject matter and perspective which challenge readers to negotiate transitions and make connections, so allowing political implications to emerge obliquely rather than as directly authorial observations. Like some of Horace's odes, Marvell's poem addresses the movement of public affairs, and through the shifts in tone and contents it speaks of the precariousness of our powers of recognition and representation, the difficulty of turning our present experiences into an historical narrative.

But as we read into the poem, its manipulation of Horatian motifs, and of other kinds of classical Roman material, becomes puzzling, teasing us in a way which is perhaps not too dissimilar to Horace's own style. The poem deploys a Latinate vocabulary and philosophical framework: we are in a world of temples (line 22), gods (line 61), Fortune (line 113) and Fate (line 37), but this classicizing is problematic. Since some had thought that it was primarily Charles I's devout adherence to the Church of England which led him to the scaffold, to associate him with "the *Gods*" is to traduce rather than translate, or is at best a tendentious translation. So too when Cromwell, who continually referred his military successes to divine Providence, is called "the Wars and Fortunes Son," this translation of English history into a Roman idiom is more than an elegant classicizing gesture, it questions the very language through which Cromwell represented his motives to himself and to observers. Later we are told that Cromwell is "still in the *Republick*'s hand," but the word "republic" is also problematic. A Latin term, it used to mean in English simply "the state" or "the public sphere." After the execution of the king in 1649 England was a republic in the usual modern sense, but the word itself was not commonly used to describe the new state, which was instead officially called the "Commonwealth and Free State."[3] It was not clear, when Marvell was writing in 1650, who or what constituted "the republic": the Roman term does not quite pass into modern English speech. Because of the poem's Roman allusions, we are more sensitive than usual to the word's Roman history and its imperfect naturalization, and so we are led to hear a strangeness in its usage. Moreover, there are unsettling associations if we trace the word back to Horace's time, for Augustus had, in effect though not in name, abolished the Roman republic with its liberties and instituted a monarchy, even while avoiding the hated name of king.

Similarly, the poem's use of allusions to Julius Caesar is problematic. Cromwell's forceful rise unseated Charles,

> And *Caesars* head at last
> Did through his Laurels blast.   (lines 23–24)

Caesar here stands for Charles I, both rulers who were killed because they were thought to pose a threat to the people's liberties; but later in the poem Caesar is now Cromwell:

> A *Caesar* he ere long to *Gaul*,
> To *Italy* an *Hannibal*.   (lines 101–02)

Here Cromwell is the Caesar who expanded the Roman empire through his foreign conquests, and yet since Caesar's untimely end has already been alluded to, it is difficult to expunge that part of his story from our memory as we ponder this image. But Cromwell is also aligned here with Hannibal, the foreigner who invaded Italy to destroy Rome, but was himself destroyed in the attempt. What does that suggest about Cromwell's future? These allusions appear at first to locate Cromwell in a clear narrative of military success, and yet if we remind ourselves of the original Roman contexts, they turn into narratives of hubris and nemesis.

These various allusions suggest parallels, both large-scale and local, between England in 1650 and Rome in the years after its civil wars had ended but before the triumph of Augustus was secure. But the parallels are fragmentary, inconsistent, and contradictory, suggestive (teasing, even) rather than definitive, disturbing us and through their interaction disturbing one another. The reader faces a complex interpretative problem, as no coherent narrative pattern is able to triumph. The experience of reading the "Horatian Ode" with Horace's own odes in mind becomes a lesson in the complexities of reading history and reading the present.

The local and structural tensions in Marvell's use of classical precedent are paralleled on a larger scale in his contemporaries' political uses of Roman material. The Parliamentarian Thomas May translated Lucan's poem on the Roman civil war,[4] Edmund Waller celebrated Cromwell as Augustus,[5] and the Protectoral coinage depicted Cromwell as a Roman emperor, but Roman history and iconography were not used with any consistency to forge a new civic idiom. Meanwhile, Royalist writers turned to the translation of Latin poetry as a way of making coded statements of their loyalty to the defeated cause.[6] And some distrusted the classics altogether: from contrasting ideological standpoints extreme Puritans condemned all classical learning as ungodly, while Hobbes blamed the discontent which led to the Civil War on too much reading of classical histories.[7] The reading of contemporary events via classical texts was as unsettled and unsettling as the times themselves.

John Dryden, too, pondered Roman examples as he wrote about Cromwell. In his *Heroic Stanzas* Cromwell's funeral becomes a Roman rite, where the sacred eagle is released to fly over the pyre, and the hero's ashes rest in a sacred urn (lines 1–4; 145). Other allusions cast Cromwell as a quasi-Roman ruler:

> When past all Offerings to *Feretrian Jove*
> He Mars depos'd, and Arms to Gowns made yield. (lines 77–78)

The first allusion associates Cromwell with Romulus, the founder of the Roman state, who dedicated arms which he had captured in battle to Jupiter Feretrius, while the phrase "Arms to Gowns made yield" echoes Cicero's description of his own consulship, *cedant arma togae* ("let arms yield to the toga" – the toga being the dress of peace). The poem's allusions and vocabulary classicize Cromwell not by suggesting a single point of comparison with Roman history (which would link past and present in an allegorical or typological reading) but by suggesting that England might be able to fashion equivalent but idiomatic classical forms and structures. Dryden may be attempting to shape a classical republican aesthetic in these sober quatrains, but like the concurrent development of a Puritan classicism in architecture,[8] it was short-lived.

The association of England and Rome is rethought in *Astraea Redux*, the poem in which Dryden greets the return of Charles II, and with him the return of Astraea, goddess of justice. Here the association which Dryden develops (in common with many of his contemporaries, who found the analogy irresistible) is that of Charles and Augustus, and the Latin quotation which Dryden places as the epigraph to his poem – *iam redit et virgo, redeunt Saturnia regna* ("now the goddess returns, the reign of Saturn returns") – brings into play Virgil's fourth *Eclogue* and its promise of a golden age under Augustus. Time present is renewed by a recovery of time past.

But the past which is being recovered in this trope is not an historical moment but an already mythologized time, not Rome but Virgil's hopes for Rome. Dryden knew, of course, that such mythologies have only an hortatory force, no predictive or definitive power, and the actual poetry which establishes such parallels is apt to underline their fictive status. As Paul de Man observes, "A literary text simultaneously asserts and denies the authority of its own rhetorical mode ... Poetic writing is the most advanced and refined mode of deconstruction."[9] Dryden's uses of classical reference – like Marvell's in the "Horatian Ode" – tend to set to work in the text a semiotic movement which cannot be contained, for these invocations of Rome lead readers into a complex world, the imaginative world of a poem in which time and space are both English and Roman, and so not quite either, and where the English language is made to disclose its Latin roots: we hear another language resonating through Dryden's English.

Annus Mirabilis is a good example of a poem which uses Latin pre-texts both to construct an interpretation of the present and at the same time to set in motion (as all true poetic language must) a deconstruction of the authority of that interpretation. A Virgilian thread running through the fabric of Dryden's poem invites us to see a parallel between the burning of London in the Great Fire of 1666 and the destruction of Troy as told in the *Aeneid*. The allusion is present in the epigraph from *Aeneid* II, *urbs antiqua ruit, multos dominata per annos* ("The ancient city falls, having dominated for many years"), and in a series of tiny echoes which shape the texture of the work. For example, when Dryden writes that the homeless Londoners "repeat what they would shun" (line 1028), he is using "repeat" in the Latin sense of "encounter again," and recalling the moment when Aeneas says *urbem repeto* ("I encounter the city again": *Aeneid* II. 749) in telling of his escape from the flames of Troy. But set alongside these Virgilian signals – which move the account toward epic, so dignifying subject, writer, and reader – there are other Latin texts drawn into the poem's imaginative world. Lines adapted from Ovid describing an exhausted hare pursued by a dog evoke our sympathy for the plight of the weary sailors in the Dutch war (lines 521–28), reminding us that military success has its human price; while verses adapted from Petronius speak of man wandering blindly in the dark empire of Fortune (lines 125–40), a philosophical vision which clearly works in tension with the poem's assertions that the hand of God is directly guiding the nation's history. What this mixing of classical material achieves is a complex texture (complex, that is, both linguistically and philosophically) which invites the reader to see parallels between his experience and Roman history, while at the same time setting to work a deconstructive movement between the various components which questions the stability of these conceptual structures. The result is neither a glib mystification of power nor a nihilistic destruction of meaning, but a responsibly complex meditation on the acts of representation and of reading. It is a poem written by a man whose study housed annotated editions of Virgil alongside newsbooks and manuscript satires, where Lucretius and St. Paul inhabited the same space.

This deployment of allusion and quotation is one kind of translation between Roman and Restoration culture: another is the formal translation of complete poems into modern English. Dryden was the unrivaled master of translation in his age, and in the course of his career he turned increasingly to this mode of writing. This was partly for commercial reasons, since translations began to find a market (ably exploited by Dryden's publisher, Jacob Tonson) among both lovers of the classics and a growing reading public which lacked Latin and Greek (including women readers). It was partly also for political reasons, since the Revolution of 1688–89 displaced Dryden from his positions as Poet Laureate and Historiographer Royal, and compelled him to find new ways of writing poetry and history: translation offered an opportunity for oblique commentary on the times. But primarily there was throughout his later life a strong imaginative and philosophical necessity for Dryden to translate the classics, since he had a dramatist's fascination with the play of different voices, and a skeptic's reluctance to adhere to any single system.

Dryden's formal translations began with versions from the *Heroides* for *Ovid's Epistles* (1680), where he took on the voices of women embroiled in tragic love affairs; then he rendered portions of Virgil, Lucretius, Horace, and Theocritus for the first two of Tonson's anthologies, *Miscellany Poems* and *Sylvae* (1684–85); several of Juvenal's satires and all of Persius for a collected translation which he supervised and prefaced with a long essay on satire (1693); then the complete works of Virgil (1697); and finally tales from Homer and Ovid alongside Chaucer and Boccaccio in the crowning achievement of his career, *Fables Ancient and Modern* (1700).

In the preface to *Ovid's Epistles* Dryden summarized the varied methods of translation current in his day. Some translators (like Ben Jonson with Horace's *Ars Poetica*) used metaphrase, a close word-by-word rendering which was liable to result in stilted, unidiomatic English; others (like Waller with the fourth book of the *Aeneid*) used paraphrase, translating with some latitude; while a third group practiced imitation, a transposition of the original not only into the English language but into the contemporary social world, peopling the text with modern references. Dryden cites Cowley's versions of Pindar as examples of imitation, and this form of translation had been practiced by Rochester in *An Allusion to Horace*, and would be developed with great verve by Oldham and Pope. Dryden's own practice as a translator generally follows the middle path, with some diversions into imitation: he seems to have been concerned to produce neither a close crib for those who wanted the bones of the Latin poem, nor a virtuoso variation on classical themes to divert contemporaries, but an imaginative recreation of the voice of the original, paying attention not only to the poet's ideas but to his persona and style.

The translations which Dryden produced in this middle way are poems which situate themselves between England and Rome. As an example we may take his translation of Horace's *Epode* 11, which tells of the delights of a country life. Dryden does not consistently preserve Horace's references to the Italian countryside as Jonson had done in his version; neither does he simply transpose it into an English setting, as Oldham had chosen to do with Horace's *Ode* 1. xxxi, which he transferred to the Cotswolds. Instead, he fashions a poetic world in which Roman references can coexist with a plausibly English life. As a sample of his working methods, here is the opening:

> How happy in his low degree,
> How rich in humble Poverty, is he,
>   Who leads a quiet country life!
>   Discharg'd of business, void of strife,
> And from the gripeing Scrivener free.
> (Thus e're the Seeds of Vice were sown,
>   Liv'd men in better Ages born,
> Who Plow'd with Oxen of their own
>   Their small paternal field of corn.)
> Nor Trumpets summon him to War
>   Nor drums disturb his morning Sleep,
> Nor knows he Merchants gainful care,
>   Nor fears the dangers of the deep.
> The clamours of contentious Law,
>   And Court and state he wisely shuns,
> Nor brib'd with hopes nor dar'd with awe
>   To servile Salutations runs.
>   ("From Horace, *Epod.* 2d.," lines 1–17)

This is neither metaphrase nor paraphrase nor imitation, but a version which is often close to the Latin while sometimes adding whole lines (lines 2–3, 7, and 11–12 are additions, while others are substantial expansions of single words or short phrases).[10] This world seems to belong recognizably to Horace's Italy, where men grow vines and plow with oxen, but also recognizably to Dryden's England, where men eat turbot and complain of scriveners. (A scrivener was a money-lender, and at the end of the poem we discover that this praise of country life has been spoken by a money-lender called Morecraft – a name from the English tradition of satirical comedy.) And many of the details of this imagined world are comfortably common to England and Italy (the sheep, the mead, the mallows). In lines 14–15 Dryden eliminates the specifically Roman reference in *forumque vitat* ("and he avoids the Forum"), and by choosing the word "Court" he allows the reader to see both the lawcourt and the king's court as oppressive places. Dryden has made the moral thought of the poem more explicit, adding the striking quasi-biblical paradox in line 2, while in line 16 he anticipates a reference later in the poem to larks who are caught by being "dared" (dazzled with mirrors), using this as an image of men helplessly intimidated by power. Some of the vocabulary is taken from the seventeenth-century English tradition of writing about the joys of rural retirement: "How happy" and "quiet" and "business" are part of this hallowed vocabulary, and help to evoke in the reader's mind that collection of morally informed meditations on the countryside. Some of the phrasing has been influenced by other Latin poets: line 7 comes not from Horace but from Virgil's *magnanimi heroes nati melioribus annis* ("great heroes born in better times") in *Aeneid* Book VI. Other ideas are prompted by the glosses in the editions which Dryden was using: from the 1605 commentary by Lubinus the phrase *lucri spe* ("hope of gain") seems to have suggested line 12, which has no equivalent in Horace. The vocabulary has occasionally resulted from a careful perusal of previous translations both in English and in French, for Dryden apparently noted down "void of" from Alexander Brome's version and "déchargé" from Otto van Veen's (which prompted "discharged"). Other phrases have been shaped by recollections of Spenser, of Cowley's *Essays*, Virgil's *Eclogues* and *Georgics*, and other poems by Horace. So what Dryden is fashioning here is not only a translation of Horace's *Epode* II, but a concentrated meditation on the poem and the questions which it raises, with its vocabulary bringing into play a tradition of both classical and contemporary thought.

   Dryden turned to classical translation particularly as a way of moving aside from the contingencies of the present to imagine other ways of living, and to manage the incoherence and instability of life. The skeptical sensibility which led him to weave together such different philosophical strands in *Annus Mirabilis* drew him also to translate parts of Lucretius's passionately argued account of the universe as a collection of atoms in random motion, a world in which the individual consciousness arises from and returns to chaos. But Lucretius's philosophy also encourages man to seek tranquillity of mind, and Dryden responded to this by selecting passages "Against the Fear of Death" and "Concerning the Nature of Love," where Lucretius urges us not to be anxiously possessed by the fear of death, or obsessed with the pursuit of sexual pleasure. Equanimity is the goal of this text, and indeed the goal of many of Dryden's translations: readers are brought to take possession of themselves more profoundly by making this detour through the philosophies of the ancient world. The movement away from contemporary England and the compromises of public life does not take us into a private world of untroubled communion with the classics, but into a variety of contrasting, competing textual worlds which challenge us to rethink ourselves.

The translation of Virgil which occupied much of Dryden's attention after the Revolution is the epic, the national poem, which the nation could not have, and did not, perhaps, deserve. While the supremacy of epic as a genre was widely acknowledged, and some writers, including Milton and Dryden, had aspired to write an epic on British history, the epics of this period all refuse, in some way, to be poems of nationhood: *Paradise Lost* meditates on the failure of the English nation to respond to its God-given freedom, while *The Rape of the Lock* and *The Dunciad* use epic strategies to reveal the impoverished values of social and literary coteries. The nation has no epic; the epic has no nation.

Dryden's *Aeneis* begins with lines which hover between Rome and England:

> Arms, and the Man I sing, who, forc'd by Fate,
> And haughty *Juno*'s unrelenting Hate,
> Expell'd and exil'd, left the *Trojan* Shoar:
> Long Labours, both by Sea and Land he bore,
> And in the doubtful War, before he won
> The *Latian* Realm, and built the destin'd Town:
> His banish'd Gods restor'd to Rites Divine,
> And setl'd sure Succession in his Line:
> From whence the Race of *Alban* Fathers come,
> And the long Glories of Majestick *Rome*.   (Book 1, lines 1–10)

While Dryden preserves the Roman proper names, some of the phrasing here invites us to recall the recent political history of England as we read. The phrase "expelled and exiled" might prompt memories of the expelled and exiled James II, while line 7 is a curiously free translation of *inferretque deos* ("and brought in his gods"): the Latin verb does not mean "brought *back*," so the stress on return and restoration is Dryden's own. Line 8 is entirely Dryden's addition, and seems to recall the disturbed succession to the English throne. "*Alban* Fathers" is an exact translation of *Albanique patres*, but readers who have by now been alerted to undercurrents in the text may remember that James had been Duke of Albany, and had been celebrated by Dryden under the allegorical title of Albanius in the opera *Albion and Albanius* (1685). Ironically, it is this absolutely faithful translation of *Albanique patres* which permits a reading which leaves faithful interpretation far behind. But then, keeping faith is exactly what both Virgil and Dryden, in their different ways, are concerned with. This teasingly unfaithful yet faithful opening to the *Aeneis* sets these issues working in the mind of the reader, and the irresolvable tensions of the initial paragraph initiate us into a complex mode of reading. Dryden is opening the poem out to include England, without making it an allegory of English history. The temporary association of Aeneas and James is quickly shown not to be allegorical as the poem itself rapidly deconstructs the rhetorical scheme which it had appeared to offer: the present tense in "come" takes the poem into a present in which the long-established glories of Rome are still flourishing. This present tense would be appropriate for Virgil, writing when Rome was indeed still glorious, though in fact the Latin lacks a verb here, and so does not specify any tense. It is Dryden's translation which, by creating this emphatic but impossible present – a time in which the Alban fathers and the glories of Rome are fully present – makes us recognize our own separation from such a time, and our displacement from such a rich kind of nationhood. It establishes for the duration of the poem a milieu which is neither Rome nor England, but a placing and displacing of both.

It was also by the translation and imitation of classical texts that Alexander Pope shaped a world which he could control, a milieu in which his friends and enemies appeared translated, some like Bottom sporting an ass's head, others made into sometimes equally unrecognizable models of sophistication and generosity. Underlying much of Pope's writing in this mode is a vision of the impossibility of Britain having an Augustan age, if that entailed taste and decency being promoted by rulers rather than flourishing in private enclaves of classical culture and embattled patriotism. *The Dunciad* is an epic not about the founding of empires, as the *Aeneid* had been, but about the displacement of literary achievements and civic values by a bizarre gallimaufry of tasteless entertainments and witless writing, presided over by a travesty king. In this empire of dulness, where "Dunce the second reigns like Dunce the first" (*The Dunciad* Book I, line 6), the responsibilities of the poet can, it seems, only be exercised through travesty: the ironic distancing of the contemporary world from the classical past is both the appropriate tribute which the modern writer pays to his classic predecessors, and the necessary means by which he asserts his own taste and judgment and independence. In *The Dunciad* Pope fills a poem with writers, scholars, actors, clowns, and publishers, and surrounds it with a critical apparatus which mimics the variorum commentaries in Renaissance classical texts. Paradoxically, the lavish *mise-en-page* of this poetry proclaims its own value at the same time as it offers itself as a satire on the encrustation of classic texts by editorial secretions. The poem comes accompanied by a ready-made critical tradition, ostensibly saving readers the labor of thinking for themselves. And yet, of course, it is precisely in order to maneuver readers into shaping their own interpretative space and fashioning their own commentary on literary and political affairs, that Pope creates such an elaborate textual playground.

In the *Imitations of Horace* Pope invites the reader to make comparisons with Horace's own epistles and satires, and to see Pope as a second Horace. In contrast with Oldham's imitations of Horace, where a lone voice spoke against the age, and was content to publish his work anonymously, Pope's collection is an exercise in self-promotion which also delineates a Horatian circle of named friends, including Arbuthnot and Swift. Yet there is a problem with replicating Horace's recurring references to his patron Maecenas. Viscount Bolingbroke is paralleled with Maecenas in "Epistles of Horace. Book I. Epistle I," but "The Seventh Epistle of the First Book of Horace" (addressed in the original to Maecenas) is addressed by Pope to an unspecified lord, while in "The Sixth Satire of the Second Book of Horace" (to which Swift and Pope both contributed) Maecenas is paralleled with Robert Harley, Earl of Oxford. The absence of a single, dominating Maecenas is partly a mark of Pope's independence, for he had had sufficient commercial success as a man of letters not to need the practical financial help of a patron. But it also suggests that the trio of ruler, patron, and poet represented classically by Augustus, Maecenas, and Horace cannot be replicated in early eighteenth-century England because there is no Augustus. Bolingbroke, who was probably the nearest equivalent to Maecenas in Pope's life, as a source of political and philosophical ideas if not of forms, was himself displaced and at odds with the country's rulers, for he was a Tory statesman whose public influence ended when the Hanoverian line succeeded, and he fled abroad to join the Pretender. When Pope was writing his imitation of Epistle I. I in 1738, Bolingbroke was back in England, but only on a brief visit before returning to his retirement in France. Readers who register Pope's difficulty in establishing a convincing modern parallel for Maecenas thereby register much of his own displacement from public affairs. And yet these local tensions between past and present cumulatively work to suggest rather that it is the rule of the Georges which has displaced the country from its true culture and its true origin.

Pope's "First Epistle of the Second Book of Horace, Imitated" defines this displacement through a teasing reworking of the Latin original which Horace had addressed to Augustus. Writing in 1737, Pope apparently addresses George II, who had been christened Augustus. At first, the coincidence looks even more heaven-sent than the Augustan parallel which delighted Dryden's contemporaries when Charles II returned in 1660. But for Pope nothing about the Hanoverians was heaven-sent. The very title warns the reader to be alert when interpreting the poem, for it includes an epigraph which comes (with disingenuous simplicity) from the Latin text: *Ne rubeam, pingui donatus munere!* ("I hope that I may not blush at having given such a stupid gift"). The gift was, in one sense, self-evidently stupid, because George II was notoriously insensitive to poetry; and so this apparent act of homage begins the work of its self-deconstruction before we have even read a line of Pope's English, simply through a straight quotation from Horace.

This imitation includes passages whose ironies even a Hanoverian might be thought capable of perceiving, but many of its deadliest effects derive from Pope's trust in the ability of his readers to compare the English with the Latin, to note subtle adjustments, and to register additions and omissions: even silence speaks. Both Horace and Pope begin with an address in the second person direct to the ruler, and Horace delays the moment when he names Augustus as the recipient of this poem until a suitably climactic moment at the end of the fourth line, when he calls him "Caesar," a title which associated Augustus with his predecessor and adoptive father Julius Caesar, warrior, statesman, and god. Pope too delays, using in the first line an ostensibly grand (but on careful inspection, vacuous and ironic) phrase "great Patron of Mankind"; but in this case there is no climactic name to follow. It is not simply that none of the names which Pope might have wished to call George II were printable, but that this refusal to implement a similarly powerful act of naming (which in Horace was an act of praise, an affirmation of Augustus's legitimacy and his place in history) deprives George II of a secure place in the poem and in the English language. This suspension places him in limbo, declining to define his relation to Augustus, as if the two names could not possibly appear together in the syntax of cultural history.

Among the various places where Pope's text diverges from that of Horace is the reference to servile writers who praise:

some monster of a King,
Or Virtue, or Religion turn to sport,
To please a lewd, or un-believing Court.   (lines 210–12)

By consulting the Latin text which was conveniently placed alongside the English, readers could see that there is no justification for this in the original. Also added to Horace here is the reference to Swift as a poet whose writings defended Ireland and made good the deficiency of the laws; by noticing that there is no precedent in Horace for this, we take the point that in the reign of Augustus poets did not need to act to defend public interests which government and law neglected. In such places we note the absence of any Latin pretext for Pope's English; elsewhere we realize that there is, damningly, no English equivalent available for Horace's Latin when he praises Augustus for his discriminating critical judgment in favoring the poets Virgil and Varius. His gifts to them have redounded to the credit of the giver, says Horace (Pope lines 389–90; Horace lines 245–47). Pope's silence tells us that no contemporary English equivalent is imaginable.

As silence speaks, so too does slyly inexact translation. A significant mismatch of English and Latin occurs at the point when Pope is describing the staging of the coronation scene from Shakespeare's *Henry VIII*. In his note to line 319, Pope observes that in a recent performance "the Armour of one of the Kings of England was borrowed from the Tower, to dress the Champion" (Pope's note at line 319), the champion being one of Pope's many *bêtes noires*, Colly Cibber. Whereas Horace is concerned only about the low Roman taste for spectacle, Pope's example extends beyond this point to suggest that in a world where the armour of the English kings can be borrowed and turned into stage props, the coronation of George II (which had taken place just two weeks before Cibber's performance) is a similarly empty charade, a borrowing of regalia and titles to which a Hanoverian has no better claim than any other actor.

Another mismatch invites interpretation when Horace's allusion to the library established by Augustus on the Palatine hill as part of the complex around the temple of Apollo is paralleled by a reference to Merlin's Cave (line 355). This was a thatched house with gothic windows established in the royal gardens at Richmond, containing wax figures of Merlin and his secretary, two Tudor queens, and two characters out of Ariosto, a poet who had celebrated the Hanoverians' ancestors. As part of the decoration of this "cave" the king ordered a collection of English books to be installed. The site is therefore an attempt to legitimize the Hanoverians by associating them with ancient British historical legend and with the Tudor monarchy.

The contrast between this self-serving and grotesque fabrication and the Palatine library makes embarrassingly clear the gap between the two cultures.

If Horace helped Pope to define culture, Homer helped him to define nature. What Pope said of Virgil might also be said of Pope himself: "*Nature* and *Homer* were, he found, the *same*" (*An Essay on Criticism*, line 135). Homer was the primary genius, not simply the first poet but the originary poet.[11] In the Preface to his translation of the *Iliad*, Pope credits Homer with supreme powers of invention (principally in the Latin sense of *inventio*, the discovery of material), for he saw nature with such clarity and reported it with such force that "no Man of a true Poetical Spirit is Master of himself while he reads him" (*Poems*, vol. VII, p. 4). Homer indeed saw the animation of the material world ("An Arrow is *impatient* to be on the Wing, a Weapon *thirsts* to drink the Blood of an Enemy" [*Poems*, vol. VII, p. 10]), but by "Nature" Pope primarily means "how the world is" or "how human beings behave": the basic nature of man is Homer's subject, and Pope's subject too.

In his translation of the *Iliad* Pope made his understanding of Homer as a moral writer explicit in notes which analyze Homer's conception of the principal characteristics of his heroes: "he has plac'd Pride with Magnanimity in *Agamemnon*, and Craft with Prudence in *Ulysses*. And thus we must take his *Achilles*, not as a meer heroick dispassion'd Character, but as compounded of Courage and Anger" (Pope's note to *Iliad* Book 1, line 155). Whether or not this now seems a plausible account of ancient Greek psychology, it is a reading which neatly fits with Pope's own understanding of man as a creature driven by ruling passions, as set out in his *Epistle to Cobham*. And it is Pope's own mode of moral thought which often shapes the way he translates the Greek verse. Here he is at a moment in Book 1 which might have specially appealed to him, when Achilles confronts Agamemnon, the supreme commander of the Greek army, who has just tried to appropriate one of Achilles' prisoners. Pope shows us a man telling his ruler that he is behaving unjustly:

> O Tyrant, arm'd with Insolence and Pride!
> Inglorious Slave to Int'rest, ever join'd
> With Fraud, unworthy of a Royal Mind.
> What gen'rous *Greek* obedient to thy Word,
> Shall form an Ambush, or shall lift the Sword?
> What Cause have I to war at thy Decree?
> The distant *Trojans* never injur'd me.
> To *Pthia*'s Realms no hostile Troops they led;

Safe in her Vales my warlike Coursers fed:
Far hence remov'd, the hoarse-resounding Main
And Walls of Rocks, secure my native Reign,
Whose fruitful Soil luxuriant Harvests grace,
Rich in her Fruits, and in her martial Race.
Hither we sail'd, a voluntary Throng,
T'avenge a private, not a publick Wrong:
What else to *Troy* th'assembled Nations draws,
But thine, Ungrateful, and thy Brother's Cause?

(Book 1, lines 194–210)

Pope's reworking of Homer begins by translating Agamemnon from a military commander into a tyrant whose behavior is paradoxically disturbing the natural hierarchy: although a ruler he has made himself morally a slave. He is all the more servile, in fact, the more he deploys his power in the service of his self-interest, which is shown to be his ruling passion. It is not control so much as self-control that concerns Pope here, a general moral lesson which he takes Homer to be illustrating. The Greek soldiers, by contrast with Agamemnon, are truly noble (the meaning of "generous" here). All this moral placing of Agamemnon has been added by Pope to Homer's confrontation between the two generals, as has the distinction between private and public in line 208. Pope's habit of expounding the moral issues in a generalized vocabulary, however, can lead him away from the unsettling directness of Homer's Greek: Pope's Achilles cannot be allowed to call Agamemnon anything like Homer's *kunopa*, metaphorically "shameless" but literally "dog-eyed." For Pope the moral force of "Ungrateful" is quite strong enough.

By way of comparison, here is Dryden's version of the same passage:

O, Impudent, regardful of thy own,
Whose Thoughts are center'd on thy self alone,
Advanc'd to Sovereign Sway, for better Ends
Than thus like abject Slaves to treat thy Friends.
What *Greek* is he, that urg'd by thy Command,
Against the *Trojan* Troops will lift his Hand?
Not I: Nor such inforc'd Respect I owe;
Nor *Pergamus* I hate, nor *Priam* is my Foe.
What Wrong from *Troy* remote, cou'd I sustain,
To leave my fruitful Soil, and happy Reign,
And plough the Surges of the stormy Main?
Thee, frontless Man, we follow'd from afar;
Thy Instruments of Death, and Tools of War.
Thine is the Triumph; ours the Toil alone:

> We bear thee on our Backs, and mount thee on the Throne.
> For thee we fall in Fight; for thee redress
> Thy baffled Brother; not the Wrongs of *Greece*.
>
> ("The First Book of Homer's Ilias," lines 225–41; in *Fables Ancient and Modern*)

Dryden was a dramatist, as we can hear in these lines which ask to be declaimed, for his rhythms are more varied than Pope's, and the passage effectively combines swelling periods with terse phrases such as "Not I." We can see that Pope has taken some of his vocabulary from Dryden, but the two translators generally find quite different interests in the passage. For Dryden, what needs to be stressed is that Agamemnon, having been made a king for the sake of the public good, has now turned his subjects into slaves. Though Pope picks up Dryden's word "slave," the moral issue for him primarily concerns the government of the passions. Dryden's Achilles harps on the theme of the Greeks being reduced to mere instruments and tools, even (in an image which makes Agamemnon into a barbarian monarch) reduced to being trodden on as the ruler ascends the throne. None of Dryden's emphasis on the individual being brutally subjected to the power of the ruler is present in Pope, or, indeed, in Homer. While these brief passages cannot be taken as representative of the two translations, they do illustrate that to translate is to transform.

The translator is, whether implicitly or explicitly, implicated in a myth of origins. He has an original text in front of him, but in only a limited sense could Pope's copy of Homer or Marvell's copy of Horace be thought of as supplying the "original" text. The text is always already reconstructed. Nor was the trope of originality itself original: what Pope said of Homer's unrivaled proximity to Nature, Dryden had already said more eloquently of Shakespeare.[12] And Dryden had also reminded his readers that the Greeks were not the originators of European culture:

> Whether the fruitful *Nile*, or *Tyrian* Shore,
> The seeds of Arts and Infant Science bore,
> 'Tis sure the noble Plant, translated first,
> Advanc'd its head in *Grecian* Gardens nurst.
>
> ("To the Earl of Roscommon, on his excellent
> *Essay on Translated Verse*," lines 1–4)

The Greeks were only the first translators.

Translation reimagines the original according to the ideals of the present, while redescribing the present in terms of this irrecoverable past. Through translation, past and present are reciprocally mythologized. But they are not thereby confused: translation demanded of its practitioners and readers a comparative movement between past and present which enabled a sharper understanding of their difference. Through poetry's recurring marks of separation from its supposed origins – its many signs that the translation is not the original, that England is not Rome, that Pope's Homer is not Homer's Homer – the culture of the present is made legible. And the disappointments of the present are made bearable by the consolation that there is a world elsewhere – even if this is, inevitably, always a Rome recomposed in each reader's imagination.

NOTES

1 Ode 1. 22 translated by the Earl of Roscommon; quoted from *Horace in English*, ed. D. S. Carne-Ross and Kenneth Haynes (Harmondsworth, 1996), p. 114.

2 *Epode* 11 was translated by Jonson, Cowley, and Dryden; for the tradition of Horatian meditation in rural retirement see Maren-Sofie Røstvig, *The Happy Man: Studies in the Metamorphoses of a Classical Ideal* (Oslo, 1954–58; second edn. 1962).

3 David Armitage, Armand Himy, and Quentin Skinner (eds.), *Milton and Republicanism* (Cambridge, 1995), pp. 15, 27–28.

4 See David Norbrook, "Lucan, Thomas May, and the Creation of a Republican Literary Culture," in Kevin Sharpe and Peter Lake (eds.), *Culture and Politics in Early Stuart England* (Basingstoke, 1994), pp. 45–66.

5 "A Panegyric to My Lord Protector," lines 169–72, in *The Poems of Edmund Waller*, ed. G. Thorn Drury, 2 vols. (London, 1901), vol. 11, p. 17.

6 Lawrence Venuti, "*The Destruction of Troy*: Translation and Royalist Cultural Politics in the Interregnum," *Journal of Medieval and Renaissance Studies*, 23 (1993), pp. 197–219; Timothy Raylor, *Cavaliers, Clubs, and Literary Culture* (Newark, 1994), pp. 183–88.

7 Thomas Hobbes, *Behemoth, or The Long Parliament*, ed. Ferdinand Tönnies (London, 1889), p. 3.

8 See Timothy Mowl and Brian Earnshaw, *Architecture without Kings* (Manchester, 1995).

9 Paul de Man, *Allegories of Reading* (New Haven, 1979), p. 17.

10 For details of Dryden's treatment of Horace's original, see the notes in *The Poems of John Dryden: Volume 11: 1682–1685*, ed. Paul Hammond (London, 1995), pp. 378–85.

11 See Kirsti Simonsuuri, *Homer's Original Genius* (Cambridge, 1979).

12 Pope's praise of Homer's originality in his Preface to the *Iliad* echoes Dryden's praise of Shakespeare's originality in his *Essay of Dramatic Poesy* (*The Works of John Dryden*, eds. E. N. Hooker and H. T. Swedenberg, Jr., 20 vols. [Berkeley and Los Angeles, 1956–], vol. XVII, p. 55), while "*Nature* and *Homer* were, he found, the *same*" is traced by the Twickenham editors to Dryden's lines on Shakespeare in his "Prologue to *The Tempest*" lines 7–8.

FURTHER READING

For a list of translations from the classics, see the relevant volumes of the *Cambridge Bibliography of English Literature*, supplemented by Stuart Gillespie's article, "A Checklist of Restoration English Translations and Adaptations of Classical Greek and Latin Poetry, 1660–1700," *Translation and Literature*, 1 (1991), pp. 52–67.

General works

Erskine-Hill, Howard, *The Augustan Idea in English Literature* (London, 1983).

Lord, George deF., *Classical Presences in Seventeenth Century English Poetry* (New Haven, 1987).

Martindale, Charles, and Hopkins, David (eds.), *Horace Made New: Horatian Influences on British Writing from the Renaissance to the Twentieth Century* (Cambridge, 1993).

Røstvig, Maren-Sofie, *The Happy Man: Studies in the Metamorphoses of a Classical Ideal, 1600–1700* (Oslo, 1954–58, revised 1962).

Sowerby, Robin, *The Classical Legacy in Renaissance Poetry* (London, 1994).

Weinbrot, Howard, *Augustus Caesar in "Augustan" England* (Princeton, 1978).

Dryden

The Works of John Dryden, eds. E. N. Hooker and H. T. Swedenberg, Jr., 20 vols. (Berkeley and Los Angeles, 1956–). This does not yet include the *Fables*.

The Poems of John Dryden, ed. James Kinsley, 4 vols. (Oxford, 1958). Particularly for the *Fables*.

The Poems of John Dryden: Volume I: 1649–1681 and *Volume II: 1682–1685*, ed. Paul Hammond (London, 1985). For detailed annotation to the early translations.

Bottkol, J. McG., "Dryden's Latin Scholarship," *Modern Philology*, 40 (1943), pp. 214–54.

Hammond, Paul, "The Integrity of Dryden's Lucretius," *Modern Language Review*, 78 (1983), pp. 1–23.

"John Dryden: The Classicist as Sceptic," *The Seventeenth Century*, 4 (1989), pp. 165–87.

John Dryden: A Literary Life (Basingstoke, 1991), chapter 7.

Hopkins, David, "Nature's Laws and Man's: The Story of Cinyras and Myrrha in Ovid and Dryden," *Modern Language Review*, 80 (1985), pp. 786–810.

"Dryden and Ovid's 'Wit out of Season,'" in Charles Martindale (ed.), *Ovid Renewed* (Cambridge, 1988), pp. 167–90.

Jones, Emrys, "A 'Perpetual Torrent': Dryden's Lucretian Style," in D. L. Patey and Timothy Keegan (eds.), *Augustan Studies: Essays in Honour of Irvin Ehrenpreis* (Newark, 1985), pp. 47–63.

Mason, H. A., "The Dream of Happiness," *Cambridge Quarterly*, 8 (1978), pp. 11–55 and 9 (1980), pp. 218–71. On the translation of Horace's *Epode* II.

"Living in the Present," *Cambridge Quarterly*, 10 (1981), pp. 91–129. On the translation of Horace's *Ode* III. 29.

"The Hallowed Hearth," *Cambridge Quarterly*, 14 (1985), pp. 205–39. On the translation of Horace's *Ode* I. 9.

Reverand, Cedric D., *Dryden's Final Poetic Mode: The "Fables"* (Philadelphia, 1988).

Sloman, Judith, *Dryden: The Poetics of Translation* (Toronto, 1985).

Zwicker, Steven N., *Politics and Language in Dryden's Poetry: The Arts of Disguise* (Princeton, 1984).

See also Martindale and Hopkins, *Horace Made New*, under "General works" above.

Marvell

The Poems and Letters of Andrew Marvell, ed. H. M. Margoliouth, third edn. revised by Pierre Legouis and E. E. Duncan-Jones, 2 vols. (Oxford, 1971).

Coolidge, J. S., "Marvell and Horace," *Modern Philology*, 63 (1965), pp. 111–20.

Wilson, A. J. N., "Andrew Marvell: *An Horatian Ode Upon Cromwell's Return from Ireland*: The Thread of the Poem and its Use of Classical Allusion," *Critical Quarterly*, 11 (1969), pp. 325–41.

See also Martindale and Hopkins, *Horace Made New*, under "General works" above.

Oldham

The Poems of John Oldham, ed. Harold F. Brooks and Raman Selden (Oxford, 1987).

Hammond, Paul, *John Oldham and the Renewal of Classical Culture* (Cambridge, 1983).

Selden, Raman, "Oldham's Versions of the Classics," in Antony Coleman and Antony Hammond (eds.), *Poetry and Drama 1570–1700: Essays in Honour of Harold F. Brooks* (London, 1981), pp. 110–35.

Pope

The Twickenham Edition of the Poems of Alexander Pope, ed. John Butt et al., 10 vols. (London, 1938–67).

Mason, H. A., *To Homer through Pope* (London, 1972).

Stack, Frank, *Pope and Horace* (Cambridge, 1985).

Williams, Carolyn D., *Pope, Homer, and Manliness* (London, 1993).

See also Martindale and Hopkins, *Horace Made New*, under "General works" above.

Part 2
WRITERS

8

CEDRIC C. BROWN

"This Islands watchful Centinel": anti-Catholicism and proto-Whiggery in Milton and Marvell

To consider the writings of John Milton and Andrew Marvell in a collection on Restoration and Augustan literature is to focus on the last part of the careers of two men who had been friends and both employed by the Cromwellian regime. With Milton this is potentially to consider all three major poems, *Paradise Lost* (1667, second edition 1674), *Paradise Regained* and *Samson Agonistes* (1671), and a small number of prose pamphlets, chiefly *Of True Religion* (1674), and some printings of earlier work issued before his death at age nearly sixty-six in late 1674. With Marvell it is to consider a range of political writing connected with his parliamentary experience until his sudden death at age fifty-seven in 1678, that is, a number of satirical poems (with many others of uncertain attribution), a few occasional poems, and some influential prose works.[1] It is also to look at the way their oppositional roles were interpreted in the politics of the 1660s and 1670s. That was influenced in turn by their earlier activities and in the case of Milton by a lot of previous well-known political writing. Beyond that it is to see, too, how those writings were appropriated by the Whigs from the late 1670s, for both Milton and Marvell, despite various prejudices against them, achieved the status of ideological authorities. For that, however, I shall glance only briefly into the 1680s and beyond.

This chapter is not a simple overview and it is selective in its treatment of texts. It examines ideological underpinnings which most clearly have to do with the appropriation of these texts by the Whig press very soon after Marvell's death. Although the writings of two politically engaged men cannot be explained from any single argument, it may be possible to discover a significant convergence of purposes by looking at the situation of the mid-1670s especially. I shall focus in particular upon a widely shared ideology, that of anti-Catholicism, together with its adjunct, a polemic against tyrannical or arbitrary government, and its accompaniment, toleration of dissent for Protestant sects. Anti-Catholicism informs a discourse without which the Whig appropriation could not have happened.

We might begin with a prose work which Marvell wrote, or in which he had a hand, in 1677. This was *An Account of the Growth of Popery, and Arbitrary Government in England*, written during a mistrustful deadlock between parliament and King Charles II. The book seems to have been organized by the oppositional group around the Earl of Shaftesbury. It offers a polemical analysis of the history of England since the Restoration, deriving the nation's ills from popish conspiracy and French connections. The opening sentence is startlingly direct:

> There has now for diverse Years, a design been carried on, to change the lawfull Government of England into an Absolute Tyranny, and to convert the established Protestant Religion into down-right Popery...[2]

This is a conspiracy theory which posits that a group associated with the court was working for those bugbears of national Protestantism, the Pope and the Jesuits ("Romish Idolatry"), channeled through the power of France under Louis XIV ("French Slavery") (*An Account*, p. 14), which in the later seventeenth century had replaced Spain as the demonized nation of the Elizabethans and Jacobeans. (Marvell himself had been to France and witnessed state persecution of the Huguenots.) The text capitalizes on the polemic of generations, seeing a repeated story of the attempted ruin of monarchs at the hand of Catholic conspirators: the excommunication of Queen Elizabeth I and the Spanish invasion of 1588; the papal exclusion of James I and the Gunpowder Plot; the Irish War fostered by Catholics to destroy Charles I; and most recently, the rumored firing of London in 1666 by Catholic French. The mid-1670s saw a large increase in anti-Catholic publications, and each crisis centering on fears of popery caused not just a rehearsal of earlier crises, but publications of books belonging to the earlier crises.[3]

This anonymously published little history touched sensitive points, and a reward was offered for information about author and printer. Several pamphlets suspected Marvell's involvement and one dubbed him "a shrewd man against Popery."[4] As scholars have delighted to tell, because the incident shows such characteristic mischief in him, Marvell himself reported the suspicions to his nephew William Popple in what is probably his latest surviving letter. Several publications, he said, had suggested that the Member of Parliament, Mr. Marvell, might have written *An Account*, "but if he had, surely he should not have escaped being questioned in Parliament, or some other Place."[5]

If this shows Marvell as parliament man and writer relishing a reputation as an English patriot, then one elegist even in 1678 could praise him as "this Islands watchful Centinel" and the brave enemy of "the grim Monster, Arbitrary power,"[6] and soon that reputation had hardened into virtual canonization. Marvell did not quite live to see the Popish Plot of 1678, in which Titus Oates's fabricated conspiracy built on just the discourses used in *An Account* and in which the whole range of fears about popery was exploited. *An Account* itself went to a second edition in 1678, a French translation in 1680, and a Whig continuation in 1682.[7] In other words, the work played a part in the Whig attempts to exclude the Catholic James from the succession, which occurred nevertheless in 1685. At the Glorious Revolution of 1688, when James II departed, it had become so useful that it was reprinted in the collection of *State Tracts* justifying the dethronement,[8] and in the flood of Protestant–patriotic literature at that time one book-seller put out (in January 1689) a little pamphlet entitled *Mr. Andrew Marvell's Character of Popery*, which reprinted a general description of Catholicism from *An Account* and offered these pages as the true dying prophecy of a patriot:

> The Author ... laboured to set it [Catholicism] forth in its proper Colours, as if he had intended it as his last Legacy to this Nation ... And as it were prophetically to let us understand what a Deliverance God has bin pleased to bless us withal, in so lately freeing the Kingdom from that Inundation of Antichristian Pomp & Vanity.[9]

The persuasiveness of this lay in its legacy as the words of a dying prophet and in the nation's sustained fears of popery.

Similar evidence of Whig assimilation can be told of some other prose works of Marvell. *A Short Historical Essay, concerning General Councils, Creeds, and Impositions in Matters of Religion* (1676) was a contribution to the toleration debate. It claims that the church itself, through the power of the bishops working with monarchs over the centuries, has been more likely to persecute fellow believers than the early pagan emperors. It was published at the end of a satirical essay about toleration, the mischievous *Mr. Smirke; Or, The Divine in Mode*. (Marvell frequently attacked estab-lishment clergymen who wished to enforce conformity in religion.) The *Essay* was on a topic of huge importance to Whigs and had posthumous printings in 1680 and again under James in 1687.

Marvell's recent writing was politically close to the Whig party which formed just after his death, and it was probably his ideological credit that led to the posthumous publication of his poems by 1681 by a Whig bookseller, Robert Boulter. The great majority of texts included in *Mis-cellaneous Poems* were social and patronage poems from the end of the

1640s through the 1650s, but there was nervousness about those in praise of Cromwell, and most copies omitted them. The publication of many of the verse satires of the Restoration period was not straightforward either: after 1688 popular satirical poems written under the Stuarts were collected and published in *Poems on Affairs of State*.[10] In these celebrated volumes, Marvell's name was given prominence, and many more poems were attributed to him than are his, so much was he championed by the now victorious Whig party.

The main focus of this chapter is, however, the late 1660s and the 1670s. In this period, Marvell was best known as a long-sitting and active Member of Parliament for Hull, between 1659 and his death. It was a career which began under some suspicion. Like Milton, he had served as a Secretary for Foreign Languages in the Cromwellian regime (from 1657 until the collapse of the Commonwealth), and had previously been employed by both leading Parliamentary Generals, Fairfax and Cromwell, as tutor in languages in their households, in the early 1650s. The Fairfax connection was not so disadvantageous for him in the Restoration, because Fairfax was a moderate who had distanced himself from the trial of Charles I, married his daughter to the second Duke of Buckingham, son of Charles's former favorite, and worked finally toward the Restoration settlement. Cromwell connections were a problem, and they had to be played down. By the time of the Restoration Marvell was in the thick of political intrigue and, as a parliament man of no independent means, supported by his constituency stipend and by whatever short-term assignments he could get, and being a man moreover of varied overseas experience, he was ripe for suspicion as an upstart modern Machiavel.

Restoration parliaments eventually came to be dominated by fears of popery to an extraordinary degree, especially from the 1670s, and the Popish Plot of 1678 was built upon assumptions way beyond rationality. In general, fears of a reimposition of Catholicism in England were hugely exaggerated: the Catholic constituency was no larger than it had been for a century and would have provided completely inadequate support for a changed orthodoxy. Romanism was mainly organized around landowners and their clients and tenants, using priests trained abroad. Some of those families held court positions. Whenever court connections with foreign Catholic powers came to notice, the way was open for a whole host of conspiratorial fears.[11]

By 1673 there had been a complete breakdown of trust between the king and parliament. It was based on two key underlying issues: Charles's policy toward toleration – trying to ease the punitive measures on recusants by linking them to measures of toleration for Protestant dissenters; and the suspicion, confirmed by 1673, that the heir to the throne had actually turned Catholic. What is more, the king had declared war on Protestant Holland in 1672 without the consent of parliament. The royal Declaration of Indulgence of 1672, allowing toleration for Dissenters, was resented as an imposition without parliamentary consent and distrusted as a blind for toleration of papists. In the Test Act of 1673 parliament effected a bar on Catholics holding high office. Oppositional groupings gradually formed which stood upon the principles of resistance to absolute monarchical power (though rarely expressing itself in terms of republicanism), associated more and more with a phobia about Catholic designs at court. By the time of the crisis of negotiation when *An Account* was written, opposition was organizing about the Earl of Shaftesbury, who was for some time imprisoned, and Buckingham, with whose family Marvell had various patronage connections. Following the hysteria of the Popish Plot, the Whig party, loosely formed though it was, was united in one aim, to exclude James from the succession. By that time, the catchphrase "Arbitrary Power" was wholly identified with popery. Parliament had cast itself as guardian of the Protestant nation, and the issue of toleration for Dissenters had become completely enmeshed with fears about letting popery loose. Into this complex Marvell's *Account* and *Essay* were received, and he was set to become "This Islands watchful Centinel."

But before looking selectively at Marvell's role in Restoration politics and the importance of anti-Catholicism as a shaping discourse, we should perhaps review the strand of anti-Catholicism in his earlier poetry. There is a story, to begin with, of Marvell's own brief fling with Romanism during his university days, from which his father, a stoutly Protestant clergyman, had to rescue him (Legouis, *Andrew Marvell*, p. 4). As if in conformist compensation, one of the early satirical poems, occasioned by his being in Italy, "Flecknoe, An English Priest at Rome" (1645 or 1646) presents Catholicism as a confirming mark of unmannerly otherness. There is an obsession especially in earlier poems with manners and refinement, and social insecurities can be felt in many of Marvell's writings. For a much lighter touch, we might note the ideological undertow in "The Nymph's Complaining for the Death of her Fawn" where, though the heartless troopers who have mortally wounded the deer are Scottish Presbyterians, the gently mocked sentimentality of the girl is figured in a kind of superstition sainting the animal and deifying virginity. Similarly to be shared with the reformist reader is the irony of "The Mower Against Gardens," where the "puritan" fieldworker, jealously disapproving of high-life sophistications up in the big house, convicts himself of superstition concerning native gods (fairies) whilst seeking to brand the statues in the garden as pagan. But the issue of anti-Catholicism becomes more seriously defining, where religion is more obviously written into current history, as in the laudatory treatments of Queen Christina of Sweden ("Letter to Ingelo" and the epigram for her), and of course in the poems to or about Fairfax and Cromwell.

The matter is particularly clear in "Upon Appleton House." The whole poem in praise of the family, probably presented to Fairfax as a thank-offering at Marvell's leaving the household,[12] is structured upon the history of the Reformation in England. The story of the family, through the house, is presented as coterminous with the progress of Reformation, transforming a wickedly portrayed corrupted nunnery into a place symbolizing heroic action for the cause of Protestantism in Europe, and allowing virtuous retirement for the general. That legitimate retirement is set off not only against the earlier unreformed monasticism but also the relative self-indulgence of the poet's sojourn there. "Upon Appleton House" meditates on the difficulties of interpreting the providential meaning of the present historical moment, in the uncertain post-Civil War period before the ascendancy of Cromwell had become clear, but one of the remarkable things about its organization is the way in which anti-Catholicism is accepted as established upon history, something certain against which present uncertainties are measured. Implicitly, much the same is true of the elusive "private" "An Horatian Ode." If victories continue, Cromwell "to all states not free / Shall climacteric be" (lines 103–04).[13] In other words, what gives credence to the idea of a new phase of history is the crushing of Catholicism in Ireland, and with Catholicism is associated regimes "not free."

This is all private or social verse, but it already seems likely that anti-Catholicism is being used as an orientation in times of uncertainty of direction, whether in Marvell's private life or in considerations of the meaning of the historical present. His Restoration writings, however, are public and political, and they follow the contours of parliamentary debate. They concern parliament itself, the court, the church, and the state of the Protestant nation. By 1678 they have also revealed a political analysis involving popery as an ideological given shared with the reader.

The poem "Last Instructions to a Painter" of 1667 is a devastatingly detailed indictment of the court party under the Earl of Clarendon, and could only have been written by a Parliamentarian.[14] The venality of these men is used as an explanation for the collapse of organization leading to the disaster in the Medway, when the Dutch fleet sailed in unchecked and fired some of the English ships there. The implied comparison is with the better naval success of the more disciplined Cromwellian regime, and the implied subject is the humiliation (ironically by another Protestant state) of English national Protestantism, so often associated with the sea. It is also, traditionally, a kind of advice document to the monarch – "Blame not the Muse that brought those spots to sight" (line 957) – and it was part of the campaign to remove Clarendon from office. When Clarendon fled to France, Marvell was equally suspicious of the new ministers, the Cabal. Warren L. Chernaik (*The Poet's Time*, p. 71) is probably right to point to the fact that the appeal of much of his political writing is in the offer to uncover what is hidden from view. By that not unfamiliar method, conspiracies are likely to be unveiled in the true interests of the Protestant state.

In "The Loyal Scot," an offshoot of "Last Instructions," written about 1669, the causes of national humiliation are now seen to lie in the worldly corruption of the bishops. The poem is based on the idea of ironically reversing John Cleveland's Royalist satire against the Presbyterian Scots: now a Scottish captain is not "The Rebel Scot" as in Cleveland's satire, but the patriotic example to the English, refusing to leave his post and dying on his burning ship. The court party must look to their own church for the roots of such laxity as had led to the judgmental disasters of 1666 or on the Medway.

By the 1670s, although many of the targets remained the same, an even greater cynicism seems to have set in about the corruptibility of parliament and church. The court was seen to be bribing parliament men, which was like giving away "the whole Land, and Liberty, of England," Marvell wrote intemperately in a letter of 1671.[15] There is a particular distaste for dishonorable turncoats, men who had compromised principle to join the crowd for reward, and some such issue may also be at stake in Marvell's biggest literary success of this period, *The Rehearsal Transpros'd* of 1672 (*Second Part*, 1673), in which the writings of the self-important careerist churchman Samuel Parker, a man of Puritan background, were subjected to merciless, witty, point-for-point satire. It is like an educated defeat at fencing. The pretentious cleric is reduced to the status of a bit part, Mr. Bayes, in one of Buckingham's plays (a tactic which will be imitated in Mr. Smirke), and convicted of madness, the slur usually reserved by the establishment for fanatics. Like "The Last Instructions," *The Rehearsal Transpros'd* offers to guide the king away from a set of false counselors, whose instincts in the matter of toleration seemed to be more tyrannical than might be expected from monarchs (*The Rehearsal Transpros'd*, p. 89). Critics have been puzzled by Marvell's continued loyalism to the king, but the method must be seen in convention and in political context, in other words in terms of the pragmatism which an MP would well understand. In the light of private sentiment about national liberty, it may be doubted whether Marvell really dissociated either the king or the king's party from analyses of something like arbitrary power, about which he would speak clearly, as we have seen, in *An Account* in 1678, on the eve of the Popish Plot, and as the Whigs were about to appropriate his writings.

To rehearse the ground Marvell and his parliament covered also brings the writings of Milton to mind. Strengthening the radical resolve of parliaments had been Milton's repeated aim in the 1640s and 1650s; the examination of the prelacy and of attempts to limit conscience and apply censorship had been a main concern of his writings since the tracts against the bishops and the debates at various times about censorship, most memorably in *Areopagitica* in 1645; analyses of tyranny and of manipulations of parliaments had been the main preoccupation of the anti-monarchical tracts from 1649; and Milton had reiterated his analyses on all these fronts in the clutch of publications on the eve of the Restoration. What is more, he had written as a schoolboy on the Gunpowder Plot and posted a watchful sentinel on Protestant England as early as 1637, with St. Michael in "Lycidas."[16] He had helped Marvell to gain his Secretaryship; Marvell had helped Milton when he was in trouble at the Restoration. It is unimaginable that Marvell's political thinking was untouched by Milton's vigorous output.

Milton's own position at the Restoration was precarious. In 1660 he was fifty-two and had already been blind for about eight years. He had retired from his government position of Secretary for Foreign Languages which he had held from 1649 to the mid-1650s. Unlike Marvell, he had for most of his life just enough private means to be more or less independent, and he eagerly cultivated, along with his high-principled authorship as civic reformer in what he hoped might be a free-speaking commonwealth, an Horatian stance, that brought with it the assumptions of the educated gentleman. But his regicide writings had made him infamous and he had problems with censorship. The great Latin *Defence* (*Defensio*) of the regicide and *Eikonoklastes* of 1650 – his attempt to counter the martyrologies of the dead king – books written at the behest of the Council of State (the ruling body of the early Commonwealth), had given him wide, if notorious, recognition in Europe. They were also picked out by the authorities in 1660, and copies of both were burned by the public hangman. (There were further burnings of his books at the failed Rye House Plot of 1683.) The episcopal licenser seems to have been reluctant about the first edition of *Paradise Lost* in 1667; the text of *The History of Britain* was pruned in 1670; when Milton himself republished his 1645 collection of shorter poems and augmented it with later poems in 1673, he omitted the sonnets to Fairfax, Cromwell, and Vane; *Of True Religion* had an anonymous imprint in 1673; and after his death the publication of his state letters and the heretical *De Doctrina Christiana* was blocked.[17]

Owning a debt to the anti-monarchical Milton was something one had to be careful about before 1688 especially, but there are many signs of his being assimilated by Whig writers.[18] Two writers on press censorship, for example, drew on *Areopagitica*, Charles Blount in 1679 and William Denton in 1681, but neither named their source, and the same thing happened as late as 1698, with Matthew Tindal's *A Letter to a Member of Parliament*.[19] Two writers of 1682 against arbitrary power seem to have used the *Defensio* without acknowledgment: Samuel Johnson, against church authority, and Thomas Hunt, against state authority.[20] There was no lack of explicit mention amongst hostile Tories, and Sir Robert Filmer's *Patriarcha* (published 1680) ranges itself openly against the *Defensio*. However, the influence of Milton's writings on key Whig writers is important, and the list includes John Locke in *Two Treatises* (1690), James Tyrrell in *Patriarcha Non Monarcha* (1680), Algernon Sidney in *Discourses Concerning Government* (early 1680s, published 1698), and Milton's editor and biographer, and radical writer, John Toland.

The pattern changed after 1688, when there was a demand to acknowledge Milton's political works: two editions of the prose writings were planned, though neither appeared until the late 1690s; the notorious *Eikonoklastes* was republished in 1690; there was an English translation of the *Defence* in 1692, and the resistance arguments of the *Tenure* had been taken over in the anonymous *Pro Populo Adversus Tyrannos* of 1689, though only the later edition of 1691 made the Miltonic connection evident. Meanwhile the fame of *Paradise Lost* took a leap with the publication of the impressive folio edition of 1688, and the literary indebtedness of such works as Sir Richard Blackmore's *Prince Arthur* (1695). *Paradise Lost* now began to take on the appearance of a great Whig epic.

When, round about 1674, Marvell wrote a commendation for the second edition of Milton's *Paradise Lost*, he fashioned a good-humored, self-deprecating poem which kept more sensitive matters of politics at arm's length. The blind singer is celebrated for the hugeness of his godly argument and the inimitable decorum of his writing. In fitting matter and manner together so perfectly, therefore, Milton proves himself, in his blindness, to have become a true prophet:

Where couldst thou words of such a compass find?
Whence furnish such a vast expense of mind?
Just heaven thee, like Tiresias, to requite,
Rewards with prophecy thy loss of sight.   (lines 41–44)

There may be several acts of friendship in this deft tribute. With his own "tinkling rhyme" (line 46) Marvell is left at the level of the merely fashionable poet about town, whereas Milton is mythologized into a figure of such independent purpose, mind, method, and faith as to seem to transcend current thoughts and manners. For a writer who had achieved notoriety as a dangerous reformer and defender of regicide, such transcendent status was a comfortable antidote, as well as a high tribute.

Although in the 1660s and 1670s Milton was no longer in the thick of political maneuverings as Marvell was, it makes sense to see not just the late prose tracts but also the three major poems as belonging to the political climate of the 1660s and 1670s. True prophets speak to their own times, and *Paradise Lost*, inscribing amongst other things forms of history, automatically encompasses in a method working with continuities, repeats, and parallels, significant traces and interpretations of its own times.[21] What is more, when the poet constructs his own prophetic presence within his text, he does so in such a way as to contextualize his seeking for the truth. The opening of Book III, where Milton mythologizes himself as blind seer-poet, is complicated by the opening to Book VII, where it is revealed that, as well as with blindness, he is beset with darkness and dangers. He makes himself a solitary and perhaps unheard witness in times of adversity. So there is an invitation to see the patterns revealed in his telling of the Fall as being implicit and ongoing in the world of poet and reader.

One might consider the impact of Milton's way of beginning his narrative, immediately exposing the reader to Satan and the gathering powers of Satan in Books I and II. No one reading *Paradise Lost* at the time could have been in any doubt after the first two books that the evil institutions initiated by Satan and his company after their fall into Hell are active, through history, into the Restoration, and that, indeed, a mid seventeenth-century political discourse is shaping that history of the world. By the end of Book I tyrannical monarchy has already been built on the basis of idolatrous religion.

As the satanic powers gather off the lake, they are defined by reference to godless tyranny or the ruin of civilization: Egyptian cruelty with Busiris (Book I, line 307); or the Pharaoh holding the Israelites in bondage (line 342); a paynim Sultan (line 348); or hordes of barbarians (line 353). Ruin follows from false religion. The roll-call of the chief fallen angels names them as idols in the Old Testament, the infections threatening to overwhelm God's people. Although the first frame of reference is Old Testament, the reader is subtly reminded at the end of the list with the slack but dangerous spirit of indiscipline, Belial, that the patterns of behavior over which he presides are to be seen through to the present day: "In courts and palaces he also reigns / And in luxurious cities" (lines 497–498).[22] A similar indication is given with Saturn, who expresses lawless license, and who long ago reached western kingdoms: "Fled over Adria to the Hesperian fields, / And o'er the Celtic roamed the utmost isles" (lines 520–21).

As with amazing speed the forces of evil create the institutions which are to replicate themselves through the history of the world, tyrannous government is set up on the base of false religion. Pandaemonium is the architectural center from which the forces of a powerful new empire are supported. The building has an aggregate design, reminding readers of the seats of tyrants over the centuries, beginning with Nimrod and the rulers of Babylon and Egypt. It is the site of secular power, but it employs for political ends the intimidating features of a temple; it is part temple, part palace, in the combination of religion and state which Milton so distrusted. The architecture and interior lighting strike admiration and the trumpets announce "awful ceremony" (line 753). Thus tyrants manipulate minds. As the hosts of angels gather, they are diminished, in Milton's withering irony: "Thus incorporeal spirits to smallest forms / Reduced their shapes immense, and were at large" (lines 789–90). The fallen angels are hoodwinked by the princely caste –

> But far within
> And in their own dimensions like themselves
> The great seraphic lords and cherubims
> In close recess and secret conclave sat.   (lines 792–95)

– and are vulnerable to exploitation. Like Marvell and others, Milton takes the lid off hidden manipulative practices. Even within the inner council chamber, when the "great consult" begins, it turns out to have been stage-managed by Satan and his henchman Beezebub: so easily are weakened minds, even of great angels, led. Confronting Satan's falsehood with his own witness, Raphael gives the appropriate analytical definition, when he calls the false monarch "idol of majesty divine" (Book VI, line 101), one who inspires awe with the trappings of false religion.

This is a polemical analysis of the way tyrannous regimes work and it uses the same discourse that Marvell relies upon in *An Account*, when he talks (p. 11) of "inslaving men by the assistance of Religion more easily." Indeed, it would be surprising if Marvell did not have Milton in mind as he wrote his oppositional pieces of the 1670s, especially perhaps *Eikonoklastes*. *Eikonoklastes* was a cultural critique, a revelatory deconstruction. It offered to show the manipulative meanings behind the language and iconography of Caroline Royalism, and the sense of danger from Catholic conspiracy is particularly clear, in its relentless focusing upon the weakening effect of Charles I's French Catholic queen, Henrietta Maria. It assumed that women are often the chief channels of Catholic influence, leading to the ruin of Protestantism and the inception of tyranny.

In this regard the sequence of events in Milton's telling of the Fall should be noted. In his temptation of Eve, Satan plants superstitious thoughts in her mind by offering to worship the "magic" tree in his speech (Book IX, lines 679ff.). The suggestion sticks: Eve's first act, after falling, is one of worship of the plant (lines 834–38). In Milton's analysis she becomes the first of many female agencies tending to weaken rational minds. Also, when Satan first breaks into Paradise in Book IV, the moment is treated as proleptic of the whole spoiling of the true church by materialistic manipulators: "So since into his church lewd hirelings climb" (line 193). *Paradise Lost* is a meditation on faith and politics over the whole of human history, as Milton had charted it, but there can be no doubt that a reader like Marvell could have seen expressed in it a polemic against popery and arbitrary government which Milton would have expected any "fit audience" to share. Adam's education by Michael in the last books begins by telling how the sons of God were ruined in marriage by godless fair women, "oppression" and "sword-law" following from these mixed marriages, diluting religious discipline, with "luxury and riot" and civil wars to follow before the Flood. Infections of true religious discipline are to be seen at the base of each successive fall, and the great fall of the Christian era is into Catholicism, as Adam is told in Book XII.

Read contextually and in the light of the anti-Catholic, anti-tyrannical discourses, Milton's *Samson Agonistes*, published in the same volume as *Paradise Regained* in 1671, is a narrative of hugely suggestive power, telling the story of one man's fraught resistance.[23] We might begin, however, as the volume does, with *Paradise Regained*. Although this four-book epic has often been read primarily as a work of religious instruction, there is much to be gained by appreciating its encouragement of spiritual discipline in the context of the religio-political discourses of the time. It is true that, like all three of Milton's major poems published

in the Restoration, it goes back to fundamentals, but it is likely that the
Whig printer who put out the second edition of *Paradise Regained* and
Samson Agonistes in 1680 saw ideological alignments with which his
readers could identify. For one thing, Milton's recasting of the story of
Jesus' temptation in the wilderness, the great educative test and prepara-
tion for his ministry, provides an enabling, encouraging narrative for the
faithful in the context of political oppression and pharisaical religion, just
as *Samson Agonistes* tells a story of doubt and faith in the context of
idolatrous oppression. Whilst we should not give too much credence to
the self-congratulatory account of Milton's young Quaker friend, Thomas
Ellwood, that he had made the crucial suggestion which led to the
writing of *Paradise Regained*,[24] it is quite likely that Dissenting readers
would have particularly identified with a poem about the "inward oracle"
(Book 1, line 463) which alone is necessary, the individual's search rather
than an obedience to established church doctrine. It is the same point
which Adam learns at the end of *Paradise Lost*, about the guiding Spirit of
God.

Some of the peculiarities of Milton's reordering of the wilderness
narrative, as told in Matthew and Luke, should be noted in this context. To
begin with, by treating separately and reinterpreting the temptation of
hunger in his first episode, Milton creates a foundation for his action which
is entirely predictable in terms of his usual arguments: a test of the
separation of truth from falsehood in matters of religion. This episode,
which rewrites his early anti-Catholic "Nativity Ode," establishes the first
challenge to be that of facing infections within the church itself. After the
temptation has failed, Satan himself acknowledges in his discomfiture that
his role has been like that of the "hypocrite or atheous priest" (line 487). In
the second day's temptation, for which different kinds of worldliness are
organized, such is the insistence on the separation of religion from all
aspects of career or state, that established connections seem more feasible
for the tempter (dressed as one from city or court) than for the tempted,
and even the use of learning is severed from considerations of secular
power.

Paradise Regained also shares with *Samson Agonistes* the influence of
the informing narrative of the Book of Job, a model for works dealing with
interlocutive tests of strength of faith. *Samson Agonistes* is an exhausting
and exhaustive study of religious states of mind in adversity, concerning
not just Samson's progress but also the divergent lines of thought of the
other Israelites, represented by his father Manoa, and the Chorus of
Danites. It debates the meaning of Providence rather as the divergent
voices in the Book of Job try, with varying degrees of enlightenment, to see

meaning in God's purposes. The fact that the poem shows attitudes to faith and doubt in adversity forms an important part of its significance, and that aspect of the text invites consideration against the background of the long struggles of Dissenters under the Clarendon Code. But the spiritual debate of Samson is also fiercely politicized: its theme of religion oppressed by idolatrous power argues the importance of anti-Catholicism to the poem as a whole. One of its teasing qualities is that as a dramatic narrative with no guiding narratorial voice it leaves its readers to do their own work in applying Old Testament to past, present, or future and in doubt as to just how the irresolute state of the tribes in the highly politicized last part of the Book of Judges might apply to the character of England.

Anti-Catholicism provides a fundamental discourse, within which the action is turned. Not only is the dramatic climax a day of games (so that the final outcome becomes, as in many Old Testament narratives, a trial of strength between true and false gods), but Samson's crucial re-encounter with and final rejection of his Philistine wife, Dalila, is sealed by religious allegiance.[25] The wife of a false idolatrous religion is meant to adopt the true religion of the husband, as in the heroic example of Ruth, celebrated in Milton's Sonnet IX. In his divorce tracts, Milton opined that there should be grounds for divorce, if the right-thinking partner had no hope of converting the other to true religion. Such thought was not simply about general matters of domestic discipline: it was informed by generations of anxieties concerning the role of idolatrous consorts in high places. What Samson achieves, if intemperately, in the episode with Dalila is the putting away of a wife beyond hope of conversion; the clarification through argument is that she had been deaf to her duty to follow her husband's one God and had also been swayed and rewarded by the priests of Dagon for reasons of state in the continuing Philistine oppression of the Israelites. Since her faithlessness is also in a sense her faithfulness, to her roots, it makes for good ironic drama.

With different degrees of acuteness, all the Israelites have a sense of religious nationalism and destiny. But, as we have seen, in the kind of analysis developed by Milton and apparently followed by Marvell, false religion is the foundation for a set of other ills. Whether the idolatry is imposed from outside the culture or embraced within the culture, it is likely to be used by a tyrannous regime to awe the populace into acceptance of arbitrary government. The Israelites are pictured in *Samson* as typical of those who have long suffered lack of discipline and morale, both before and after falling into servitude to foreign oppressors:

> But what more oft in nations grown corrupt,
> And by their vices brought to servitude,
> Than to love bondage more than liberty,
> Bondage with ease than strenuous liberty.
>
> (*Samson Agonistes*, lines 269–72)

The part of the Book of Judges which deals with Samson is a study of national disunity and lack of morale, and, perhaps most ironically, the educated reader of Milton's poem will know that even the temple disaster inflicted on the Philistines did not fuel a national resurgence. The Israelites, like the English perhaps, had God-given opportunities, but were not good at taking their chances. The poem engages the morale and spirit of a nation.[26]

Some of the subtlest effects of the poem concern the varying moods of the Israelites, their wonderfully differentiated states of doubt, disagreement, and resolve. In a cathartic rehearsal of conflicting opinion in a community of nevertheless pious men, it may be as important that there is communication between the Hebrews as that there is disagreement in the understanding of the mysteries of Providence. This is in agreement with *Of True Religion, Heresy, Schism, Toleration*, Milton's contribution of 1673 to the debate about toleration.[27] All men err, including God's champions, and it is more important for Protestants to seek together, in debate, than it is to labor divisions and define heresies in the adverse circumstances of the Clarendon Code, the series of measures seeking to control Puritan radicalism through the 1660s, fettering Dissenters, ejecting ministers, banning meetings, stopping academies, and forcing conformity on lay officials as well. To reforming spirits, this was a new bondage of conscience, Israel in a new idolatrous tyranny; and better toleration of Dissenters would form a major plank in Whig policy. As we have seen, the issue got entangled with the king's desire to ease penalties on Catholics.

In the context of fears of popery, Milton's participation in the debate over toleration was timed to encourage the right outcome of that debate. Following the Declaration of Indulgence of March 1672, he was supporting the more radical position, discriminating fundamentally between Protestant and Catholic schism, and bringing into play the old discourses of fear about Catholic effects on courts, citing the Gunpowder Plot and the infiltrations before the Civil War and opining that if England had been more disciplined in its true religion, it would not have invited the judgments of plague, fire, and war. "True Religion is the true Worship and Service of God, learnt and believed from the Word of God only," whilst "Popery is the only, or the greatest, heresy" (*The Complete Prose Works*, vol. VIII, p. 421). Here are the familiar associations, to be exploited by the Whigs. Catholicism is tainted with worldly power. What is needed is zealous laboring toward the truth, and as long as men seek diligently by their own lights in the Word of God schismatics should be tolerated, for only when such conscienceful seeking takes place can there be any hope of better religious discipline. Church authorities need not always be followed: "Every member of the Church, at least of any breeding or capacity, so well ought to be grounded in spiritual knowledg, as, if need be to examine their Teachers themselves" (p. 435). His arguments repeated many positions he had taken up in the 1640s and 1650s: in particular, he recast material he had used in *Of Civil Powers* (1659).

It is quite clear that this searching has a special purpose in times of adversity, as in this passage, referring to Job:

> But so long as all these profess to set the Word of God only before them as the Rule of faith and obedience; and use all diligence and sincerity of heart, by reading, by learning, by study, by prayer for Illumination of the holy spirit, to understand the Rule and obey it, they have done what man can do: God will assuredly pardon them, as he did the friends of *Job*, good and pious men, though much mistaken, as there it appears, in some Points of Doctrin.
>
> (*Of True Religion, The Complete Prose Works*, vol. VIII, p. 424)

This distinctive interpretation expresses a general situation in which, as in *Samson Agonistes*, the elect find it hard to understand the "unsearchable dispose" of God, and yet must for all that trust in divine justice and benevolence. On such bases of obedience and searching in times of trial, the actions turn in *Paradise Regained* and *Samson Agonistes*. Jesus' final triumph over Satan in the brief epic is in a trial of strength on the pinnacle in which the crucial factor is a total trust in the power of the true God. As with *Paradise Lost* these works show no simple retreat into an unpolitical world: they exploit deeply embedded ideological discourses and make statements about the fundamental disciplines of the mind, even as freedom of conscience for the Dissenters was being debated.

This chapter has suggested a convergence of discourses centering particularly on the 1670s. It does not seek to make the writings of Marvell and Milton say all the same things: despite the evident connections, it is obvious, for example, that Milton's determined republicanism,[28] as expressed particularly in his writings of 1659, is not quite matched by Marvell's more pragmatic dealings with limited monarchy (shared with most Whigs), and it would be wrong to seek unchanging politics in the writings of either, during the bewildering changes of this period. Nor is there a neat Whig consensus. What we seem to have is a crucial informing anti-Catholic discourse, a given base around which other arguments are organized and from which orientation is sought. On the one hand, this is a widely shared cultural discourse automatically shaping the utterances of those who identified with national Protestantism; on the other, it is a propagandistic counter which is obviously being used for political persuasion. In Milton's texts, it is part of a whole analysis of political process, which was understood by Marvell and others. This informing discourse is not marginal: it stands at the center of many texts, some of them very well-known texts, and the beginnings of Whiggery are as much founded on fear of Papists as they are on any more comfortable notions of liberalism.

NOTES

1 The canon of Marvell's poems is notoriously difficult to establish and particularly for the Restoration period. There is a brief summary in Warren L. Chernaik, *The Poet's Time: Politics and Religion in the Work of Andrew Marvell* (Cambridge: Cambridge University Press, 1983), Appendix A, pp. 206–14.

2 *An Account of the Growth of Popery, and Arbitrary Government in England, More Particularly, from the long Prorogation of November, 1675 ...* (London, 1677), p. 3. There has been no modern collected edition of Marvell's prose works since *The Complete Works in Verse and Prose of Andrew Marvell*, ed. A. B. Grosart, 4 vols. (London, 1872–75).

3 For example, in relation to the Gunpowder Plot alone: *A true and perfect relation of the whole proceedings against the late more barbarous traitors, Garnet a Jesuite, and his confederats ...* (London, 1679); Robert Widdrington, *The tryal and execution of Father Henry Garnet ...* (London, 1679); Antoine Arnauld, *The king-killing doctrine of the Jesuites ...* (London, 1679); Thomas Morton, *An exact account of the Romish doctrine: in the case of conspiracy and rebellion ...* (London, 1679). My thanks to Arthur F. Marotti for these references.

4 See Pierre Legouis, *Andrew Marvell: Poet, Patriot, Puritan*, second edn. (Oxford: Oxford University Press, 1968), p. 160. The phrase comes from the anonymous pamphlet, *A letter from Amsterdam, to a Friend in England* (London, 1678).

5 Letter to William Popple, 10 June 1678, in *The Poems and Letters of Andrew Marvell*, ed. H. M. Margoliouth, third edn., revised by Pierre Legouis with the collaboration of E. E. Duncan-Jones, 2 vols. (Oxford: Oxford University Press, 1971), vol. II, p. 357. Quoted in Legouis, *Andrew Marvell*, p. 160.

6 Legouis, *Andrew Marvell*, p. 225. The poem was first printed in *Poems on Affairs of State* (see note 10, below). It can be found in George de F. Lord et al. (eds.) *Poems on Affairs of State: Augustan Satirical Verse, 1660–1714*, 7 vols. (New Haven: Yale University Press, 1963–75), vol. I, pp. 436–37.

7 Legouis, *Andrew Marvell*, p. 227. The last chapter, "After Death" (pp. 224–44), is a brief review of Marvell's subsequent reputation.

8 *State Tracts: in two parts ... being a collection of several treatises relating to the government ...* (London, 1693).

9 *Mr. Andrew Marvell's Character of Popery* ... Printed for Richard Baldwin (London, 1689), pp. 3–4.

10 *Poems on Affairs of State: From the Time of Oliver Cromwell, to the Abdication of K. James the Second* (London, 1689, 1697, and later editions). In the 1697 edition, twelve satires were attributed to Marvell.

11 For a general account on Catholicism and Restoration politics, see John Miller, *Popery and Politics in England, 1660–1688* (Cambridge: Cambridge University Press, 1973).

12 An essay arguing a precise date for "Upon Appleton House" is Derek Hirst and Steven Zwicker, "High Summer at Nun Appleton, 1651: Andrew Marvell and Lord Fairfax's Occasions," *Historical Journal*, 36, 2 (1993), pp. 247–70.

13 Quotations are from *Andrew Marvell: a Critical Edition of the Major Works*, ed. Frank Kermode and Keith Walker (Oxford: Oxford University Press, 1990).

14 Chernaik's (*The Poet's Time*) is the only study devoted specifically to the Restoration writing of Marvell.

15 Letter of 9 August 1671, "To a Friend in Persia": Margoliouth, *Poems and Letters*, vol. II, pp. 324–25; Chernaik, *The Poet's Time*, p. 75.

16 "In Quintum Novembris"; "Lycidas," lines 161–63. See also the early verse paraphrases on Psalm 94 and Psalm 136, joining in the rejoicing at the failure of the Spanish Match.

17 An interesting case of an indirect contribution to the succession debate, not discussed here, is provided by Milton's issuing *A Declaration, or Letters Patent* (London, 1674), a translation of a document urging elective monarchy in Poland.

18 For a detailed analysis of the late seventeenth-century Whig assimilation of Milton's writings, see Nicholas von Maltzahn, "The Whig Milton, 1667–1700," in David Armitage, Armand Himy, and Quentin Skinner (eds.), *Milton and Republicanism* (Cambridge: Cambridge University Press, 1995), pp. 229–53. An earlier and less discriminating analysis of Milton's career in relation to the Whig tradition is George Senabaugh, *That Grand Whig Milton* (Stanford, CA: Stanford University Press, 1952).

19 Charles Blount, *A Just Vindication of Learning* (London, 1679); William Denton, *Jus Caesaris* (London, 1681); Matthew Tindal, *A Letter to a Member of Parliament* (London, 1698).

20 Thomas Hunt, *Mr. Hunt's Postscript* (London, 1682); Samuel Johnson, *Julian the Apostate* (London, 1682).

21 The line of evidence on *Paradise Lost* closely follows that in my *John Milton: A Literary Life* (Basingstoke and London: Macmillan, 1995), chapter 8, pp. 155–81. See also Mary Ann Radzinowicz, "The Politics of *Paradise Lost*," in Kevin Sharpe and Steven N. Zwicker (eds.), *Politics of Discourse: The Literature and History of Seventeenth-Century England* (Berkeley and Los Angeles: University of California Press, 1987), pp. 204–29; reprinted in Annabel Patterson (ed.), *John Milton* (London: Longman, 1992), pp. 120–41.

22 Quotations from *Milton: The Shorter Poems*, ed. John Carey (London and New York: Longman, second edn., 1997); and the companion volume *Milton: Paradise Lost*, ed. Alastair Fowler (revised edn., London and New York: Longman, 1971).

23 The line of evidence in this section is similar to that in my *John Milton*, chapter 9, pp. 182–207.

24 C. G. Crump (ed.), *The History of the Life of Thomas Ellwood* (New York and London, 1900), pp. 144–45.

25 See Cedric C. Brown, "Milton and the Idolatrous Consort," in Cedric C. Brown (ed.), "The Politics of Literature in Early Modern English Culture," a special number of *Criticism*, 35, 3 (1993), pp. 441–62.

26 The parallel analysis, not discussed in this chapter, is in *The History of Britain*, which has a fascinating publication history in the late seventeenth century. See Nicholas von Maltzahn, *Milton's "History of Britain": Republican Historiography in the English Revolution* (Oxford: Oxford University Press, 1991). See also Gary D. Hamilton, "The History of Britain and its Restoration Audience," in David Loewenstein and James G. Turner (eds.), *Politics, Poetics and Hermeneutics in Milton's Prose* (Cambridge: Cambridge University Press, 1990), pp. 241–55.

27 *The Complete Prose Works of John Milton*, ed. D. M. Wolfe et al., 8 vols. (New Haven: Yale University Press, 1953–82), vol. VIII, p. 421. On some effects of *Of True Religion* see Martin Dzelzainis, "Milton's Of True Religion and the Earl of Castlemaine," *The Seventeenth Century*, 7 (1992), pp. 53–69.

28 For a varied collection of essays on Milton's politics, see Armitage, Himy, Skinner, *Milton and Republicanism*. On republicanism see also Blair Worden, "Milton's Republicanism and the Tyranny of Heaven," in Gisela Block, Quentin Skinner, and Maurizio Viroli (eds.), *Machiavelli and Republicanism* (Cambridge: Cambridge University Press, 1990), pp. 225–45.

FURTHER READING

Achinstein, Sharon, *Milton and the Revolutionary Reader* (Princeton: Princeton University Press, 1994), esp. chapter 5, pp. 177–223.

Armitage, David, Himy, Armand, and Skinner, Quentin (eds.), *Milton and Republicanism* (Cambridge: Cambridge University Press, 1995).

Brown, Cedric C., *John Milton: A Literary Life* (Basingstoke and London: Macmillan, 1995).

Chernaik, Warren L., *The Poet's Time: Politics and Religion in the Work of Andrew Marvell* (Cambridge: Cambridge University Press, 1983).

Condren, Conal, and Cousins, A. D. (eds.), *The Political Identity of Andrew Marvell* (Aldershot and Brookfield, Vermont: Scolar Press, 1990).

Davies, Stevie, *Images of Kingship in "Paradise Lost": Milton's Politics and Christian Liberty* (Columbia, Missouri: University of Missouri Press, 1983).

Griffin, Dustin, *Regaining Paradise: Milton in the Eighteenth Century* (Cambridge: Cambridge University Press, 1986).

Hill, Christopher, *The Experience of Defeat: Milton and Some Contemporaries* (London and New York: Faber, 1984).

Keeble, N. H., *The Literary Culture of Nonconformity in Later Seventeenth-Century England* (Leicester: Leicester University Press, 1987).

Legouis, Pierre, *Andrew Marvell: Poet, Patriot, Puritan* (second edn., Oxford: Oxford University Press, 1968).

Loewenstein, David, *Milton and the Drama of History: Historical Vision, Iconoclasm and the Literary Imagination* (Cambridge: Cambridge University Press, 1990).

Miller, John, *Popery and Politics in England, 1660–1688* (Cambridge: Cambridge University Press, 1973).

Patterson, Annabel, *Marvell and the Civic Crown* (Princeton: Princeton University Press, 1978).

Patterson, Annabel (ed.), *John Milton* (Harlow: Longman, 1992).

Radzinowicz, Mary Ann, "The Politics of *Paradise Lost*," in Kevin Sharpe and Steven N. Zwicker (eds.), *Politics of Discourse: The Literature and History of Seventeenth-Century England* (Berkeley and Los Angeles: University of California Press, 1987).

9

STEVEN N. ZWICKER

John Dryden

Is there a writer in the history of English letters who more completely defines an age than John Dryden? His writing life coincides exactly with the second half of the seventeenth century: he was eighteen in 1649 when he published his first poem; his last work was finished a few weeks before his death in May 1700. Between the elegy for Lord Hastings and *The Secular Masque*, Dryden created what we have come to know as Restoration literature. He wrote in every mode and genre that thrived in these years; in most cases, Dryden's contributions outgo all rivals.

The creation of the poetry and drama, the translations and literary criticism, what we have come to know as *The Works of John Dryden*,[1] is an incomparable achievement from a writer whose early verse gave little indication of incomparability and whose career was variously driven by partisanship and faction, by professional alliance and literary rivalry, and by the incursion of something like a modern commercial market into the aristocratic precincts of literary patronage.[2] Without his writing, Restoration literature would be difficult to recognize; without his example, Augustan literature would have developed in quite different ways. Next to his, the careers of Marvell and Rochester seem brilliant but slight; even Milton's career, an achievement of which Dryden was sharply aware, does not display the variety of his younger rival's work. In prose Dryden excelled all others. What began as sheer enterprise came to conclusion in remarkable creation. Dryden's career shows unswerving development. Milton began after long delay; he had read in leisure, toured Italy, and aimed at the classical model: pastoral to epic. Dryden was hurried under the hand of Dr. Busby from Westminster School to Cambridge University and thence to London, minor service in Cromwell's government, and to his debut as public poet on the death of Oliver Cromwell.[3] Within months of the publication of *Heroique Stanza's to the Glorious Memory of ... Oliver Cromwell Late Lord Protector* (1659), Dryden began a career as Stuart apologist that would end only with his death in 1700.

There was not a moment in his career when Dryden lacked enterprise. There are times when the writing lacked, if not ambition, then genius. But he pursued the idea of literary profession unflaggingly, with learning and daring, and through every turn of Restoration politics. He wrote quickly and brilliantly; he could produce verse almost to order. Rather than constraining him, the demands, the intrigues, and the personalities of national and of literary politics released in Dryden the full measure of his talent. He was able to pursue sublime genres and exalted expression in compromising circumstance, often in defense of programs and positions that struck later generations – and more than a few of his contemporaries – as compromised, shabby, perhaps wishful and deluded. Out of such circumstances, and often in the midst of turmoil, came Dryden's quartos and folios, his plays, translations, and miscellanies. Dryden commemorated the death of the Lord Protector in 1659; he celebrated the return of Charles Stuart in 1660; he early courted the Lord Chancellor and the Lord Chancellor's daughter, the Duchess of York: throughout his career he attached himself to aristocratic patrons. He celebrated a damaging commercial war in the 1660s; he defended the court's impolitic moves toward Indulgence in the 1670s; he excoriated the king's enemies, denigrated the Popish Plot, and derided Exclusion in the 1680s; he mounted a brilliant and nearly unintelligible defense of James II and of his own conversion to Rome late in that king's reign; and after the revolution that deprived the king and his laureate of office (1688–89), Dryden spent a decade regretting the revolution and meditating on its politics and motives in a set of remarkable translations.

In triumph and humiliation Dryden was able to summon the muse. But the beginnings did not augur anything so lofty as Dryden's career, in fact they seemed to augur hardly anything at all. The beginnings are recorded in the verse that Dryden contributed to *Lachrymae Musarum* (1649), a collection of elegies on the death of Henry, Lord Hastings. Son and heir of the Earl of Huntingdon, Henry died on 24 June 1649; his death was lamented by aristocrats and Royalist poets, among them the Earl of Westmorland and Lord Falkland, Charles Cotton, Robert Herrick, and John Denham.[4] What prompted such a group to lament the death by smallpox of this nineteen-year-old? Six months earlier, Charles I had been executed. That event was not only a political climacteric, it changed the course of writing. The most immediate evidence was the production in 1649 of thirty-five editions of the king's own book, the *Eikon Basilike*. But on other occasions, and in less direct forms, the death was also recorded. The demise of Lord Hastings offered such an opportunity to recall that "unforgettable blasphemy"; the conflation of the two deaths is echoed throughout *Lachrymae Musarum*. Dryden joined the chorus of outrage in an ambitious appearance. The verse elegy would become one of Dryden's most expressive and elastic forms, but the elegy on Hastings is thoroughly conventional. What are of interest, though strained and self-conscious, are the rhetorical figures, the materials of classical antiquity, the allusions to science, history, and art, and of course the shadow of contemporary politics.

Between the elegy on Hastings and Dryden's next poem, *Heroique Stanza's* (1659), almost a decade elapsed: the only hiatus in this career. Perhaps *Heroique Stanza's* should be considered the real beginning of the career for the poem is remarkably poised. The rhymed quatrains are borrowed from Sir William Davenant's *Gondibert* (1651), but the quality of expression is Dryden's own, fluent and exact. Dryden surveys the achievements of the Lord Protector; he admires the boldness, the military prowess, and political force, but by contrast with Marvell's bathos in *A Poem upon the Death of O.C.*, Dryden seems unmoved. The debut in *Heroique Stanza's* must have been a calculation, an effort to win attention by a young poet who joined Edmund Waller and John Denham as junior partner in an enterprise called *Three Poems on the Death of His Lord Highness* (1659).[5] The poem was a gamble and it turned out to be a mistake. His detractors never let Dryden forget that in 1659 he had lamented the death of the "usurper," and within months composed an elaborate panegyric to welcome home the son and heir of Charles I.

One more beginning: *Astraea Redux* (1660), Dryden's poem on the return of Charles II. Here finally affect and technique are joined. The nation as a whole celebrated the bloodless restoration of the person of the king and the institution of monarchy. Dryden's poem stands out among the more than one hundred panegyrics composed for the occasion. It is long, a third as long as some books of *Paradise Lost*; it is learned, full of analogies, of mythology, and Scripture; and here first appears that most telling comparison between two kings, "Thus banish'd *David* spent abroad his time, / When to be Gods Anointed was his Crime."[6] Dryden was not the only poet to see in the careers and persons of David and Charles an invitation to compare; but in years to come he would exploit the analogy in ways none could have imagined in 1660. In *Astraea Redux* the Davidic analogy and, more broadly, scriptural allusion argue a prophetic order for restored monarchy. But the recourse to sacred history raises more complex historiographical and interpretive issues for the whole of Restoration culture: after a decade of Puritan scripturalism, after the repudiation of the politics of inspiration, and after the restoration of a court fixed from early days on oblivion and pleasure what public force might Scripture hold? Much has been made of the hardened libertinism, even the pornographic character, of court culture in the years after the king's return; what also needs to be acknowledged is the continued presence of Scripture, the force of sacred history in so many articulations of Restoration programs and personalities. The true model of this culture insists both on the tensions and the colloquy between sacred and profane texts.

Scripture and prophecy have recuperative force in *Astraea Redux*, but the poem plays out other restorative themes: "Oh Happy Age! Oh times like those alone / By Fate reserv'd for Great *Augustus* Throne! / When the joint growth of Armes and Arts foreshew / The world a Monarch, and that Monarch *You*" (vol. 1, p. 24). Virgil is resonant in these lines, so too is the conjoining of arts and empire. The intimacy of the first Caroline court with visual and literary culture was not to be ignored in polemicizing the second. Perhaps Dryden's lines are a bid for personal favor, but they also announce the cultural meaning of monarchy as a system of patronage that assured the revival of arts within the refurbishing empire. Such an assertion blandly elides the cultural, to say nothing of the military, achievements of the Commonwealth and Protectorate, but we could hardly expect evenhanded appraisal in these acts of oblivion.

Dryden produced more occasional verse and several influential plays in the first years of the Restoration, but the most significant achievements were *Annus Mirabilis* (1666) and the *Essay of Dramatic Poesy* (1668). The poem is ambitious and clever, an experiment in which Dryden practiced intellection and strategy. The *Essay of Dramatic Poesy*, by contrast, is mature and brilliant. It is Dryden's first effort at literary theory and one of the most elegant and important contributions to criticism between Sidney's *Apology for Poesy* (1587) and Pope's *Essay On Criticism* (1711). We might see *Annus Mirabilis* and *An Essay of Dramatic Poesy* as companion pieces, experiments in new forms, but the prose is more knowing, more sophisticated than the verse.

There are however effects in *Annus Mirabilis* worth noting. It occupied an important moment in Dryden's career and in the career of Restoration literature. Dryden's subjects are military exploit and civic fortitude: the triumph of the English navy over the Dutch, the triumph of London over war, fire, and plague. The poem also celebrates the heroism, suffering, and magnanimity of the king; but its real aim is less celebration than defense and diffusion.

Faced with war, fire, and plague, and with poems, pamphlets, and sermons savagely denouncing its quality, the court struck back, and *Annus Mirabilis* was one of its most important texts. The poem would refurbish and reinterpret: it uses the schemes and devices of providential history to denounce political radicalism, to rehearse the effects of the usurper's hand, to see fire and plague as the last vestiges of a program that had, in the 1650s, brought the nation low. Whatever its value as polemical warfare, the poem proved an invaluable exercise in the creation of a high polemical style. With the Restoration, myths of commonweal and commonality had been restored; the king proposed and parliament voted an Act of Indemnity and Oblivion (1660). But few had forgotten the past, and by the mid-1660s, in fierce satire, in the truculent responses of parliament, and in the hounding from office of Lord Chancellor Clarendon, a sense of formidable opposition had begun to coalesce. None, however, proposed a return to civil war. What emerged, rather, was the first evidence of party politics. By the end of this century, the facts of opposition had become central to politics as well as to aesthetics. The first moves toward acknowledging a political culture of opposition were taken in the satires of the 1660s. *Annus Mirabilis* suggested that it was not the opposition alone that could invoke such a muse.

We have said nothing of the dedication and elaborate preface to *Annus Mirabilis*, and the role such texts would play in Dryden's mature work and in Restoration literature more generally. The dedication of *Annus Mirabilis* and Dryden's "account of the poem" are central to its polemical work; the preface indicates a shrewd awareness of the role of literary theory in the production and reception of poetry, in the twinning of aesthetics and politics, and an expanded notion of what constitute the texts of a work of literature. In the brilliant reprisals of Swift's *Tale of a Tub* (1704) and in the apparatus to Pope's *Dunciad* (1728) we see the legacy of Dryden's performance in prefaces and dedications. They provided sites for the development of literary theory and for literary experimentation, and they leave us a record of the relations between patronage and production, and between production and consumption.

An Essay of Dramatic Poesy (1668) is Dryden's first sustained work in literary theory and in practical criticism. Here Dryden reviews the topics that will become central themes of Restoration criticism: wit, rhyme, and the dramatic unities; the mixing of genres and the imitation of nature; the war of the ancients and moderns; and the rivalry of French and English aesthetics. Dryden's rehearsal of these topics is casual and brilliant, and they recur throughout the criticism of the age: in Milton's truncated critical exercises that preface *Paradise Lost* and *Samson Agonistes* and in more sustained pieces of critical writing from Sir Robert Howard and Thomas Rymer to Jeremy Collier and John Dennis. The *Essay* not only fixes the topics of critical debate, it helps formulate a national style, that loose and flexible aesthetic that defines so much of Restoration literary practice. The king's taste for French whores and French manners may have inflected the tone, even the politics, of the Restoration court, but the *Essay* reminds us that the relations between native and foreign sensibilities, even sensualities, were very much in negotiation in the 1660s, that French neoclassicism did not sweep native genius aside, and that earlier English drama would prove crucial to the unfolding of English aesthetics.

Such issues are central to the *Essay of Dramatic Poesy* as well as to the practical business of creating a new drama for the English stage in the 1660s, an effort that includes Dryden's *The Rival Ladies* (1664); *The Indian Queen* (1665), which Dryden wrote in collaboration with Sir Robert Howard; the *Indian Emperour* (1667); Howard's *The Duke of Lerma* (1668); and the Earl of Orrery's *Mustapha* (1665). But the *Essay* seems the theatrical masterpiece of the 1660s, a drama whose subject is literary theory, whose setting is Anglo-Dutch war, and whose method is colloquy and contest. The characterizations of Lord Buckhurst, Sir Robert Howard, Sir Charles Sedley, and Dryden's own self-presentation as Neander are pointed, subtle, and sustained. The *Essay* displays not only Dryden's capacity to orchestrate ideas and dramatize abstractions, but his wide and sophisticated knowledge of English and European drama. It illustrates Dryden's fluent knowledge of both theory and practice and his grasp of the state of English theatre. Late in the decade he began to think more directly on how that drama could combine the concerns of epic literature with the resources of the stage.

Restoration culture, we were once told, denied epic invention. The turmoil of civil war, the barrenness of the Commonwealth, the libertinism of the restored court could hardly sustain the heroic imagination. Such literary history was naive in its cultural biases and wrong in many of its particulars, but it forces us to think about the emergence of the sublime after 1660. The formulation of an epic drama, the perfection of the genre, and the vivid critical debate over its character and quality all point to the status of epic in this age. Rather than witness their demise, the Restoration witnessed the flourishing of epic forms. Surely *Paradise Lost* (1667) and Dryden's translation of Virgil's *Aeneas* (1697) rival Spenser's *Faerie Queene* (1590) and Edward Fairfax's translation of *La Gerusalemme Liberata* (1600) as they do Pope's *Dunciad* (1728) and his *Homer* (1715). But neither *Paradise Lost* nor Dryden's *Virgil* are now placed at the center of Restoration culture. *Paradise Lost* was written against that center; rather than a celebration of imperium, it is a hymn to forbearance and denial, an epic of exile and loss. We have been taught to imagine *Paradise Lost* as a leviathan beached on the shores of an alien culture, but Restoration readers heard in this text a powerful engagement with the themes and sources of their own political authority. The poem may not have won broad acceptance at publication (it would be more than two decades before the epic was taken up as cultural icon), but it surely registered in the literary awareness of its contemporaries, and with no one more vividly than with Dryden.[7]

Indeed, Dryden's most pointed encounter with Milton took place over the body of *Paradise Lost* in an adaptation that Dryden called *The State of Innocence* (1677). Milton's thousands of lines are here reduced to a handful of theatrical scenes, his masterful Protestant epic narrowed, indeed miniaturized – perhaps even mocked – in Dryden's dedication of the *State of Innocence* to the Roman Catholic bride of the Roman Catholic Duke of York, to the point of irony. Not all of Dryden's literary relations are so dominated by his competitive drive. His responses to Shakespeare are deeper and more sympathetic; surely *All for Love* (1678) is the great theatrical adaptation of the age. Like *The State of Innocence*, it condenses a vast amount of material; unlike *The State of Innocence*, the result is not trivializing. *All for Love* concentrates the power of *Antony and Cleopatra*: the movement is unified, the freedom of Shakespeare's blank verse maintained, the language richly figurative. Dryden's meditation on pleasure and on civic care is mindful both of the Jacobean complexity of the original and of the contemporary meaning of such themes. Dryden's encounters with Jonson and Shakespeare, like his meditations on Latin poetry, are dominated by the will to reshape the past but in ways that might accommodate the pleasures and the anxieties – literary as well as political – of the present.

Indeed the virulence of literary politics in the Restoration certainly outgoes even the jealousies and rivalries that run through Jacobean letters. That very rivalry opened a space for epic energies but now in inverted, mocked, and miniaturized forms. Literary mockery had a distinguished history, but Dryden's *Mac Flecknoe* (1682) is the opening move in something rather grander than mockery. Not only does Dryden treat his contemporaries to a brilliant and topical routing of dulness, he enlarges the scope of literary satire into a near epic kind. The attack on Richard Flecknoe and Thomas Shadwell is blunt and damaging, at points wonderfully crude, but the literary texture of the poem is unnervingly elegant. The poet's sources are elevated and disparate: Virgil, Horace, and Juvenal; Shakespeare and Jonson; Milton, Cowley, Waller, and Cleveland; Shadwell and Flecknoe. The machinery is elaborate, outsized; the target might seem hardly worth the effort. But the aim of mock heroic is not simply to crush the opposition beneath classical culture and contemporary letters; it is to indict the whole quality of the opposition, to call into question their aesthetic principles and practices, their manners and morals, and of course to implicate art in politics and here in political succession. *The Dunciad* (1728) is the masterpiece of the genre, but Swift too understood the implications of *Mac Flecknoe*.

Dryden's work in the 1670s had been largely theatrical, and there is no question that the stage encouraged literary sophistication and economy. But neither the nondramatic verse nor the theatrical writing of the first two decades prepares us for the masterpiece of 1681. Indeed there is nothing in all of Dryden's verse quite as brilliant, capacious, and nuanced as the opening dozen lines of *Absalom and Achitophel*. Certainly there is no partisan verse that can make the claims of high art so rightly allowed for this poem. Andrew Marvell had posed, with the utmost delicacy, questions of political legitimacy and engagement in *An Horatian Ode* (1650); but *An Horatian Ode* seems to argue the impossibility of partisanship in the midst of crisis. *Absalom and Achitophel* does not have the luxury of disinterestedness; it claims the protection of political neutrality, but Dryden's poem is bitterly and brilliantly partisan. Dryden seems to be the instrument of all the energy and anxiety, the suspicion, even distemper released by the Popish Plot, that baroque fabrication of "evidence" that the king's Roman Catholic wife and brother had hatched a plot to murder Charles and place the Duke of York on the throne. Written in extremely close quarters to the Exclusion Crisis – and perhaps at the behest of the king himself and certainly with the knowledge and approval of the court[8] – the poem engages with all the principals of Exclusion. It is crowded with contemporary portraits and caricature, with slanders and accusations and set pieces of praise; with civic theory and political argument; with speeches and dramatic colloquy – that is, with all the intimacy and particulars to which this servant of the court was privy. Could the daring slight to the queen – "a Soyl ungrateful to the Tiller's care" (line 12) – have been written without the knowledge of the king? But for all the poem's proximity to civic authority, it is set neither at Whitehall nor Oxford, but in an indeterminate biblical past. While its plots and portraits may be those of Charles II's reign, the poem claims sacred history throughout. But the allegory of *Absalom and Achitophel* does not hide the politics or arguments of the laureate; nor does sacred history render oblique or obscure the application of tenor to vehicle. Dryden's biblical analogy exploits a long tradition of scriptural parallel at once to suggest the sanctity of Royalist politics and to mock the heated scripturalism of the crown's enemies and opponents. The applications of sacred history to English politics reach back to the middle decades of the century, and earlier; such scripturalism had achieved a frenzied height in the triumph of the Puritan theocracy:

Cromwell's army marched to battle singing David's psalms; they took Lord Jesus to be their king. But the appropriation of sacred history was not confined to one party, nor can the role of Scripture in political life be narrowed to one decade. Of course, by 1681 we need to allow irony as well as admonition in proximity to sacred metaphor, but *Absalom and Achitophel* gives vivid evidence of the flexibility and continuing power of sacred politics late in the century, fully three decades after the execution of the king and the triumph of militant Puritanism.

Absalom and Achitophel was not the only essay in the politics of sacred history to emerge from the Exclusion Crisis. John Locke's *Two Treatises of Government* (c. 1679–80) was in many ways a similar act of imagination, and the text that most clearly links Locke's radical tenets and Dryden's Tory apologetics is Sir Robert Filmer's *Patriarcha* (1680). That treatise was conceived half a century before Exclusion; its language is archly Royalist and absolutist.[9] *Patriarcha* conjures up a Jacobean political world more than it does Exclusionary politics, but it was in fact a text first published in 1681 and then widely read, often quoted, and vigorously refuted in Exclusion. Indeed, the quality and thoroughness of the refutation are as much an acknowledgment of the power of scriptural politics in the 1680s as are the actual uses of patriarchalism in Royalist polemic.

If we were to judge the status of patriarchalism by that touchstone of Royalist poetry, *Absalom and Achitophel*, we might well be surprised by the central role of patriarchalism in the pamphlet literature of Exclusion. Dryden's poem handles patriarchalism cautiously, often ironically. The poet is aware of the absolutist implications of Filmer's text, perhaps even of its French overtones, but he understands as well the authority of foundational myths and histories. *Absalom and Achitophel* has much to teach us about the uses of poetry for polemic and about the management of political satire. The poem also instructs us in the character of political thought late in this age. While it is hardly a sustained piece of political argument – its theory of governance is threadbare, all compromise, metaphor, and innuendo – the text is shrewdly attuned to all the idioms of political argumentation. It suggests both the conservatism of the late seventeenth century and the precariousness of Royalist political theory.

The months following the defeat of Exclusion were buoyant and optimistic for the crown and for the Tory cause. The king's authority had been reaffirmed, and he ruled for the next three years without summoning a parliament. When the Duke of York came to the throne, his first parliament voted him the largest annuity that any monarch had yet enjoyed. And this renewed sense of authority is certainly expressed in the literature. *Absalom and Achitophel* is its masterpiece, but there is a substantial and an exuberant literature of the Exclusion Crisis which includes not only pamphlets, broadsides, and squibs but the satires of John Oldham, Tom Durfey, Nahum Tate, and Roger L'Estrange, and the brilliant and intricate theatrical allegory of Thomas Otway's *Venice Preserv'd* (1682).

Dryden himself produced not only *Absalom and Achitophel* but a number of theatrical prologues and epilogues that reflected on the crisis; he collaborated with Nahum Tate on *The Second Part* of *Absalom and Achitophel* (1682), and he produced a vindictive political satire called *The Medal*. The harsh tone of this satire should not surprise in the context of Exclusion pamphleteering, but set against the remarks regretting partisanship and passion that the poet himself makes in the preface to *Absalom and Achitophel*, the spirit of *The Medal* might seem disturbing. Dryden's satire is a vivid reminder that politics in the 1680s were hardly polite; losing a political struggle meant more than the diminution of civic authority: one anti-court satirist was executed for a libel against the king (1681), and theorists of republicanism in these years risked the block.

Yet in 1682 Dryden also began a short career as a religious poet; in the midst of Exclusion Crisis turmoil came the first of Dryden's two major religious poems: *Religio Laici*. The poem seems a halcyon moment within a partisan whirlwind:

> Dim, as the borrow'd beams of Moon and Stars
> To lonely, weary, wandring Travellers,
> Is Reason to the Soul: And as on high,
> Those rowling Fires discover but the Sky
> Not light us here; So Reason's glimmering Ray
> Was lent, not to assure our doubtfull way,
> But guide us upward to a better Day.   (vol. I, p. 311)

The body of *Religio Laici* engages seriously and sagaciously with issues of faith and belief: it offers a history of religious thought, weighs the rival claims of natural religion and pagan piety, and addresses the infallibility of Scripture and the status of tradition in revealed religion. These themes reappear in *The Hind and the Panther* (1687); and the learning in divinity that Dryden displays in both texts suggests the depth of his intellectual engagement with religious vocation. Indeed the Restoration saw the production and consumption of enormous quantities of religious writing: sermons and religious pamphlets, scriptural manuals, redactions, and paraphrases. And yet religious poetry published by a servant of the court who had achieved not simply a civic voice but public notoriety could not easily have been received as the meditations of a private man.

In *Religio Laici* Dryden makes strenuous profession of privacy and laity;

and the text of his poem provides an elegant demonstration of his ability to write meditative as well as satiric verse. But in both preface and poem *Religio Laici* often veers closer to satire than to meditation. A man might prefer the quiet of his study to polemical tumult, but to publish a confession of faith in 1682 was to pronounce civic engagement. The civil wars had powerful religious motives; the Exclusion Crisis was an effort to bar a Roman Catholic from the throne; the Glorious Revolution aimed to remove that Roman Catholic and his heirs from rule; and the Act of Settlement (1701) forever barred Roman Catholics from the English monarchy. *Religio Laici* is the laureate's expression of the Anglican confession at a moment when he must have found the argument of religious quietism as strategic as the expression of polemical savagery. More such expression would be forthcoming in James II's reign.

How are we to understand *The Hind and the Panther*? The poem was written in 1687, a time if not verging on crisis, certainly of political anxiety. The poem is a defense of James II's policy of Indulgence – the king's efforts to remove by royal declaration the restrictions and penalties levied by parliament against Roman Catholics; but more largely it is a defense of Roman Catholicism itself and of a monarch who was alienating his most powerful allies and who would soon make flight under cover of darkness from London to St. Germain. *The Hind and the Panther* is also an act of self-defense and spiritual redefinition. The Protestant laureate who had been raised in a Puritan household and educated at a university that was a stronghold of Puritanism in the 1650s was now a Roman Catholic. The exact date of the conversion is not known, but by the time Dryden wrote *The Hind and the Panther* he was willing to make the conversion public. There is a body of scholarship on the question of Dryden's conversion, much of it an effort to show the logical steps between *Religio Laici* and the conversion to the Roman faith.[10] But *Religio Laici* is a confession of Anglican faith. Dryden had long made a case for deploring the politics, if not the spirituality, of sectarian dissent. But the Anglican quietism of *Religio Laici* is no step on the road to Rome. In a political community scarred by religious controversy, a nation that held pope-burning processions and hailed the memory of Queen Elizabeth as defender against the Roman antichrist, conversion to Roman Catholicism was no simple matter. And Dryden was among the very few converts at the court of James II. Perhaps the Earl of Sunderland was a more important catch; but Sunderland promptly converted back after James's flight. Dryden alone among the prominent converts remained attached to his new faith. As he poignantly noted after the Revolution, "I know not what Church to go to, if I leave the Catholique."[11] Nor would the public relations involved in the reclamation of Protestant faith have been an easy matter for Dryden at this date in a career of conversion and partisanship.

But *The Hind and the Panther* is more than apologetics and self-defense. It is Dryden's most ambitious piece of original verse. The poem is composed of allegories, parables, puzzles, mysteries, and prophecies; it is formally a beast fable, but the fable is so outsized, so intricate and learned that its relations to fable seem ironic and distant. Such complexity afforded cover and aesthetic enterprise; into its turning structure Dryden folded personal apologia, official defense, religious satire, spiritual meditation, and a variety of prophecies and anxieties. The poem is a device of wonderful complexity and invention; and its determinedly literary character shows us a poet fully conversant with the native fabling tradition, in the debt of Chaucer and Spenser, and ever the keen student of Virgil. *The Hind and the Panther* is Dryden's most confessional piece of writing, and it marks a turning point in his career. It accurately predicts the political disasters of James's regime, though the prediction is so closeted within the fable of the poem that it makes but a very oblique appearance. What the poem openly foretells is the brilliant last turn of Dryden's career. Who could have predicted literary triumph out of displacement and defeat? Dryden seemed, by the end of James's reign, old and out of luck. He had lost pension and prestige in the Revolution of 1688, yet now would begin the most remarkable phase of his literary career: a return to the theatre, 24,000 lines of the best English Virgil yet made, and a brilliant collection of translations from ancient and modern poets known as *Fables*. The sheer production of the last decade is remarkable; more remarkable is the quality of the writing, the expressiveness of the poetry, the intimacy and candor of the prose, and always the sense of continuous invention.

The theatrical masterpiece of the 1690s is Dryden's *Don Sebastian*. Or rather, since the former laureate would encourage the work of a coterie of young dramatists – among them Southerne, Etherege, and Congreve – it would be more accurate to call *Don Sebastian* the theatrical masterpiece of the Glorious Revolution. In fact, it is the literary masterpiece of that crisis, for the Glorious Revolution was a political crisis unlike any other in this century. It has been argued that the Glorious Revolution wrought a more profound change on the body politic than the civil wars;[12] certainly the Revolution was a momentous event compared with the Exclusion Crisis. The earlier crises of this century produced civic turmoil and cultural ferment; we rightly associate the crises at mid-century with the literary, political, and intellectual careers of John Milton and Andrew Marvell. The Restoration and nearly every significant crisis for the next thirty years are forcefully articulated in cultural forms. The Exclusion Crisis produced a feast of narrations and representations. But the Glorious Revolution was acceded to in near silence. There were of course conventional efforts – official panegyrics, crudely satirical squibs on James and his wife, Mary of Modena, on the birth of their son, James Francis Edward Stuart, and then on William and Mary. But the muse was remarkably silent in the days and months following William's landing at Torbay. The outstanding cultural monument of the Glorious Revolution turns out not to have been a celebration of the triumph of liberty but a tragedy which discovers in the failed heroics of a Portuguese king and the brutality of an infidel warrior the long shadow of English politics.

Such a conjunction of affairs predicts much of the fate of high culture in the coming decade. Not that the production of great literature excludes political defeat, or exile and despair. Consider Hobbes writing *Leviathan* in Paris, Milton's remarkable productivity in the 1660s, or the example of Edward Hyde, the Earl of Clarendon, writing his subtle and brilliant history of the Revolution in exile, first after civil war, and then in personal ruin in France when he had been driven from office in 1667. Dryden's career evokes exactly this model. But the 1690s were not a propitious time altogether for high culture. Profound structural changes in English politics were underway: a European war would determine the course of its politics, economy, and foreign policy for the next century and more. The 1690s proved to be years not so much for literary invention as for fabling, paraphrase, and translation.

Jacobites remained true to the cause of James II, but the nation as a whole had no such political mission. Yet it was not Jacobites alone who took cover under fabling and translation. More editions of Aesop were produced in the 1690s than in any previous decade of the century. One conclusion we might draw about the relations between politics and culture from this decade is that wariness and uncertainty, more than turmoil and change, quelled the muse. The legitimacy of William III's authority and title was worried throughout the decade: in satires, in assassination attempts, in votes of association. Programs of moral reform, societies for the improvement of manners, and charitable foundations flourished in the 1690s, but alongside the decade's overt moralism lay an uncertainty about the legal authority of the government. The unsteady relations between moral reform and political legitimacy surely recall the 1650s; both decades had begun in usurpation and conquest; and both were undermined by moral uncertainty and defined in their literatures by indirection and unsteadiness. Obliqueness and innuendo are the safest modes for troubled times. Whether you are intent on hiding dangerous opinions or simply uncertain of what to say, fable and translation offer shelter, a space in which to negotiate a voice.

How prescient of Dryden to have begun a career of fabling not in the winter of 1689 but in the summer of 1687 when he must have sensed that the girders underpinning the Stuart regime were beginning to tremble. He would later write in *Fables* (1700):

> What should the People do, when left alone?
> The Governor, and Government are gone.
> The publick Wealth to Foreign Parts convey'd;
> Some Troops disbanded, and the rest unpaid.
> Rhodes is the Soveraign of the Sea no more;
> Their Ships unrigg'd, and spent their Naval Store;
> They neither could defend, nor can pursue,
> But grind their Teeth, and cast a helpless view. (vol. IV, p. 1757)

The verse is Boccaccio's but the language clearly intimates the Revolution and its settlement. The mood, poignant and bitter, is one that we find throughout the 1690s. What is to be done when authority has been wrested from weak but legitimate hands? Marvell had posed the question in 1649; the relations between power and legitimacy are crucial to Dryden's writing in the whole of the 1690s: they drive *Don Sebastian* and they are at the center of the *Aeneid* or, rather, at the center of how Dryden sought to translate the epic of Latin empire and eternity. The troubled relations between power and authority run like a bright thread through his Virgil and through the translations and original verse of *Fables*. And though they were not Dryden's alone, the answers he achieved in the 1690s form the most moving legacy of the Revolution and the most enduring expression of Jacobitism.

New work of course appeared late in the decade; Swift began the *Tale of A Tub* in 1697; Defoe had begun to write in the 1690s, and the most perfect examples of the comedy of manners date from the last years of this decade. But for students of high culture, the center of the 1690s must be Dryden's *Virgil*.

> What Virgil wrote in the vigour of his Age, in Plenty and at Ease, I have undertaken to Translate in my Declining Years: struling with Wants, oppress'd with Sickness, curb'd in my Genius, lyable to be misconstrued in all I write; and my Judges, if they are not very equitable, already prejudic'd against me, by the Lying Character which has been given them of my Morals.
>
> (vol. III, p. 1424)

Perhaps there is self-dramatization here, a hint of self-pity, but it must have seemed daunting, even to so prodigious a worker as Dryden, to begin a project late in his life, late in his century, that he may have suspected he would not live to complete. It turned out not to be Dryden's last project, not in fact by some measure. But there are summative effects in the Virgilian project that are worth noting as we look back across the decades of Dryden's career and his time.

The poet's apprenticeship in the Virgilian line began early.[13] There is a suggestion of Virgil in the Cromwell verses and in *Astraea Redux*; we can hear Virgil in *Annus Mirabilis* and in the heroic drama; Virgil is a subtext in *Mac Flecknoe*, a presence in *Absalom and Achitophel*, and crucial to the political and prophetic gestures in *The Hind and the Panther*. We can watch Dryden experimenting with the translation of Virgil in *Sylvae* (1685), and in the miscellanies that Jacob Tonson published in 1693 and 1694. The consolidation of this work began in the spring of 1694 when Dryden signed a contract with Tonson for a translation to consist of the *Georgics*, *Pastorals*, and the *Aeneid*. The 1697 *Virgil* is then a culmination of years of affiliation and affinity. Some have thought it was the epic which Dryden could never bring off, but if we see *The Works of Virgil* as substitution or displacement, we construct a false model not only of Dryden's career but as well of the mood of the late seventeenth century. For three decades Dryden worked rapidly and steadily as public poet, as dramatist to a commercial theatre, and as literary theorist. His career bore no resemblance to the careful constructions that Spenser and Milton made of their work. They were epic poets by design, literary career was an important act of self-fashioning. Jonson's career, in a different way, also suggests studious self-presentation. Dryden could not have entertained such designs when he contributed to *Lachrymae Musarum* or *Three Poems on the Death of O.C.*. These he conceived as opportunities, not for a career as Renaissance poet but for something humbler, not yet for Grub Street but for patronage and profession. The late seventeenth century saw the transformation of the career in letters from membership in the priesthood of Mount Parnassus to commercial enterprise, and Dryden's ambition for place, his work in the theatre both early in his career and late, even his *Virgil* we must understand in terms both of professional needs and something akin to poetic furor. He did everything to qualify himself for both worlds, but he belonged fully to neither. He was not completely the patronized servant of the great man, not a Spenser in the household of a magnate, but neither was he Swift, Defoe, or Johnson. And the way in which he would go about producing his *Virgil* is an emblem of the transitional point that his career identifies.

The *Virgil* is a translation of one culture into the idioms of another; it is a steady and lofty and moving meditation on the price that empire exacts from a nation. But the *Virgil* is also a business transaction. And happily for our awareness of its position both in the life of the poet and in his culture, the contract for the *Virgil* has been preserved: so many lines for so many guineas.[14] Dryden was writing not only to claim his identity as the English Virgil, he was also working as a professional and ever, as writers are, suspicious of the motives of his publisher. The correspondence that survives between Dryden and Tonson is brusque and wary on both sides, concerned with the production of a book and not with the transmission of a culture. But clearly, the poet, if not the publisher, had both aims in mind.

In the transmission of antiquity, this English *Virgil* occupies a crucial place. The seventeenth century was a time in England, and throughout Europe, when Virgil stood very high. The number of Virgil translations into modern languages from this age is striking as is the number of efforts in England alone, from Richard Stanyhurst in 1582 to Dryden's contemporary, Richard Maitland, fourth Earl of Lauderdale. Dryden was aware of the cultural preeminence of Virgil as a European master. But surely the presence of Virgil in English literary and political culture was not the same at the beginning of Dryden's career as by its end. We are familiar with the term Augustan as a description of literature of the late seventeenth and early eighteenth centuries. But that literature was not Augustan in 1660. The central book of English literary culture at mid-century was the Bible. Scripture dominated the idioms of culture and politics. This was not quite so in 1700. The turn in English culture between 1650 and 1700 might best be understood by considering how Virgil's *Aeneid* replaced the Holy Scriptures as the central book of literature. By the late seventeenth century we are steadily aware of the Roman idioms of English literature; *pietas* had replaced piety, and the Virgilian sublime had replaced sacred passion as the height of literary expression. Of course, the displacement of Scripture by Virgil is a signature, an emblem rather than an outline or an anatomy. But the creation of an Augustan age depended on the honoring of certain texts, and Virgil's epic poem occupied the most important place.

Dryden tells us that he had hoped to lay the new *Virgil* at the feet of his old master, but he knew by 1697 that he could not delay for that event. He would not, however, dedicate the book to William III. Perhaps William was the best of a bad lot – language which Dryden gives to Virgil as the Latin poet instructs the elective monarch, Augustus Caesar, on the proprieties and dangers of such an office. But in his patrons and among the aristocrats to whom he dedicates various pieces of his book, Dryden celebrates the political world that he had lost. Dorset, Ormonde, Abingdon, Orrery, Ailesbury – these were the men and the families whom he had long honored and whose names would be affixed to his book.[15] Dryden's *Virgil* was both a commercial success and a literary masterpiece, a fitting text for solace and fame. The *Virgil* was a summary of the career and a crucial point in the creation of Augustan literature.

But the career was not over when Dryden made the corrections and postscript to the *Virgil*. He signed another contract with Tonson for more translations, this time from ancient and modern authors. *Fables* (1700) is a more miscellaneous effort than *The Works of Virgil*, but not a lesser masterpiece. There is a trial here for a new Homer and translations from Boccaccio, Ovid, and Chaucer. There are also several original pieces, including an elegant verse epistle to his cousin John Driden and a lavish panegyric to the Duchess of Ormonde. Best of all is the capacious *Preface* to *Fables*, Dryden's most beautiful piece of critical writing:

> 'Tis with a Poet, as with a Man who designs to build, and is very exact, as he supposes, in casting up the Cost beforehand: But, generally speaking, he is mistaken in his Account, and reckons short of the Expence he first intended: He alters his Mind as the Work proceeds, and will have this or that Convenience more, of which he had not thought when he began. So has it hapned to me; I have built a House, where I intended a Lodge: Yet with better Success than a certain Nobleman, who beginning with a Dog-kennil, never liv'd to finish the Palace he had contriv'd.   (vol. IV, p. 1444)

The intimacy and ease of voice are characteristic of the whole; it is as if Dryden spoke directly across these pages. While the prose is informal, even digressive, it has a superb economy; there is not a wasted breath here. The effects are now second nature, for we have the illusion of the poet's words wholly without art. And this is true for much of the writing of the last decade. Not all is so condensed and fluent as the prose of the *Preface* to *Fables*, but the best of Dryden's work of the 1690s achieves exactly this effect. And it is an aesthetic – a simplification and clarification – toward which the whole of the age had moved. We associate the term neoclassical with literature of brilliant artifice; but the *Preface* and the verse translations – steady, fluent, utterly idiomatic in effect, condensed, and lucid – convey as exactly the ideals of neoclassicism as the pointed juxtapositions and archness of what is often celebrated under that rubric.

Dryden began his life as a poet wholly dependent on materials that were ready to hand, on devices and conceits that none could have mistaken for his own. The prose and verse of *Fables* reveal the identity of its author at every turn, and yet the writing is without idiosyncrasy. But the creation of a literary voice was more than a personal triumph. Would it be naive to accept Dryden's own estimate of his work, that it was a national treasure, an act of patriotism, and an enrichment of "our native language"? Because the writing is so varied and the poet intent both on theory and invention, he was able to produce a body of literary texts and to create a literary culture. He enabled his younger contemporaries to invent the next age as he now allows us to imagine his own. The "works" of John Dryden may have begun as an unlikely venture, but it came to embody an idea of national culture at a moment when ideas of empire and nationhood had more than begun to hold sway.

NOTES

Some material in this chapter has appeared in my "John Dryden e la Restaurazione," in Franco Marenco (ed.), *Storia della Civiltà Letteraria Inglese*, 4 vols. (Turin, 1996).

1 I refer to what is still the only complete edition of Dryden's writing, ed. Sir Walter Scott, 18 vols. (Edinburgh, 1808), revised and corrected by George Saintsbury (Edinburgh, 1882–93). The "California" Dryden, edited by E. N. Hooker and H. T. Swedenberg, Jr., et al. (Berkeley and Los Angeles, 1956–), bears the same name.

2 Dryden's relations with his publishers Henry Herringman and Jacob Tonson have been thoroughly examined; see Clarence Miller, "Henry Herringman, Restoration Bookseller-Publisher," *Papers of the Bibliographical Society of America* (New York, 1948); Harry M. Geduld, *Prince of Publishers* (Bloomington, 1969); Kathleen Lynch, *Jacob Tonson, Kit-Cat Publisher* (Knoxville, 1971); and the exhibition catalogue, *Annus Notabilis* (Los Angeles, 1981). We still await – Anne Barbeau Gardiner's "Dryden's Patrons," in R. P. Maccubbin and M. Hamilton-Phillips (eds.), *The Age of William and Mary* (Williamsburg, 1989) notwithstanding – a full study of Dryden and his aristocratic patrons.

3 For the early years through Cambridge and the 1650s, see James A. Winn, *John Dryden and His World* (New Haven and London, 1987), pp. 1–103.

4 See Hugh Macdonald, *John Dryden: A Bibliography of Early Editions and of Drydeniana* (Oxford, 1939), pp. 1–2.

5 For bibliographical details, see *ibid.*, pp. 3–4.

6 *The Poems of John Dryden*, ed. James Kinsley, 4 vols. (Oxford, 1958), vol. 1, p. 18; subsequent citations will be to volume and page number in the Kinsley edition and included in parentheses in my text.

7 Dryden's supposed response to *Paradise Lost*, "That Poet had cutt us all out" was recorded in a MS note by Jonathan Richardson, Sr., p. cxxix of his annotated copy of *Remarks on Milton's Paradise Lost by Jonathan Richardson Father and Son* (London, 1734), now in the London Library. Reproduced in V. de Sola Pinto, *Sir Charles Sedley, 1639–1701* (London, 1927), p. 94n.

8 See Macdonald, *John Dryden*, p. 19.

9 On the dating of Filmer, see *Sir Robert Filmer, "Patriarcha" and Other Writings*, ed. Johann P. Sommerville (Cambridge, 1991), pp. xxxii–xxxiv.

10 The argument can be traced to Louis I. Bredvold, *The Intellectual Milieu of John Dryden* (Ann Arbor, 1934).

11 *The Letters of John Dryden*, ed. Charles Ward (Durham, 1942), p. 123.

12 See J. G. A. Pocock, *Three British Revolutions: 1641, 1688, 1776* (Princeton, 1980).

13 See, among others, Reuben Brower, "Dryden's Epic Manner and Virgil," *PMLA*, 55 (1940), pp. 119–38; Brower, "An Allusion to Europe: Dryden and Poetic Tradition," *ELH*, 19 (1952), pp. 38–48 (reprinted in *Alexander Pope: Poetry of Allusion* [Oxford, 1959]); and, more recently, the remarks on Dryden and Virgil in Geoffrey Hill's *The Enemy's Country* (Stanford, 1991), and the notes in Paul Hammond (ed.), *The Poems of John Dryden* (London and New York, 1995–).

14 The contract between Dryden and Tonson is reproduced in Hooker and Swedenberg (eds.), *The Works of John Dryden*, vol. VI, *Poems: The Works of Virgil in English, 1697*, ed. William Frost (1987), pp. 1179–83.

15 See the two subscription lists to Dryden's *Virgil* reproduced in Hooker and Swedenberg (eds.), *The Works of John Dryden*, vol. V, *Poems: The Works of Virgil in English, 1697*, ed. William Frost (1987), pp. 67–71, as well as Dryden's dedications of the *Georgics* and the *Aeneid*.

FURTHER READING

Brower, Reuben, "An Allusion to Europe: Dryden and Poetic Tradition," *ELH*, 19 (1952), pp. 38–48.

Bywaters, David, *Dryden in Revolutionary England* (Berkeley and Los Angeles, 1991).

Hammond, Paul, *John Dryden: A Literary Life* (New York, 1991).

Hill, Geoffrey, *The Enemy's Country* (Stanford, 1991).

Macdonald, Hugh, *John Dryden: A Bibliography of Early Editions and of Drydeniana* (Oxford, 1939).

McKeon, Michael, *Politics and Poetry in Restoration England* (Cambridge, MA, 1975).

Miner, Earl, *Dryden's Poetry* (Bloomington, 1967).

Verrall, A. W., *Lectures on Dryden* (Cambridge, 1914).

Winn, James A., *John Dryden and His World* (New Haven, 1987).

Zwicker, Steven N., *Politics and Language in Dryden's Poetry: The Arts of Disguise* (Princeton, 1984).

IO

ROS BALLASTER

John Wilmot, Earl of Rochester

> He that can rail at one he calls his *Friend*,
> Or hear him absent wrong'd, and not defend;
> Who for the sake of some ill natur'd Jeast,
> Tells what he shou'd conceal, Invents the rest;
> To fatal *Mid-night* quarrels, can betray,
> His brave *Companion*, and then run away;
> Leaving him to be murder'd in the *Street*,
> Then put it off, with some *Buffoone* Conceit;
> This, this is he, you shou'd beware of all,
> Yet him a pleasant, witty *Man*, you call
> To whet your dull Debauches up, and down,
> You seek him as top *Fidler* of the *Town*.[1]

Carr Scroope, frequent object of Rochester's scorn, here summarizes the character that has been handed down to posterity: rake-hell, misanthropist, fantasist, orchestrator and recorder of the "dull Debauches" of Restoration London. These dramatic roles, which Rochester himself both contributed to and colluded in, have for some time obscured the writer. Born in 1647 in the midst of one political crisis, the English Civil War, and dying in 1680 after the onset of another (the Popish Plot and the Exclusion Crisis), Rochester's short life was attended by contradiction. He was the son of a Cavalier ennobled for his service to the exiled Stuarts, although his mother, Anne, came from a Parliamentarian family and had been previously married to a Parliamentarian. Reputed a brilliant scholar, Rochester (he acceded to his father's title on the latter's death in 1658) toured Europe in the early 1660s, returning to England to be introduced at court with a letter from Charles II's sister in 1664. The following year he was confined to the Tower for the attempted abduction of an heiress, Elizabeth Malet, the same woman who agreed to marry him in 1667, and went on to bear him a son and three daughters. Notwithstanding the early passion and later evident affection between Rochester and his wife, in 1675 he entered into a liaison with Elizabeth Barry, who later became the leading actress of the Restoration stage and bore him a daughter in 1677. His martial, like his sexual life, indicates paradoxes. He distinguished himself by notable heroism in the second Dutch war in 1665 and 1666, but, in the incident to which Scroope referred, Rochester drew his sword upon the watch and seems to have killed his friend Captain Downes in a drunken brawl at Epsom in 1676; he earned the contempt of John Sheffield, Duke of Mulgrave by failing (through ill-health) to attend a duel; and he was rumored to have hired ruffians to set upon Dryden in an alley as revenge for an anonymous satire in fact authored by Mulgrave. A close friend of the king's mistress, Nell Gwynne, and leading member of a circle of court wits including Sir Charles Sedley, the Duke of Buckingham, and Lord Buckhurst, Rochester incurred the displeasure of Charles II on a number of occasions, and was repeatedly exiled from the court, first in 1673 for a satirical poem on Charles II which apparently went too far; then in 1675 for smashing the king's pyramidal chronometer; and again in 1676 as a result of the infamy following the Epsom brawl. His facility with disguise and persona touched not only his verse but also his life; his best-known exploit in the second period of exile entailed the impersonation of a mountebank, Doctor Alexander Bendo, who purveyed his cures by the Tower of London.

If the impressive scholarship of David Vieth and Keith Walker has wrested a relatively secure canon of some 80 poems from the 250 once attributed to Rochester, the works themselves defy secure categories of tenor and vehicle, voice and persona. We can with relative confidence assert that Rochester produced (at least) the following: a collection of some thirty-six attractive Cavalier lyrics often comic and often obscene; twenty-one satires and lampoons on topics philosophical, political, sexual, religious, aesthetic, and scandalous, five of which exceed 120 lines ("Artemiza to Chloe," "A Satyr against Reason and Mankind," "Timon," "Tunbridge Wells," "An Allusion to Horace"); one tragedy (*Valentinian*) and one pornographic comedy (*Sodom*); a few fragments of translation from Ovid, Lucretius, and Seneca; three prologues and epilogues; a handful of epigrams and impromptu verses. Some twenty-two of his poems were published during his lifetime, but most circulated in manuscript, and none appeared collected under his name until after his death. Approximately one hundred of his letters have been identified, addressed in the main to his wife, his mistress Elizabeth Barry, and his closest friend Henry Savile.[2]

Despite Rochester's evident expertise in stagecraft (he supposedly taught Elizabeth Barry to act) and, in particular, his deftness in staging himself, he is the least flamboyant, the most restrained, of Restoration writers, his strength located in "adroit syntax, diction and cadence" as Bernard Beatty notes, by contrast with the extravagance of image associated with his contemporary, John Dryden.[3] It is this remarkable economy of expression and, more generally, a discernible preoccupation with an economics of the body politic and private, with which the following argument will be principally concerned.

The language of economy permeates Rochester's writing, nowhere more obviously than in the representation of sexual exchange as a form of economic trade, usually entailing "loss" for the male lover. "A Ramble in Saint James's Parke" complains that Corinna has sex with foolish fops, devaluing the currency of her lover's sperm. She is, he expostulates, "a Whore in understanding / A passive pott for Fools to spend in" (lines 101–02). Rochester's male speakers insistently remind their female addressees that they must capitalize on their beauty while it is worth something (see for example "The Advice" to Celia), yet an aristocratic subtext of contempt for all forms of measure associated with vulgar mercantilism ultimately discredits the addressee for assenting at all to the validity of an "economy" of sexual practice. When her lover ejaculates prematurely, Corinna of "The Imperfect Enjoyment" cries "All this to Love, and *Rapture's* due, / Must we not pay a debt to pleasure too?" (lines 23–24). Strephon (a name frequently applied to Rochester by members of his circle) tells his past mistress, Daphne, that his new one flies "Tedious, trading, Constancy" ("A Dialogue between Strephon and Daphne," line 56). Thus, Rochester's poetry seems at once to contravene, while participating in, the ascendancy of a vocabulary of debt, exchange, and commerce.

This vocabulary might be associated with the emergent language of political and sexual contract, now associated with John Locke, whose own thinking was informed by that of those latitudinarian advocates to whom Rochester was so bitterly opposed. Stephen Clark draws our attention to Rochester's marked preference in philosophy and political thought for a Hobbesian spendthrift pursuit of sensation, by contrast with the Lockean philosophy of accumulation, with its imperative to hoard, conserve, and protect.[4] Rochester's debt to Thomas Hobbes extends to a critique of the tendency in more tolerant and nascently liberal thinking to attempt to distinguish between different spheres of culture, the private and public, the political and the domestic. Hobbes's totalizing political theory makes no distinction between state relations, sexual relations, and aesthetic relations as objects of sovereign power.[5] Rochester's lampoons and satires insistently refuse all distinctions between state and sexual politics. Thus, a lampoon "To longe the Wise Commons" of 1673 fuses topical and sexual innuendo expertly and, for the modern reader, confusingly:

> To longe the Wise Commons have been in debate
> About Money, and Conscience (those Trifles of State)
> Whilst dangerous Greyvances daily increase,

And the Subject can't riott in Safety, and peace.
Unlesse (as agaynst Irish Cattle before)
You now make an Act, to forbid Irish whore.   (lines 1–6)

Parliament in 1673 obliged Charles to abandon his policy of toleration of Nonconformists ("Conscience") in exchange for granting him money to continue his war against the Dutch ("Money"). The poem asserts these are "Trifles of State," however, beside the threat posed by pox-ridden Irish whores. It proceeds to cite some Irish court ladies as evidence, and advises the Commons to extend a law it had passed in January 1666/7 against importing cattle into England from Ireland to such human "cattle." The proposal is, of course, ironic, but the juxtaposition serves to cast a cynical light on the process of government itself which operates through the mean-spirited trading of one unlike thing for another: "Money" can be traded for "Conscience," and hence why not ban Irish whores as well as Irish cattle? In his letters, Rochester frequently expresses contempt for statecraft; he comments in spring 1676 to Savile that "They who would be great in our little government seem as ridiculous to me as schoolboys who with much endeavour and some danger climb a crab-tree, venturing their necks for fruit which solid pigs would disdain if they were not starving" (*Letters*, p. 119). Rather than concluding Rochester's disinterestedness or independence from the intense political fissures of his period,[6] it might be more exact to observe that he found the available models of statecraft constraining and diminishing.

In Rochester's poetic and dramatic works we can identify a consistent tendency toward critique of the very discourse of commerce and exchange within which he is writing, a restless unhappiness with the demarcation of boundaries between the social, sexual, and political, condemning such discriminatory activities as part and parcel of a culture that continually balances its books, and attempts to value and delimit its component parts. James Turner has marked this general tendency in libertinism to resubmit to the terms that it challenges: "the rebellious display of illicit sexuality is linked, by latent associations and ghostly companionships of language, to the religious and moral systems it purports to reject."[7] In Rochester's case the escape from such resubmission, although ostensibly a call to hedonistic excess, ultimately manifests itself by retreat into forms of extreme minimalism, nihilism, and non-entity.[8] These gestures of negativity attend the two primary forms of figuration that dominate his writing and become the subject of both investigation and critique: first, a figuration of waste or emission identified with the physical and symbolic properties of the penis/phallus; and second, a figuration of surfeit and absorption identified with the physical and symbolic properties of the vagina/cunt. If Rochester's famous misogyny can be located anywhere it is here: in the repetitive assignment of gendered psychological identities, indeed agency, on the basis of fixed mechanical sexual properties.[9] That Rochester's writing is preoccupied with the physical mechanics of sexuality yet repeatedly eschews issues of procreation and generation indicates the ultimate barrenness of the totalizing philosophy it pursues. As Marianne Thormählen shrewdly observes: "At the centre of Rochester's poems on love, there is an empty space."[10] Apparent materialism dissolves into abstraction, and physical body parts are revealed to be the chimeric products of mental processes and intellect.

Waste

In Rochester's poetry, emission and loss are consistently associated with male sexuality and, especially, the penis. His most famous poem on this theme, "The Imperfect Enjoyment," partakes of a lengthy tradition stemming from Ovid and Petronius and developed by the French poets, Rémy Belleau and Mathurin Regnier in the late sixteenth and early seventeenth centuries.[11] However, Rochester also departs from the tradition in that the "debt to pleasure" that the speaker has failed to pay, the achievement of orgasm in his partner, is the result of premature ejaculation rather than impotence. His failure is one of self-control and timing rather than the machinery itself. However, the speaker's invective, commencing on line 46, displaces anger from its rightful target, the mind, to the body part. And the punishment the speaker calls down upon his/its head is a fitting one, that future emissions should be the result of disease, or should fail outright:

> May'st thou to rav'nous *Shankers*, be a *Prey*,
> Or in consuming *Weepings* waste away.
> May *Strangury*, and *Stone*, thy *Days* attend.
> May'st thou ne're Piss, who didst refuse to spend,
> When all my joys, did on false thee depend.   (lines 66–70)

Rochester frequently deploys mock-heroic conventions to figure the comic failure of the penis to fulfil its single purpose. The speaker of "The Imperfect Enjoyment" figures his penis as a failed street bully who shrinks from his military duty when called upon by king and country:

> Like a Rude roaring *Hector*, in the *Streets*,
> That Scuffles, Cuffs, and Ruffles all he meets;
> But if his *King*, or *Country*, claim his Aid,
> The *Rakehell Villain*, shrinks, and hides his head:

Ev'n so thy *Brutal Valor*, is displaid,
Breaks ev'ry *Stew*, does each small *Whore* invade,
But when great *Love*, the onset does command,
Base Recreant, to thy *Prince*, thou darst not stand. (lines 54–61)

Similarly, the speaker of "The Disabled Debauchee" adopts the conceit that he is a war-scarred admiral admiring the military prowess of younger combatants from a distance, which casts light on "His present glory, and his past delight" (line 8). The only emissions he is now capable of are "flashes of rage" from "his fierce *Eyes*" (line 9) and words from his mouth in the shape of stories of his past exploits used to "fire [the] Blood" (line 31) of the "cold complexion'd *Sot*" (line 29) who shrinks from the fray. Again, the language of commerce is smuggled into the military metaphor; despite falling victim to venereal sufferings, he claims, "Past joys have more than paid what I endure" (line 24). The agency of the speakers in both these poems lies in their utterance, which comes to substitute for the physical act in which they have failed. Male speech compensates for mechanical sexual failure. And the potency of speech is considerable. The "disabled debauchee" claims that, in passing on his tales to the younger man, he can lead him toward blasphemy and obscenity: "I'll make him long some *Antient Church* to fire, / And fear no lewdness he's called to by *Wine*" (lines 43–44).

Evidently, we must understand both the disabled debauchee and the speaker of "The Imperfect Enjoyment" as subject to their creator's irony: preoccupied with sensual pleasures, they trivialize political and military glory by invoking the comparison and reveal themselves to be trivial in the process. Perhaps the scabrous lampooning, invective, and obscenity in this period even carried specific overtones of resistance to latitudinarian attempts to promote civility and appeasement as a means of furthering the rational religion seen as favorable to the increase of trade, empire, and science. In aligning his poetry with "wanton expression," satiric invective rather than the kind of civil satire that Dryden promotes in his "Discourse concerning the Original and Progress of Satire," Rochester is repudiating this latitudinarian model of political and state culture (most overtly of course in his "Satyr against Reason and Mankind").[12] Speech is then characterized as a form of effective emission for the male agent, but only when the sexual body fails to perform. Ineffective speech is also figured as a debased form of emission which substitutes for sexual prowess. The speaker of "An Epistolary Essay" – perhaps a send-up of Rochester's enemy, John Sheffield, Duke of Mulgrave[13] – refers to his writing as a form of excretion:

> Perhaps ill Verses, ought to be confin'd,
> In meere good Breeding, like unsav'ry Wind;
> Were Reading forc'd, I shou'd be apt to thinke
> Men might noe more write scurvily, than stinke:
> But 'tis your choyce, whether you'll Read, or noe,
> If likewise of your smelling it were soe,
> I'd Fart just as I write, for my owne ease,
> Nor shou'd you be concern'd, unlesse you please:
> I'll owne, that you write better than I doe,
> But I have as much need to write, as you,
> What though the Excrement of my dull Braine,
> Runns in a harsh, insipid Straine,
> Whilst your rich Head, eases it self of Witt?
> Must none but Civet-Catts, have leave to shit?   (lines 30–43)

Here then writing is, like the physical act of farting, shitting, or ejaculating, beyond the mental control of the poet.

In Rochester's writing, male "tackle" consistently fails its owner as he seeks to have it figure his own power and authority. The comedy of both the "Satire on Charles II" and "Signior Dildo" lies in the acknowledgment of "bollocks" as undermining the regal symbolism and unified authority of the penis/phallus. "Signior Dildo" – an anti-Yorkist satire which lays the import of dildoes and their enthusiastic embrace by the ladies of the English court at the door of James Duke of York's Italian bride of 1673, Mary of Modena – concludes with another mock-heroic scene in which "Count Cazzo" (the fleshly penis) and his "Rabble of Pricks" attempt to chase "Signior Dildo" out of town. Nell Gwynne's friend, Lady Sandys, is described as bursting into laughter:

> To see how the Ballocks came wobbling after,
> And had not their weight retarded the Fo
> Indeed't had gone hard with Signior Dildo.   (lines 90–92)

Similarly, in the "Satire on Charles II," it is the king's bollocks that undermine his magisterial prick. When impregnating his Catholic mistress, Louise de Keroualle, Duchess of Portsmouth, we are told "For though he setles well his Tarse [penis] / Yett his dull graceless Ballocks hang an arse" (lines 26–27). To "hang an arse" according to Johnson's dictionary is "to be tardy, sluggish, or dilatory." In both these cases, then, the physical machinery of reproduction (the bollocks) slows down the organ of pleasure, the penis, preventing it from completing its task, bringing the woman to orgasm. The bollock-less efficient machine of the dildo directed by the woman outstrips the penis, freed of the encumbrance ("weight") of the spermatic juices carried in the testes.

Anal penetration does not discriminate between male and female as sources of gratification for the male protagonist. In "The Imperfect Enjoyment" the speaker remembers his penis's previous mastery of coition regardless of the sex of his partner:

> Stiffly resolv'd, twou'd carelessly invade,
> *Woman* or *Man*, nor ought its fury staid,
> Where e're it pierc'd, a *Cunt* it found or made.   (lines 41–43)

As Harold Weber notes, "The feminized object of desire remains essential to the procurement of male pleasure within this libertine sexual economy."[14] Yet, ultimately, and paradoxically, the magisterial phallus is undermined by the materiality of the penis, the object for which it stands, which emits (whether piss, venereal weepings, or sperm) uncontrollably.[15]

The political implications of this economy of waste in the poetry are made overt in the comic closet drama, *Sodom*.[16] Bolloximian, King of Sodom, passes an edict that men may only bugger and must abstain from cunt, an edict which his wife, Cuntigratia, and her maids of honor, Fuckadilla, Cunticula, and Clitoris, as well as his heir, Prince Prickett, and the Princess Swivia, proceed to ignore. On the authority of his physician, Flux, Bolloximian declares "Products spoil cunts. Flux does allow / That what like woman was, it makes like cow" (Act 3, lines 157–58, Lyons [ed.], *Complete Poems and Plays*, p. 146). The paradox here is that emission in a cunt results in "products" (babies) which "spoil" the sexual gratifications it might offer so that total abstention is seen as preferable. The play humorously reveals the paradoxical force of "liberty"; Bolloximian, in a sideswipe at Charles II's pursuit of religious toleration in his reign, must act tyrannously in order to ensure freedom:

> Let conscience have its force of liberty.
> I do proclaim, that buggery may be used
> O'er all the land, so cunt be not abused.
>   (Act 1, lines 68–70, Lyons [ed.], *Complete Poems and Plays*, p. 131)

Sexual freedom is here seen to result in, precisely, a dead-end, in non-procreative anal sex. In order to prevent "spoiling" the cunt by using it for purposes other than pure sexual pleasure (procreation), male seed must be wastefully expended in the anus. However, this leaves the state in a condition of permanent revolt and chaos, deprived of the sovereign phallic power the king set out to assert. The play concludes with Bolloximian agreeing to share his dynastic potential with his fellow-king, Tarsehole (Louis XIV), who is given the freedom to "command like me what cunts do live / Within my precincts that are fit to swive" (Act 3, lines 179–80, Lyons [ed.], *Complete Poems and Plays*, p. 46) in exchange for the forty young men he has sent for his brother-in-law to use. Heterosexual procreative activity is frequently rejected by Rochester's speakers in a gesture of aristocratic disdain, similar to that of Bolloximian here, who considers it below his dignity. Likewise, in the song "Love a *Woman*! y're an *Ass*," the speaker announces his preference for his "sweet soft *Page*" (line 15) and pronounces:

> Let the *Porter*, and the *Groome*,
>> Things design'd for dirty *Slaves*,
> Drudge in fair *Aurelias Womb*,
>> To get supplies for Age, and Graves.   (lines 5–8)

Yet, in the case of the king of Sodom and the aristocracy in general it is precisely the need to stoop to the "labour" of ensuring legitimate heirs through conjugal intercourse to which Rochester is calling attention.[17] The authority of the phallus is, paradoxically, secured only through its reduction to the menial task of marital reproduction.

Sodom also asserts the independence and threatening power of the female cunt which challenges the symbolic authority of the phallus through its potential inexhaustibility. Where vaginal sex with women is figured as a form of unwelcome labor by Buggeranthus, who complains that "toils of cunt are more than toils of war" (Act 3, line 35, Lyons [ed.], *Complete Poems and Plays*, p. 142), Cuntigratia responds "Fucking a toil! Good lord! you do mistake. / Of ease and pleasure it does all partake" (Act 3, lines 36–37, Lyons [ed.], *Complete Poems and Plays*, p. 142). Both Weber and Thormählen note that Rochester's representations of eroticism are less concerned with sexual pleasure than the struggle for power, which figured as a conflict over which determines the action of the other's body, penis or cunt (Weber, "Drudging," pp. 104–05), or between animal (associated with women) and cerebral (associated with men) pleasure (Thormählen, *Rochester*, p. 27). The autonomy of the female cunt is figured in Rochester's obscene verse and drama as a suffusing greed which ultimately cannot be satisfied by the feeble emissions of the penis.

Surfeit

If "The Imperfect Enjoyment" shifts its course mid-stream to an invective against the speaker's penis, "A Ramble in Saint James's Parke" enacts an equivalent movement in relation to the female vagina. As in "The Imperfect Enjoyment" the poem's speaker is a male lover spurred to sexual excitement who suddenly experiences a reversal of desire and emotion, here not through premature ejaculation but rather the sight of his mistress, Corinna, allowing three foolish lovers "With wriggling tailes [make] up to her" (line 44). At line 109, the speaker shifts to apostrophize his mistress in an invective as obscene and perverse as that directed toward the penis in "The Imperfect Enjoyment." If the penis is complained of for its shortcomings and its too nice discriminations (it can perform for a common whore but not a loved mistress), the cunt is figured as an exorbitant and indiscriminate agent. It is the combination of these two attributes that particularly enrages the speaker who complains that:

> Had she pickt out to rub her Arse on
> Some stiff prickt Clown or well hung Parson
> Each jobb of whose spermatique sluce
> Had fill'd her Cunt while wholesome Juice
> I the proceeding should have praisd
> In hope she had quench'd a fire I rais'd.   (lines 91–96)

However, Corinna's cunt proves neither quenchable nor capable of discriminating between "wholesome" and corrupting "Juice." She sleeps with fops for reasons other than sexual pleasure:

> Did ever I refuse to bear
> The meanest part your Lust could spare
> When your lewd Cunt came spewing home
> Drench't with the seed of halfe the Town
> My dram of sperm was sup't up after
> For the digestive surfeit water.
> Full gorged at another time
> With a vast meal of nasty slime
> Which your devouring Cunt had drawn
> From Porters Backs and Footmens brawn
> I was content to serve you up
> My Ballock full for your Grace cupp
> Nor even thought it an abuse
> While you had pleasure for excuse.   (lines 111–24)

The speaker's objection is that Corinna's activities indicate insatiability (his sperm can no longer act as "surfeit water," a digestive taken after excessive consumption) and blasphemy (her cunt is "prophaned" [line 166] in that his spermatic "offering" no longer has the priority over others' unconsecrated juices). The "curse" on Corinna is, like that on the speaker's penis in "The Imperfect Enjoyment," fitting. Since her cunt cannot be satisfied and she allows "whiffling Fools" (line 136) to copulate with her, he prays:

> You may goe madd for the North wind
> And fixing all your hopes upont
> To have him bluster in your Cunt
> Turn up your longing Arse to the Air
> And perrish in a wild despair.   (lines 138–42)

The paradoxical desire to be filled by an absence, air, will, the speaker threatens, result in expiry.

Rochester's poetry constructs female desire as unfulfillable precisely because it is a desire to be filled to excess. Hence, it never imagines the possibility of female same-sex desire or indeed sexual gratification not organized around the penis or a phallic substitute: dildo or thumb. Hence, in the mock-pastoral song, "Fair Chloris in a pigsty lay," Chloris is prompted to masturbation by a dream of penetration by an amorous swain in which the grunts of the pigs she tends are equated with her lover's cries:

> Frighted she wakes and wakeing Friggs
>   Nature thus kindly eas'd
> In dreams rais'd by her murmring Piggs
> And her own Thumb between her leggs
>   She's Innocent and pleas'd.   (lines 36–40)

Strikingly, however, those few poems that Rochester puts in the female voice rarely imply such uncomplicated desire for the penis or its substitutes on the part of women. Those women who do express such desires are treated satirically. Of the six women who are shown to actively use the dildo in "Signior Dildo," four belong to the York sphere against whom Rochester aligned himself with his friend, Buckingham, whereas those women associated with the king or Buckingham reject the artificial phallus.[18] "Mistress Knights Advice to the Dutchess of Cleavland in Distress for a Prick" is a satirical attack on Barbara Palmer, Duchess of Cleveland, who made an enemy of Rochester by having an affair with Mulgrave. By contrast, female speakers with a modicum of intellect show a marked preference for power over pleasure in their sexual choices. "The Platonick Lady" expresses her preference for loveplay without penetration and implies that only here can her sexuality be active rather than receptive:

> I love a youth, will give mee leave
>   His Body in my arms to wreath;
> To presse him Gently and to kisse,
>   To sigh and looke with Eyes that wish.
>   For what if I could once Obtaine,
>   I would neglect with flatt disdaine. (lines 13–18)

In "A Letter from Artemiza in the Towne to Chloe in the Countrey," one of Rochester's longest and most complex poems, the poet takes the unusual move of allowing the critique of the reduction of love to a form of economic exchange in the mouth of a woman. Artemiza relates to Chloe an account in verse of her encounter with a fine lady married to a foolish knight. The lady in turn tells the brief story of Corinna, seduced and abandoned by a man of wit, who obtains and fleeces a married country bumpkin as a lover, poisoning him once she is secure in the house, plate, and jewels he has bought for her by mortgaging his estate. Like the Corinna in "A Ramble in Saint James's Parke," the fine lady and this Corinna prefer foolish lovers to men of wit. However, as Artemiza concludes, the woman of intelligence who chooses the fool as her sexual partner is ultimately more to blame than the driven cunt who indiscriminately hosts fool, man of wit, dildo, or thumb. While the fine lady plays with a monkey admiring it as a "curious Miniature of Man" (line 143), Artemiza comments:

> I took this tyme, to thinke, what Nature meant,
> When this mixt thinge into the World shee sent,
> Soe very wise, yet soe impertinent.
> One, who knew ev'ry thinge, who, God thought fitt,
> Should bee an Asse through choyce, not want of Witt.   (lines 147–51)

It is not insignificant that Artemiza is a poet, for Rochester ascribes a negative aesthetics to female sexuality which might be paralleled to the image of male writing as excretive substitute for the failed mechanics of coition. Artemiza figures poetry as a form of madness in pursuit of insubstantial gratification for women. This image might be paralleled with that conjured in "A Ramble in Saint James's Parke" of Corinna's impossible desire for the north wind:

> Deare Artemiza, poetry's a snare:
> Bedlam has many Mansions: have a Care.
> Your Muse diverts you, makes the Reader sad;
> You Fancy, you'r inspir'd, he thinkes, you mad.
> Consider too, 'twill be discreetly done,
> To make your Selfe the Fiddle of the Towne,
> To fynd th'ill-humour'd pleasure att their need,
> Curst, if you fayle, and scorn'd, though you succeede.   (lines 16–23)

Although writing by women can be figured as a form of agency which transgresses cultural taboo, like maids wooing or men marrying (line 28), it results in a more familiar objectification and passivity, making the writer into "the Fiddle of the Towne" not far removed from the "passive Pott for men to spend in" ("A Ramble in Saint James's Parke," line 102).

If women themselves rarely figure as linguistic agents in Rochester's poetry (recall Corinna's only speech act in "A Ramble in Saint James's Parke": "at her Mouth her Cunt cries yes" [line 78]), the emissions of the female body do provide a source for male writing. "On Mistress Willis" imagines the poet as drawing on the excess materials of the female body, and in particular female sexuality, to produce his own bawdy writing:

> Whom that I may describe throughout
>   Assist me Bawdy Powers
> I'le write upon a double Clowt
>   And dipp my Pen in Flowers.   (lines 5–8)

The poet here writes on a sanitary towel and dips his pen in menstrual blood in order to produce his image of the court prostitute, Sue Willis, yet that image comes surprisingly, and uncomfortably, close to that of the author himself:[19]

> A Prostitute to all the Town
>   And yet with no man Freinds
> She rails and scolds when she lyes down
>   And Curses when she Spends.   (lines 13–16)

The attempt to draw the fine line between promiscuity and indiscriminacy proves a task less easy for Rochester's poetic speakers than might first appear, not least when applied to male aesthetic activity in the analogy with female sexuality. In the satire known as "Timon," in imitation of a satire by Rochester's favorite poet, Nicholas Boileau,[20] the speaker encounters a man who invites him to a dinner on the basis of a libel he admires and wrongly believes to be written by the speaker. The speaker admits his own error in keeping silent rather than vigorously denying authorship:

> Which he, by this, has spread o're the whole Town,
> And me, with an officious Lye, undone.
> Of a well meaning *Fool*, I'm most afraid,
> Who sillily repeats, what was well said.   (lines 29–32)

He joins his host, the host's wife, and group of ignorant and loud-mouthed friends for dinner to find himself regaled with precisely the silly repetitions of the "well said" lines of Orrery, Etherege, Settle, Crowne, and Dryden. The poet, Rochester, manages by contrast with these pretentious literati, to do more than passively imitate; he transforms his favorite poet's lines, ending, not as Boileau does, on a dispute about literary value but rather one about military glory: the company comes to blows over the question of whether the French army is courageous or not. Mechanical repetition, passive imitation, are the marks of folly in Rochester's poetry, and these vices magically slip from association with femininity to male protagonists, even in all-male social groupings; the host's wife whose only interest is in discussing love and love poetry (by contrast with the men who take more pleasure in the martial lines of heroic tragedy) has departed from the scene by line 110 of the 177-line poem.

At other points in Rochester's writing, the distinction between male and female desire and sexuality dissolves and reverses. If the cunt is seen as an inexhaustible repository of liquid in Rochester's obscene poetry, it might be paralleled with the male drinker of his anacreontic verse (poetry in praise of love and wine in imitation of the Greek lyric poet, Anacreon). In a letter to George Savile of 22 June (?)1671, Rochester famously observed:

> I have seriously considerd one thinge, that of the three Buisnisses of this Age, Woemen, Polliticks & drinking, the last is the only exercise att wch you & I have nott prouv'd our selves Errant fumblers; if you have the vanity to thinke otherwise, when we meete next lett us appeale to freinds of both sexes & as they shall determine, live & dye sheere drunkards, or intire Lovers.   (p. 67)

The song "How happy Cloris (were they free)" explicitly equates female appetite for sperm with male capacity for drink, encouraging a fair trade with Chloris:

> Whilst I, my Passion to pursue
> Am whole Nights takeing in
> The lusty Juice of Grapes, take you
> The lusty Juice of Men.   (lines 21–24)

Again, an attempt is made to distinguish between an indiscriminacy associated with female as opposed to male consumption. The three versions of this "Song" not only demonstrate the care with which Rochester crafted his verse but also the consistent slippage between mercenary and sexual metaphor through association with promiscuous female sexuality, against which is pitted the true liberty of the male wit devoted to wine and boys. Stanza 4 of "How happy Cloris (were they free)," stanza 4 of "How perfect Cloris, and how free," and stanza 6 of "Such perfect Blisse fair Chloris, wee" (also known as "To a Lady in a Letter" and the only version to be published in Rochester's lifetime, anonymously in the 1676 *A New Collection of the Choicest Songs*) are virtually identical except for a significant choice of word in the last line. The first version runs:

> You never thinke it worth your care,
> How empty nor how dull,

> The heads of your Admirers are,
> Soe that their Codds be full. (lines 13–16)

The second version, a manuscript text, replaces "Codds" with "backs" written above an uncanceled "purse" and the third version offers "bags," with "Codds" preferred again in a manuscript variant of the same version. "Codds," "bags," and "purse" thus seem interchangeable, not only as slang terms for the testes but in terms of Cloris's sexual pursuit, which is covetous (whether of sperm or money) by contrast with her lover's pursuit of drink, figured as a form of homosocial bonding which excludes women and can be indulged to excess without ill-effect.

However, the desire for surfeit associated with the female cunt and imitated in homosocial drinking ultimately induces a state of indiscriminacy or chaos which Rochester designates as nothingness. "Upon his Drinking a Bowl" concludes on the inescapable return to "cunt" which recognises the temporary nature of the retreat to boys and the goblet:

> *Cupid*, and *Bacchus*, my Saints are,
> May drink, and Love, still reign,
> With *Wine*, I wash away my cares,
> And then to *Cunt* again. (lines 21–24)

And it is this paradox of nothingness as the product of the pursuit of material sensuous pleasure that finally confounds the attempt to designate Rochester's writing utopian or Epicurean.

Nothing

Conventional though the paradox of the creation of the world from nothing may be, Rochester's "Upon Nothing," when considered in the context of his other writings, reveals echoes of the gendered distribution of symbolism discussed earlier.[21] Though described as "Elder Brother even to Shade" (line 1), "Nothing" is figured as sharing the attributes of the boundless female cunt, activating the familiar Renaissance pun on whores and female sex organs as "Nothing"; the pun on "twat" in the phrase "all proceeded from the great united what" (line 6)[22] leads on to references to "Nothing's" "boundless selfe" (line 9), its "fruitfull Emptinesses" (line 11), and "hungry wombe" (line 21). Similarly, Rochester expands the allusion in the second chorus of Act 2 of Seneca's "Troas" to original chaos into an image of a vast nihilistic womb:

> Dead, wee become the Lumber of the World,
> And to that Masse of matter shall be swept,
> Where things destroy'd, with things unborne, are kept. (lines 8–10)

Rochester's poetry insistently demonstrates itself to be grounded upon, and to conclude in, nothingness. Apostrophizing "Nothing" in "Upon Nothing," the speaker explains that, "Thou hadst a being ere the world was made / And (well fixt) art alone of ending not afraid" (lines 2–3). The failed dialectic of the argument – Nothing produces Something which reverts back to Nothing – is mimicked in the very structure of the poem written in rhymed triplets, whereby the third line repeatedly fails to deliver anything but a collapse back into the "nothing" of the first.

The only sure and certain "knowledge" in Rochester's universe is of "Nothingness." Rochester takes Hobbes's grounding argument that man's life is "nasty, brutish and short" a step further, toward a representation of culture as unremitting chaos and nihilism. In this bleak cosmos, pain provides the only source of "truth" and it is this insight into pain as knowledge that colors so much of Rochester's poetry. The song "Insulting *Beauty*, you mispend" concludes with a characteristic piece of assertion through negativity. His mistress, the speaker claims, should not frown upon him, because he gives full credit to the power of her beauty, where others claim to be protected from it by their preference for rival women. Her rejection of him, however, makes him the victor in defeat:

> Nor am I unreveng'd, though lost;
> Nor are you unpunish'd, though unjust,
> When I alone, who love you most,
>   Am kill'd with your Disdain.   (lines 15–18)

Indeed, Rochester's aesthetics and morality seem to center on reserve and pain.[23] Ultimately, the void of the vagina or anus figures as no more than an empty space into which the speaker projects his fantasies of identity and power. If Rochester is consistent it is in his critique of forms of egotism and self-assertion; in "A Very Heroicall Epistle in Answer to Ephelia," Mulgrave is satirized through the mouth of Bajazet, who declares: "In my deare self, I center ev'ry thing" (line 7) and "'tis my Maxim, to avoyd all paine" (line 13). Pain, "The Mistress" asserts, is the only site where a "truth" derived from the senses can be found:

> Fantastick Fancies fondly move;
>   And in frail Joys believe:
> Taking false Pleasure for true Love;
>   But Pain can ne're deceive.   (lines 29–32)

This logic of necessary pain at the heart of Rochester's libertinism extends to his representation of political order, and kingship in particular. *Valentinian*, Rochester's reworking of Fletcher's *Tragedy of Valentinian* (1610–14), provides the tragic equivalent to the comic treatment of despotism in *Sodom*. Written between 1675 and 1676, but not performed until 1684, the play criticizes Charles II through the figure of Valentinian not so much for his sexual appetite as for his love of ease. Maximus, at the play's opening, comments that "the whole world, dissolved into, a peace, / Owes its security to this man's pleasures" (Act 1, lines 96–97, Lyons [ed.], *Complete Poems and Plays*, p. 162). When Valentinian, with the collusion of his councilors, rapes Maximus's wife, the army rebels and kills him, notwithstanding the loyalty of the general, Aecius. As the satire of "A Very Heroicall Epistle" reinforces, Rochester's libertinism did not extend to an admiration for a sovereign's exploitation of absolute power for purely selfish ends:

> Oh happy Sultan! whom wee Barb'rous call!
> How much refin'd art thou above us all?
> Who Envys not the joys of thy Seraill?
> Thee, like some God, the trembling Crowd adore,
> Each Man's thy Slave, and Woman-kind, thy Whore.
> Methinkes I see thee underneath the shade,
> Of Golden Cannopies, supinely laid:
> Thy crowching Slaves, all silent as the Night,
> But at the Nod, all Active as the Light!
> Secure in Solid Sloth, thou there dost Reigne,
> And feel'st the joys of Love, without the paine.   (lines 32–42)

If pain is the source of "truth" in erotic and civil relations, the withholding of egotism and virtual retreat from language, particularly public language, is the key to aesthetic value in Rochester's writing. The "Allusion to Horace," which might be seen to represent Rochester's manifesto for culture, criticizes Dryden for overexposing his talent: "forbeare / With uselesse Words, t'oppresse the wearyed Eare" (lines 22–23). By contrast, Shadwell is admired for his "Shewing great Mastery with little care" (line 47). Rochester's aesthetic centers on creating an impression of not trying and a satirical style that brilliantly mimics the rhythms of speech.[24] Modeling himself on the urbane courtier satirist, Horace, the speaker of "An Allusion" makes the argument for economy and restraint, the avoidance of surfeit and excess, in both words and audience. Once more, assertion comes about through negative disclaimer and the positive claim for pain. The poem concludes:

> I loath the Rabble, 'tis enough for me,
> If Sidley, Shadwell, Shepherd, Witcherley,
> Godolphin, Buttler, Buckhurst, Buckingham,

> And some few more, whom I omit to name
> Approve my Sense, I count their Censure Fame.   (lines 120–24)

Omission and censure become markers of "value." This conventional claim of the aristocratic courtier-poet acquires larger significance once the threads of Rochester's writing life are laid alongside each other. In representing aesthetic as well as sexual and political life, Rochester consistently inquires into the failure of an active masculine agency to produce positive value as it oscillates between waste – copious but exhaustible non-generative emission – and surfeit – indiscriminate and equally non-generative absorption of all matter.

This most fragmentary, restless, and intellectual of Restoration authors subjects his modern-day reader, as he did his contemporaries, to a series of reversals and logical paradoxes under the guise of an accessible hedonism. We are left convinced of a powerful intelligence, but one which keeps itself hidden behind the deft invocations of and allusions to others' arguments, techniques, and materials. From his letters we discern an idealism embedded in friendship, and true affection for his wife and children as well as passion for his mistress. Yet his poetry and dramatic writing reveal a waspish cynicism which can turn swiftly against friends and patrons in the service of its skeptical convictions. In a hand-bill, one of Rochester's many personae, the mountebank Alexander Bendo announces: "if I appear to anyone like a counterfeit, even for the sake of that chiefly ought I to be construed a true man. Who is the counterfeit's example, his original, and that which he employs his industry and pains to imitate and copy? Is it therefore my fault if the cheat by his wits and endeavours makes himself so like me that consequently I cannot avoid resembing of him?"[25] Such acts of impersonation and self-invention must trouble any attempt at conclusive reading of either Rochester's text or life.

NOTES

1 Carr Scroope, "In Defence of Satyr," Appendix II in *The Poems of John Wilmot, Earl of Rochester*, ed. Keith Walker (Oxford: Basil Blackwell, 1984), p. 137, lines 48–59. All poetry by Rochester cited in this article is from Walker's edition and referenced by line. Walker identifies three poems by Rochester targeting Scroope (1649–80): "The Mock Song," parodying Scroope's song "I cannot change as others do" (itself ascribed to Rochester in the editions of his *Poems* that appeared in 1680); "On the suppos'd Authour of a late Poem in defence of Satyr" in response to Scroope's poem quoted here; and "On Poet Ninny." David M. Vieth argues for Scroope's authorship and attempts to date the personal and literary rivalry of the two writers in chapters 5, 8, and 13 of his *Attribution in Restoration Poetry: A Study of Rochester's Poems of 1680* (New Haven and London: Yale University Press, 1963).

2 See *The Letters of John Wilmot Earl of Rochester*, ed. Jeremy Treglown (Oxford: Basil Blackwell, 1980), p. 166. Savile was a highly successful diplomat, a Member of Parliament for Newark, Nottinghamshire, and shared Rochester's critical stance toward James, Duke of York, despite (or perhaps because of) having served as groom of the bedchamber to the duke. His regular mistress was Carr Scroope's widowed mother.

3 Bernard Beatty, "'The Present Moment' and 'Times Whiter Series': Rochester and Dryden," in Edward Burns (ed.), *Reading Rochester* (Liverpool: Liverpool University Press, 1995), pp. 207–26, esp. p. 214.

4 Stephen Clark, "'Something Genrous in Meer Lust?' Rochester and Misogyny," in Burns (ed.), *Reading Rochester*, pp. 21–41, esp. p. 23.

5 See Thomas Hobbes, *Leviathan* (1651), Part II, chapter 29: "what is it to divide the Power of a Commonwealth, but to Dissolve it; for Powers divided mutually destroy each other" (ed. C. B. MacPherson [London: Penguin, 1968], p. 368).

6 See Frank H. Ellis in his edition of *John Wilmot Earl of Rochester: The Complete Works* (London: Penguin, 1994), p. 239.

7 James G. Turner, "The Properties of Libertinism," in Robert Purk Maccubbin (ed.), *'Tis Nature's Fault: Unauthorized Sexuality during the Enlightenment* (Cambridge: Cambridge University Press, 1987), pp. 75–87, esp. p. 80.

8 Numerous critics have noticed the skepticism, colored by a philosophical materialism inherited from Hobbes, Lucretius, and Seneca, which informs Rochester's writing, and results in a position of negativity. See, in particular, Barbara Everett, "The Sense of Nothing," in Jeremy Treglown (ed.), *Spirit of Wit: Reconsiderations of Rochester* (Hamden, CT: Archon Books, 1982), pp. 1–41; Simon Dentith, "Negativity and Affirmation in Rochester's Lyric Poetry," and Tony Barley, "'Upon Nothing': Rochester and the Fear of Non-Entity," both in Burns (ed.), *Reading Rochester*, pp. 84–97, and pp. 98–113.

9 For discussions of Rochester's misogyny (and not all concur with the accusation of misogyny), see Sarah Wintle, "Libertinism and Sexual Politics," in Treglown (ed.), *Spirit of Wit*, pp. 133–65; Clark, "'Something Genrous in Meer Lust?'," pp. 21–41; Reba Wilcoxon, "Rochester's Sexual Politics," *Studies in Eighteenth-Century Culture*, 8 (1979), pp. 137–49, rpt. in David M. Vieth (ed.), *John Wilmot, Earl of Rochester: Critical Essays* (New York: Garland, 1988), pp. 113–26.

10 Marianne Thormählen, *Rochester: The Poems in Context* (Cambridge: Cambridge University Press, 1993), p. 83.

11 Richard E. Quaintance, "French Sources of the Restoration 'Imperfect Enjoyment' Poem," *Philological Quarterly*, 42 (1963), pp. 190–99.

12 David Trotter, "Wanton Expressions," in Treglown (ed.), *Spirit of Wit*, pp. 111–32.

13 See Vieth, *Attribution*, pp. 119–36.

14 Harold Weber, "'Drudging in Fair Aurelia's Womb': Constructing Homosexual Economies in Rochester's Poetry," *The Eighteenth Century*, 33 (1992), pp. 99–117, esp. pp. 114–15.

15 The pedophilic aspect of the process whereby anus is metamorphosed into cunt by the adult male penis has been somewhat obscured as Marianne Thormählen notes, by the editorial decision on the part of both Vieth and Walker to

substitute in line 42 the "boy" of their copy-text (the 1680 *Poems*) with the "Man" of the extant manuscripts they consult (*Rochester*, p. 21).

16 Paddy Lyons (ed.), *Rochester: Complete Poems and Plays* (London: Everyman, 1993). See Lyons's comment in his Introduction which associates the play with the sodomitical circle, known to Rochester, of Monsieur, brother of Louis XIV and husband to Charles II's sister, Henrietta-Anne (pp. xv–xvi); and his notes on the play's authorship, that three of the seven early manuscripts identify Rochester as author (p. 314).

17 Charles II's inability to father a child with his wife, Catherine of Braganza, remained the single most disturbing aspect of his reign in particular to an anti-Yorkist such as Rochester, who aligned himself with Buckingham against the prospect of James's Catholic succession, more on the grounds of James's temperament than his religion it seems (see Thormählen, *Rochester*, pp. 291–94).

18 See *ibid.*, pp. 289–91.

19 See Clark, "'Something Genrous in Meer Lust?'," p. 36.

20 On the similarities and differences between "Timon" and Boileau's third satire, see Dustin Griffin, *Satires against Man: The Poems of Rochester* (Berkeley and Los Angeles: University of California Press, 1973), pp. 36–41; David Farley-Hills's *Rochester's Poetry* (London: Bell and Hyman, 1978), pp. 150–55 and 186–90; and Harold Love, "Rochester and the Traditions of Satire," in Harold Love (ed.), *Restoration Literature: Critical Approaches* (London: Methuen, 1972), pp. 158–63.

21 For the tradition of the paradox of the creation of the world from "Nothing" from Erasmus's *Praise of Folly* (1511) onward, see Farley-Hills, *Rochester's Poetry*, p. 170. For Rochester's reworking of accounts of Genesis in Milton's *Paradise Lost* and Cowley's *Davideis*, see Griffin, *Satires against Man*, pp. 266–80.

22 For this suggestion, see Kristoffer Paulson, "Pun Intended: Rochester's 'Upon Nothing'," *English Language Notes*, 9 (1971), pp. 118–21.

23 See Thormählen, *Rochester*, pp. 76–77.

24 Jeremy Treglown, "'He knew my style, he swore'," in Treglown (ed.), *Spirit of Wit*, pp. 75–91.

25 "To all Gentlemen, Ladies and Others, whether of City, Town or Country, Alexander Bendo wisheth all Health and Prosperity," in *The Complete Works*, ed. Ellis, lines 48–51, p. 93.

FURTHER READING

Braudy, Leo, "Remembering Masculinity: Premature Ejaculation Poetry of the Seventeenth Century," *Michigan Quarterly Review*, 33 (1994), pp. 177–201.

Burns, Edward (ed.), *Reading Rochester* (Liverpool: Liverpool University Press, 1995).

Donaldson, Ian, "The Argument of 'The Disabled Debauchee'," *Modern Language Review*, 82 (1987), pp. 30–34.

Farley-Hills, David, *Rochester's Poetry* (London: Bell and Hyman, 1978).

Love, Harold, "Refining Rochester," *Harvard Library Bulletin*, 7 (1996), pp. 40–49.

Thormählen, Marianne, *Rochester: The Poems in Context* (Cambridge: Cambridge University Press, 1993).

Treglown, Jeremy (ed.), *The Letters of John Wilmot Earl of Rochester* (Oxford: Basil Blackwell, 1980).

(ed.), *Spirit of Wit: Reconsiderations of Rochester* (Hamden, CT: Archon Books, 1982).

Vieth, David M., *Attribution in Restoration Poetry: A Study of Rochester's Poems of 1680* (New Haven and London: Yale University Press, 1963).

Rochester Studies, 1925–1982: An Annotated Bibliography (New York: Garland, 1984).

Vieth, David M. and Griffin, Dustin, *Rochester and Court Poetry: Papers Presented at a Clark Library Seminar* (Los Angeles: William Andrews Clark Memorial Library, University of California, 1988).

11

MARGARET FERGUSON

The authorial ciphers of Aphra Behn

"Aphra Behn has always been an enigma," Paul Salzman observes at the outset of his introduction to a new edition of her novella *Oroonoko*.[1] The wild fluctuations in her literary reputation, tied to changing sexual mores, changing views of women writers, and changing moral and political judgments of the Restoration period itself, comprise one part of this enigma.[2] Another (and related) part is comprised of the problem of her biography. This problem arises from the many shady moments in her life story, moments that have teased readers from her own time to ours to fill in and thus to "master" the gaps. The problem this poses for the critic has both theoretical and strategic implications: how much and what kind of attention should the serious student of her writing expend on the story (or rather, competing stories) of her life?

For some the debates about Behn's biography have contributed substantially "to the devaluation – and neglect – of [her] ... *writing*."[3] Even the recent feminist focus on "reconstructing" her life has not remedied the neglect of her literary techniques typical of older critical emphases on her alleged moral "looseness" and on the question of whether or not she was "truthful" ("realistic").[4] Robert Chibka wittily wonders why critics have been so doggedly concerned with the historical truth or falsity of Behn's claim, at the beginning of *Oroonoko*, that "I was myself an eye-witness to a great part of what you will find here set down,"[5] when similar autobiographical truth-claims – by Defoe, for instance, in *Robinson Crusoe*, or by Swift, in *Gulliver's Travels* – have tended to prompt sophisticated attention to the feints and ruses of seventeenth-century prose-fictional narrators ("Oh! Do Not Fear," p. 511). Chibka contrasts the many studies of *Oroonoko* focusing on whether Behn "really" went to the British colony of Surinam with the history of criticism of *Robinson Crusoe*; it is, he remarks, "hard to imagine an article concerning whether Defoe lived in goatskins near the mouth of the Orinoco River entitled, 'New Evidence of the Realism of Mr. Defoe's *Robinson Crusoe*'" (p. 512).

While I agree with Chibka that Behn's gender – and other (related) aspects of her biography – have colored critical approaches to her works in all sorts of troublesome ways, I do not think that separating the author from the works is the solution to the problem. "Believe the tale, not the teller," said Henry James – but in a Jamesian text like *The Turn of the Screw*, as in many of Aphra Behn's texts, the "authority" of the tale is intimately bound up with the representation of a narrator with a distinct "interest" (psychological and economic) in her materials. While it is true that attention to Behn's biography has often worked to impede analyses of "the premises and structure" of the quite remarkable body of writing – prose fiction, translation, drama, and lyric poetry – which she produced between 1670 and her death in 1688, it nonetheless seems possible, at this historical juncture when sophisticated criticism of Behn's works is burgeoning, to repose the question of biography in a way that can not only notice but also attempt critically to account for her numerous if always partial self-representations. These occur not only in her prose fictions and poetry, but also in her translations of others' works and even in her drama, that most apparently non-autobiographical of genres. The Restoration theatre, however, had a socioeconomic structure that solicited, even depended on, authorial self-advertisement in the small world of London's theatre-goers. Behn, as Catherine Gallagher has forcefully shown, developed dramatic personae designed to attract spectators and sustain their interest in a production until the "third night" of the run, when playwrights finally received house receipts.[6] Behn's authorial personae both build on and seek to revise contemporary images (mostly negative) of the female playwright, especially the image of the "public" woman writer as a prostitute: "Punk and Poesie agree so pat," one of Behn's male contemporaries wrote in 1691, "you cannot well be *this*, and not be *that*."[7] Making some of her authorial personae complement characters represented in her plays (mostly comedies, but also some tragicomedies and one tragedy), she sought to transform the liability of her gender into an asset. Quite insistently in the prologues, epilogues, and epistles that frame her plays; in her unusual preoccupation with sexualized "discovery" scenes in which an actor or actress is revealed – undressing for bed – behind painted "Scenes"; and in her construction of striking "breeches" parts for actresses,[8] Behn invited her contemporary readers and spectators to perceive authorial self-references and to enjoy the titillating pleasures of decoding those allusions, recognizing "likenesses" in the texts to the shape-shifting public character known variously as "A." or "Astrea" or "Aphra" Behn.[9] Moreover, the question of whether the spectator or reader should *believe* a given persona created by Behn's "female pen" is central to the interpretive knots she so often creates by tying fictional images with ones that seem to be drawn from the (authorial) life, itself being constructed and constantly altered in texts by Behn and others.

In this essay, I propose, then, to look at some of the ways in which she creates what might be called "cipher" or "enigma" effects; I will also look at some of the reasons – both social and aesthetic – for her fashioning of herself as a "cipher" in two senses of that term. The first is the meaning of "nothing" or zero (from the Arabic *sifr*), a meaning traditionally associated with the female genitals.[10] The second meaning of cipher relevant to my essay – and to Behn's many literary allusions to her biographical experience as a spy – is that of a type of code or secret writing that invites (but may also resist) full deciphering by readers and spectators with varying amounts of information about the authorial subject(s). This is the meaning elaborated by several Renaissance men of letters who seem to have regarded cipher-systems as a second-order mode of literacy, like Latin, which had for centuries served as a social as well as an epistemological marker distinguishing elite literate men, priestly or secular, from others.[11] As vernacular literacy spread in the early modern period, as scripts became standardized and easier to read through the technology of print, and as even women and some lower-class men were able to pick up some Latin, the men of letters who served as diplomats, letter-writers, and spies for the monarchs of Europe grew increasingly interested in a "Renaissance" of the ancient art of ciphers. Behn participated in this Renaissance, I argue, albeit from a necessarily eccentric subject position and in ways that have been little remarked.

There is no scholarly consensus about Behn's parents' identity, their social class, the year of her birth,[12] or how she acquired the unusually good education her writings display. Like most seventeenth-century women, she seems not to have had access to the education in classical languages that gave one "full" literacy in her era; Dryden says that she knew no Latin, but his statement, like many about Behn by contemporaries, raises more questions than it answers: "I was desired to say that the author, who is of the fair sex, understood not Latin. But if she does not, I am afraid she has given us occasion to be ashamed who do," Dryden wrote in his preface to a collaborative translation of Ovid's Epistles; his preface is a sort of advertisement for the volume at a moment in the early 1680s when he like Behn and other dramatists had fallen on hard economic times.[13] If Behn herself "desired" Dryden to say that she understood no Latin, she may have been slyly displaying herself both as a "typically" uneducated person and as an unusual scholar; and Dryden's gallant rhetoric may well signal his awareness of this female writer's value in advertising his book to a range of readers.[14]

Despite her alleged lack of Latin, Behn was mysteriously able to add classical allusions absent from the original to her translation of the Abbé Paul Tallement's *A Voyage to the Island of Love*; and she seems, intriguingly, to have known enough of the Greek alphabet to make the code she invented for her Netherlands spying activities resemble Greek characters.[15]

Her early history has provoked much scholarly speculation; so have many other moments in the life story she herself did much to shape *as* a mystery and, probably, as one of those socially "self-improving" stories so common in her era.[16] Shakespeare made himself a second-generation gentleman by purchasing a knighthood for his father, and Behn was suspected early on, it seems, of not truly being (as she claimed in *Oroonoko*) the daughter of a gentleman named Johnson with high aristocratic connections. Behn's self-positioning in her fictions was confirmed by a biography written soon after her death. The anonymous biographer described her as a "gentlewoman by birth, of a good family in the city of Canterbury in Kent";[17] her father or adoptive father, Mr. Johnson, is said to have been related to Lord Willoughby, through which connection Johnson acquired the position he was about to assume when he died at sea: the position of deputy governor of the colony of Surinam.

Behn's (and her biographer's) claims about her gentle birth were disputed in a rhetorical sequence that uncannily anticipates much subsequent criticism of Behn: in a poem called "The Circuit of Apollo," Anne Finch, Countess of Winchilsea praised the wit but deprecated the loose morals displayed in Behn's writings ("amongst women," says Finch's Apollo, "there was none on earth / Her superior in fancy, in language, or wit, / Yet owned that a little too loosely she writ"); a marginal note to Finch's poem completes the sequence by suggesting that Behn's biographer, and by implication the author of *Oroonoko* who claims gentle birth, are liars: "Mrs Behn was daughter to a barber, who lived formerly in Wye, a little market town in Kent. Though the account of her life before her works pretends otherwise, some persons now alive do testify upon their knowledge that to be her original."[18] Lying, pretense, and the problem of belief or "credit": these are themes that recur again and again in Behn's *oeuvre*, as they do in the historical documents that would-be decoders of her biography have unearthed to make various and competing cases for (and against) her. Although she was, after Dryden, "the most prolific and probably the most popular writer of her time, with at least eighteen plays, several volumes of poetry, and numerous works of fiction that were in vogue for decades after her death,"[19] she was more like Defoe than Dryden in keeping her "true" identity an enigma.

Critical debate has swirled not only around the circumstances of her birth but also, as I have already suggested, around her (alleged) voyage to Surinam in the early 1660s, during which sojourn, novelistically re-presented by Behn herself in the year of her death, she was said by a hostile observer – William Byam, the man who replaced her supposed father as deputy governor of the colony – to have had a love affair in the colony with the Republican William Scot. I consider Scot, the son of a regicide executed for treason after the Restoration, a significant albeit shadowy presence in *Oroonoko*. Although Scot is not named in that text, other Republicans are, and in a remarkably favorable light, given Behn's apparent Tory loyalism and ardent Royalism in the 1670s and 1680s.[20] Behn's memory of Scot arguably colors the novella's concern with epistemological and economic credit – a key issue for Oroonoko himself and for the white female narrator who tells his story in Behn's exercise in "memorial reconstruction." The black prince loses his freedom because he naively accepts the invitation of an English sea captain – with whom Oroonoko has engaged in slave trading – to dine aboard ship. Behn excoriates the "treachery" of the captain, who entraps the too-credulous prince and transports him to Surinam. There he is bought by Trefry, the manager of the absent governor's plantation. Although Trefry and the narrator assure Oroonoko that he will be freed when the governor arrives, the promised emancipation never occurs; instead Oroonoko leads a slave revolt against the deputy governor, Byam, and is punished by torture and execution.

Oroonoko's story alludes cryptically to that of the historical Scot, for though we know little about Behn's youthful encounter with Scot in Surinam (nothing other than Byam's mocking testimony to a romance between "Celadon" and "Astrea," as he called Scot and Behn), we do have holograph letters from Behn describing later encounters with Scot when she was in the Netherlands in 1666, shortly after her return from Surinam. Her epistolary rhetoric in reports home, describing her efforts to persuade Scot to give information against the Dutch and the exiled English Republicans in Holland, suggests that the question of who should believe whom in an erotically charged and tensely dangerous game of "ciphers" – a game in which neither player could be quite sure of the other's intentions – made a profound impression on Behn. The experience of spying with (and perhaps against) Scot had a strong effect on the woman who would turn to writing for her living upon discovering that she herself had been financially duped in her labors as a spy for the Crown, and the memory of her complex relations to Scot haunted her particularly when she imaginatively revisited Surinam in the year of her own death, writing about the dead and betrayed Oroonoko.

It was highly uncommon for a young woman of ambiguous class origins to be recruited for intelligence work in this era, as Behn herself pointed out in a late poem:

> by the Arcadian King's Commands
> I left these Shores, to visit Foreign Lands;
> Employed in public toils of State Affairs,
> Unusual with my Sex, or to my Years.[21]

Her acquaintance with Scot in Surinam may well have led Thomas Killigrew, Groom of the Bedchamber, to recruit her for the king's spying service (see Goreau, *Reconstructing Aphra*, pp. 93–94). Under the code-name "Astrea," ironically, the very name given her by her enemy Byam, she sought to convince Scot (code name "Celadon") that the Royalists would protect and – equally important – reward him for information about his fellow Republicans and about the Dutch, who were supporting the anti-Royalist English forces in the second Anglo-Dutch War. In her reports Aphra calls Scot a "Rogue" and at one point says she "must not trust him in Holland"; but at another point she assures her handlers, and perhaps herself, that "I really do believe that his intentt is very reall and will be very diligent in the way of doing you all the service in the world for the ffuter [future]; he expresses him self very hansomly: and I beleeve him in all things: I am sure he wants no witt nor adress: nor anything to manage this affaire with, but money."[22] If *Oroonoko* dramatizes a naive hero's "education in skepticism," as Robert Chibka calls it ("Oh! Do Not Fear," p. 515), the education is tragic because the hero learns too late that the "good" Christians – the apparently admiring estate manager Trefry, for instance, or the narrator herself, who is explicitly enlisted to spy on him and to distract him from thoughts of rebellion – have repeatedly if perhaps not fully consciously deceived him. The narrator herself doesn't trust Oroonoko as fully (or as foolishly) as he trusts her: although she says that he had "entire confidence" in her and called her his "great mistress" (*Oroonoko*, pp. 46, 45), she tells the reader that she did not think "it convenient to trust him much out of our view, nor did the country, who feared him" (p. 46); she arranges to have him "accompanied by some that should be rather in appearance attendants than spies" (p. 47). Is Oroonoko playing Scot's role to Aphra's recreation of Astrea the spy's role – or vice versa? Do we believe her when she says Oroonoko believed her? He was of course long dead in 1688, so we have no way of knowing if she altered anything that came "from [his] mouth" (p. 6); Scot too was long dead by 1688, and hence could not challenge any refraction of his relation to her in Oroonoko's complex relation to the woman who appropriates his story. In any case, one of her first letters about Scot to her Royalist employers describes his movements as being extremely constricted – as Oroonoko's are – by the spies who surround him.[23]

It is the narrative refraction of an epistemological and visual *situation*, rather than any simple allegorical correspondence between characters in *Oroonoko* and the characters in this episode of Behn's life, that seems significant to me. Someone is looking at someone looking back (and over his/her shoulder) – and neither party knows who exactly knows what, although both are bound by affection as well as by political and economic designs that may require each, at any moment, to "use" the other. The spying chapter of her biography is enigmatically inscribed in *Oroonoko*; and the enigma exists not only to titillate the reader but also to mirror a still perplexing and libidinally unresolved situation for the narrator/author. If in her representation of Oroonoko's and the narrator's vexed relation to each other and to other manipulators of words in the colonial setting Behn represents aspects of her own youthful naivety *vis-à-vis* Scot (in Surinam as well as a few years later, perhaps, in the Netherlands) and at the same time probes the problems of her "credit" with the Royalists who hired her but broke their promises to pay her, the authorial self-allusions Behn embeds in her novella are neither politically nor psychologically straightforward; sometimes the ciphers contain guilty or even self-critical charges, and sometimes they are tinged by anger and hurt at the images of the female author minted by others.

Many questions remain unanswered about Behn's spying mission to Flanders and about the imprisonment for debt – or near-imprisonment – that ensued upon her return to England.[24] Between her return in 1666 and 1670, when her first play, *The Forc'd Marriage, or the Jealous Bridegroom*, was produced by the Duke's Company in London (one of two licensed theatre companies in the city), her biographers surmise that she married a Mr. Behn (or Ben or Bhen or Beene). Some have speculated that he was one of those wealthy, sexually greedy but repellant "old" husbands depicted so often, and with such scathing irony, in Behn's comedies. There is, however, not one shred of historical evidence for his existence, much less his character, other than the posthumous biography, which describes him as "a merchant of this city through Dutch extraction." Behn herself never mentions a husband, and I suspect that he was an invention of convenience, as was his apparently prompt demise;[25] being a widow was more respectable than being an unmarried woman working in a public arena, and being a widow certainly was less constricting than being someone's wife: according to the Common Law doctrine of *feme covert*, the wife was owned by the husband, her being literally "covered" by his.

A series of *Love-Letters* ("by Mrs. A. Behn," first published post-humously as a short story in *The Histories and Novels of the Late Ingenious Mrs. Behn: In One Volume* [1696]), dramatizes the difficulty of distinguishing fiction from fact in Behn's life story or stories; in the second edition of *The Histories and Novels* (1698), the *Love-Letters* – allegedly addressed to a bisexual lawyer named John Hoyle, with whom Behn is supposed to have had an affair in the 1670s – are no longer printed as a piece of short fiction; rather, they have become part of the biography of Behn prefacing (and advertising) the new edition of the works and probably based – as the shorter version in the 1696 volume also was – on a two-and-a-half page "Account of the Life of the Incomparable Mrs. BEHN" included with the posthumously printed play, *The Younger Brother* (1696).[26] All subsequent biographies depend on these textually variable early bio-graphies, published completely without authorial attribution in the *Younger Brother*; ascribed to "A Gentlewoman of Her Acquaintance" in the eighteen-page "Memoir on the Life" of the 1696 *Histories and Novels*, and then ascribed, in the sixty-page version of the biography published in 1698 and entitled "Life and Memoirs," to "One of the Fair Sex."[27]

The ambiguity and gaps in the evidence provided by the early biographies make it quite understandable that even twentieth-century accounts of Behn's life, as well as assessments of her place in literary history, should offer competing narratives; many modern as well as earlier accounts of her life and works read like novels gemmed with clues that readers are invited to pursue, with satisfaction of our curiosity a prize always just around the next corner. Instead of defending or refuting absolute positions critics would do well, I think, to analyze the possible aims as well as the aesthetic and political effects of the intermixing of fiction and biography in works by Behn and in many contemporary (not to mention later) works about her.

Given the strong likelihood that the early posthumous biographies were based largely on materials written by Behn herself (and found among her literary "remains"), it does indeed seem that many of that biography's lurid details were part of her own economically, politically, aesthetically, and erotically motivated efforts at self-fashioning. The early biography's denial of a rumor that she had had a romantic liaison with the black hero of *Oroonoko*, for instance (a denial present in the 1696 and 1698 versions of the "Memoirs," and rearticulated both in the *Dictionary of National Biography* article about her by Edmund Gosse and in the introduction to the Norton edition of *Oroonoko* of 1973), is a striking example of a narrative device that piques the reader's curiosity without satisfying it. The rumor clearly builds on hints from the novella itself, which Thomas Southerne had revised and produced as a play in the very year that the posthumous edition of Behn's work, with the "advertising" biography, first appeared.[28] Critics often register some sense that Behn is deliberately withholding information from them, but I propose that we take that refusal to tell all – on Behn's part as well as on that of her first biographer, her "intimate" acquaintance and perhaps her double – as part of an intriguing authorial strategy aimed at generating "news" or, as Behn calls the commodity, "novelty": "for where there is no novelty, there can be no curiosity," as she remarks in *Oroonoko* (p. 8). The strategy of generating curiosity and novelty is prompted both by individual authorial agency and by the social circumstances of Behn's writing, circumstances shaped by her gender and mysterious class origins among other factors.

Catherine Gallagher has taken just this interpretive tack by relating the specific economic requirements of the Restoration London theatre – in particular the requirement that a play "survive" until the third night's performance – to Behn's development of a scandalous and intriguing persona that Gallagher calls the "newfangled whore" (*Nobody's Story*, p. 14). To fashion this persona, and a related one based on the figure of the (oppressed Stuart) monarch, Behn deliberately played on the "early modern concept of female 'nothingness,'" what I have referred to as the first meaning of "cipher." This concept encompasses both women's presumed genital lack (with its bawdy figuration as a hole or zero) and women's "secondary ontological status in relation to men" (p. xv). The idea of woman as a "nothing" is famously articulated in canonical texts such as *Hamlet* and *Clarissa*.[29] In Gallagher's view, Behn plays in innovative ways on the notion of female nothingness, portraying the author as a commodity (and seller of commodities) in an expanding international market and hence dramatizing the links between the female author and "the conceptual disembodiment that all commodities achieve at the moment of exchange"; this overlap between different kinds of "nothingness" allows Behn to construct remarkable composite personae that are characterized by identity-effects designed to pique and hold an audience's interest and, however paradoxical it may seem, to generate outraged criticism from her political opponents (p. 14).

Behn's use of autobiographical personae in her drama (including many prologues and epilogues, some written for others' plays), her lyric poetry, and her prose fiction, which ranges in length from short stories (e.g., "The Black Lady") through novellas (*Oroonoko*, *The Fair Jilt*) to the long, generically hybrid *Love-Letters between a Nobleman and his Sister* (1683–86?), is intricately bound up with her allegorical use of historical "facts" for political purposes; what she writes might justly be called "factional" in at least two senses of that word. Deliberately exploiting her reputation as a

Tory in many plays attacking Puritans or "Roundheads,"[30] Behn nonetheless displays in some of her writings, especially, I think, those set in the
"American" colonies (the posthumously produced *Widow Ranter, or the
History of Bacon in Virginia*, and *Oroonoko*), a more complex political
perspective than most critics allowed until recently. The complexities arise
in part because Behn's dramatic representations of women's economic
oppression by patriarchal marriage make her views of male absolutism at
times more fractured than those of contemporaries like Thomas Hobbes or
Robert Filmer. And although she relentlessly satirizes Cromwell's followers
and their Whig descendants, she differs from Rochester and other Tory
writers in her analysis of the cost of masculine libertinism for the women
who fall for men like the rake Willmore in *The Rover*. Critics are beginning
to explore the ways in which "Behn's treatment of gender often seems to
complicate and refract, if not indeed to contradict, her party politics,
creating in her work the sense of multiple and incommensurate ideological
agenda."[31] Moreover, as several recent critics have remarked, the differences between Whig and Tory views in the late seventeenth century were
not always clear; certainly the modern stereotype of the Tories as committed to "antiquated notions of hierarchy and patriarchy," in contrast to
Whigs committed to "bourgeois individualism"[32] is challenged by Behn's
sympathy for characters oppressed by a "bad" monarch or monarchical
representative, as Oroonoko and his wife Imoinda are, for example, in the
part of the novella set in Oroonoko's grandfather's absolutist court, and as
Oroonoko, Imoinda, and the white female narrator all are in the Surinam
colony ruled by Byam, the English king's corrupt representative. Decoding
the political allegory of *Oroonoko* is in short very difficult: the black prince
has sometimes been read as a composite symbol for Stuart monarchs such
as the "martyred" Charles I and the soon-to-be-deposed James II;[33] the
Stuarts' color was black, and there is no doubt that the novella attaches
complex and perhaps competing meanings to the "ebony" color of Oroonoko's and his wife Imoinda's skin. Parts of *Oroonoko*, moreover – the
opening depiction of innocent Indians living like Adam and Eve – remind
us that Behn's deep fascination with an ideal "golden age" – an ideal fueled
by her knowledge of South and North American colonial sites – sometimes
works against a coherent articulation of a recognizably Royalist political
view. In "The Golden Age: A Paraphrase on a Translation out of the
French" (1684), she elaborates on Tasso's evocation (in his pastoral drama,
the *Aminta*, 1573) of a paradisal realm in which "Each Swain was Lord
o'er his own will alone, / His Innocence Religion was, and Laws," and
neither "Right" nor "Property" – much less "Honour" – existed.[34] Behn's
abiding concern with relations of erotic equality and her attacks on the

institution of marriage – a fundamental element in the patriarchal absolutism advocated by Robert Filmer among others – make her at times a
highly idiosyncratic defender of the monarchy and the Tory party.

It remains difficult to decipher not only her party politics but also, on a
more local level, her politically charged relations with literary contemporaries. She is usually described as a great admirer of the free-thinking Tory
the Earl of Rochester, for instance – but since Behn encoded aspects of John
Wilmot, Earl of Rochester's character and name, especially with the pun on
"will" and the French "mot," word, in her portrait of Willmore in *The
Rover* Part 1 (1677) and Part 2 (1681),[35] we may surmise that her
admiration was leavened with a certain critical irony. Willmore, the
penniless Cavalier "rover" of the play's title, is a witty, ebullient fortune-
hunter with great sexual charisma. The prostitute Angellica Bianca – who
bears Aphra Behn's initials and hangs out a "sign," significantly, a self-
portrait, to advertise her wares – swiftly falls in love with Willmore but
also interrogates some of his most egregiously self-serving and misogynist
views. Having fallen in love with her picture (which a man "may gaze on"
for "nothing," he bawdily remarks[36]), Willmore berates her for charging
money for her favors rather than offering them for free, as a true lover
would: "Though I admire you strangely for your beauty," he says to
Angellica, "Yet I condemn your mind" (p. 185). Specifically, he condemns
her mercenary practice as a prostitute, but his words place him in a long
tradition of men who criticize women's mental powers as inferior to men's
– a tradition that the historical Rochester had wittily illustrated in a poem
arguing for the superiority of men's erotic (and conversational) relations to
each other over relations to any woman:

> Love a *Woman*! y'are an *Ass*,
>   'Tis a most insipid Passion,
> To choose out for your happiness
>   The idlest part of *Gods creation!*[37]

Behn's Angellica Bianca, whose name wittily inverts the traditional
association of prostitutes with the color black and with devils' agents,
clearly emerges from a cultural context that equated women writers and
actresses – *public* women – with whores. But Angellica's rhetorical skills,
like those of the author Angellica figures, allow her to parry if not perfectly
destroy Willmore's opinion of her "trade": he is the man with the mote in
his eye, she suggests, with a scathing glance at the rake who marries an
heiress to remedy a chronic absence of funds, as the historical Rochester
did, at the king's request: "Pray tell me, sir," says Angellica to Willmore,
"are not you guilty of the same mercenary crime [as what you accuse me of

committing], when a lady is proposed to you for a wife, you never ask, how fair – discreet – or virtuous she is; but what's her fortune – which if but small, you cry – she will not do my business – and basely leave her, though she languish for you – say, is this as poor?" He grants that it is – but goes on to marry the heiress Helena, who is reported dead from childbirth in the first scene of *The Rover*, Part 2. Loving Willmore is dangerous to women, it seems. But for those who can read her allegorical signs, Behn probes Rochester/Willmore's character here (and perhaps also in the portrait of Philander in *Love-Letters*) without offering any clear moral judgment for or against it. Critique lurks in admiration until she comes to write her elegy for Rochester, where – with the subject dead – the portrait becomes more unequivocally positive – and completely silent on the supposed death-bed conversion to Christianity that preoccupied Rochester's biographer Gilbert Burnet.[38] Perhaps she didn't credit it.

Her relations to Dryden were, in their lifetimes, even more complex than her relations to Rochester. Critics disagree about whether she wrote a poem satirizing Dryden's conversion to Catholicism, "A Satyr on Doctor Dryden."[39] Since Behn herself may have been raised as a Catholic – which doesn't mean that as an adult she "believed" in Catholic doctrine – and since we have a letter from her to the publisher Jacob Tonson stating that she would rather be esteemed by Dryden than by anybody in the world,[40] some critics have felt that she could not have written the satire, which is quite bitterly critical of Dryden. The riddle of Behn's possible authorship of the satire on Dryden cannot, I suspect, be empirically resolved.[41] It does, however, seem symptomatic of the problem of "deciphering," in the sense of finding a single fixed meaning, Behn's political, religious, and social views at various moments in her career. The satire on Dryden, unpublished in Behn's lifetime, exists in only two manuscript copies, and only one of these has Behn's name on it; does the name signal authorship or simply that she copied it out in a book?[42] I suspect that Behn could well have written the satire – and could have regretted offending Dryden too. The poem is quite within her stylistic register(s), and an author capable of mocking even her revered king – as she does in a satire entitled "Caesar's Ghost"[43] – would have been perfectly able to criticize Dryden for what appeared to many to be an opportunistic, even favor-currying act. A few courtiers converted to Catholicism under the Catholic James II, and Dryden himself had to protest, in *The Hind and the Panther* (III. lines 376–85), that such conversion brought no worldly rewards. After the Glorious Revolution, when the Protestant William of Orange and his wife Mary came to the throne, Roman Catholicism once again became a serious social liability – and indeed Dryden experienced it as such, but that was after Behn's death.

Hypocrisy in religious matters seems to have been something that deeply angered Behn; herself accused of atheism by Rochester's pious biographer Burnet, she excoriates the so-called "Christians" who break their word to Oroonoko in her novella. The satire attacks Dryden for an act of hypocritical opportunism unworthy of "a poet" of "great heroick th[e]ames" and inspiration, and suggests that Dryden was content to be a Protestant when the king was one, but converted after the king did: "for when the act is done and finish't cleane / what should the poet doe but shift the scene[?]" (Todd, *Works*, vol. I, p. 231).

Leaving the question of Behn's authorship of this poem open – as I think we must, given the extant evidence – we can use the attribution problem to address once more the larger question of her authorial ciphers: the fact cited by Mary Ann O'Donnell as conclusive proof against Behn's authorship of the satire – namely that she copied satires not her own into a miscellany[44] – seems to me to point precisely to a question central to her writing career and its critical reception: how do we tell the difference between a copy and an "original"? Several poems now attributed to Behn (the witty poem on male impotence, for instance, entitled "The Disappointment") were originally published as Rochester's, and the question of her "canon" is still highly unsettled, partly because so many of her poems and fictional works were published posthumously.[45]

The question of how to distinguish genuine from counterfeit texts clearly preoccupied Behn's age, when works circulated in manuscript as well as in print and multiple copies of anonymous works often made attribution very difficult.[46] In her Textual Introduction Janet Todd cites a note preceding a poem in the March 1707 issue of *The Muses Mercury*, a miscellany printed in 1707–08, inviting any suspicious reader "to inspect the manuscripts 'at the Booksellers who publishes this Paper.'" The manuscripts in question were by Behn, and contrary to the claim "Never before printed" on the title page, "all but two of the twelve poems by Behn had already appeared," albeit in somewhat different forms (Todd, *Works*, vol. I, pp. xliii–xliv). The text included the following general note about the problem of "certifying" Behn's texts as her property:

> If it were proper to make publick what we have learnt of the Story of the Author of the following Verses, 'twou'd be an unquestionable Proof of their being *genuine*. For they are all writ with her own Hand in a Person's Book who was very much her Friend; and from thence are now transcrib'd for the
> *Mercury*.　　　　　　　　　　　　　(cited in Todd, *Works*, vol. I, p. xliii)

Behn often raises questions about what constitutes literary originality. Forced, like other women writers (Katherine Philips and Anne Bradstreet, for example), to defend herself against charges that she had "stolen" material from men (the lines between translation, imitation, and plagiarism being even blurrier in Behn's time, before copyright laws were formally introduced, than they are today), she defended herself vigorously in various prefaces and epistles to readers.[47] In the epilogue to *Sir Patient Fancy* (1678), she yoked a defense against "bawdiness" with a discussion of "copying" that defines the latter as a positive (and original) act. In the original production, the famous actress Nell Gwynne spoke Behn's words defending her (their) play against a "coxcomb" who cried:

> Ah, Rot it – 'tis a Woman's Comedy,
> One, who because she lately chanc'd to please us,
> With her damn'd Stuff, will never cease to teeze us.
> What has poor Woman done, that she must be
> Debar'd from Sense, and sacred Poetry?
> Why in this Age has Heaven allow'd you more,
> And Women less of Wit than heretofore?
> We once were fam'd in story, and could write
> Equal to Men; cou'd govern, nay, could fight.
> We still have passive Valour, and can show,
> Wou'd Custom give us leave, the active too . . .
> We'll let you see, whate'er besides we do,
> How artfully we copy some of you:
> And if you're drawn to th' Life, pray tell me then,
> Why Women should not write as well as Men.[48]

With such a defense of the actress's or writer's right to "copy" men artfully, the female author portrays her mimetic work positively while giving notice that she will adopt different genders as well as different costumes for different occasions. Indeed she often plays the role of a "hermaphrodite" or member of what one contemporary called a "third sex," as, for instance, in her witty poem "To the Fair Clarinda, who made love to me, imagin'd more than a Woman."[49]

Behn's ciphers, as they pertain to the realms of national (and colonial) politics, interpersonal relations, gender roles, and textual issues, are no less difficult to interpret than are her biographical ciphers. And these various strands, I have been arguing, are often complexly intertwined. The interconnections or allegorical "translations" among these realms seem, indeed, to be at the heart of the verbal wit she used to delight – and covertly to instruct – her theatre audiences and, in the last decade of her life, the "unseen" public that comprised the (potential) audience for her lyrics, translations, and prose fictions. The theatre itself functioned as a kind of allegory for court politics; in Behn's era "political relationships were acted out in tableaux in the boxes under the same illumination as the stage, while references were made onstage to events in the bedrooms of Whitehall" (Todd, *Works*, vol. I, p. xxv). Alert to the links between plots onstage and at court, comically willing to suggest that masked prostitutes in the audience were the "Poetess's spies," bringing her rich material for dramatization and interpretation, Behn often constructed her prologues and epilogues to frustrate readers' attempts neatly to define her views or identity and to insinuate allegorical political messages to members of her audience or readership. Plays, she wrote, "are secret instructions to the people, in things that 'tis impossible to insinuate into them in other way."[50]

Behn's authorial personae are at once remarkably disembodied and tantalizingly carnal; they frequently occupy an eroticized subject position *vis-à-vis* the male or female spectator or reader.[51] They include not only the prostitute and the monarch so well analyzed by Gallagher but also the lusty, economically independent widow (as in *The Widow Ranter* or the *City Heiress*) and the related persona of the "scheming" woman who manages the "property" of the female body, her own or another's. In *Oroonoko*, for instance, the aging courtesan Onahal becomes a striking figure for the author when she exclaims to a man, "Oh, do not fear a woman's invention!" (p. 23). Onahal uses her inventive powers both to manage Imoinda's body by smuggling her into Oroonoko's chamber so he can take the prize of her maidenhead and to pursue a complex erotic and epistemological game with a young man Onahal herself fancies – and upon whom she spies, even as he thinks he is spying on her. Another example of a woman who learns to manage the property of the female body is Sylvia in *Love-Letters between a Nobleman and His Sister*. Here Behn creates a morally complex portrait of a lady: Sylvia's "education" in vice goes hand-in-hand with an increasing awareness that she must depend on her wit and counterfeiting talents to survive in a world where no man can or will provide for her.

Behn's ciphers – in the sense both of figures for the author and a coded type of writing – seem to amalgamate an emergent (Baconian) notion of a cipher as a second order of literacy similar to the humanist man of letters' ability to communicate in Latin or Greek with an older notion of allegorical writing as a sugar-coating of difficult theological doctrines – or dangerous philosophical ones. In this hybrid notion of cipher-allegory, aimed at an audience mixed along lines of class as well as gender, the writer simultaneously *deciphers* problematic ideas for ordinary readers or spectators and *hides* (reciphers) certain aspects of the meaning. The double hermeneutic activity is as dangerous as spying, for the authorities may misconstrue one's allegorical efforts, seeing in them ambitions to seduce and usurp. Behn herself acknowledges the potential danger of a type of writing – vernacular translation of the classics – that puts certain kinds of elite knowledge in the hands of lower-class people and, in particular, of women. In a poem of 1683 commending Sir Thomas Creech on his translation of Lucretius's *De Rerum Naturae* (*On the Nature of Things*), she initially depicts herself as an "unlearn'd" woman who benefits from Creech's work; as she develops a parallel between Creech's female reader and Eve, however, we realize that the poem explores a relation between author and reader that could pertain as well to her relations to her own readers as Creech's to her or Satan's to Eve:

> The god-like *Virgil*, and great *Homers* Muse,
> Like Divine Mysteries are conceal'd from us.
>   We are forbid all grateful Theames,
> No ravishing thoughts approach our Ear...
> [until Creech comes]
> ... by this *Translation* ... [to] advance
> our knowledge from the State of Ignorance
>   And Equallst Us to Man!
>   (Todd, *Works*, vol. I, pp. 25–28, lines 29–32, 41–43)

Here she wittily and subversively plays on Milton's characterization of Eve falling because of her ambition to equal Adam through the acquisition of forbidden knowledge. In this poem and elsewhere in her writing, Behn probes a fear that Creech himself articulated in his defensive preface to the second edition of his translation. There he worried that the "pill" of his translation might be covered in "venom" rather than in sugar for (some) Christian readers. Lucretius's proto-libertine arguments that "there was no life after death and that happiness should be gained on earth" (Todd, *Works*, vol. I, p. 384) clearly challenged Christian doctrines, as Behn indicates when she compares the translation of the pagan philosopher to something "As strong as Faiths resistless Oracles . . . / Faith the secure Retreat of Routed Argument" (lines 56–58). Praising Creech for decking "The Mystick Terms of Rough *Philosophy*" in "so soft and Gay a Dress, / So Intelligent to each Capacity; / That They at once Instruct, and charm the Sense" (lines 45, 47–49), Behn follows Sidney and Milton in exploring the knotty aesthetic and social problem of the potentially amoral – or worse, morally subversive – power of poetry or of rhetoric more generally. As a kind of cipher, allegorical writing could protect the free-thinking writer against censorship even as it allegedly supported that writer's traditional claim to teach (in a socially acceptable fashion) through delighting. If in her early writing Behn firmly eschewed a moral aim for her playwriting, polemically aligning herself with Shakespeare as opposed to the "well-educated" Jonson,[52] by the time of Creech's translation of Lucretius, when she herself had been attacked for a politically "incorrect" position expressed in the epilogue to the anonymous play *Romulus and Hersilia*, Behn was evidently developing a notion of secret allegorical writing to define a specifically political educative function for the drama. As she wrote in the Dedicatory Epistle to *The Lucky Chance* (cited in note 50), " 'Tis example that prevails above reason or DIVINE PRECEPTS ... I have myself known a man, whom neither conscience nor religion cou'd perswade to loyalty, who with beholding in our theatre a modern politician set forth in all his colours, was converted ... and quitted the party." To promote herself and her political agenda, she developed many tactics of partly exposing, partly concealing "secrets" about her life and self in her writings. These tactics constitute a symbolic cryptography that reveals Behn's fascination with modes of disguise, deceit, and such para-cryptographic practices as "counterfeiting" one's handwriting – her character Philander, for instance, in *Love-Letters Between a Nobleman and His Sister*, begs his illicit lover Sylvia to burn one of his letters because "writing in haste I have not counterfeited my hand."[53]

Approaching Behn as an adept in versions of cipher writing understood broadly as including esoteric types of writing such as political and autobiographical allegory decodable to greater and lesser degrees by different members of the audience may help us gain a sharpened perspective not only on some of her characteristic themes and writing practices, but also on the vexed question of her names. "Name" had a double metaphorical meaning in Behn's time, signifying both personal virtue and renown. Since, for women, personal virtue was defined as a sexual modesty incompatible with any appearance in the public sphere of the sort that would lead to "renown," women with literary ambitions could not pursue fame without risking the loss of their "good name." This dilemma underlies some women's decisions to write anonymously or to deny their responsibility for their works' publication. Although Behn developed authorial personae very different from those more "chaste" ones constructed by aristocratic near-contemporaries such as Katherine Philips (the "matchless Orinda") or Anne Finch ("Ardelia"), Behn like these other women assumed a pen name to gain some of the prerogatives of naming ascribed to Adam and exercised by many of his sons.[54] Designated "A. Behn" or "Ann Behn" on most title pages of her early printed works,[55] she referred to herself as "Astrea," as did her early biographer. Although the name had initially been used as a weapon against her by Byam, in his letters from Surinam, Behn appropriated it for new purposes, conjuring up not only the heroine of a popular French romance by Honoré d'Urfé but also the historical Elizabeth Tudor. That famous queen had been honorifically associated with Astraea, the classical and virgin goddess of justice who fled the earth after the end of the Golden Age and whose imagined return was celebrated by Virgil in his Fourth Eclogue.[56]

Although most readers have assumed that "Astrea" is somehow more fictional than "Aphra" is, a few recent critics share my suspicion that "Aphra" is also a *nom de plume*.[57] However the name came to be attached to the writer, "Aphra" works as a particularly appropriate and ironic counter to "Astrea," for the latter name is associated with royal virgins, while the former is associated with prostitutes. A third-century courtesan named "Afra" or "Aphra" was worshipped as the patron saint of prostitutes during the Renaissance, although her existence (and hence her popular cult) was deemed a fiction by the Counter-reformation church – another detail Aphra Behn might have relished.[58]

Margaret Cavendish, Duchess of Newcastle, had remarked that daughters were like "moveable goods," unable to keep or preserve a family "name" (in the sense of honor).[59] I want to conclude by suggesting that Behn's last name as well as her first ones are part of the specular and rhetorical cipher-field we have been exploring. In one of the first documents mentioning "Behn" as her surname, a syntactically enigmatic diary entry by one Thomas Culpepper probably made in the 1690s, the name is the occasion for a witty allusion to the Hebrew word for son and to an earlier writer in whose footsteps Behn hoped that her "masculine part, the poet" (preface to *The Lucky Chance*) would be able to tread: "BEENE the famos female Poet di[e]d 29 April 1689," Culpepper remarks. "Her mother was Colonell Culpeper's nurse and gave him suck for some-time, Mrs. Been was Borne at Sturry or Canterbury, her name was Johnson, so that she might be called Ben Johnson, she has also a fayer sister maryed to Capt. [there follows an illegible name which could be Wrils, Eris, Erile, or Write] their names were frfranck, & Aphora, was Mr. Beene."[60] "Mr. Beene," perhaps a scribal error for "Mrs. Behn," since it is in apposition to "Aphora," seems like a curious and tenuous grammatical appendage to this sentence. Most scholars who cite the diary entry have done so to argue for the historical existence not of Mr. Behn but of a father named "Johnson";[61] I want to focus attention, however, on Culpepper's play on "Ben Johnson," with its suggestions of a literary identification based on the past tense of the verb "to be" and on the notion of a literary genealogy: Aphra *son of* ("ben") Johnson. For Astrea or Aphra Behn seems to me quite capable of presenting herself as a somewhat unruly son of Ben by using a name that plays on his Christian one and that, moreover, neatly rhymes with the instrument both writers deployed to construct their name in the sense of fame: the pen. That Behn pronounced her name to rhyme with "pen" seems likely, on the evidence of Culpepper's play with "Ben Johnson."

The author who for some still mysterious reason took the name Behn, and who, in *Oroonoko*, called attention to the power of her "female pen" to make a subject live beyond death, had a playfully Oedipal relation to the historical Ben Jonson. In *The Amorous Prince* of 1671 she defiantly anticipated criticism from educated male readers and spectators who admired "rule-bound" authors like Jonson and Dryden: "you grave Dons, who love no Play / But what is regular, Great Johnson's way."[62] Nonetheless, although she set her mode of playwriting against Jonson's in various polemical passages, she also aspired to a professional renown like Jonson's, and mockingly suggested that he was not so different from Shakespeare and herself (the "unlearned" dramatists) as one might think. She yoked Jonson's and Shakespeare's great names together in the "Epistle to the Reader" prefixed to her early play *The Dutch Lover*; there she remarked that "Plays have no great room for that which is men's great advantage over women, that is Learning. We all well know that the immortal Shakespeare's plays (who was not guilty of much more of that [i.e., learning] than often falls to women's share) have better pleas'd the World than Johnson's works, though by the way 'tis said that Benjamin was no such Rabbi neither, for I am inform'd that his Learning was but Grammar high; (sufficient indeed to rob poor Salust of his best orations")."[63] Through the playful undermining of Jonson's claims to be a learned poet – by accusing him of plagiarizing Sallust Behn actually brings Jonson closer to herself and Shakespeare, both of whom were accused of stealing others' materials – Behn assumes just that "hermaphroditical authority" Jonson had attacked in his play *Epicoene, or the Silent Woman*.[64] Anything but a "silent woman," Behn is nonetheless a writer whose authentic voice is hard to find, for she changes her voices and names with Shakespearean or Ovidian finesse. And since, as Shakespeare's Titus Andronicus says, quoting Ovid, "Terras Astraea reliquit" ("Astrea has left the earth," *Metamorphoses* Book 1, line 150), the modern quest for Aphra Behn takes us inevitably to the ciphers of identity she left us in the products of her pen.

NOTES

1 Aphra Behn, *Oroonoko and Other Writings*, ed. Paul Salzman (Oxford: Oxford University Press, 1994), p. ix.
2 For discussions of her reputation, see Catherine Gallagher, *Nobody's Story: The Vanishing Acts of Women Writers in the Marketplace, 1670–1820* (Berkeley: University of California Press, 1994), pp. 1–4; Jacqueline Pearson, "History of

the *History of the Nun*," in Heidi Hutner (ed.), *Rereading Aphra Behn: History, Theory, and Criticism* (Charlottesville: University Press of Virginia, 1993), pp. 234–52; Pearson, *The Prostituted Muse: Images of Women and Women Dramatists, 1642–1737* (Brighton: Harvester Press, 1988); Jeslyn Medoff, "The Daughters of Behn and the Problem of Reputation," in Isobel Grundy and Susan Wiseman (eds.), *Women, Writing, and History 1640–1740* (London: B. T. Batsford, 1992); Nancy Cotton, *Women Playwrights in England, c. 1363–1750* (London: Associated University Presses, 1980); Frederick M. Link, *Aphra Behn* (New York: Twayne Publishers, 1968), chapter 9; Angeline Goreau, *Reconstructing Aphra: A Social Biography of Aphra Behn* (New York: Dial Press, 1980); and Janet Todd, *The Secret Life of Aphra Behn* (London: André Deutsch, 1996).

3 Quoted from Dale Spender, *Mothers of the Novel: One Hundred Good Women Writers Before Jane Austen* (London: Pandora, 1956), p. 50. See also Robert Chibka, "Oh! Do Not Fear a Woman's Invention: Truth, Falsehood, and Fiction in Aphra Behn's *Oroonoko*," *Texas Studies in Literature and Language*, 30, 4 (1988), p. 511.

4 "As contemporary standards of female chastity often overshadowed Behn's work" in the past, Robert Chibka remarks, "so our century's fear that she lacked another sort of fidelity, to the ideal of historical truth, has distracted attention from her work" ("Oh! Do Not Fear," p. 511).

5 All quotations from *Oroonoko* are from the text edited by Paul Salzman, cited above, note 1.

6 See Gallagher, *Nobody's Story*, pp. 10–11, and the introduction by Emmett L. Avery and Arthur H. Scouten to *The London Stage, 1600–1800*, Part 1: *1660–1700*, ed. William Van Lennep (Carbondale: Southern Illinois University Press, 1965), pp. lxxix–lxxxiv.

7 Robert Gould, "Satirical Epistle to the Female Author of a Poem called 'Sylvia's Revenge'"; the connection between female writer and whore is a commonplace of the age, as Catherine Gallagher, who quotes these lines, notes in *Nobody's Story*, p. 23.

8 In *The Ornament of Action: Text and Performance in Restoration Comedy* (Cambridge: Cambridge University Press, 1979), p. 41, Peter Holland argues that no other Restoration dramatist is "even half as preoccupied with bedroom scenes" as Behn is. Gallagher discusses the significance of Holland's observation in *Nobody's Story*, p. 32, and Elin Diamond, in "*Gestus* and Signature in Aphra Behn's *The Rover*," *ELH*, 56 (1989), pp. 519–41, discusses the technical innovation of discovery scenes. See also Pat Rogers, "The Breeches Part," in Gabriel Bouce (ed.), *Sexuality in Eighteenth-Century Britain* (Manchester: Manchester University Press, 1982), pp. 244–58.

9 My argument here parallels that of Diamond, "*Gestus* and Signature," although I seek to historicize the notion of "deciphering" an authorial "signature" more than she does.

10 This meaning has recently been explored by Edward Tayler, "*King Lear* and Negation," *English Literary Renaissance*, 20 (1990), pp. 17–39; by Terry Castle, *Clarissa's Ciphers: Meaning and Disruption in Richardson's Clarissa* (Ithaca: Cornell University Press, 1982); and by Catherine Gallagher in *Nobody's Story*.

11 The best-known Renaissance cryptographer was John Trithemius, whose *Polygraphia*, published in 1518, inspired Francis Bacon's work on the "double cipher" system of cryptography. For a useful general history of cryptography, see David Kahn, *The Codebreakers: The Story of Secret Writing* (New York: Macmillan, 1967).

12 Maureen Duffy thinks Behn was born in 1640 (*The Passionate Shepherdess: Aphra Behn, 1640–89* [New York: Dial Press, 1980]), p. 16, whereas Sara Mendelson proposes 1649 in *The Mental World of Stuart Women* (Brighton: Harvester Press, 1987), p. 2. Behn's grave in Westminster Abbey states that she died on 16 April 1689.

13 The theatrical depression was the result, in part, of the amalgamation of the two great theatre companies (the King's Company and the Duke's Company, for which latter Behn chiefly wrote) in 1682. With the lessening demand for new plays, many playwrights turned to translation.

14 Dryden, *Of Dramatic Poesy, etc.*, ed. George Watson (London, 1692), p. 273. Janet Todd also suspects that Behn knew some Latin; see Todd's introduction to *Seneca Unmasqued and Other Prose Translations*, in *The Works of Aphra Behn*, ed. Janet Todd, 7 vols. (Columbus: Ohio State University Press, 1992–96), vol. IV, p. x.

15 Introduction to *The Poems of Aphra Behn: A Selection*, ed. Janet Todd (London: Pickering, 1994), pp. xviii–xix. On Behn's code, see Duffy, *The Passionate Shepherdess*, p. 76.

16 For a discussion of her mysterious origins see Mendelson, *The Mental World of Stuart Women*, pp. 117ff.

17 *On the Life of Mrs. Behn, Written by a Gentlewoman of her Acquaintance*, in *Histories and Novels* (London: printed for S. Briscoe, 1696), sig. A7v.

18 Cited and discussed in Goreau, *Reconstructing Aphra*, p. 9.

19 Gallagher, *Nobody's Story*, p. 3. Gallagher also remarks that four of her plays were produced at court – an accomplishment only Dryden, again, surpassed. See Fidelis Morgan (ed.), *The Female Wits: Women Playwrights of the Restoration* (London: Virago, 1981), p. 12.

20 See Mendelson, *The Mental World of Stuart Women*, p. 123, for a discussion of the "unexpected" Republican perspective in *Oroonoko*. Mendelson, however, oversimplifies the question of the novella's political allegory by explaining the republicanism of the narrative just as a function of Behn's youth and the fact that she loved William Scot.

21 Entitled "A Pastoral to Mr. Stafford, Under the Name of Silvio, on his Translation of the Death of Camilla: Out of Virgil," the poem is addressed to John, son of William Howard, Viscount Stafford and is printed in full in Janet Todd (ed.), *Works*, vol. I, pp. 185–98 (no. 64).

22 Public Record Office, State Papers, 29/169, 117; cited in Goreau, *Reconstructing Aphra*, p. 101.

23 Scot is "not suffered to go out of [Colonel Bampfield's] ... sight," according to the letter (cited in Goreau, *Reconstructing Aphra*, p. 96).

24 For information on Behn's spying activities, including reprinted documents, see William J. Cameron, *New Light on Aphra Behn* (Auckland: University of Auckland Press, 1961); Janet Todd and Francis McKee, "'The Shee Spy' and *The Younger Brother*," *Times Literary Supplement*, July 1993.

25 Maureen Duffy, who has expended much labor in trying to track Mr. Behn down in shipping records and other documents, rightly remarks that he has "less substance than any character [Behn] ... invented" (*The Passionate Shepherdess*, p. 48).

26 On the "Account" and the 1696 "Life," see *Poems, A Selection*, ed. Todd, pp. viii–ix; for a detailed description of the different versions of the biography in different editions of the *Histories and Novels*, see Robert Day Adams, "Aphra Behn's First Biographer," *Studies in Bibliography*, 22 (1969), pp. 227–40.

27 Janet Todd follows Behn's previous editor, Montague Summers, in suspecting that all three accounts were written by Charles Gilden, "the main editor of the posthumous Aphra Behn and himself a playwright, manipulator of the literary marketplace, and author of well-known 'fictional letters and tales'" (Todd, *Works*, vol. i, p. x).

28 See *On the Life of Mrs. Behn* by a "Gentlewoman of Her Acquaintance," in *Histories and Novels*, 1696, sig. bi^r: "I knew her intimately well, and I believe she wo'd not have conceal'd any Love-affair from me ... which makes me assure the World, there was no Affair between that Prince and Astraea." Behn hints in her own story of Oroonoko at the possibility of a romance between herself and the hero; for an elaboration of this argument, see my "News from the New World: Miscegenous Romance in Aphra Behn's *Oroonoko* and *The Widow Ranter*," in David Lee Miller, Sharon O'Dair, and Harold Weber (eds.), *The Production of English Renaissance Culture* (Ithaca, NY: Cornell University Press, 1994), esp. pp. 185–86.

29 Terry Castle's study of *Clarissa* take its title from the heroine's statement, "I am but a cypher, to give *him* [Lovelace] significance, and *myself* pain." See *Clarissa's Ciphers*, p. 15; see also *Hamlet*, Act 3, scene 2, lines 117–18, where Hamlet plays with bawdy double meanings and entraps Ophelia into saying "I think nothing" – to which Hamlet responds, "That's a fair thought to lie between maids' legs" (cited from *The Riverside Shakespeare*, ed. G. Blakemore Evans et al. [Boston: Houghton Mifflin, 1974], p. 1163).

30 See Robert Markley, "'Be Impudent, Be Saucy, Forward, Bold, Touzing, and Leud': The Politics of Masculine Sexuality and Feminine Desire in Behn's Tory Comedies," in J. Douglas Canfield and Deborah C. Payne (eds.), *Cultural Readings of Restoration and Eighteenth-Century Theater* (Athens: University of Georgia Press, 1995), pp. 115–40.

31 Ellen Pollak, "Beyond Incest: Gender and the Politics of Transgression in Aphra Behn's *Love-Letters between a Nobleman and his Sister*," in Hutner (ed.), *Rereading Aphra Behn*, p. 155; see also Robert Markley and Molly Rothenberg, "Contestations of Nature; Aphra Behn's 'The Golden Age' and the Sexualizing of Politics," in Hutner (ed.), *Rereading Aphra Behn*, pp. 301–21.

32 Ros Ballaster, "Aphra Behn and the Female Plot," in Hutner (ed.), *Rereading Aphra Behn*, p. 189; see also Susan Staves, *Players' Scepters: Fictions of Authority in the Restoration* (London and Lincoln: University of Nebraska Press, 1979).

33 For a reading of the novella as a Stuart allegory, see George Guffey, "Aphra Behn's *Oroonoko*: Occasion and Accomplishment," in George Guffey and Andrew White, *Two English Novelists: Aphra Behn and Anthony Trollope* (Los Angeles: William Andrews Clark Memorial Library, 1975).

34 Cited from Todd (ed.), *Works*, vol. 1, pp. 31–32 (the poem is no. 12 in her edition); she notes that Behn expanded from Tasso's play's the famous opening chorus evoking a primitive paradise where the only law was pleasure.

35 See Diamond's "*Gestus* and Signature," p. 528; for a longer discussion of Rochester's place in Behn's life and works – and for a discussion of the accusations against Behn made by Rochester's biographer Burnet – see Duffy, *Passionate Shepherdess*, pp. 195–203.

36 *The Rover*, in *Oroonoko, The Rover, and Other Works*, ed. Janet Todd (London: Penguin, 1992), p. 175. All citations are to this edition of the play.

37 Rochester, "Song," in *The Poems of John Wilmot, Earl of Rochester*, ed. Keith Walker (Oxford: Basil Blackwell, 1984), p. 25.

38 For a text of the Rochester elegy, see Todd (ed.), *Works*, vol. 1, pp. 161–63 (no. 53); although she wrote a moving "pindarick" to Burnet at the end of her life, after he had inquired about her health, her earlier relations to him were troubled; he wrote to Anne Wharton, Rochester's cousin, whom Behn had commended in verse, that "some of Mrs. Behn's songs are very tender; but she is so abominably vile a woman, and rallies not only all religion but all virtue in so odious and obscene a manner, that I am heartily sorry she has writ anything in your commendation" (cited in Goreau, *Reconstructing Aphra*, p. 245).

39 For a text of this poem, which is sometimes printed under the title "On Doctor Dryden, Renegade," see Todd (ed.), *Works*, vol. 1, p. 231.

40 See Todd, *Works*, vol. 1, p. xxiii. Dryden's relations to Behn were certainly marked by an ambivalence equal to that which she displayed toward him, if indeed she wrote the "Satyr": his commissioning of her work for his volume of Ovid's *Epistles* indicates some degree of esteem, and he wrote a prologue and epilogue after Behn's death for her play *The Widow Ranter*; on the other hand, he advised Elizabeth Thomas in a letter not to write so "loosely" as Behn had. The letter is quoted and discussed in James A. Winn, *"When Beauty Fires the Blood": Love and the Arts in the Age of Dryden* (Ann Arbor: University of Michigan Press, 1992), p. 430.

41 Mary Ann O'Donnell argues that the poem's "mistaken" attribution to Behn "probably came about because of the presence of this poem in ... a commonplace book into which Behn copied many contemporary satires, of which only a few are hers" (Mary Ann O'Donnell, *Aphra Behn: An Annotated Bibliography* [New York: Garland, 1986], p. 308). Janet Todd (*Works*, vol. 1, p. xxiii), however, follows Montague Summers in printing the poem as Behn's, though she notes that it seems "at odds" with Behn's other expressions of admiration for Dryden.

42 Although in her introduction to the *Works* Todd suggests that Behn's failure to publish the satire may be evidence that she regretted writing it, in her headnote on the poem itself (no. 71 in her edition of the *Works*, vol. 1, p. 427), she notes that many satires were circulated in manuscript in this era, often unsigned.

43 See Mendelson, *The Mental World of Stuart Women*, p. 174, for a discussion of this poem and its implications for an understanding of Behn's complex political stance.

44 See O'Donnell, *Aphra Behn: An Annotated Bibliography*, pp. 308–10.

45 Todd discusses for instance the "eight rather dubious letters, supposedly by Behn," printed in 1718 in a volume entitled *Familiar Letters of Love, Gallantry, and Several Occasions, by the Wits of the last and present Age ...* (*Works*, vol. 1, p. xliv).

46 See Harold Love, *Scribal Publication in Seventeenth-Century England* (Oxford: Clarendon Press, 1993) and also Arthur F. Marotti, "Malleable and Fixed Texts: Manuscript and Printed Miscellanies and the Transmission of Lyric Poetry in the English Renaissance," in W. Speed Hill (ed.), *New Ways of Looking at Old Texts*, Papers of the Renaissance English Text Society, 1985–93 (Binghamton, NY: Renaissance Texts and Studies, 1993), pp. 159–73.

47 See, e.g., her defense against charges of plagiarism in the postscript to *The Rover* Part 1; the "sign of Angellica," Behn claims, is the "only stolen object" from the play she was charged with appropriating, Thomas Killigrew's *Thomaso* (cited from *The Rover*, ed. Todd, p. 248).

48 Cited from *The Works of Aphra Behn*, ed. Montague Summers, 6 vols. (1915; rpt. New York: Phaeton Press, 1967), vol. IV, pp. 115–16.

49 For a text of "To the Fair Clarinda," see Todd (ed.), *Works*, vol. I, p. 288 (no. 80); for the poem (by Daniel Kendrick) praising Behn as the sole exemplar of a super "Third Sex," see Montague Summers (ed.), *Works*, vol. VI, p. 363.

50 Dedicatory Epistle to *The Lucky Chance*, *Works*, ed. Summers, vol. III, p. 183.

51 See Jessica Munns, "'Good Sweet, Honey, Sugar-Candied Reader': Aphra Behn's Foreplay in Forewords," in Hutner (ed.), *Rereading Aphra Behn*, pp. 44–62; Gallagher studies some of the same erotic dynamics in "Who Was that Masked Woman: The Prostitute and Playwright in Aphra Behn," chapter 1 of *Nobody's Story* and also reproduced in Hutner (ed.), *Rereading Aphra Behn*.

52 For a discussion of this self-positioning passage, from Behn's preface to *The Dutch Lover*, see below, p. 243.

53 Cited from Maureen Duffy's edition of the *Love-Letters between a Nobleman and his Sister* (London: Virago, 1987), p. 41. Ellen Pollak discusses an analogous instance of semiotic disguising in *Love-Letters*; see her "Beyond Incest," cited above n. 1, p. 178.

54 See Dorothy Mermin, "Women Becoming Poets: Katherine Philips, Aphra Behn, Anne Finch," *ELH*, 57 (1990), pp. 335–55.

55 See O'Donnell, *Aphra Behn*, p. 2, on the appearance of "Ann."

56 See Frances Yates, *Astraea: The Imperial Theme in the Sixteenth Century* (London: Routledge and Kegan Paul, 1975), pp. 9–10.

57 Both Janet Todd and Sara Mendelson suggest that "Aphra" (variously spelled) may be an assumed name, despite literary historians' efforts to link "Aphra Behn" with an Aphra mentioned in baptismal records in the 1640s.

58 Angeline Goreau notes that the original "Aphra" had been a "sacred prostitute in the temple of Venus in Augsburg on the Rhine in the third century A.D. until her conversion by Saint Narcissus" (*Reconstructing Aphra*, p. 17), but Goreau does not link the name with Behn's own creation of "virtuous" prostitute figures in her plays, figures like Angellica Bianca and La Nuche in Part I and Part II of *The Rover* respectively.

59 Margaret Cavendish, Duchess of Newcastle, *Sociable Letters* (London, 1664), pp. 183–84.

60 *Adversaria*, MS. Harley 75988, f. 453v. Cited from Todd (ed.), *Poems: A Selection*, p. vii; see also Mendelson, *The Mental World of Stuart Women*, p. 16, and n. 3, p. 208.

61 See, e.g., Duffy, *The Passionate Shepherdess*, pp. 18–21.

62 *Works*, ed. Summers, vol. IV, p. 121.

63 *Ibid.*, vol. I, p. 224.
64 See *Epicoene*, Act I, scene i, line 76, and Paula Backsheider's discussion of the passage in *Spectacular Poetics: Theatrical Power and Mass Culture in Early Modern England* (Baltimore: Johns Hopkins University Press, 1993), p. 27.

FURTHER READING

Behn, Aphra, *Love-Letters Between a Nobleman and His Sister*, ed. Maureen Duffy (London: Virago, 1986).
   Oroonoko, The Rover, and Other Works, ed. Janet Todd (London: Penguin, 1992).
Cotton, Nancy, *Women Playwrights in England, c. 1363–1750* (London: Associated University Presses, 1980).
Diamond, Elin, "*Gestus* and Signature in Aphra Behn's *The Rover*," *ELH*, 56 (1989), pp. 519–41.
Duffy, Maureen, *The Passionate Shepherdess: Aphra Behn, 1640–89* (New York: Dial Press, 1980).
Ferguson, Margaret, "News from the New World: Miscegenous Romance in Aphra Behn's *Oroonoko* and *The Widow Ranter*," in David Lee Miller, Sharon O'Dair, and Harold Weber (eds.), *The Production of English Renaissance Culture* (Ithaca, NY: Cornell University Press, 1994).
Gallagher, Catherine, *Nobody's Story: The Vanishing Acts of Women Writers in the Marketplace, 1670–1820* (Berkeley: University of California Press, 1994).
Goreau, Angeline, *Reconstructing Aphra: A Social Biography of Aphra Behn* (New York: Dial Press, 1980).
Holland, Peter, *The Ornament of Action: Text and Performance in Restoration Comedy* (Cambridge: Cambridge University Press, 1979).
Hutner, Heidi (ed.), *Rereading Aphra Behn: History, Theory, and Criticism* (Charlottesville: University Press of Virginia, 1993).
Kahn, David, *The Codebreakers: The Story of Secret Writing* (New York: Macmillan, 1967).
Medoff, Jeslyn, "The Daughters of Behn and the Problem of Reputation," in Isobel Grundy and Susan Wisemen (eds.), *Women, Writing, and History 1640–1740* (London: B. T. Batsford, 1992).
Mendelson, Sara, *The Mental World of Stuart Women* (Brighton: Harvester Press, 1987).
Pearson, Jacqueline, *The Prostituted Muse: Images of Women and Women Dramatists, 1642–1737* (Brighton: Harvester Press, 1988).
Todd, Janet, *The Secret Life of Aphra Behn* (London: André Deutsch, 1996).

12

JOHN MULLAN

Swift, Defoe, and narrative forms

I walk'd about on the Shore, lifting up my Hands, and my whole Being, as I may say, wrapt up in the Contemplation of my Deliverance, making a Thousand Gestures and Motions which I cannot describe, reflecting upon all my Comerades that were drown'd, and that there should be not one Soul sav'd but my self; for, as for them, I never saw them afterwards, or any Sign of them, except three of their Hats, one Cap, and two Shoes that were not Fellows.[1]

What became of my Companions in the Boat, as well as of those who escaped on the Rock, or were left in the Vessel, I cannot tell; but conclude they were all lost. For my own Part, I swam as Fortune directed me, and was pushed forward by Wind and Tide. I often let my Legs drop; and could feel no Bottom: But when I was almost gone, and able to struggle no longer, I found myself within my Depth; and this Time the Storm was much abated. The Declivity was so small, that I walked near a Mile before I got to the Shore, which I conjectured was about Eight o'Clock in the Evening.[2]

Two of literature's most famous adventurers have struggled ashore. Both have been singled out; both live to tell stories of self-reliance. Washed up alone in an alien place, each brings to his predicament an undauntedness that we often hear in the very rhythm of narration. Each will go on to tell us of the means by which he managed to survive, and even prosper, in a strange land, ruefully reflecting on his weakness and vulnerability, as well as proudly recalling his resourcefulness. Practicality and determination also shape their narrations. The drama of their stories is not so much in what they contain as in how they are told. We read of their struggles to survive, but we also listen to their struggles to get their stories to make sense – their struggles to form a narrative.

These two imagined travelers, Robinson Crusoe and Lemuel Gulliver, are also imagined narrators. Each tries to find level tones to tell us of the strangest things (the original title page of *Robinson Crusoe* announced its hero's "strange surprizing adventures"). In the first of the passages above, Crusoe characteristically "cannot describe" his reactions; elsewhere in his narrative, he frequently marks his recollection of feelings he cannot exactly represent. "I believe it is impossible to express to the Life what the Extasies and Transports of the Soul are, when it is so sav'd, as I may say, out of the very Grave."[3] Yet, in all these "Transports of the Soul," there is something else that can be recalled: the sharply remembered, palpable world of objects – "three of their Hats, one Cap, and two Shoes that were not Fellows." Crusoe could notice, and can remember noticing, that those two shoes on the beach were sadly and ludicrously mismatched. The details he offers are evidence of his concern for authenticity, and so his story – like the stories told by all Defoe's other resilient adventurers – is full of measurements and inventories.

Gulliver too likes to think about facts ("... near a Mile ... about Eight o'Clock ..."), and his tale of shrunken and expanded dimensions will supply plenty of its own incredible but pedantically recorded measurements. We might say that both Gulliver and Crusoe are pragmatic Enlightenment Englishmen, and that each is representative of the values of his age and nation in keeping a steady head for facts in the face of the unknown. Except that Gulliver's prose, apparently fashioned like Crusoe's to subdue the world to its particulars, leads to an amazing failure to be amazed. Crusoe's sentences set off in exploratory fashion, adding details and qualifications as they occur; Gulliver's aim at solid testimony – a string of factual statements. His narrative rhythm is bizarrely undistracted by what he narrates: "I was extremely tired ... I lay down on the Grass, which was very short and soft ... when I awaked, it was just Day-light. I attempted to rise, but was not able to stir ... I found my Arms and Legs were strongly fastened on each Side to the Ground ... I could only look upwards ... I heard a confused Noise about me ... I felt something alive moving on my left Leg ... I perceived it to be a human Creature not six Inches high, with a Bow and Arrow in his Hands, and a Quiver at his Back."[4]

This is the point at which Gulliver's narrative becomes something radically different from Crusoe's. In part, this is simply because we have left behind us the world of "probability" that Defoe's protagonists inhabit (whatever their supernatural beliefs). It is also because we must now realize that the very steadiness of the narrative ("the style is very plain and simple" writes the supposed "Publisher") is what is most disturbing and ludicrous about it.[5] It is not a novel but a mock-travel book; it is a satire whose object is its narrator. It is quite possible that, to the modern reader, Gulliver's narration of his arrival in Lilliput would have seemed unremarkable until his first encounter with a Lilliputian, but, alongside Crusoe's narrative, we might see something else that is perturbing about its flatness. Crusoe senses that his "Deliverance," as the word implies, might have been more than fortuitous. As well as the natural laws that a novel must obey, there is Providence. His narrative will tell of the saving not just of a person, but of a "Soul" – the word that he cannot help using of himself. Gulliver simply says, "I swam as Fortune directed me." Nowhere is he to be surprised, as Crusoe often is, by the strange evidence of God's will. There is no God in his prose. On that fact, we will find, Swift's satirical experiment is based. In contrast, the coherence of Defoe's fictional autobiographies requires the presence of God to his sinful narrators. It is on this sense of Providence that the development of what we now call "the novel" is founded.

It seems natural to begin a discussion of the narrative forms adapted or invented by Daniel Defoe and Jonathan Swift with *Robinson Crusoe* and *Gulliver's Travels*. These two works, which epitomize their authors' narrative innovations, became famous beyond any of their other writings, and probably beyond any other books first published during the eighteenth century. Measured by numbers of editions and adaptations, *Robinson Crusoe* and *Gulliver's Travels* have no rivals from this period. Over 70 different editions of *Robinson Crusoe* had been published by 1800; over 100 separate editions of *Gulliver's Travels* had appeared by 1815.[6] (These figures do not include the cheap, hugely simplified chap-book versions, illustrated with crude woodcuts, in which both tales circulated amongst readers who did not belong to the polite classes.)[7] The standard catalogue of eighteenth-century publications in English, the *Eighteenth-Century Short Title Catalogue*, lists over 200 editions and abridgments of *Robinson Crusoe* by 1800, if we include Defoe's own sequels to his book. Both were soon translated in many other European languages, and new translations continue to appear.

Measured in this way – rather than by actual numbers of copies – they are two of the most reproduced works in history. Figures for the nineteenth and twentieth centuries are harder to ascertain, but the British Library catalogue lists 330 versions of *Gulliver's Travels* since 1815 and almost 300 versions of *Robinson Crusoe* (excluding translations).[8] Many editions of both books are illustrated, and many are adaptations for children.[9] Given its notorious misanthropy and scatology (Thackeray called it "filthy in word, filthy in thought, furious, raging, obscene") *Gulliver's Travels* has a particularly interesting history of being, in the words of a 1908 title, "Retold for little folk."[10] In the nineteenth century, typical editions declared themselves "Carefully edited by a Clergyman" or "Revised for family reading."[11] As one Victorian editor said in his preface to a typical adaptation, Swift had "a liking for saying nasty things ... such as are in bad taste and offensive. These have been omitted in this publication."[12]

These two works stand for the achievements of their two authors because they have become mythical narratives, known in some of their elements by many who have never read what Defoe and Swift actually wrote. It is natural to put them together because they display both the proximity and the antagonism of the two writers' narrative forms. In their different imitations of what we might call "factuality," they both draw on a contemporary fascination for detailed accounts of voyages.[13] These voyages provided writers as well as readers with new imaginative opportunities, but opportunities sanctioned by their concern for matters-of-fact. "As the fresh wonders of travel opened a more credible escape than the faded wonders of romance, the way was paved with factual exactitude."[14] The philosopher Shaftesbury remarked in 1710 that voyages "are in our present days what books of chivalry were in those of our forefathers."[15] Narratives, he implied, no longer appealed by being fantastic. In a world in which factual report had a high status, readers were learning to delight in what seemed strange but true.

Defoe's and Swift's imaginary voyages have outlived the factual accounts that they imitated. The vogue for voyages was set in motion by William Dampier's *A New Voyage Round the World*, first published in 1697.[16] In the prefatory "Letter from Capt. Gulliver, to His Cousin Sympson," which Swift added to the 1735 edition of *Gulliver's Travels*, Gulliver writes of having given directions "to hire some young Gentleman of either University" to "correct the Style" of his account "as my Cousin Dampier did by my Advice, in his Book called *A Voyage round the World*."[17] It is indeed the *style* of Dampier that we can hear in *Gulliver's Travels*. Dampier tells of a voyage, or series of voyages, lasting some twelve years and taking him buccaneering around the globe. Yet, as he says in his Dedication, though he brings knowledge of "Remote Regions," his account is "this plain piece of mine."[18] This is not just conventional modesty. Plainness is the guarantee of what his Preface calls "the Truth and Sincerity of my Relation." However exotic the places visited and however strange the peoples encountered, the mariner sets down "such Observables as I met with." "Choosing to be more particular than might be needful," the undistracted narrator has stuck to the facts. At the beginning of the final chapter of *Gulliver's Travels*, Gulliver declares that he has "not been so studious of Ornament as of Truth." "I could perhaps, like others, have astonished thee with strange improbable Tales; but I rather chose to relate plain Matter of Fact in the simplest Manner and Style; because my principal Design was to inform, and not to amuse thee."[19] He might be remembering the proud plainness of his "cousin" Dampier in *A New Voyage*: "As to my Stile, it cannot be expected, that a Seaman should affect Politeness; for were I able to do it, yet I think I should be little sollicitous about it, in a work of this Nature."[20]

"Politeness," by which Dampier means literary refinement and elegance of expression, was, as he well knew, an important value of the age. His own writing presented itself as credible by having no room for considerations of taste. (As a joke at the expense of such proud inelegance, Swift inserted an unreadable paragraph from Samuel Sturmy's *Mariner's Magazine* into Gulliver's narration of the storm at sea in Part II of his *Travels*.)[21] Dampier says in his Preface to his later *Voyage to New Holland* (1703) that he offers, instead of "a Polite and Rhetorical Narrative," only "a Plain and Just Account of the true Nature and State of the Things described." The "true Nature" of what has been seen includes what we might call "scientific" information. Dampier dedicated his *New Voyage* to the President of the Royal Society, the official body that represented the prestige of what was then called "natural philosophy." Dampier hoped that his "Gleanings" could be added to its "general Magazine, of the knowledge of Foreign Parts," and his book is full of descriptions of exotic plants and animals, as well as of observations of tides and winds. (We might notice Gulliver promising, as a sequel to his *Travels*, "a greater Work" – "a particular Account" of the Lilliputians and their history: "their Plants and Animals, their peculiar Manners and Customs, with other Matters very curious and useful."[22]) In pursuit of "curious" facts, Dampier lies hidden to observe the nesting habits of flamingoes on the Cape Verde islands, calculates the weight of turtles on the Gallapagos, and measures the wingspans of "great Batts, with Bodies as big as Ducks" in the Philippines.[23] It is as if he were inspired to travel by a love of natural history (if it were not for his habit of eating most of the strange animals that he describes). In reality, Dampier had been a buccaneer, who traveled around the world in search of profit, attacking Spanish possessions. His account may seem a dogged record of all that he saw, but is not quite the uncontrived log that it purports to be – it took him several years after he returned to turn his notes into this *New Voyage*.[24]

The attachment to the *factual* (however careful a fiction) is what Defoe and Swift exploit. The Preface to *Robinson Crusoe* declares that "The Editor believes the thing to be a just History of Fact," just as the prefaces to Defoe's other novels claim that we are about to read actual records of events (albeit, in the case of *Moll Flanders*, records that have had to be rewritten in "Language fit to be read").[25] These prefaces are themselves part of the fiction – part of the apparatus of authenticity – just like Swift's publisher's note at the front of *Gulliver's Travels*. Yet, though they are fictional, they do guide us to the sense of probability that Defoe creates. In these works of fiction as in Dampier's travel narratives, detail is presented as if it were synonymous with credibility. In Defoe's case, one can see the writer's earlier experience as what we might call a "reporter" informing his fiction. A work like *The Storm*, Defoe's account of the great storm of 1703, seems close to a fiction like his *Journal of the Plague Year* in its sense of particularity, by turns vivid and plodding. The narrator of the former tells us, as he counts fallen trees, that "the Author of this was an Eye-Witness and Sharer of the Particulars."[26] The narrator of the latter, H.F., tries to sort fact from the fantastic stories that spread through plague-stricken London by looking for the circumstantial details that constitute a tale's "probability." Defoe's narratives are full of what De Quincey called "little circumstantiations of any character or incident as seem, by their apparent inertness of effect, to verify themselves":

> where the reader is told that such a person was the posthumous son of a tanner, that his mother married afterwards a Presbyterian schoolmaster, who gave him a smattering of Latin, but, the schoolmaster dying of the plague, that he was compelled at sixteen to enlist for bread – in all this, as there is nothing at all amusing, we conclude that the author could have no reason to detain us with such particulars but simply because they were true.[27]

Defoe's preface to his *Memoirs of a Cavalier* tells us that, while "the Facts" of history that it contains "are confirmed for their general Part by all the Writers of those Times," "the Beauty" of the account is that it is "embellished with Particulars, which are no where else to be found."[28] The ambition of his fiction is to be fact-like.

We associate the particularity of Defoe's narrators with this ambition. Crusoe and the rest measure and count and catalogue because Defoe seems to be trying to do justice to the particularity of the material world. Whatever the debates of literary historians, he will always seem the pioneer novelist because he makes "probability" his creed and has his protagonists, who are also his narrators, provide all the detail and exactitude that will testify to that probability. Crusoe-the-narrator details the provisions that he recovered from his ship as carefully as Crusoe-the-protagonist once paddled them ashore. Telling his story, he sees again each valuable object: those "two very good Fowling-pieces" and the "three Dutch cheeses."[29] As both narrator and character in her own story, Moll Flanders has the same "tenacity of the realist," as Peter Conrad puts it – she "will only believe in things if she can grasp them. That is why she pilfers."[30] Narrating her transactions with "my Mother Midnight," midwife to "Ladies" with something to conceal, she provides copies of the woman's itemized bills for her "Lying-Inn" – as if "the particulars of her Bill" were what made the episode vivid again.[31] Roxana cannot individualize her various lovers (the Jeweler, the Prince, and so on), but she seems to recall exactly how many crowns, pistoles, and livres each of them gave her, and to count them up lovingly all over again in the business of narration.

In *Gulliver's Travels*, the ambition to be fact-like is the object as well as the means of Swift's satire, and in a work of deadly attention to the forms of human pride, Gulliver's proudest boast in his "Veracity" – his faithfulness to "Matter of Fact."[32] At the end of his travels, after his stay with the Houyhnhnms, this sustains the misanthropy that is the logical consequence of the collapse of his vanity: he prides himself on sparing the reader nothing. This is also true in his accounts of his first three voyages. When he has told us of having "discharged the Necessities of Nature" between two sorrel leaves in a Brobdingnagian garden, his apologia is ludicrously close to Dampier's preface to *New Voyage* (see above).

> I hope, the gentle Reader will excuse me for dwelling on these and the like Particulars; which however insignificant they may appear to grovelling vulgar Minds, yet will certainly help a Philosopher to enlarge his Thoughts and Imagination, and apply them to the Benefit of publick as well as private Life; which was my sole Design in presenting this and other Accounts of my Travels to the World; wherein I have been chiefly studious of Truth, without affecting any Ornaments of Learning, or of Style.[33]

Gulliver's sense of the factual truth of what he tells is what enables him not to recognize the worlds that he visits. Since the book's first publication, readers have felt compelled to identify the particular characters and events that it mirrors, and today's standard edition has seventy-three pages of notes pursuing this compulsion. At the end of the *Travels*, the narrator dismisses "the Tribes of Answerers, Considerers, Observers, Reflecters, Detecters, Remarkers" who are ready to find references to eighteenth-century England in the book: "what Objections can be made against a Writer who relates only plain Facts that happened in such distant Countries . . . ?"[34]

So it is that the same influences can have such different effects in the narratives of Swift and of Defoe. Defoe imitates factual accounts to provide us with the means of believing in his stories. In his composition of *Robinson Crusoe* he was probably influenced by a "true story" that had become well known a few years earlier: the case of Alexander Selkirk, who had been marooned for four years on the Pacific island of Juan Fernandez. Several had told Selkirk's story, including the captain of the ship that had rescued him, Woodes Rogers, in his *A Cruising Voyage Round the World* (1712). Here too Dampier, the father of such accounts, was involved. He had captained the ship accompanying that by which Selkirk had originally been abandoned, and four years later he was a member of Roger's crew when Selkirk was picked up. What is more, in his *New Voyage* he had himself told of "a *Moskito Indian*" who had been marooned on the same island from 1681 to 1684 and had survived by his great "sagacity."[35] Defoe seemed to acknowledge his debt to both these voyage writers when he declared in his *Compleat English Gentleman* that an inquisitive person "may go round the globe with Dampier and Rogers, and kno' a thousand times more in doing it than all those illiterate sailors."[36] Likely sources can be found for all Defoe's novels: he used historical accounts for *Memoirs of a Cavalier*; he probably based some of *Moll Flanders* on the exploits of a notorious thief of the period; he drew on bills of mortality for *A Journal of the Plague Year*.[37] Later eighteenth-century novels do not have sources in this way. Even when, like the novels of Richardson, they are presented as authentic documents, they do not reach out for other, known histories. In this sense, Defoe builds the bridge from fact to fiction.[38] Identification of his sources is important only inasmuch as it confirms the ambition of that fiction: to find the factual "particulars" that make a narrative individual – and thence the shapes of providential design that his narrators must discover amidst all the details.

Defoe was so successful that some of what we now call his "novels" were only recognized as fiction long after his death. Late in the eighteenth century, there was still discussion of the authorship of both *Memoirs of a Cavalier* and *A Journal of the Plague Year* that clearly indicates that they were widely considered to be "genuine" recollections, written in the seventeenth century.[39] In 1724, he published a "voyage," directly in the line of Dampier and Rogers: *A New Voyage Round the World*. Only in the 1770s did this begin to be treated as a work of the imagination ("plagiarism" would be more accurate) written by Defoe. Of course, he did not put his name to any of his novels (Moll Flanders and the rest are presented as authors of their own narratives), but he was not necessarily trying to impose on his readers, even if he sometimes did so. In his (also anonymous) *Serious Reflections During the Life and Surprising Adventures of Robinson Crusoe* (1720), he acknowledges that the original is an "imaginary story," but says that there is a "real History" behind it. It may be "Allegorical," but it is not "Romance." What he calls "allegorick History" is morally justifiable: "Such are the historical Parables in the Holy Scripture, such the Pilgrim's Progress, and such in a Word the Adventures of your fugitive Friend, Robinson Crusoe."[40]

This disavowal of "Romance" is a deep-seated need of eighteenth-century fiction. "Romance" stands for an older kind of fictional narrative, with no allegiance to probability. When Fielding, in *Tom Jones*, wishes to justify his fiction, he writes that "truth distinguishes our writings from those idle romances which are filled with monsters."[41] The style is mock-self-important, but relies on the contrast between "truth" and "romance." When Clara Reeve published the first history of the novel in 1785, she called it *The Progress of Romance* to indicate that an entertaining but childish genre had indeed "progressed," and, by discovering a new rigor and new scruples, become, in effect, a new genre. "Romance" elements remain part of this new fiction: the magical transformation of Richardson's Pamela from servant to lady; the discovery of the birthmarks that tell us that Fielding's Joseph Andrews is really a gentleman.[42] Yet Defoe's striving after both factual accuracy and "allegorick" moralism, even if it did not directly influence these later novelists, does tell of a project whose development we can call "the rise of the novel" – even if, of course, Defoe himself cannot have known that he was inventing this genre.

We can better understand the novelty of both Defoe and Swift by returning to some of the narrative forms and conventions that they were adapting (and that the triumphant march of the novel has long since left behind). As well as the new "voyages," with their facts and observations there were journeys of the imagination. Defoe wrote one himself, earlier in his career. In 1705 he published an anonymous prose satire, *The consolidator: or, memoirs of sundry transactions from the world in the moon.* Defoe's "consolidator" is the name for the machine that flies him to the moon, where he observes a society whose political squabbles and religious disputes crudely but vividly parallel the divisions in post-Glorious Revolution England. Defoe's satirical purposes are always so clear that the world he imagines cannot come to life for the modern reader. In large measure, the work is a Whiggish polemic about the dangers of "Absolute Submission" to a monarch (the lunar Prince is "bubl'd" by those who advise him to assume absolute sovereignty) and religious intolerance (Defoe even dramatizes himself as "A certain *Author*" who defends Dissenters against "*high Solunarian Zeal*").[43] Yet, even if it has no aspiration to escape mere topicality, this "voyage" of Defoe's seems to belong to a literary tradition – one much older than the proudly prosaic accounts of Dampier and his ilk. The imaginary voyage, to places beyond belief as well as beyond experience, had been a natural vehicle for satire from classical times.[44] While the determinedly factual accounts of voyages that began with Dampier have a genealogical relationships to novels, novels have no such kinship with the fantastic journeys of which *The consolidator* might have reminded eighteenth-century readers.

The earliest of these that has survived is "A True Story" by Lucian, a satirist who wrote in Greek in the second century A.D. and who was one of Swift's favorite authors.[45] Lucian's also tells of a journey to the moon. The account contains much that is outlandish mischief in the guise of diligent report ("Moonmen have artificial penises, generally of ivory but, in the case of the poor, of wood") and a certain amount that exploits the satirical possibilities of relativism (on the moon "A bald pate or no hair at all is considered a mark of beauty"[46] – clearly an amusingly incredible notion for Lucian). As in *Gulliver's Travels*, there is the constant possibility – in Defoe's *The consolidator* this is a simple necessity – that the narrative is glancing at "real" historical events. In Lucian's case, unlike Swift's, the events are safely distant: the history of Ancient Greece rather than of the Roman Empire in which he lived. As also in *Gulliver's Travels*, the fantastic voyage allows for a celebratory or, more interestingly, debunking encounter with historical characters. In an episode on which Swift must have drawn for Gulliver's visit to Glubbdubdrib in Part III of *Gulliver's Travels*, Lucian's narrator visits "the Isle of the Blest," where he encounters the spirits of great men and can compare them with their reputations.

Lucian greatly influenced a famous English adaptor of the fantastic voyage, Thomas More. More's *Utopia*, first published in 1516, is in the same tradition of *serio ludere* – learned playfulness – as much of Lucian's work, including "A True Story." In modern times it has been called "the tradition of learned wit"[47] – a tradition in which allusive learning is deployed facetiously or deflatingly. In such writings scholarly authors can abandon the religious or political commitments that their scholarship would usually serve. *Utopia* begins with a fiction that licenses its author's purposeful irresponsibility. More's Preface says that his "little book" has avoided stylistic sophistication and merely reproduced the "casual simplicity" of the account of Utopia given him by a traveler, Raphael Hythloday. "Truth in fact is the only quality at which I should have aimed, or did aim, in writing this book."[48] It is a satirical assertion that Swift might have remembered when he invented his proudly truthful Gulliver, having his "publisher" tell us that Gulliver "was so distinguished for his veracity, that it became a sort of proverb amongst his neighbours at Redriff, when any one affirmed a thing, to say, it was as true as if Mr. Gulliver had spoke it."[49] The point of More's irony is that he can write as if he were dutifully repeating what he has been told of the utopian commonwealth. "Truthfulness" is a mischief-making disclaimer. Hythloday has told him in simple terms of a happy land without Christianity (and the "lazy gang of priests and so-called religious men") and without landlords.[50] Its citizens rationally adopt some practices which More himself, in his own world, would have condemned (public officials encouraging the terminally ill to commit suicide, for instance). But "truth" is what is offered us, however uncomfortable or difficult to square with our own ways.

Hythloday's description of Utopia takes up almost all of Book II of More's work. As in Swift's prose satires, the text relies on the distance of the author from what he has imagined. Hythloday (from a Greek compound meaning "expert in nonsense") describes an ideal commonwealth long dreamt of by Ancient, as well as humanist, thinkers. It is a place where vanity and superfluity are renounced. He admiringly tells More and his friend Peter Giles that, in Utopia, "The chief aim of their constitution is that ... all citizens should be free to withdraw as much time as possible from the service of the body and devote them selves to the freedom and culture of the mind."[51] The Utopians are stoics: virtuous ascetics who disdain luxury and who treasure only what is useful. In Utopia, iron is valued, but not gold and silver; children play with pearls and diamonds, but adults scorn them. Utopians never waste time in idling; there are no taverns or brothels, no corruption (because no secrecy), no envy or competition, because all "life's good things" are shared equally (so, without luxury, there is no poverty).

This particular dream – which has, of course, given its name to the very act of dreaming of a better world – is recognizable in Part IV of *Gulliver's Travels*, where Gulliver readily learns to love the rational frugality of the Houyhnhnms. These talking horses are another version of the stoic ideal: passions conquered, appetites subjugated, reason revered. As in Utopia, what readers will recognize as worldly wealth is valueless:

> in some fields of his country, there are certain *shining stones* of several colours, whereof the Yahoos are violently fond ... My master said, he could never discover the reason of this unnatural appetite, or how these *stones* could be of any use to a Yahoo ... My master further assured me, which I also observed my self; that in the fields where these *shining stones* abound, the fiercest and most frequent battles are fought, occasioned by perpetual inroads of the neighbouring Yahoos.[52]

What Swift has learned from More is not, however, the thought that gold and jewels are but "shining stones." Rather, he has learned the art of satire as intellectual experiment, where a narrator tells us in wonder of a wonderful land, but the author is lost. Utopia is (literally, in Greek) "no place," and there is no place for Gulliver in the land of ever-truthful, dispassionate horses. More invented Utopia not as a proposal, but as a provocation. The reader is left to see why it might be admirable, and to understand why it is impossible. "I was left thinking that quite a few of the laws and customs he had described as existing among the Utopians were really absurd," comments More at the end of Hythloday's "afternoon discourse."[53] Yet we cannot be sure that even this conclusion is unironical.

More pretends to reject Utopia on the grounds that its economic egalitarianism "utterly subverts all the nobility, magnificence, splendour and majesty which (in the popular view) are the true ornaments and glory of any commonwealth." But does this not invite us to rise above the "popular view," knowing – as More's Christian humanist readers would know – the true smallness of worldly "magnificence"? The better world that More has invented is not a true alternative to the one in which he lived and made his worldly career; it is a satirical counterpart. In *Gulliver's Travels*, Swift has learned from this device. Yet, in his hands, the absurdity of that gap between the utopian and the real becomes something terrible. Gulliver too sees a better world, and his return to reality, to the world of his fellow yahoos, drives him to live in a stable with herbs up his nose.

A couple of years after *Utopia* was first published, an edition that was almost certainly authorized by More appeared with marginal annotations by one of his friends, perhaps Erasmus. At the point in the book where Raphael Hythloday tells how the Utopians work hard, avoid all senseless pleasures, and hide nothing from each other, the annotator cries "O sacred society, worthy of imitation, especially by Christians!"[54] Influenced by Lucian (who, we are told, is a favorite author in Utopia)[55] More's method allows him to make Utopia a salutary counter-example of the workings of a commonwealth. He invents his traveler, Hythloday, so that his account of the perfect commonwealth can tease the reader into recognition of the corruption or irrationality of his own commonwealth. The separation of author and narrator is as important here as it was in *In Praise of Folly*, written by More's friend Erasmus, six years earlier. In Erasmus's most famous work, Folly herself celebrates folly. Again, we have a text in which mischief is married to learning – an experiment upon the values of its readers. Writings in such a tradition of learned wit were entirely congenial to Swift. It is a tradition to which *A Tale of A Tub* and *Gulliver's Travels* belong. (Later in the eighteenth century, Laurence Sterne, in *Tristram Shandy*, would recover some of the resources of this tradition for the novel.) Defoe's fiction is something new and different because it sets itself different rules. The playfully learned narratives of Lucian, More, Erasmus, Rabelais, or Swift have no regard to the standard of "probability" that Defoe's narrators expect to apply to their stories. Their truth is intellectual, not circumstantial. They bend all their details to their satirical purposes.

The non-novelistic character of Swift's prose satires can also be seen if one thinks about their infamous (if only occasional) scatology. While novels may deal with the facts of life, it is not until Joyce's *Ulysses* that these include defecating. Gulliver, of course, feels impelled to inform us how he dealt with "the Necessities of Nature," hoping that the "candid

Reader" will approve the "Cleanliness" of his behavior.[56] (Gulliver likes to feel that there is nothing that he shirks telling us.) Elsewhere in Swift's satires, pissing, shitting, farting, and belching feature as natural analogies for what we might otherwise like to think of as intellectual processes. In his *Discourse Concerning the Mechanical Operation of the Spirit* (1704), an unknown author purports to find the material causes of "Enthusiasm" – what we might call "divine inspiration." It is both a satirical parody of materialist explanations of human action, offered in particular by the philosopher Thomas Hobbes, and an attack on Protestant sects that trusted to the "Inward Light" of individual believers. Such congregations will be easily possessed by an "inspired" preacher.

> A Master Work-man shall *blow his Nose so powerfully*, as to pierce the Hearts of his People, who are disposed to receive the *Excrements* of his Brain with the same Reverence, as the *Issue* of it. Hawking, Spitting, and Belching, the Defects of other Mens Rhetorick, are the Flowers, and Figures, and Ornaments of his.[57]

In *A Tale of A Tub*, religious enthusiasts are taken literally when they speak of the breath of inspiration, and all their ecstasies are treated as "*Effluviums of Wind*."[58] These "Wise *Aeolists*," as the *Tale* dubs them, "affirm the gift of BELCHING, to be the noblest Act of a Rational Creature."[59] The "author" of the *Tale* treats the bodily spasms and "eructations" that accompany inspiration as its causes rather than its symptoms. Prophetic convulsion is just breaking wind.

Swift has an important model for his reduction of human vanity and folly to the body's baser functions. Perhaps his favorite writer was the learned, facetious French satirist, François Rabelais. When Alexander Pope, Swift's friend and erstwhile collaborator, wished to compliment him at the opening of *The Dunciad*, he imagined him laughing at the world from "Rabelais' easy chair," while Voltaire described Swift as "Rabelais perfectionné."[60] In his satirical application of learning, Rabelais has something in common with his contemporaries More and Erasmus (significantly, all three men translated Lucian, the father of this tradition), although they had neither his taste for vulgarity nor quite his enjoyment of dense parodies of erudition – both features of Swift's satire. Rabelais's "chronicle" of the adventures of the giants Gargantua and Pantagruel was a series of books published over the course of some thirty years, the last of them appearing eleven years after the author's death. This fact of its publishing history is itself some indication of how Rabelais's "chronicle" was something different from what we usually think of as a novel: it was held together not by a plot, but by its capacity to find new opportunities for parody; not by the inner life of its characters but by their capacity to make mischief. As in *A Tale of a Tub* and *Gulliver's Travels* these characters are just ways of encountering arguments, follies, beliefs, and vices.

It is not surprising, then, that one of the Books of Rabelais's chronicle, his "Quart Livre," is an imaginary voyage. In search of advice about marriage, Pantagruel and his companions travel to find the Oracle of the Holy Bottle. In the lands they visit, values or vices are embodied; Rabelais's readers are invited, like eighteenth-century readers of *Gulliver's Travels*, to recognize what they already know in these strange beings and places: the "land of Clerkship," inhabited by the Chiquanous (those who live off "la chicane" – legal chicanery), "men who will hang their fathers for a shilling";[61] the country of the "Papimanes," who have forgotten the Bible because of their reverence for papal law – the decretals – and adore the Pope ("We would kiss his bare bum and his ballocks into the bargain. For he's got ballocks, has the Holy Father. We found that out from our great Decretals");[62] the island of Messer Gaster (Signor Belly), whose subjects, possessed by gluttony, "looked up to Gaster as their great God, worshipped him as a God, sacrificed to him as their God almighty."[63] This voyage through follies and vices, personified in grotesque forms, is behind *Gulliver's Travels* in particular. More generally, Swift has learned from Rabelais a style of incongruity. He has none of Rabelais's celebratory enjoyment of absurdity, which is why Coleridge referred to him as *"anima Rabelaisii in sicco,* – the soul of Rabelais dwelling in a dry place."[64] But his narratives, just like Rabelais', conspire to combine the intellectual and the bodily, the elevated and the ignominious, the spirit and the bowels. In this way too they are unlike Defoe's narratives, or indeed later novels, which purchase the right to tell us of sexual passion by keeping clear, as the Preface to *Roxana* has it, of all "Indecencies, and immodest Expressions."[65]

Yet, while Swift's satires and Defoe's novels may seem opposites, they are as intimately related as all antagonists. The narrative forms that they develop are, we might say, alternative responses to the same challenges. So *Gulliver's Travels* mocks the trust in fact that makes the world credible in *Robinson Crusoe*. *A Tale of A Tub* and *The Mechanical Operation of the Spirit* hold up to (perhaps horrified) ridicule that confidence in an individual's immediate commerce with God that is learned by all Defoe's protagonists and that was essential to their inventor's dissenting Protestantism. Most fundamentally, Swift turns an enthusiasm for progress, improvement, and innovation that seems characteristic of the period, and that we find expressed in many of Defoe's writings, into dark comedy. In one of Swift's earliest satires, *The Battle of the Books*, he brings to life in ludicrous miniature a war between Ancients and Moderns – books-as-warriors, fighting for precedence in the library – whose echoes rumble on through his later works. Swift is with the Ancients (all too clearly, in *The Battle of the Books*, many "modern" readers might feel). The Moderns are the writers of the post-classical world; those "of the Modern party" are those who are ready to believe that the achievements of Modern learning outdo those of the Ancients. Such enthusiasts for intellectual progress "being light-headed ... have in Speculation a wonderful Agility, and conceive nothing too high for them to mount."[66] The nameless "author" of *A Tale of A Tub* is proud to be one of those "whom the World is pleased to honor with the Title of *Modern Authors*."[67] He belongs to an "Illustrious Age" in which learning is not remembered and imitated, but newly coined; in which "the Learned ... deal entirely with *Invention*, and strike all Things out of themselves, or at least, by Collision, from each other."[68] It is an age of "Wit," but then even the enthusiastic "author" of the *Tale* ruefully acknowledges that "nothing is so very tender as a *Modern* Piece of Wit": "Some things are extreamly witty *to day*, or *fasting*, or *in this place*, or *at eight a clock*, or *over a Bottle*, or *spoke by Mr.* What d'y'call'm, or *in a Summer's Morning*: Any of which, by the smallest Transposal or Misapplication, is utterly annihilate."[69] *A Tale of A Tub*, with its layers of preface and apology, its mock-footnotes and inventively substanceless digressions, is not just a description of this modern world but a product of it. It is the most extreme of the mock-books composed by Swift and his fellow "Scriblerians," Pope, Gay, and Arbuthnot.[70]

The modernity to which Swift was an enemy included, of course, "natural philosophy" – what we would call "science." In Part III of *Gulliver's Travels*, the narrator tells us how, on the island of Glubbdubdrib, the ghost of Aristotle talked of the various scientific theories that have been "exploded" over the centuries, and "predicted the same fate to *attraction*, whereof the present learned are such zealous asserters."[71] "Attraction" was the name given, in Newtonian mechanics, to what we now call "gravity." Gulliver reports, from Aristotle's own mouth, the attitude of an advocate of the Ancients to new theories of the workings of nature. "He said, that new systems of nature were but new fashions, which would vary in every age; and even those who pretend to demonstrate them from mathematical principles, would flourish but a short period of time, and be out of vogue when that was determined."[72] Newtonian theory is still in mind, for Aristotle's ghost, referring to "mathematical principles," reminds the eighteenth-century reader of the title of Newton's greatest work: *Philosophiae naturalis principia mathematica*. *A Tale of A Tub* mockingly declares itself, on its title page, to be "Written for the Universal Improvement of Mankind," for it is the fantasy of "improvement" that characterizes modernity. Those who believed in "improvement," whether it be intellectual or economic, were called "projectors," and Swift's preoccupation with the energies of projectors gave shape to several of his satires.

Swift mocked projectors, most famously in his account of the experimenters in the Academy of Lagado. Defoe, on the other hand, wrote a hopeful *Essay upon Projects*, first published in 1697. "Necessity," he says in the Introduction to this book, "has so violently agitated the Wits of men at this time, that it seems not at all improper, by way of distinction, to call it, *The Projecting Age.*"[73] He calls "Projecting and Inventing" a "Modern Art," and while happy to pay his respects to the wisdom of "our Forefathers," is even happier to declare that "some parts of Knowledge in Science as well as Art, has [*sic*] received Improvements in this Age, altogether conceal'd from the former."[74] Appropriately given the acquisitive ingenuity of the protagonists of his fiction, Defoe sees the age's, and the nation's, inventive energies largely in economic terms. Several of the projects that he outlines in the *Essay* – state pensions, Friendly Societies, provincial banks – are designed to improve the country's economy. The best kind of projector is, indeed, a merchant, whose business ensures that he "converses with all Parts of the known World." "This, and Travel, makes a True-bred Merchant the most Intelligent Man in the World, and consequently the most capable, when urg'd by Necessity, to Contrive New Ways to live."[75]

Projectors can be dangerous, especially those who excite other men's hopes with impossible schemes. A new invention is proposed; the projector "gets a Patent for it, divides it into Shares, and *they must be Sold*; ways and means are not wanting to Swell the new Whim to a vast Magnitude; Thousands, and Hundreds of thousands are the least of his discourse, and sometimes Millions; till the Ambition of some honest Coxcomb is wheedl'd to part with his Money for it."[76] The "Honest Projector," however, is someone like Defoe, who proceeds to fill his book with honest projects: a state commission for bankruptcies, a lunatic asylum funded by a tax on books, schemes for the education of women, an academy "to polish and refine the *English* Tongue."[77] A few years later, Swift was to echo the last of these with a project of his own. In 1712 he published *A proposal for correcting, improving and ascertaining the English tongue*, in which he too proposed a national academy, empowered to pronounce on the use and misuse of the English language. "I see no absolute Necessity why any Language should be perpetually changing," writes Swift.[78] Even here, where his imagined academy is a new scheme, it is designed to stand against innovation.

Swift's project is framed as a letter to the Earl of Oxford, who was the leading minister in the government and a personal friend. (He was also intimate with Defoe, whom he employed at various times as a propagandist and secret agent.)[79] Swift has to trust to this friendship to distinguish his scheme from all the other projects of the age, and ends his text, therefore, as "Humble Servant" to a legislator wiser than himself: "But I forget my Province; and find my self turning Projector before I am aware; although it be one of the last Characters under which I should desire to appear before your Lordship."[80] For all his conservative purposes, his academy is designed, as he says, for "the improvement of Knowledge and Politeness."[81] Swift uneasily recognizes that he lives in an age of "improvement." Three years earlier, he had anonymously published *A project for the advancement of religion, and the reformation of manners* which is full of this uneasiness.

> Among all the Schemes offered to the Publick in this projecting Age, I have observed with some Displeasure, that there have never been any for the Improvement of Religion and Morals: Which beside the Piety of the Design from the Consequences of such a Reformation in a future Life, would be the best natural Means for advancing the Publick Felicity of the State, as well as the present Happyness of every Individual.[82]

The idealist proposals that make up this "project" would more probably belong in Brobdingnag than Britain: commissioners should inquire into the "Morals and Religion" of all office-holders; only persons of "distinguisht Piety" should be allowed to become ministers; all plays should be subject to the harshest censorship.

It is strange to find Swift writing with a projector's hopeful enthusiasm, even if it has a characteristic edge of desperation. His sense of the dangers of that enthusiasm forms his satirical personae; they are invented to demonstrate the deadly vanity of those who would improve the world and all our knowledge – those who would, in Defoe's optimistic words, "contrive New Ways to live." It is not just that projectors are often Swift's targets, though indeed they are. It is also that several of his most brilliant satires are, in effect, mock projects. The best known is *A Modest Proposal*, an argument for feeding their own babies to the starving Irish, written by one who has "turned my thoughts for many years upon this important subject and maturely weighed the several *schemes of other projectors*."[83] This projector, with his proud show of modesty ("I shall now therefore humbly propose my own thoughts, which I hope will not be liable to the least objection")[84] is buoyed up by his sense of his own ingenuity. As often in Swift's satires, an argument, once set loose, begins to discover justifica-tions. This projector is supported in his "computation" by his professions of humanity – anything "bordering upon cruelty" would be, he says, "the strongest objection against any project, however so well intended."[85] He is also carried along simply by the projector's occupational zeal, finding more reasons to support his proposal the more he thinks about it.

Similarly, when Swift attacks the religious skeptic William Collins it is by writing a mock-proposal for spreading his ideas more widely, *Mr. C___ns's discourse of free-thinking put into plain English, by way of abstract for use of the poor* (1713). "I have another Project in my Head which ought to be put in execution, in order to make us *Free-thinkers*" announces Swift's invented author, as he mulls over schemes to persuade the clergy out of any old-fashioned belief in the divinity of Christ.[86] When he turns to the debasement of the language that once spurred him to his scheme of a national academy, he produces a mock-instruction book: *A complete collection of genteel and ingenious conversation, according to the most polite mode and method now used at court, and in the best companies of England* (1738). The work's introduction offers this collection of jargon, neologism, cliché, pretended wit, and linguistic affectation as a "standard Grammar in the publick Schools" that it proposes for the nation's benefit. The author ("Simon Wagstaff, Esq.") adds that he has a living to earn and therefore claims for his scheme "a Patent, granted of Course to all useful Projectors."[87] More dizzyingly, his *Argument against abolishing Christianity* (1708) is a mock-reply to an imagined "project," in which the proposer recruits a series of merely pragmatic or fatalistic reasons for sustaining, nominally at least, Christian religion. "I hope no Reader imagines me so weak to stand up in the Defence of real Christianity, such as used in primitive Times (if we may believe the Authors of those Ages) to have an influence upon men's beliefs and actions. To offer at the restoring of that would indeed be a wild Project."[88]

The imaginative achievement of the *Argument against abolishing Christianity*, as of many of Swift's satires, is the scandal of its very existence. Things must be bad indeed if such an argument is even possible. It is as if modernity (rather than Swift) makes these texts. The very title of *The Mechanical Operation of the Spirit* tells us that it should be an offense to our religious sensibilities – and yet, like the *Argument against abolishing Christianity* or the *Modest Proposal*, the speculation ("narrative" seems hardly the right word), once set going, has a momentum all its own. *A Tale of A Tub*, declaring itself one of the "Productions of the *Grub-street* Brotherhood,"[89] is composed of such a variety of origin-less writings as to seem a bewildering, inadvertently inventive testimony to a debased culture. All Swift's satires were at first anonymous, and, thanks to the "modern" world of pseudo-learning that it mocks, *A Tale of A Tub* seems the most anonymous of all – a truly authorless work of the imagination. (Arguments about its authorship indeed continued long after Swift's death.)[90] It takes to an extreme what was always Swift's method: to let loose his satirical inventions, severed from authorial responsibility.

Swift and Defoe both used anonymity (or pseudonymity) creatively. By absenting themselves from their narratives they both brought to life the failings and limitations of their narrators. In Swift's satire, the effect is what is usually called "irony" (Gulliver's failures to recognize his own world in what he encounters – and then his overpowering readiness to recognize the Yahoos as his own species in his last voyage). In Defoe's novels, the narrators' limitations testify to the authenticity of their experiences. H.F., in *A Journal of the Plague Year*, tells of the day when "my Curiosity led, or rather drove me" to see one of the huge burial pits into which victims of the plague were tipped. He attempts a description "tho' it is impossible to say any Thing that is able to give a true Idea of it to those who did not see it, other than this; that it was indeed *very, very, very* dreadful, and such as no Tongue can express."[91] Defoe's narrators grapple with their recollections of their experiences, and often the drama of their engagement with their own histories is in their not being able to describe things. Defoe was a resourceful writer, and has managed to create a narrator who can only say "*very, very, very* dreadful."

Defoe's narrators look back in amazement at their lives, struggling to explain themselves and their destinies. Though protagonist and narrator are one and the same person, there is a gap between them. Invariably, the protagonist is a sinner, the narrator a penitent. To some, Defoe has seemed to be turning into fiction a genre of "spiritual autobiography": an account of the self in which the devout Protestant, like Bunyan in *Grace Abounding*, religiously examines his or her past life.[92] Perhaps even closer to works like *Moll Flanders*, *Colonel Jack*, and *Roxana* were the tales of criminals popular in the early eighteenth century, and in particular the supposed confessions of condemned criminals published by the Ordinary (i.e. chaplain) of Newgate (in *Moll Flanders* he is depicted as a drunk who keeps telling Moll to confess). These criminal biographies were distinguished by what John Richetti has called "religious sensationalism."[93] Their point was to register the horror with which the malefactor now recognized how he had ignored Providence. In his fiction, Defoe went beyond criminal biography of the period, with its "lack of fusion between the two narrative purposes of realistic depiction and moral generalization."[94] Defoe's penitent narrators condemn themselves, but also explain themselves. They sinned, but they had reasons. Moll sums up the complexity of this in her dry reference to "the wise Man's Prayer, *Give me not Poverty least I Steal*."[95] Realism and moralism fuse in her story because, though she has repented, no reader could be more suspicious than her of the opportunism of conscience. As she says when she recalls being sent to Newgate, "I repented heartily of all my Life past," but "it was repenting after the Power of farther Sinning was taken away."[96]

Penitent narration also means detecting Providence in the small accidents of one's life. The sense that the will of God was at work is what makes incident into narrative. "How strange a Chequer Work of Providence is the Life of Man!" exclaims Crusoe as he recalls his adventures.[97] "Strange" and "surprizing" are the words he uses to recognize the "secret Intimations of Providence."[98] When Moll receives the "strange News" that her mother has left her a valuable plantation in Virginia, she recognizes "the Hand of Providence."[99] Narration often means finding "Providences" amongst remembered particulars. Crusoe even manages this when he records the key dates in his life: "I remember that there was a strange Concurrence of Days, in the various Providences which befel me."[100] *Memoirs of a Cavalier* ends with a list of such "Providences," in which the "just Judgment of God" is visible.[101] *A Journal of the Plague Year*, describing a city in which plague-inspired terror of divine retribution is everywhere, is largely given over to the narrator's attempts to recognize "Intimation from Heaven," whilst not succumbing to superstition and credulity.[102] Defoe's protagonists cannot make either their destinies as individuals or their stories without "Providence." Truly to rely on yourself is to rely on God. Here we can return to that initial contrast between Crusoe and Gulliver. For Swift's most famous book is a satirical, pessimistic enactment of self-reliance. With only his own resources, Gulliver knows only pride (Parts i–iii) or the misanthropy that is one step away from pride (Part iv). *Gulliver's Travels* is an experiment in godlessness that leaves its narrator without humility or hope. It is a mockery of individualism. In this respect, as in so many others, Swift seems to ridicule the modern world, the world to which Defoe's narratives look forward – the world of novels.

NOTES

1 Daniel Defoe, *Robinson Crusoe*, ed. J. Donald Crowley (Oxford: Oxford University Press, 1972; rpt. Oxford: Oxford University Press, World's Classics, 1990), p. 46.

2 Jonathan Swift, *Gulliver's Travels*, ed. Paul Turner (Oxford: Oxford University Press, 1971; rpt. Oxford: Oxford University Press, World's Classics, 1991), p. 5.

3 *Robinson Crusoe*, p. 46.

4 *Gulliver's Travels*, pp. 5–6.

5 *Ibid.*, p. xl.

6 In the absence of actual sales figures, and with a relatively tiny book-buying public, it is customary to measure the success of works in this period by numbers of editions. A typical work of fiction might be printed in an edition of

1,000 copies; one that was expected to sell particularly well in an edition of 2,000 copies. The figure for *Robinson Crusoe* is for editions recorded in James Raven, *British Fiction 1750–1770, A Chronological Check-List of Prose Fiction Printed in Britain and Ireland* (London & Toronto: Associated University Presses, 1987). Raven indicates that there are certainly editions that he has not traced. The figure for *Gulliver's Travels* is based on editions recorded in H. Teerink, *A Bibliography of the Writings of Jonathan Swift* (Hague: Martinus Nijhoff, 1937); second edn., revised by A. H. Scouten (Philadelphia: University of Pennsylvania Press, 1963) and includes versions published in editions of Swift's *Works*.

7 See, for instance, Pat Rogers, "Moll in the Chapbooks," in *Literature and Popular Culture in Eighteenth-Century England* (Brighton: Harvester Press, 1985). It is notable that the only now-canonical works of the period that made their way into these "penny histories" were *Moll Flanders, Robinson Crusoe, Gulliver's Travels*, and *Pilgrim's Progress*. I am grateful to David Goldthorpe for this observation.

8 See also Robert W. Lovett (ed.), *A Bibliographical Checklist of English Language Editions of Robinson Crusoe* (New York: Greenwood Press, 1991).

9 For discussion of illustrations of *Robinson Crusoe*, see David Blewett, "The Illustration of *Robinson Crusoe*," in Joachim Moller (ed.), *Imagination on a Long Rein: English Literature Illustrated* (Marburg: Jonas, 1988). For *Gulliver's Travels*, see Jeanne K. Welcher, "Eighteenth-Century Views of Gulliver: Some Contrasts between Illustrations and Prints," also in Moller (ed.), *Imagination on a Long Rein*.

10 *Gulliver's Travels*, "Retold for little folk by Agnes P. Herberton" (London: Blackie and Son, 1908).

11 The first is an illustrated abridgment of *Gulliver's Travels*, ed. James Lupton, published in 1867. The second is an abridgment published in 1873. From the late nineteenth century onwards, there are more abridged versions of Swift's book than "full" ones.

12 *Gulliver's Travels*, "An Illustrated Edition for the Rising Generation" (London and New York: G. Routledge & Sons, 1874), p. viii.

13 Two recent accounts have explored this fascination: Philip Edwards, *The Story of the Voyage. Sea-Narratives in Eighteenth-Century England* (Cambridge: Cambridge University Press, 1994) and Neil Rennie, *Far-Fetched Facts. The Literature of Travel and the Idea of the South Seas* (Oxford: Clarendon Press, 1995). The former is largely descriptive, and gives a good sense of the number and variety of "voyages" published in the eighteenth century. The latter is intellectually more ambitious and challenging, exploring the relations between "voyages" and the works of fiction that used or imitated them.

14 Rennie, *Far-Fetched Facts*, p. 59.

15 See Edwards, *The Story of the Voyage*, p. 3.

16 Swift owned a copy of this, as well as of other "voyages." See Harold Williams, *Dean Swift's Library* (Cambridge: Cambridge University Press, 1932), p. 72.

17 *Gulliver's Travels*, p. xxxv.

18 William Dampier, *A New Voyage Round the World*, ed. Sir Albert Gray (London: The Argonaut Press, 1927), p. 1.

19 *Gulliver's Travels*, p. 299.

20 Dampier, *A New Voyage*, 1697 edn., sig. A3^v.
21 *Gulliver's Travels*, p. 74, and Paul Turner's note, p. 324.
22 *Ibid.*, p. 34.
23 Dampier, *A New Voyage*, pp. 56–57, 77 and 258.
24 From manuscript evidence, Philip Edwards gives a convincing account of Dampier's "manipulation of the record" to make a satisfying narrative: see Edwards, *The Story of the Voyage*, pp. 20–28.
25 Daniel Defoe, "The Preface," *Moll Flanders* (London: Penguin, 1989).
26 [Danie Defoe,] *The Storm* (1704), p. 83.
27 In Pat Rogers (ed.), *Defoe. The Critical Heritage* (London: Routledge and Kegan Paul, 1972), pp. 117–18.
28 Daniel Defoe, *Memoirs of a Cavalier*, ed. James T. Boulton (Oxford: Oxford University Press, 1972; rpt. Oxford: Oxford University Press, World's Classics, 1991), p. 4.
29 *Robinson Crusoe*, p. 50.
30 Peter Conrad, "Inventing the Novel: Defoe," in *The Everyman History of English Literature* (London: J. M. Dent & Sons, 1985, rpt. 1987), p. 333.
31 *Moll Flanders*, pp. 223–24.
32 *Gulliver's Travels*, p. 299.
33 *Ibid.*, pp. 84–85.
34 *Ibid.*, p. 301.
35 Dampier, *A New Voyage*, pp. 65–67.
36 *Selected Writings of Daniel Defoe*, ed. James T. Boulton (Cambridge: Cambridge University Press, 1967, rpt. 1975), p. 255.
37 For sources of *Memoirs of a Cavalier*, see Arthur W. Secord, "The Origins of Defoe's *Memoirs of a Cavalier*," in *Robert Drury's Journal and Other Studies* (Urbana: University of Illinois Press, 1961). For *Moll Flanders* and the life of Moll King, see Gerald Howson, *Thief-Taker General: The Rise and Fall of Jonathan Wild* (London: Hutchinson, 1970), chapter 16. For *A Journal of the Plague Year*, see Watson Nicholson, *The Historical Sources of Defoe's Journal of the Plague Year* (Boston: Stratford Company, 1919).
38 This idea is imaginatively pursued in Lennard J. Davis, *Factual Fictions: Origins of the English Novel* (New York: Columbia University Press, 1983).
39 See my introduction to *Memoirs of a Cavalier*, ed. Boulton.
40 [Daniel Defoe,] *Serious Reflections During the Life and Surprising Adventures of Robinson Crusoe* (1720), Preface and pp. 115–16.
41 Henry Fielding, *Tom Jones*, ed. John Bender and Simon Stern (Oxford: Oxford University Press, World's Classics, 1996), IV, i, p. 131.
42 The persisting power of "romance" in eighteenth-century fiction is argued in Michael McKeon, *The Origins of the English Novel* (Baltimore: Johns Hopkins University Press, 1987). See especially chapter 1, "The Destabilization of Generic Categories," pp. 25–64.
43 [Daniel Defoe,] *The consolidator: or, memoirs of sundry transactions from the world in the moon* (1705), pp. 170 and 208.
44 For renewed interest in the seventeenth century, see Howard Erskine-Hill, *Jonathan Swift. Gulliver's Travels* (Cambridge: Cambridge University Press, 1993), pp. 12–20.
45 See Williams, *Dean Swift's Library*, p. 46.

46 *Selected Satires of Lucian*, ed. and trans. Lionel Casson (Garden City, NY: Anchor Books, 1962; rpt. New York: Norton, 1968), p. 24.

47 See D. W. Jefferson, "*Tristram Shandy* and the Tradition of Learned Wit," *Essays in Criticism*, 1 (1951), pp. 225–48.

48 Thomas More, *Utopia*, ed. George M. Logan and Robert M. Adams (Cambridge: Cambridge University Press, 1989), p. 3.

49 *Gulliver's Travels*, p. xl.

50 *Utopia*, p. 52.

51 *Ibid.*, p. 55.

52 *Gulliver's Travels*, p. 265.

53 *Utopia*, p. 110.

54 *Ibid.*, p. 60.

55 "They ... are delighted with the witty persiflage of Lucian," *ibid.*, p. 78.

56 *Gulliver's Travels*, pp. 14–15.

57 Both the *Mechanical Operation of the Spirit* and *The Battle of the Books* were published in a volume also containing *A Tale of A Tub* in 1704. The standard modern edition also contains all three: *A Tale of A Tub, to which is added, the Battle of the Books, and, The Mechanical Operation of the Spirit*, ed. David Nichol Smith and A. C. Guthkelch (Oxford: Clarendon Press, 1950). This passage is on p. 279.

58 *Ibid.*, p. 157.

59 *Ibid.*, p. 153.

60 Alexander Pope, *The Dunciad. In Four Books* (1743) Book 1, line 22, and Williams, *Dean Swift's Library*, p. 64. Pope's address to Swift is also to be found in the three-book *Dunciad* of 1727.

61 François Rabelais, *Gargantua and Pantagruel*, trans. J. M. Cohen (Harmondsworth: Penguin, 1955), p. 475.

62 *Ibid.*, p. 551.

63 *Ibid.*, p. 574.

64 Cited in Denis Donoghue, *Jonathan Swift. A Critical Introduction* (Cambridge: Cambridge University Press, 1969), p. 24. Rabelais' influence on Swift has not been adequately described, perhaps because of what the modern Anglophone reader finds Rabelais' intellectual and linguistic obscurity. For such a reader, a useful introduction is M. A. Screech, *Rabelais* (London: Duckworth, 1979).

65 Daniel Defoe, *Roxana*, ed. John Mullan (Oxford: Oxford University Press, World's Classics, 1996), p. 2.

66 *A Tale of A Tub*, ed. Nichol Smith and Guthkelch, p. 225.

67 *Ibid.*, p. 123.

68 *Ibid.*, pp. 134–35.

69 *Ibid.*, p. 43.

70 Their most notable collective work was *The Memoirs of Martinus Scriblerus*, a parody of stupid learnedness published in 1741, though mostly written a good deal earlier. A modern edition is edited by Charles Kerby-Miller (New Haven: Yale University Press, 1950; rpt. Oxford: Oxford University Press, 1988).

71 *Gulliver's Travels*, p. 198.

72 *Gulliver's Travels*, p. 190.

73 Daniel Defoe, *An Essay upon Projects 1697*, Scolar Press Facsimile (Menston: The Scolar Press, 1969), p. 1.

74 *Ibid.*, p. 2.

75 *Ibid.*, p. 8.

76 *Ibid.*, p. 34.

77 *Ibid.*, p. 233. Near the end of his career, Defoe was still fancying himself such a useful innovator, publishing a collection of projects under the title *Augusta Triumphans: or, the Way to Make London the Most Flourishing City in the Universe* (1728). This included projects for a university in the capital, a hospital for foundlings, a national academy of music, the suppression of prostitution and gambling, and the provision of adequate street lighting. In its second edition it was retitled *The Generous Projector.*

78 Jonathan Swift, *The Prose Works of Jonathan Swift*, ed. Herbert Davis et al., 14 vols. (Oxford: Blackwell, 1939–68), vol. IV, p. 9.

79 See J. A. Downie, *Robert Harley and the Press. Propaganda and Public Opinion in the Age of Swift and Defoe* (Cambridge: Cambridge University Press, 1979).

80 Swift, *Prose Works*, ed. Davis, vol. IV, pp. 20–21.

81 *Ibid.*, p. 5.

82 [Jonathan Swift,] *A project for the advancement of religion, and the reformation of manners. By a person of quality* (London, 1709), p. 7.

83 [Jonathan Swift,] *A modest proposal for preventing the children of poor people from being a burden to their parents or the country, and for making them beneficial to the public* (1729), in Swift, *Prose Works*, ed. Davis, vol. XII, p. 110.

84 *Ibid.*, p. 111.

85 *Ibid.*

86 *Mr. C_ _ _ns's discourse of free-thinking put into plain English, by way of abstract for use of the poor* (1713), in Swift, *Prose Works*, ed. Davis, vol. IV, p. 31.

87 Swift, *Prose Works*, ed. Davis, vol. IV, pp. 112–22.

88 Swift, *Prose Works*, ed. Davis, vol. II, p. 27.

89 *A Tale of A Tub*, ed. Nichol Smith and Guthkelch, p. 66.

90 In his "Life of Swift," first published in 1781, Samuel Johnson can still write of the authorship of *A Tale of a Tub* being open to doubt. See *Lives of the English Poets*, ed. G. Birkbeck Hill, 3 vols. (Oxford: Clarendon Press, 1905), vol. III, p. 10.

91 Daniel Defoe, *A Journal of the Plague Year*, ed. Louis Landa (Oxford: Oxford University Press, 1969; rpt. Oxford: Oxford University Press, World's Classics, 1990), p. 60.

92 See G. A. Starr, *Defoe and Spiritual Autobiography* (Princeton, NJ: Princeton University Press, 1965).

93 John J. Richetti, *Popular Fiction Before Richardson. Narrative Patterns: 1700–1739* (Oxford: Clarendon Press, 1969, rpt. 1992), p. 30. His chapter in this book, "Rogues and Whores: Heroes and Anti-Heroes," is an excellent introduction to the topic.

94 *Ibid.*, p. 32.

95 *Moll Flanders*, p. 191.

96 *Ibid.*, p. 274.

97 *Robinson Crusoe*, p. 156.

98 *Ibid.*, p. 176.

99 *Moll Flanders*, p. 336.
100 *Robinson Crusoe*, p. 133.
101 *Memoirs of a Cavalier*, p. 272.
102 *Journal*, p. 11.

FURTHER READING

Primary texts

Defoe's novels have been published individually by Oxford University Press in the World's Classics series, and these are the editions to which reference is made in this essay. In the same series is Swift's *Gulliver's Travels*, ed. Paul Turner (Oxford: Oxford University Press, 1971; rpt. Oxford: Oxford University Press, World's Classics, 1991). The standard edition of Swift's prose is *The Prose Works of Jonathan Swift*, ed. Herbert Davis et al., 14 vols. (Oxford: Blackwell, 1939–68), and reference has been made to individual volumes of this edition. Individual satirical essays can found in many anthologies; particularly useful is the volume in *The Oxford Authors* series: *Jonathan Swift*, ed. Angus Ross and David Woolley (Oxford: Oxford University Press, 1984). *A Discourse upon the Mechanical Operation of the Spirit* and *The Battle of the Books* can be found together with *A Tale of a Tub* in the standard edition of all three works: *A Tale of a Tub, to which is added, the Battle of the Books, and, The Mechanical Operation of the Spirit*, ed. David Nichol Smith and A. C. Guthkelch (Oxford: Clarendon Press, 1950).

Secondary texts

For Swift, two biographies are invaluable: I. Ehrenpreis, *Swift: the Man, his Works and the Age*, 3 vols. (London: Methuen, 1962–83) is authoritative; David Nokes, *Jonathan Swift. A Hypocrite Reversed* (Oxford: Oxford University Press, 1985) is briefer but more accessible. An introduction to the history of the reception of Swift's satire is Kathleen Williams, *Swift. The Critical Heritage* (London: Routledge and Kegan Paul, 1970). General treatments of Swift's narrative devices are Denis Donoghue, *Jonathan Swift. A Critical Introduction* (Cambridge: Cambridge University Press, 1969); R. Quintana, *The Mind and Art of Jonathan Swift* (London and New York: Oxford University Press, 1936; rpt. London: Methuen, 1953); E. Zimmerman, *Swift's Narrative Strategies: Author and Authority* (Ithaca, NY: Cornell University Press, 1983). Amongst many books and essays on *Gulliver's Travels*, Angus Ross, *Gulliver's Travels* (London: Edward Arnold, 1968); Howard Erskine-Hill, *Jonathan Swift. Gulliver's Travels* (Cambridge: Cambridge University Press, 1993); and Richard Gravil (ed.), *Swift: Gulliver's Travels*, Casebook Series (London: Macmillan, 1974) are all good introductions. For discussions that relate *Gulliver's Travels* to the development of the eighteenth-century novel, see Ronald Paulson, *Satire and the Novel in Eighteenth-Century England* (New Haven: Yale University Press, 1967) and J. Paul Hunter, "*Gulliver's Travels* and the Novel," in Frederick N. Smith (ed.), *The Genres of Gulliver's Travels* (Newark: University of Delaware Press, 1990).

For Defoe, Paula R. Backscheider, *Daniel Defoe. A Life* (Baltimore and London: Johns Hopkins University Press, 1989) is now standard, though James Sutherland, *Daniel Defoe* (London: Methuen, 1937) is readable and good. Maximillian E. Novak, *Defoe and the Nature of Man* (Oxford: Oxford University Press, 1963) treats Defoe's fiction in relation to other genres in which he wrote. The structure and artfulness of his narratives began to be treated with a new respect in the 1970s. Stimulating studies are John J. Richetti, *Defoe's Narratives: Situations and Structures* (Oxford: Oxford University Press, 1975); Everett Zimmerman, *Defoe and the Novel* (Berkeley and Los Angeles: University of California Press, 1975); Paul Alkon, *Defoe and Fictional Time* (Athens: University of Georgia Press, 1979); and David Blewett, *Defoe's Art of Fiction* (Toronto: University of Toronto Press, 1979). Highly influential are two books by G. A. Starr on the religious patterning of Defoe's novels: *Defoe and Spiritual Autobiography* (Princeton, NJ: Princeton University Press, 1965) and *Defoe and Casuistry* (Princeton, NJ: Princeton University Press, 1971). Lincoln B. Faller, *Crime and Defoe. A New Kind of Writing* (Cambridge: Cambridge University Press, 1993) compares Defoe's novels with criminal biographies of the time.

Defoe plays a pioneering role in Ian Watt's hugely influential, much challenged, still impressive *The Rise of the Novel* (Berkeley and Los Angeles: University of California Press, 1957). Good alternative accounts, in which Defoe has an important part, are Lennard J. Davis's idiosyncratic *Factual Fictions: Origins of the English Novel* (New York: Columbia University Press, 1983) and Michael McKeon's challenging, sometimes dense, *The Origins of the English Novel* (Baltimore: Johns Hopkins University Press, 1987). John Richetti's *Popular Fiction before Richardson. Narrative Patterns: 1700–1739* (Oxford: Clarendon Press, 1969, rpt. 1992) is the best account of the nature and range of English prose fiction in the early decades of the eighteenth century.

Interesting discussion of the importance and popularity of travel narratives in the period is to be found in Philip Edwards, *The Story of the Voyage. Sea-narratives in Eighteenth-century England* (Cambridge: Cambridge University Press, 1994) and Neil Rennie, *Far-Fetched Facts. The Literature of Travel and the Idea of the South Seas* (Oxford: Clarendon Press, 1995).

13

PATRICIA SPRINGBORG

Mary Astell and John Locke

A poor Northern English gentlewoman, Mary Astell was born in 1666 of a mother from an old Newcastle Catholic gentry family, and of a father who had barely completed his apprenticeship with the company of Hostman of Newcastle upon Tyne, before he died leaving the family debt-ridden when Mary was twelve. With customary spiritedness Mary Astell moved to London when she was twenty, making her literary debut by presenting to the Archbishop of Canterbury, William Sancroft, a collection of her girlhood poems, dedicated to him, accompanied by a request for financial assistance.[1] Whether or not the Archbishop, who numbered among the prominent members of the clergy who had refused to swear allegiance to William and Mary, became Astell's patron in fact, we do not know. But Astell entered a circle of High Church prelates and intellectual and aristocratic women, including Lady Anne Coventry, Lady Elizabeth Hastings, Lady Mary Wortley Montagu, and Lady Catherine Jones. To Lady Catherine Jones Astell dedicated the *Letters Concerning the Love of God* (1695) and her *magnum opus*, *The Christian Religion as Profess'd by a Daughter of the Church* (1705). Later, as a known literary figure, Astell was to contribute a preface to Mary Wortley Montagu's *Embassy Letters: The Travels of an English Lady in Europe, Asia and Africa* (1724, 1725), a work now famous in the literature surrounding the "invention" of Eastern Europe.

Astell established herself with an impressively diverse array of canonical works, beginning with a tract on women's education, *A Serious Proposal to the Ladies* (1694, 1697),[2] which very nearly won funding support for an exclusively female academy from Queen Anne. In *Reflections upon Marriage* (1700), written in response to the scandalous divorce of Hortense Mazarin, Astell displayed her powers as a social critic, for which she was emulated and imitated. Meanwhile the philosophical and theological seriousness of a carefully focused and strongly centered writer was manifested in correspondence with the Cambridge Platonist, John Norris,

Rector of Bemerton, begun in 1693, and published at his instigation in 1695 as *Letters Concerning the Love of God*.[3]

On the strength of these credentials Astell entered the political and constitutional controversy over Occasional Conformity. Her three pamphlets of 1704, published, and probably commissioned by, the High Church printer Richard Wilkin, *Moderation truly Stated*, *A Fair Way with the Dissenters and their Patrons*, and *An Impartial Enquiry into the Causes of Rebellion and Civil War*,[4] entered the Tory canon as specific responses to Whiggish works by James Owen, Daniel Defoe, and Bishop White Kennett, respectively.[5] And in 1705 Astell published what she herself regarded as her *magnum opus*, her long and systematic philosophical and theological critique of Locke's *Reasonableness of Christianity*, entitled *The Christian Religion as Profess'd by a Daughter of the Church*.[6]

Astell's last major published work, *Bart'lemy Fair* of 1709, is in a different genre altogether, an essay in Augustan *belles lettres*. Subtitled *An Enquiry after Wit in which due Respect is had to a Letter Concerning Enthusiasm*, *Bart'lemy Fair* directly addressed the *Letter*, a work by the third Earl of Shaftesbury, Locke's pupil. But Astell took it in fact to be the work of Jonathan Swift and so wrote under the name of William Wotton, the author parodied by Swift in *A Tale of A Tub*. She thus entered the Battle of the Books, that literary controversy, begun in France and then transported to England, which marked the watershed between modernity and pre-modernity, as a self-conscious contender on the side of the moderns.[7] Astell lived on until 1731, seeing her works reissued and debated. We have evidence that she continued to pursue Tory causes, although not in published works of her own, but in the research (for which she is acknowledged) for John Walker's massive study, *The Sufferings of the Clergy* (1714).[8]

Commentators have noted the capacity of Restoration women to live in the interstices of social institutions, in new literary and critical spaces created out of the great upheaval of the Civil War, as novelists, dramatists, and political pamphleteers. Astell's is a curious case. On the one hand she undertook a self-conscious critique of the very institutions at the root of female oppression: contemporary education and marriage practices. On the other she was a commissioned Tory pamphleteer. How do we explain this? It does little justice to the capacity of women to fabricate an existence amid the legal and structural constraints within which they found themselves to harp too much on their absence from the official record, if this were even true. To some extent the problem is definitional. But that we so readily acquiesce to a definition of the public realm that restricts it to the *polis* and its forms, is a story in itself. For this narrowness in the definition of public life excludes not only women. The Elizabethan period, one of the richest flowerings of commentary on the changing forms of public life in all their social and political dimensions, has been virtually expunged from the history of political thought. This is due to exclusions on the basis of genre, rather than gender. The works of Marlowe, Kyd, Spenser, and Shakespeare, intensely "political" in the broad sense, were cast for the stage or in verse, for a complex of reasons which included forms of lyric expression favored by Renaissance writers, a preference for "veiled allegory" due to religious and magical beliefs, involvement in foreign and sometimes treasonable causes and, not least, the activities of Elizabethan secret police under Secretary of State Walsingham. The New Historicists[9] have sought to rectify the loss for which the Old Historians are guilty. But political theorists have yet to leap into the fray.

As further testimony to the power of our categories to frame history, early modern liberal theory set out to entrench the public/private split which had the consequence of expunging women from the public record. Mary Astell stands as a living witness to the artificiality of this distinction and the untruthfulness of its ramifications. For in Astell we have the curious case of a mainstream religious thinker and political pamphleteer, celebrated in her day, whose works in some cases ran through four editions and only gradually lost currency. Her most celebrated persona was as "Madonella," the founder of an academy for "superannuated virgins" in Steele's satire of A Serious Proposal to the Ladies in Tatler, nos. 32 and 63.[10] As author of a project to "erect a monastery or religious retirement" for women, Astell was lampooned on the stage by Mrs. Centlivre in Basset Table,[11] although lionized by Samuel Richardson in Sir Charles Grandison[12] and as the model for Clarissa.[13] It was this persona to which Alfred, Lord Tennyson's Lilia of The Princess (1847) refers, imitated in turn by Gilbert and Sullivan's Princess Ida, their lampoon of a female academy over whose doors was emblazoned the motto "Let no man enter on pain of death."[14]

To give some indication of the reception and circulation of Astell's works, Part I of A Serious Proposal to the Ladies, of 1694, was reprinted four times and plagiarized at least as many. A Serious Proposal to the Ladies, Part II, which followed in 1697, was even more notoriously pirated. Some 147 pages of chapter three, sections 1–5 of the 1697 edition of A Serious Proposal, Part II, were excerpted without acknowledgment in The Ladies' Library of 1714, a work widely circulated, which went through eight impressions up to 1772 and was translated into French and Dutch. Steele was until recently believed to be the compiler of The Ladies' Library, and the man to whom Astell herself, in the 1722 Preface to

Bart'lemy Fair, attributed the plagiarism. But *The Ladies' Library,* according to the title page, "published by Mr. R[ichard] Steele," who supplied a preface, and "written by a Lady," was in fact compiled by George Berkeley (1685–1753), Bishop of Cloyne in Ireland, philosopher, and polymath, as recent scholarship establishes.[15] Meanwhile, Astell's *Reflections upon Marriage*[16] was to run to four editions, to the third of which (1706) she added a controversial preface, expanding her arguments of 1697 and 1700 to furnish one of the earliest and most percipient critiques of John Locke's political arguments.

Astell's revival as a positive model has largely been the work of feminists; Catherine Macaulay, Mary Wollstonecraft, and their associates, in the first instance; and the great wave of late twentieth-century feminists, in the second. Here we will briefly review the contexts for Mary Astell's feminism, her contribution to political debates in the Augustan age, her religiosity, and her enduring contribution to Augustan letters.

Mary Astell had an overwhelming concern to persuade general citizens of the sanity of Tory arguments and the dangers to the public interest of theories of social contract and resistance; theories that had ever gained but a little advocacy. New ideas were abroad, unsettling to old Tory views, and it is a mark of the complexity of Astell's thought that she reflects these tendencies also. John Pocock[17] and Mark Goldie[18] both remark on the inroads made in the second half of the seventeenth century by doctrines of natural right. They intruded into an environment of fairly parochial argument about the legitimacy of monarchy, where case and counter-case were argued in terms of English history: the ancient constitution, whether king or parliament were the true repository of immemorial custom, and claims made for the English common law as a fund of equity and justice and on behalf of the lawyer practitioners who articulated it. To the Continental legal tradition belonged the great European natural rights theorists, Hugo Grotius (1583–1645) and Samuel Pufendorf (1632–94), the former of whom Astell cites,[19] along with their English counterparts, Thomas Hobbes and John Locke, whose sojourns on the Continent had acquainted them with their European contemporaries.

It would oversimplify the position to argue that the English legal tradition had been parochial for long. As Pocock in his *Ancient Constitution and the Feudal Law* well shows, the Continental feudal law tradition had early been inserted into the debate against the common law parliamentarians. The "ancient constitution" lived on as a conceit, which it may always have been, against the onslaught of the rationalists, whether they be canon law proponents of popular sovereignty, earlier, or Whiggish adherents of natural rights, latterly, whom Astell wisely lumps together. And many conservative arguments, including those of Astell, were philosophical, not historical, and grounded in an appeal to reason.[20]

Natural rights doctrines, although less immediately recognized, and more narrowly subscribed to, were to prove more devastating. Drawn in initially as resources in the constitutional crisis of 1688 and developed in the refinement of the Whig position, they were to open a new chapter in political debate. Notwithstanding the fact that she uses it to entrench traditional positions, Astell participates in a rationalism that is ultimately corrosive of Tory causes, to the extent – which is not as great as sometimes claimed – that they depended on historicist arguments. Here we have the anomaly of a theorist contributing to the very movement that was to render her political philosophy obsolete – supplying perhaps an explanation for the removal from the political theory canon of a woman whose works in her day regularly ran to five editions.

Astell is among the most trenchant critics of Locke and Hobbes. Yet she participated in the Continental philosophical tradition out of which Hobbism and Lockeanism grew. Under the tutelage of John Norris, and through the medium of such contemporary popularizers as Richard Allestree (1619–81), Astell was an early convert to the view of Descartes that introspection, complemented by faith, provided the fundamental truths of philosophy.[21] English philosophy of her day represented commentary on Descartes. Hobbes, most famous of the early modern atomists and materialists, had supplied *Objections* to Descartes's *Discourse on Method* (1637), later published with the French philosopher's *Meditations on First Philosophy* (1641). It was in exile in France, as a member of the circle gathered around Marin Mersenne, that Hobbes had first sought to establish his credentials as a philosopher, in the company of the like-minded Epicurean and sceptic, Pierre Gassendi and others. To a greater extent than is usually acknowledged Hobbes's metaphysics belong to the history of the reception of Descartes, so many of whose ideas he absorbed. It was this tradition of epistemology to which Locke contributed so greatly with his *Essay Concerning Human Understanding* (1690): an epistemology, like that of Hobbes, which laid the foundations of modern behaviorism, pioneering the notion of the mind as a black box, which processed sensations as inputs and produced ideas, simple and complex, as outputs.

Astell satirized Locke's theory of the association of ideas, atomist, materialist, and Gassendist, as it was.[22] Too frequently modern commentators have missed this, tracing Astell's feminist reformism, like that of Mary Wollstonecraft and Harriet Taylor, whose views are otherwise so different, to an epistemology founded on Lockean principles. For the philosophies of both Descartes and Locke provided the foundations for a gender-neutral theory of mind. If, as Descartes maintained, the great truths of existence were affirmed by the solitary thinking subject, and if the mental processes of the thinking subject facilitated reason, the claims of men to rule women were baseless. The equality of all believers, which Protestantism preached, and to which Descartes was responding, had to include women or its very foundations were breached. Alternatively, if as Locke maintained, Descartes was wrong about ideas of existence being pre-theoretically imprinted in the human mind; and if, as Locke asserted, the mind was a clean slate receptive to sense impressions, gendered mind was once again an incoherent concept. It was Descartes, whose Platonist idealism Locke followed Hobbes in rejecting, who so profoundly influenced Astell.[23] And Astell's critique of Locke on "thinking matter" in *The Christian Religion as Profess'd by a Daughter of the Church*, lies at the heart of her refutation of Locke's *The Reasonableness of Christianity* in particular and his epistemology in general.[24]

In the realm of social theory, Astell made that particular politico-juridical legacy of Hobbes and Locke, the theory of social contract, the target of her attack. Designed to explain the relation between subjects and rulers as the outcome of a pact by which subjects exchanged obedience for protection, social contract relied for its force on the only form of legal contract with which ordinary people had experience, the marriage contract. In doing so, social contract theory drew an implicit parallel between the voluntary submission of wives, who enter the marriage contract as free and equal partners but emerge as radical unequals in the marriage estate; and subjects, who contract as free and equal individuals, but enter the political estate bound to an absolute sovereign. The marriage contract/social contract homology, which Hobbes and Locke bequeathed to liberalism as a paradigm for the future,[25] was subject to Astell's assault in *Reflections Upon Marriage*; a sortie as deadly as her assault on the Whig fabrications of a Popish Plot and the French alliance in *An Impartial Enquiry*.[26] She thus attacked the program of Locke and the Shaftesbury circle on all fronts.

Astell, Locke, and the problem of resistance

Astell's critique of social contract may well be one of the first published critiques of arguments central to Locke's *Two Treatises of Government*. Certain it is that Astell's *Impartial Enquiry* belongs to a genre that deals no less with the Exclusion Crisis, the Glorious Revolution, and the succession crises in the reign of Anne, than it does with the Civil War of the mid-seventeenth century. Thus Locke's and Astell's works belong to the same political milieu, a politics which, from the Exclusion Crisis to the end of Anne's reign is, in many respects, a seamless whole.

The greater issues on which these particular debates turned were the following. The ultimate source of law: was it customary right enshrined in common law, or the will of the prince? The true guardian of the law: was it the parliament as representative of the people, or the Crown, with its duty of protection in exchange for allegiance? The provenance of the ancient constitution: did it lie in immemorial custom or the institutions of the Crown? The nature of the relationship between the Crown and its subjects: was it contractual, or was it defined by submission to providential rights or rights of conquest? The entitlement rights of subjects in their own person and to their property: did they exist by nature, or by contract? Another set of questions concerned the respective antiquity of the institutions under contest and their historical status. Were they relatively indigenous, native to Englishmen; were they feudal, or rooted in Roman Law; or were they ahistorical, originating in the "natural right" of individuals, belonging to the human condition itself?

The long contest begun in the 1640s between parliament and the Crown had seen a disaggregation of customary rights and the ancient constitution.[27] The upshot of the contest was the hijacking of customary right by the parliamentary party (later the Whigs) and of the ancient constitution by the Royalists (later the Tories). If such a characterization seems too crude, it is worth noting that party politics in the age of Anne, in which Astell participated, turned on just these principles, and are barely comprehensible without them. From Sir Edward Coke's time on, juridical thought had conceived of the ancient constitution as comprising the Crown, its institutions, and the entirety of common law, and statutory law enacted by parliament sitting as a high court. But the heightening conflict between the Crown and the parliament over the royal prerogative brought with it a contest over their antiquity and, therefore, the superior claims of one against the other.

The long process of disaggregating the ancient constitution and customary rights, marked the juridically most sophisticated, perhaps the politically most participatory, certainly the party-politically most polarized, and the most vigorous pamphlet war in the history of the early modern English state. It was ultimately won by the Whig side, with limitations on royal prerogative put in place successively from 1649 to 1702. Goldie, in his review of politics and the press for the period concludes, "Between 1689 and 1714, newspapers apart, the figure of five to six thousand, or on average four per week, would not be an unrealistic guess at the total number of polemical pieces coming off the presses."[28]

Astell was implacably opposed to the removal of James II from the throne and hostile to William and Mary as imposters. Her allies numbered prominent non-jurors, and her early works are replete with *double entendre* aimed at William III and his apologists. Much of Astell's case against the fickleness with which men treat their marriage vows in *Reflections upon Marriage* can be read at another level as criticism of the fickleness of those who undertook oaths of allegiance to William and Mary despite solemn and binding oaths to James II still in force. In this way Astell characteristically turned to her advantage the marriage contract/social contract homology. So for instance in the famous 1706 Introduction to *Reflections upon Marriage*, Astell combines insistence on the rule of queens as affirmed by Salic Law in general, and endorsement of the rule of Queen Anne in particular, with jibes at Locke, Defoe, and William's propagandists who, in forsaking James II, forsook the lineage of the great Queen Elizabeth I:

> If they mean that *some* Men are superior to *some* Women this is no great Discovery;[29] had they turn'd the Tables they might have seen that *some* Women are Superior to *some* Men. Or had they been pleased to remember their Oaths of Allegiance and Supremacy, they might have known that *One* Woman is superior to *All* the Men in these Nations, or else they have sworn to very little purpose. And it must not be suppos'd, that their Reason and Religion wou'd suffer them to take Oaths, contrary to the Law of Nature and Reason of things.[30]

Only the radical Whigs, among whom Locke of the *Two Treatises of Government* belongs, along with Tyrrell, Samuel Johnson, Atwood, Blount, and Defoe, "used a natural law case for resistance or right of deposition" – although a Whig middle group used contractual resistance in some form.[31] Astell mounts against them a brilliant case, calling upon distinctions between authorization and designation that are to be found in Hobbes and Filmer, drawn ultimately from scholastic debate and now put to similar use by thinkers otherwise very much at odds, to deny a right to dethrone kings, even bad kings.

In this, as in other instances, Astell demonstrated her consistency and care in argumentation preparatory to her great attack by ridicule on the social contract/marriage contract analogue in *Reflections upon Marriage* and *An Impartial Enquiry*. The attempt, in scholastic theory, to drive a wedge between authorization and consent as sanctions for institutions public and private, had its legacy in Hobbes's finely crafted theory of simultaneous authorization and consent in the moment of social contract. If for Hobbes popular consent was the necessary but not sufficient condition for legitimacy, the fabric of social institutions could nevertheless not be allowed to hang by such slender threads. Mainstream scholastic theory had sought to secure the social power of even secular institutions, the magistracies of state, and semi-secular ones, notably the family, by separating out as different acts the authorizing of an institution and the appointment of an incumbent to it. Authorization fell to God alone, but in the act of designation the people had their day. Where the Roman Catholics Robert Cardinal Bellarmine and Francisco Suarez took the more radical position that only a community could authorize the transfer of power from a community to a ruler, Hobbes fell back on the older scholastic position that vests power to authorize with the author (in this case God), leaving only the designation of an incumbent to popular choice.[32] Hobbes's extension of contract theory to the recesses of household and family was not necessarily inconsistent. Scholastic theory held, correspondingly, that entry to the estate of marriage could only be divinely authorized, as registered in the marriage vows, but that the choice of incumbents could be left to consent, as recognized by the marriage contract between the parties.

Astell, who tipped her hand against the marriage contract/social contract analogue in *Reflections upon Marriage*, argued her case systematically in *An Impartial Enquiry* and *The Christian Religion as Profess'd by a Daughter of the Church*. Themes from contemporary parliamentary and pamphlet controversy dominate these works. In *An Impartial Enquiry*, she proceeded to invoke Paul, Romans 13,[33] although not by name, the very text canonically recited by the rationalists and pragmatists of her day, who claimed as a practical necessity of government that God, while ordaining good governors, also permitted bad ones to be obeyed. It was once again an argument only permitted on the grounds of the scholastic distinction between *ordinatio commissionis*, and *ordinatio permissionis*[34] which absolved the Deity of whatever bad choices the people might make in choosing incumbents to offices. Since these were offices that only God could authorize, and because their continued stability was in his care, the consent of the people was a non-revocable act: once made it could not be withdrawn. This was precisely the argument made by Hobbes. It was also the basis for the Christian case against divorce. Astell in *Reflections upon Marriage*, by no accident, used the opportunity of a celebrated divorce case between the courtesan Hortense Mazarine and her husband, a close relative of Louis XIV's famous Cardinal, to reflect on duty and contract in the public and private spheres.

Astell and the "Glorious Revolution" of 1688

It is ironic that Locke's *Two Treatises*, written, it is now argued, between 1681 and 1683, constantly revised and secretly guarded until their release was safe after 1689, may have been disguised as the mysterious work *Tractatus de Morbo Gallico*, "Concerning the French Disease," which had a double meaning: syphilis in one sense, despotism in another, both considered by the English to be peculiarly French.[35] But then the Whigs trumped up threats of a French alliance, popery, and despotism, as justifications for the deposition of James II and grounds for continuing fears of reinstatement of the Pretender, latterly in exile in France. Mary Astell reserved her most stinging invective for such subterfuges. Presbyters, not Popes, were the greatest threats to the prevailing civil order, she charged; and Presbyterians were more than popish in their tactics. Just as Whigs charged Tories with popery and francophilia, so Tories charged Whigs with Presbyterian–Calvinist plots against church and state.

The Act of Allegiance of 1689, in its first wording, had raised the specter of "Jesuits and other wicked persons" advising James II "to subvert the constitution of the kingdom by breaking the original contract between king and people."[36] It was on the basis of such calumnies, admittedly moderated somewhat in the final form of the bill, that clerics mindful of their oaths to the Stuarts had been deprived of their livings. Among them Mary Astell numbered her most revered authorities, Archbishop Sancroft, her earliest patron, Lord Clarendon, upon whose *History* she relied, Henry Dodwell, and Bishop George Hickes. Astell's anti-Whig treatise, *An Impartial Enquiry*, the weightiest rebuttal that White Kennett's inflammatory sermon to commemorate the death of Charles I ever received, is firmly anchored in the politics of the Glorious Revolution.

Political events in 1701 had conspired to give Lockean arguments a rerun, heralded by the reissue of radical tracts from 1649 and 1689. The Tories, enjoying the heady powers conceded to the parliament by the Revolution of 1688 which fell to them after their electoral victory of 1701, provided the conditions. They sought to curtail William III's campaign against the French by denying him funds and by seeking to impeach the Lords Somers, Halifax, Portland, and Orford for their Continental involvement. The Kentish Petitioners, who demanded the Crown fund a new war with France and were jailed for their efforts, were the catalyst.[37] Somers and the indefatigable Daniel Defoe, a publicist for Locke, leapt to the defense of the right of subjects to petition. Somers, citing Locke's *Two Treatises*, argued precisely for government as a pact between property-owners, whereby consent of the governed to government as a species of protection agency entailed that the people might also submit grievances where their liberties seemed to be jeopardized. Charles Davenant, in *Essays upon Peace at Home and War Abroad* (1704), on which Mary Astell comments in the long prefatory discourse to her pamphlet *Moderation Truly Stated* (1704), pointed out that, in the Civil War itself, radical proponents of consent had not more loudly proclaimed rights of resistance and parliamentary accountability.[38] Davenant, preoccupied with Machiavellian theories on corruption engendered by war, followed up with the trenchant *True Picture of the Modern Whig*, which showed modern Whigs to be careerists prosecuting war with France to gain political place and personal profit,[39] just the line of argument followed by Astell in *An Impartial Enquiry*. This was also the argument made by Astell, in *Moderation Truly Stated*, where her target appears to be Locke, although her tract was read by contemporaries as a refutation of Davenant.[40]

The Kentish Petitioners had raised in the minds of pamphleteers on both sides constitutional issues which never lay far beneath the surface. But Whig strategies to keep alive the threat of French despotism and the Pretender as a pretext for war, cast serious doubt on their credentials as defenders of immemorial rights, while "Tory writers manipulated the ancient constitution myth by levelling it at its perpetrators."[41] Hence we have Charles Davenant, and even Mary Astell, declaring the English constitution to be a mixed constitution consisting of "the harmony of a prince 'who is Head of the Republick', the lords and the commons."[42] Davenant, using Machiavellian language, speaks of a constitution balanced between arbitrary government and democracy (Crown and Commons), arguing that a fourth estate for the common people with separate rights, such as the Kentish Petitioners had pressed for, would be destabilizing. Mary Astell, in *An Impartial Enquiry*, argues similarly against "the People's Supremacy":

> And since our Constitution lodges the Legislative Power in the Prince and the Three Estates assembled in Parliament; as it is not in the Power of the Prince and one of the Houses, to Make or Abrogate any Law, without the Concurrence of the other House, so neither can it be Lawfully done by the Prince alone, or by the two Houses without the Prince.[43]

Whatever Locke's position on the ancient constitution may have been – and his official position is, as usual, silence, despite the role he played in drafting a constitution for the American Carolinas – Mary Astell was quick to convict him of opportunism. She observed the antinomy between the reductionism of his sensationalist psychology that placed collectivities for ever out of reach, and his predilection for the fictions of the "state of nature" and "natural rights." This was the point of her constant parody of appeals to "the rights of freeborn Englishmen" made by Locke, Defoe, and John Tutchin.[44] If Locke in fact endorsed a "mixed constitution,"[45] he would not have endorsed that peculiar version of "mixarchy" to which Lord Clarendon or Astell subscribed, a version of the ancient constitution as comprised of king, Lords, and Commons. For Clarendon, like the bishops who promulgated the theory under Charles II, the Lords included the bishops of the Anglican Church, jealous in the protection of their ecclesiastical power,[46] something Astell supported and Locke denied. If Locke's constitutional monarchy looked down the centuries in its anticipation of modern constitutional forms, it did so precisely by virtue of a lack of commitment to the constitutional niceties of which Astell and Clarendon, along with those Whigs who tried to reconcile contract and conquest, were zealously protective.

Mary Astell's political pamphlets gravitate around the twin pillars of Toryism: abhorrence of the doctrine of right of resistance and abhorrence of Nonconformity. They also represent a response to the upsurge of Lockean language occasioned by the two events already mentioned as critical: the demands of the Kentish Petitioners, who raised again the question of Ancient Liberties, a constitutional myth which the Whigs defended and the Tories manipulated; and the Occasional Conformity Bill, introduced into parliament in 1703, but not passed until 1711. For Mary Astell, the Occasional Conformity crisis presented the true test of theological seriousness. On this subject two of her three important pamphlets of 1704 turn. In *Moderation Truly Stated* (1704), her 185-page rebuttal of James Owen's pamphlet, *Moderation a Virtue* (1703), whose defense of Occasional Conformity was not unreasonable, Astell adopts the extreme tactic of representing this sort of reasonableness as treason. If the Church of England was established by law, then attempts to bypass the requirement that office-holders must be communing Anglicans were unconstitutional at the very least, she maintained. Astell dealt a particularly stinging and belittling riposte to Daniel Defoe, himself a Dissenter, whose string of satirical pamphlets on the hysterical harangues of Henry Sacheverell, Charles Leslie, and others drew her ire in *A Fair Way with Dissenters and their Patrons*.

On the issue of Occasional Conformity Astell was at one with some of the most conservative writers. Goldie has suggested that the real roots of Tory constitutionalism in the revolt against James lay in the choice of church over king.[47] Archbishop Sancroft and Edward Hyde (1609–74), first Earl of Clarendon, the former Mary Astell's patron, the latter her intellectual mentor and much cited source, were representative of the Anglican hierarchy of the 1680s, uncompromising on the status and independence of Anglicanism, and hostile to Presbyterianism and popery.[48] The language of toleration was, to Astell, the language of schism: schism in religion and schism in politics. Occasional Conformity meant opening the door to religious and patriotic slackness, one of her most sustained objections to it. Thomas Edwards, author of *Gangraena*, and "the most voluble opponent" of the religious sects,[49] is among her most cited sources. Astell agrees with John Nalson, whom she cites in *An Impartial Enquiry*, that religion, in the household as in the commonwealth, is what makes people observe the covenants they have made. The moderate Earl of Clarendon, Astell's intellectual mentor, who also lay the disorder of the Great Rebellion at the door of the Protestant sects, saw the same consequences: "Children asked not blessing of their parents ... The young women conversed without any circumspection or modesty ... Parents had no manner of authority over their children."[50]

In *An Impartial Enquiry*, Astell introduces her onslaught on Lockean principles, for which White Kennett is the surrogate. It is no accident that the occasion of Mary Astell's pamphlet should have been the memorial day for the commemoration of the death of "the Royal King and Martyr." Tory iconography depicting Charles I "as a mythological but appealing figure"[51] dates in fact to the work *Eikon Basilike* of 1649 – a sentimental and embroidered version of Charles's last reflections. Its authorship was entangled in debates over the Civil War to which Mary Astell contributed, for glorification of "the Royal Martyr" had been a calculated Tory stratagem.[52]

Astell, Locke, Sherlock, and the allegiance debate

Astell entered public debate at the end of a century of biblical patriarchalism which had never been more baldly stated than in Sir Robert Filmer's *Patriarcha* of 1680, the work of a man desperate to restore his standing with the Crown.[53] Filmer categorically denied the view argued by Aristotle and entrenched by Aristotelianism that different power sets establish qualitatively different spheres. Aristotle, in his distinctions in the *Politics* between forms of paternal, marital, despotic, and political power (as the power of a father, husband, slave owner, and magistrate, respectively) had created a distinction between private and public spheres that Hobbes and Locke, for different reasons, were keen to revive. Ignoring Aristotle's caution against confusing the rule of a large household for that of a small kingdom,[54] Filmer claimed in fact that men were born into states by being born into families and that the power of kings was the power of fathers and nothing more. Filmer's claim raised the counter-claim that if fathers were indeed kings, the sovereign was superfluous.

Not only was such a notion intolerable to Hobbes and Locke, but so were the assumptions of biblical fundamentalism associated with Puritanism that underpinned it. Moreover, the separation of public and private spheres on which they insisted had a larger purpose. The great stress Hobbes laid on the state being "artificial" rather than natural was designed to erode any self-authenticating powers the Scriptures may be claimed to have in the Protestant community of believers. At the same time it prepared the way for an analysis of the particular artifice in terms of which the creation of the state was brought about: a contract. Scripture had its uses in acclimating people to negotiation by covenant or contract, of which marriage was the most immediate experience in the everyday life of most people. For the marriage contract to function as an analogue for social contract as an institution-creating artifice, the spheres had to be categorically distinct.

Astell, who had much in common with Filmer, and whose mentor, Archbishop Sancroft, had assisted Edmund Bohun in arranging the 1685 publication of *Patriarcha*, was nevertheless gravely offended by his patriarchalism. She shared Filmer's concern to distinguish the separate moments of authorization and designation, noting however the propensity of the Presbyterians to borrow scholastic casuistry:

> Yet upon the grounds of this doctrine both Jesuits and some over zealous favourers of the Geneva discipline have built a perilous conclusion, which is "that the people or multitude have power to punish or deprive the prince if he transgress the laws of the kingdom". Witness Parsons and Buchanan ... Cardinal Bellarmine and Mr Calvin both look asquint this way.[55]

Like Filmer she supported the notion of a unitary state, divided not into spheres but into power zones in which power was distributed hierarchically. But she marshaled an impressive line of biblical women to remonstrate against the misogyny of the Apostle Paul and those adherents who argued the natural inferiority of women.[56] And here Astell appealed to canons of reason established by Descartes and vouchsafed by Hobbes and Locke, for whom men and women were naturally equal but made radically unequal by the marriage contract, as the model for the radical inequality of citizen and sovereign powers achieved by the social contract.

Astell with characteristic irony enlisted the support of Bishop William Sherlock (1641?–1707), Dean of St. Paul's, against Locke. Sherlock, whom she names among the three Whig bishops who preached the 31 January memorial sermon for Charles I,[57] might have been thought of as in Locke's camp. But Astell invokes him for his distinction between authority and title made against Locke. She phrases the distinction thus: "For, allowing that the People have a Right to Design the Person of their Governour; it does by no means follow that they Give him his Authority, or that they may when they please resume it."[58]

Astell could not have known that Locke had actually put into print a rebuttal of Sherlock's distinction, which he considered it important to refute. Sherlock had argued quite cogently that the necessity of government was logically prior to the title of any particular sovereign. If authority was the right to command obedience, decided, it turned out, on *de facto* grounds, legitimate title was a question of constitutional law, *de jure*.[59] Sherlock then carefully distinguished three modes of political empowerment: patriarchal, on the grant of authority made to Adam, Noah, Moses, and all subsequent fathers; by divine command (as to a Chosen People); and by consent. He dismissed the patriarchal argument and the argument from consent; the former because it ignored all the usurpations, beginning with Nimrod; the latter because consent, once given, could be withdrawn. He dismissed any historical arguments concerning legitimate title as "carrying men into such dark Labyrinths of Law and History, etc., as very few know how to find their way out of again."[60] He came down rather on the side of the Hobbesian reciprocity of protection/allegiance, citing Paul, Romans 13, and concluding, "If the prince can't Govern, the Subject can't Obey,"[61] a view shared by the secular Engagers, Anthony Ascham and Marchmont Nedham. Sherlock tried to distance himself from the controversial Hobbes, however, for whom "dominion is naturally annexed to Power," whereas he, Sherlock, was at pains to stress the *moral duty* of allegiance.[62]

Locke, whose comments on Sherlock constitute his only recorded remarks on political obedience postdating the *Two Treatises* of 1689, ridiculed Sherlock for attempting to separate legal title and God's authority – as if the law could breach the latter – seeming certainly to subscribe to obedience and non-resistance in this instance: "Q. Does not god['s] authority whch the actuall K[ing] has bar all other human claims & are not the subjects bound to maintain the right of such a prince as far as they can."[63]

Locke, like Sherlock, distanced himself from Hobbism, but this time Sherlock's "submission" was not enough for legal title; it had to be consent: "Where there is noe resistance ther is a generall Submission. but there may be a general submission without a general consent wch is an other thing."[64]

Sherlock had argued, quite to the contrary, and indistinguishably from Hobbes on conquest: "All Mankind have this natural Right to submit for their own preservation"; a submission that "is a voluntary Consent, tho' extorted by Force."[65] Astell does not even deal with Sherlock's argument, but she demolishes Locke's, turning against him exactly the argument he uses against slavery. Locke's case for freedom was based on the eloquently expressed argument against slavery:

> For a Man, not having the Power of his own Life, *cannot*, by Compact, or his own Consent, *enslave himself* to any one, nor put himself under the Absolute, Arbitrary Power of another, to take away his Life, when he pleases. No body can give more power than he has himself; and he that cannot take away his own Life cannot give another power over it.[66]

This is just the argument that Astell uses to make the case for a distinction between authority and title, but on assumptions that are otherwise directly contrary to Locke on authorization. People may choose the person of the governor, but they cannot empower him, because: "None can give what they have not: The People have no Authority over their own Lives, consequently they can't invest such an Authority in their Governours."[67] The argument with which Astell then proceeds seems to be explicitly aimed at Locke:

> And tho' we shou'd grant that People, when they first enter into Society, may frame their Laws as they think fit; yet these Laws being once Establish'd, they can't Legally and Honestly be chang'd, but by that Authority in which the Founders of the Society thought fit to place the Legislature. Otherwise we have been miserably impos'd upon by all those Arguments that were urg'd against a Dispensing Power.[68]

Astell on the inconsistencies of contractarianism

Astell cogently argues the Tory case, interspersing her exegesis of the Tory canon, in the form of her authorities, the Bible, the Earl of Clarendon, and Henry Foulis, with broadsides in all directions. On the subject of factiousness she lashes out at fanatics: "Malignants, High-flyers and what not."[69] She takes a shot at Hobbesian mechanism as voiced by White Kennett: "we are told, that the *Prime Engines* were *Men of Craft, dreadful Dissemblers with GOD* (what is meant by adding *and Heaven*, I know not, for the Dr. is too zealous against Popery, to suffer us to imagine that he takes in Angels and Saints)."[70] Then she dares to turn against Dissenters and regicides Hobbesian charges of demonology: "They shou'd not suffer Men to infect the Peoples Minds with evil Principles and Representations, with Speeches that have double Meanings and Equivocal Expressions, *Innuendo's* and secret Hints and Insinuations."[71] It is not the only time that she uses explicitly Hobbesian language to hoist the famous author on his own petard. Nowhere is her parody of Hobbes more explicit than in her defense of popery against the worst charges of the Presbyterians, notoriously popish casuists. There she echoes the great master's comments about hay and stubble and straw men:[72]

> Now they who are curious to know what Popery is, and who do not rail at it at a venture, know very well, that every Doctrine which is profess'd by the Church of *Rome*, is not Popish; GOD forbid it shou'd, for they receive the Holy Scriptures, and teach the Creeds. But that Superstructure of Hay and Stubble, those Doctrines of Men or Devils, which they have built upon this good Foundation, this is Popery.[73]

Having demolished faction, Astell recommends against democracy: "For we have the sad Experience of our Civil Wars to inform us, that all the Concessions the King and his Loyal Subjects cou'd make to the Factious and Rebellious, cou'd not satisfie."[74] She even suggests that the outspoken, and presumably the press, should be muzzled: "Governours therefore may very justly animadvert upon, and suppress it. For it is as much their Duty, and as necessary a Service to the Public, to restrain the Turbulent and Seditious, as it is to protect the Innocent, and to reward the Deserving."[75]

Astell's charge that the Scots, John Pym, and the French Cardinal Richelieu had conspired to trump up the French threat in the 1630s and 1640s is a constant refrain. At one point she even enlists Grotius against "factious, turbulent, and Rebellious Spirits," by which she means Pym and company, otherwise known as *"Presbyterians, or Whiggs, or whatever you will call them."*[76] Having produced a litany of offenders against political obedience and supporters of passive resistance outstanding in this particular debate, she proceeds to give an equally impressive list of evil ministers, intent on "appeas[ing] the Party ... obstruct[ing] the King's Business, and ... weaken[ing] his authority"; the cause, as Henry Foulis instructs us, of "'perpetual Hurly-burly ... and ... Leap-frog Government.'"[77] She does not mention Locke by name, but he could well be chief among "those Mercenary Scriblers whom all sober Men condemn, and who only write after the Fact, or in order to it, to make their own Fortunes, or to justifie their own Wickedness."[78] Locke it was who, in his anonymous and unpublished Minute for Edward Clarke, declared:

> Every one, and that with reason, begins our delivery from popery and slavery from the arrival of the prince of Orange and the compleating of it is, by all that wish well to him and it, dated from King William's settlement in the throne. This is the fence set up against popery and France, for King James's name, however made use of, can be but a stale to these two. If ever he returne, under what pretences soever, Jesuits must governe and France be our master. He is too much wedded to the one and relyes too much on the other ever to part with either. He that has ventured and lost three crowns for his

blinde obedience to those guides of his conscience and for his following the counsels and pattern of the French King cannot be hoped, after the provocations he has had to heighten his natural aversion, should ever returne with calme thoughts and good intentions to Englishmen, their libertys, and religion. And then I desire the boldest or most negligent amongst us, who can not resolve to be a contemned popish convert and a miserable French peasant, to consider with himself what security, what help, what hopes he can have, if by the ambition and artifice of any great man he depends on and is led by, he be once brought to this market, a poore, innocent sheepe to this shambles; for whatever advantageous bargains the leaders may make for them selves, tis eternally true that the dull heard of followers are always bought and sold.[79]

These do not sound like the words of a democrat, or even of an abstract political theorist. Locke's reputation for being overly philosophical is not something he necessarily enjoyed in his own day. Astell quite clearly sees him as a polemical political theorist, whatever the undoubted merits of his psychological theory might be. As James Farr and Clayton Roberts note, even passages in the *Two Treatises* apparently concerned with obligation in the abstract take on a different significance, seen in the light of this private document. And so do apparently contradictory statements, such as his claim in his criticism of Sherlock's *The case of allegiance due to soveraign powers*, that, "Allegiance is neither due nor paid to Right or to Government which are abstract notions but only to persons having right of government."[80] While such a statement might seem to deny all attempts to provide a *de jure* rather than *de facto* basis for government, more closely scrutinized it reads differently. The "Right or ... Government" deemed abstract are in fact Divine Right and hereditary monarchy.

The virtue of the Williamite settlement was that it could be presented as virtually an elective monarchy if the right construction was put upon the empowering oaths; in other words, the notoriously unstable Stuart patrilineal line had suffered an interloper in the form of William III, on the strength of popular sentiment. Much of Locke's effort in the brief to Clarke was to ensure that the Whig project to convert a *de facto* into a *de jure* settlement was accomplished.[81] Such a purpose casts Locke's claims in the *Two Treatises* concerning *de facto* power and the basis of citizenship in a new light. There he asserted both that "An Usurper ... [can never] have a Title, till the People are both at liberty to consent, and have actually consented,"[82] and concerning how individuals "come to be *Subjects or Members of [any] Commonwealth*," that, "Nothing can make any Man so, but his actually entering into it by positive Engagement, and express Promise and Compact."[83]

Locke's critique of Sherlock, and his political behavior more generally, might seem to fly in the face of his claim in the *Two Treatises*, that "there cannot be done a greater Mischief to Prince and People, than the Propagating wrong Notions concerning Government." But he was consistent in his view, as the brief to Clarke demonstrates, that royal claims to rule by divine right should be treated with "public condemnation and abhorrence."[84] His critique of Sherlock merely affirmed what he elsewhere asserted, that oaths of allegiance took precedence over hereditary right, as supplying that element of consent prerequisite to social contract. However, for those who were not willing to swear allegiance, the alternative was "separation from the Government"[85] – a position perilously close to the sanctions against Occasional Conformity which Locke could not have approved. The more immediate problem was to cut a swathe through the conflicting oaths that tied the non-jurors to the Stuart dynasty, and this Locke could do.

It had been the accomplishment of Thomas Hobbes to justify government on non-providential grounds.[86] Locke was in this respect a successor to Hobbes, but one who argued less for the necessity of government than for its conventionality – both prongs of the Hobbesian position – emphasizing not the injunction of reason on citizens to obey, but the motivations for governments to contract and citizens to consent. The elaborate juridical artifice by means of which citizens, like wives, children, and servants, were deemed voluntarily to have contracted into subordination had as little credibility in the late seventeenth and early eighteenth centuries as it does today, but for different reasons. In the early modern era providential arguments still reigned supreme; in ours different conclusions are drawn from contractarian arguments, which seem to have won the day.

NOTES

1 Mary Astell's *Collections of Poems Dedicated to the most Reverend Father in God William by Divine Providence Lord Archbishop of Canterbury* (1689), Rawlinson MSS poet. 154:50, Oxford: The Bodleian Library; excerpted in Bridget Hill, *The First English Feminist: "Reflections Upon Marriage" and other Writings by Mary Astell* (Aldershot: Gower Publishing, 1986), pp. 183–84, and printed in full in Ruth Perry, *The Celebrated Mary Astell: An Early English Feminist* (Chicago: Chicago University Press, 1986), pp. 400–54. I would like to thank Bridget Hill, Mark Goldie, John Pocock, Quentin Skinner, and Lois Schwoerer, and my editor, Steven Zwicker, for their comments on an earlier version of this piece. Sincere thanks to the Australian Research Council, the Folger Shakespeare Library, The Woodrow Wilson International Center for Scholars, and The John D. and Catherine T. MacArthur Foundation, under whose joint auspices it was written.

2 Mary Astell's *A Serious Proposal to the Ladies for the Advancement of their True and Greatest Interest*, London, Printed for R. Wilkin, 1694 (Folger Library, 140765 [Wing A4063]). Second edition corrected, 1695, London, Printed for R. Wilkin (Folger Library, 145912 [Wing A4063]). Fourth edition, 1701, London, Printed by J.R. for R. Wilkin (Folger Library, PR3316.A655.S3.Cage).

3 Mary Astell, *Letters Concerning the Love of God, between the Author of the Proposal to the Ladies and Mr. John Norris*, Published by J. Norris, Rector of Bemerton nr. Sarum, London, Printed for Samuel Manship, 1695 (Wing 1254).

4 Astell's three commissioned Tory tracts of 1704 are in order of publication: *Moderation truly Stated: or a Review of a Late Pamphlet, Entitul'd Moderation a Virtue, or, The Occasional Conformist Justified from the Imputation of Hypocricy ... With a Prefatory Discourse to Dr. D'Avenant, Concerning His Late Essays on Peace and War*, London, Printed by J.L. for Richard Wilkin, at the King's-Head, in St. Paul's Church-yard, 1704 (Folger Library, BX5202.A8.Cage); *A Fair Way with the Dissenters and their Patrons*, London, Printed by E.P. for R. Wilkin, at the King's Head in St. Paul's Church-yard, 1704 (Folger Library, BX5202.A7.Cage); and *An Impartial Enquiry into the Causes of Rebellion and Civil War in this Kingdom in an Examination of Dr. Kennett's Sermon, Jan. 31, 1703/4, and Vindication of the Royal Martyr*, London, Printed by E.P. for R. Wilkin, at the King's Head in St. Paul's Churchyard, 1704 (Folger Library, BV 4253.K4.C75.Cage).

5 See James Owen, *Moderation a Vertue: Or, the Occasional Conformist Justify'd from the Imputation of Hypocrisy* (London, 1703); Daniel Defoe, *The Shortest Way with the Dissenters: Or Proposals for the Establishment of the Church* (London, 1702) and *More Short-Ways with the Dissenters* (London, 1703); and White Kennett's *A Compassionate Enquiry into the Causes of the Civil War: In a Sermon Preached in the Church of St. Botolph Aldgate, On January 31, 1704, the Day of the Fast of the Martyrdom of King Charles I* (London, 1704).

6 Mary Astell, *The Christian Religion as Profess'd by a Daughter of the Church of England in a Letter to the Right Honourable T.L., C.I.*, London, Printed by S.H. for R. Wilkin, at the King's Head in St. Paul's Churchyard, 1705 (Folger Library, 216595).

7 See Joseph M. Levine's magisterial *The Battle of the Books: History and Literature in the Augustan Age* (Ithaca, NY: Cornell University Press, 1991). It is symptomatic that women should have participated in pathbreaking ways in this discourse on the cusp of modernity. Astell recognized the particular contribution of her acknowledged role model, Anne Lefvre Dacier (1654–1720), a French scholar and classics translator (see *A Serious Proposal*, p. 10). And she must have valued the contribution of her Chelsea acquaintance, the English antiquarian and linguist, Elizabeth Elstob (see Levine, *The Battle of the Books*, pp. 378–79).

8 Hill, *The First English Feminist*, p. 48.

9 Formative works of the New Historicists include Stephen Greenblatt's *Renaissance Self-Fashioning: From More to Shakespeare* (Chicago: University of Chicago Press, 1980) and *Shakespearean Negotiations: The Circulation of Social Energy in Renaissance England* (Berkeley: University of California Press, 1987); the Shakespearean studies of contributors to Jean E. Howard and

Marian F. O'Connor (eds.), *Shakespeare Reproduced: The Text in History and Ideology* (London: Routledge, 1987); and Don Wayne's work on Renaissance country-house poetry, especially that of Ben Jonson, in *Penshurst: The Semiotics of Place and the Poetics of History* (London: Methuen, 1984). "Cultural Materialism," in the works of British scholars such as Alan Sinfield and Jonathan Dollimore shares a similar emphasis on the material circumstances of texts, their social function in society, and the ways in which cultural texts enact the work of subversion and containment. See Sinfield and Dollimore (eds.), *Political Shakespeare: New Essays in Cultural Materialism* (Manchester: Manchester University Press; Ithaca, NY: Cornell University Press, 1985). I owe these observations to Steven Zwicker and thank him for his kind assistance.

10 See Astell's Forward to the second edition of *Bart'lemy Fair*, 1722 (p. A2a), on how Swift put Steele up to the satire of her *A Serious Proposal to the Ladies* in *Tatler*, No. 32, from White's Chocolate-house, 22 June 1709, "a little after the Enquiry [*Bart'lemy Fair*] appear'd." See also *Tatler*, No. 63, 1–3 September 1709. Ruth Perry, in *The Celebrated Mary Astell* (pp. 229–30, 516 n. 81), and Bridget Hill, in "A Refuge from Men: The Idea of a Protestant Nunnery," *Past and Present*, 117 (1987), pp. 107–30 (esp. p. 118, nn. 47 and 48), ascribe authorship of the *Tatler* pieces to Swift, but the revised *Tatler* does not, and Astell clearly believes them to be the work of Steele:

> But tho' the *Enquirer* had offended the *Tatler*, and his great Friends, on whom he so liberally bestows his Panegyrics, by turning their Ridicule very justly upon themselves; what had any of her Acquaintances done to provoke him? Who does he point at? For she knows of none who ever attempted to *erect a Nunnery*, or declar'd *That Virginity was to be their State of Life*.

11 *The Works of the Celebrated Mrs. Centlivre*, 3 vols. (London, 1761), vol. I, pp. 210, 218, cited in Hill, "A Refuge from Men," p. 120. Susannah Centlivre, a gentlewoman whose family fled to Ireland at the Restoration, may have disliked Astell's politics, *Basset Table* having been written after the publication of Astell's Royalist political pamphlets of 1704. The widow of two husbands, Centlivre had raised herself from obscurity by writing plays, was a friend of Richard Steele, and in 1706 married Queen Anne's chief cook, Joseph Centlivre (*Encyclopaedia Britannica*, 11th edn., vol. v, p. 674).

12 *The Works of Samuel Richardson*, 19 vols. (London, 1811), vol. XVI, pp. 155–56, cited in Hill, "A Refuge from Men," p. 121. See also the authoritative modern edition of Richardson's *History of Sir Charles Grandison*, ed. Jocelyn Harris, 3 vols. (Oxford: Oxford University Press, 1972), vol. II, pp. 255–56 and notes.

13 See A. H. Upham, "A Parallel Case for Richardson's *Clarissa*," *Modern Language Notes*, 28 (1913), pp. 103–05. It is notable, however, that standard works on Richardson, including the authoritative biography by T. C. Duncan Eaves and Ben D. Kimpel, *Samuel Richardson: A Biography* (Oxford: Clarendon Press, 1971), and Tom Keymer's study *Clarissa and the Eighteenth Century Reader* (Cambridge: Cambridge University Press, 1992), do not even include Astell in the index.

14 *The Works of Alfred, Lord Tennyson* (London, 1905), pp. 167, 176, cited by Hill, "A Refuge from Men," p. 107.

15 See E.J.F. and D.B., "George Berkeley and *The Ladies Library*," *Berkeley Newsletter* (Dublin), (1980), pp. 5–13; and G. A. Aitken, in "Steele's 'Ladies' Library'," *The Athenaeum*, 2958 (1884), pp. 16–17.

16 Mary Astell, *Some Reflections upon Marriage, Occasion'd by the Duke & Dutchess of Mazarine's Case* ..., London, Printed for John Nutt, 1700 (Wing A4067). Second edition (no known copies extant). Third edition, *Reflections Upon Marriage. To which is added a Preface in Answer to Some Objections*, London, Printed for R. Wilkin, at the King's Head in St. Paul's Church Yard, 1706. Fourth edition, 1730.

17 J. G. A. Pocock, *The Ancient Constitution and the Feudal Law* (Cambridge: Cambridge University Press, 1957).

18 Mark Goldie, "Tory Political Thought 1689–1714," Ph.D. dissertation, University of Cambridge (1978).

19 Astell in *An Impartial Enquiry*, p. 48, cites Henry Foulis, *The History of the Wicked Plots and Conspiracies of Our Pretended Saints* ... 2nd edn., Oxford, Printed by Henry Hall for Ric. Davis, 1674 (Folger Library, F1643, 204, 205): "The Blood of many thousand Christians, shed in these Wars and before, crieth aloud against Presbytery, as the People only guilty of the first occasion of Quarrel ... Of whom *Grotius* says, 'That he looks upon them as factious, turbulent, and Rebellious Spirits.'"

20 This is emphasized in Johann Sommerville, "History and Theory: the Norman Conquest in Early Stuart Political Thought," *Political Studies*, 34 (1986), pp. 249–61.

21 For instance, Astell both cites and paraphrases Richard Allestree's *The Ladies Calling* in *A Serious Proposal to the Ladies*, as on pp. 4, 9, 37, 122, 148, 153ff. of the 1694 edition, which correspond to the following sections of Allestree: part 1, section 5 (1673), 1705 edition, p. 100; part 2, sections 2 and 3, "Of Wives" and "Of Widows," 1703 edition, pp. 201ff., 231ff.; part 2, section 3, 1705 edition, p. 257; part 2, section 1, "Of Virgins," 1705 edition, p. 172; part 2, section 3, 1705 edition, p. 232; part 2, section 3, 1705 edition, p. 125, respectively. On many substantive points Astell's program for women echoes Allestree, who in *The Ladies Calling* had remonstrated against the reduction of women, denied education, to menial status and had argued in favor of "Home-education" and against sending children abroad.

22 See for instance her sarcastic remark in *An Impartial Enquiry*, p. 40: "Only let me recommend to all such Thinkers, Mr. *Lock's* Chapter *of the Association of Ideas*; they need not be afraid to read it, for that ingenious Author is on the right side, and by no means in a *French* Interest!"

23 Astell in *A Serious Proposal to the Ladies*, Part I, 1694 edn., pp. 85–86, recommends Englishwomen were better to improve themselves with the "study of Philosophy (as I hear the *French Ladies* do) *Des Cartes, Malebranch* and others." In *A Serious Proposal to the Ladies, Part II*, she draws heavily on Descartes, citing "*Les Principes del la Philosofie de M. Des Cartes*, Pt. I. 45," at some length on p. 134 (1697 edn.), declaring on pp. 250–51: "But this being already accounted for by *Des Cartes* [*Les Passions de l'Ame*] and *Dr. More*, in his excellent *Account of Vertue*, I cannot pretend to add any thing to what they have so well Discours'd."

24 "Mr. *Locke's* Supposition that it is possible for Matter to Think, consider'd"

comprises sections 259 to 271 of Astell's *The Christian Religion as Profess'd by a Daughter of the Church*, pp. 250–63, the first two parts of which (sections 1–105, pp. 1–95) are devoted to establishing "What it is that a late Book concerning the *Reasonableness of Christianity*, etc., pretends to drive at." For commentary by modern philosophers see the excellent articles by K. M. Squadrito, "Mary Astell's Critique of Locke's View of Thinking Matter," *Journal of the History of Philosophy*, 25 (1987), pp. 433–40; and Patricia Ward Scaltas, "Women as Ends – Women as Means in the Enlightenment," in A. J. Arnaud and E. Kingdom (eds.), *Women's Rights and the Rights of Man* (Aberdeen: Aberdeen University Press, 1990).

25 See R. W. K. Hinton, "Husbands, Fathers and Conquerors," *Political Studies*, 15, 3 (1967), pp. 291–300 and 16, 1 (1968), pp. 55–67; Mary Lyndon Shanley, "Marriage Contract and Social Contract in Seventeenth-Century English Political Thought," *Western Political Quarterly*, 32 (1979), pp. 79–91; Carole Pateman, *The Sexual Contract* (Cambridge: Polity Press, 1988).

26 See Patricia Springborg, "Mary Astell (1666–1731), Critic of Locke," *American Political Science Review*, 89, 3 (1995), pp. 621–33; and my introductions to *Mary Astell (1666–1731): Political Writings* (Cambridge: Cambridge University Press, 1996) and *Mary Astell, A Serious Proposal to the Ladies, Parts I and II* (London, Pickering and Chatto: 1997).

27 See Pocock, *The Ancient Constitution*, pp. 233ff.

28 Goldie, "Tory Political Thought," p. 38.

29 Astell may well be referring to theories of Nicolas Malebranche, 1638–1715, *De la Recherche de la Verit, ou l'on traitte de la nature de l'esprit de l'homme, & de l'usage qu'il en doit faire pour viter l'erreur dans les sciences*, 4th revised and enlarged edn. (Folger Library B 1893.R.3.1678.Cage). Astell treats Malebranche's principle of "seeing all things in God" at length in her correspondence with John Norris, *Letters Concerning the Love of God*, of 1693, published in 1695. She addresses Malebranche's revisions to Descartes in *A Serious Proposal to the Ladies, Part II*, of 1697, and no more critically than on the subject of sex differences. Malebranche deals with the different structures of mind between the sexes in part 2 of the *The Search for Truth*, "Concerning the Imagination," 1.1, "Of the Imagination of Women." See the 1700 translation by Thomas Taylor, *Father Malebranche his treatise concerning the search after truth …* Printed by W. Bowyer, for Thomas Bennet, and T. Leigh and D. Midwinter, 2nd corrected edn., London (Folger Library M318), which Astell may well have used. Discussing the greater excitability of women, Taylor, *Father Malebranche*, p. 64, accurately translates Malebranche, 1678 edn., pp. 105–06:

> But though it be certain, that this Delicacy of the Fibres of the Brain is the principal Cause of all these Effects; yet it is not equally certain, that it is universally to be found in all women. Or if it be to be found, yet their Animal Spirits are sometimes so exactly proportion'd to the Fibres of their Brain, that there are women to be met with, who have a greater solidity of Mind than some Men. 'Tis in a certain Temperature of the Largeness and Agitation of the Animal Spirits, and Conformity with the Fibres of the Brain, that the strength of parts consists: And Women have sometimes that just Temperature. There are women Strong and constant, and there are Men that

are Weak and Fickle. There are Women that are Learned, Couragious, and capable of every thing. And on the contrary, there are men that are Soft Effeminate, incapable of any Penetration, or dispatch of any Business. In Fine, when we attribute any Failures to a certain Sex, Age, or Condition, they are only to be understood of the generality; it being ever suppos'd, there is no general Rule without Exception.

30 Preface to the third edition of *Reflections upon Marriage*, p. iv.
31 See Mark Goldie, "The Revolution of 1689 and the Structure of Political Argument," *Bulletin of Research in the Humanities*, 83 (1980), pp. 473–564, esp. pp. 508–09.
32 See Patricia Springborg, "Thomas Hobbes and Cardinal Bellarmine: *Leviathan* and the Ghost of the Roman Empire," *History of Political Thought*, 16, 4 (1995), pp. 503–31.
33 "Let every person render obedience to the governing authorities; for there is no authority except from God, and those in authority are divinely constituted," *The Holy Bible* (Nashville, Tennessee: Giddeons International, 1986), p. 843.
34 Goldie, "Tory Political Thought," p. 100. See especially Johann Sommerville's perceptive treatment of Hobbes and Bellarmine in *Thomas Hobbes: Political Ideas in Context* (London: Macmillan, 1992), pp. 113–19, which complements his overview of papalist theory and Anglican responses in his *Politics and Ideology in England, 1603–40* (London: Longman, 1986), pp. 189–203. On the perceived convergence of Presbyterianism and popery on the power to depose kings, see Sommerville's "From Suarez to Filmer: a Reappraisal," *Historical Journal*, 25 (1982), pp. 525–40; and the Introduction to his edition of *Sir Robert Filmer, Patriarcha and Other Writings* (Cambridge: Cambridge University Press, 1991), esp. pp. xv, xxi–xxiv. On the medieval roots of consent theory see Francis Oakley, "Legitimation by Consent: the Question of the Medieval Roots," *Viator*, 14 (1983), pp. 303–35, and *Omnipotence, Covenants, and Order* (Ithaca, NY: Cornell University Press, 1984), esp. pp. 48–91.
35 See Peter Laslett's Introduction to his edition of Locke's *Two Treatises of Government* (Cambridge: Cambridge University Press, 1988), pp. 62–65.
36 See Goldie, "The Revolution of 1689," pp. 473–564, esp. p. 476.
37 Goldie, "Tory Political Thought," p. 167. For the more general political context see Lois Schwoerer, "The Right to Resist: Whig Resistance Theory, 1688 to 1694," in Nicholas Phillipson and Quentin Skinner (eds.), *Political Discourse in Early Modern Britain* (Cambridge: Cambridge University Press, 1993), pp. 232–52; and on the legal ramifications of the Kentish Petitioners' claims, see Philip A. Hamburger, "Revolution and Judicial Review: Chief Justice Holt's Opinion in *City of London v. Wood*," *Columbia Law Review*, 94, 7 (1994), pp. 2091–153.
38 Goldie, "Tory Political Thought," p. 168.
39 See John Pocock, *The Ancient Constitution*, pp. 436–48; Goldie, "Tory Political Thought," p. 168.
40 See the remarks of the eighteenth-century commentator George Ballard, in his *Memoirs of Several Ladies of Great Britain Who have been Celebrated for their Writings or Skill in the Learned Languages, Arts and Sciences* (1752), cited by Ruth Perry, *The Celebrated Mary Astell*, p. 196.

41 Goldie, "Tory Political Thought," pp. 169, 173.

42 Davenant, *Essays upon Peace at Home and War Abroad*, 1704, in *Works*, 5 vols. (London, 1771), vol. IV, sections 1 and 13.

43 Astell, *An Impartial Enquiry*, p. 34.

44 *Ibid.*, pp. 8, 14, 30, etc., mocks the language of the country Whig, exemplified in particular by John Tutchin (1661?–1707) who combined reverence for the ancient constitution, parliament, and "native right" with xenophobia, declaring of the constitution "she's as well beloved now by all true *Englishmen*, as she was by our Forefathers a Thousand Years ago" (*Observator*, 7–10 April 1703). His views were set out in the *Observator* from 29 September to 7 November 1703, focusing on resistance and targeted at Charles Leslie (see Phillipson and Skinner [eds.], *Political Discourse*, p. 217). They were bound for this reason to have come to the attention of Astell, who includes a poke at Leslie in the title to *A Fair Way with the Dissenters*, claiming her work "Not Writ by Mr. L——y, or any other *Furious Jacobite*, whether Clergyman or Layman; but by a very Moderate Person and Dutiful Subject to the QUEEN." Astell complained in her Postscript to that work (*A Fair Way with the Dissenters*, pp. 24–27), that the "High Flyer" Leslie had gotten the credit for her own *Moderation truly Stated*. And in *An Impartial Enquiry* (pp. 8ff.) Astell gives the impression that Kennett held the same views as Tutchin. Tutchin, it is true, admired "those two great men, Mr. Sidney and Mr. Locke," defenders of ancient liberty, "the one against Sir Robert Filmer, and the other against a whole Company of Slaves." (See Tutchin, *Observator*, 14–18 September 1706, cited in Nicholas Phillipson, "Politeness and Politics in the Reigns of Anne and the Early Hanoverians," in J. G. A. Pocock, Gordon J. Schochet, and Lois G. Schwoerer [eds.], *The Varieties of British Political Thought, 1500–1800* [Washington, DC: Folger Institute, 1993], pp. 211–45, esp. p. 218.) But this, the only occasion on which Tutchin names Locke, is too late for Astell's pamphlet.

45 See Martin Thompson, "Significant Silences in Locke's *Two Treatises of Government*: Constitutional History, Contract and Law," *The Historical Journal*, 31 (1987), pp. 275–94, esp. pp. 291–92; and Lois Schwoerer, "Locke, Lockean Ideas and the Glorious Revolution," *Journal of the History of Ideas*, 51, 4 (1990), pp. 531–48, esp. pp. 540–41.

46 See Richard Tuck's Review of Michael Mendle, *Dangerous Positions: Mixed Government, the Estates of the Realm, and the Answer to the XIX Propositions* (Tuscaloosa: University of Alabama Press, 1985), *Journal of Modern History*, 59, 3 (1987), pp. 570–2.

47 Goldie, "Tory Political Thought," p. 64.

48 *Ibid.*, p. 63.

49 Keith Thomas, "Women and the Civil War Sects," *Past and Present*, 13 (1958), pp. 42–62, esp. p. 55.

50 Clarendon, *Life*, vol. I (London, 1827), pp. 358–59, cited in *ibid.*, p. 57.

51 See Quentin Skinner, "Conquest and Consent: Thomas Hobbes and the Engagement Controversy," in G. E. Aylmer (ed.), *The Interregnum: the Quest for Settlement 1646–1660* (London: Macmillan, 1972), p. 85.

52 Goldie, "Tory Political Thought," p. 195.

53 See Sommerville, Introduction to *Sir Robert Filmer, Patriarcha and Other*

Writings. See also Gordon Schochet's authoritative treatment, *Patriarchalism and Political Thought* (Oxford: Blackwell, 1975).

54 Aristotle, *Politics*, Book 1, paragraph 2, 1252a 9–15, Loeb Classical Library edn., ed. H. Rackham (London: Heinemann, 1932), p. 3:

> Those then who think that the natures of the statesman [*politikon*], the royal ruler [*basilikon*], the head of an estate [*oikonomikon*] and the master of a family [*despotikon*] are the same, are mistaken (they imagine that the difference between these various forms of authority is between greater and smaller numbers, not a difference in kind – that is, that the ruler over a few people is a master, over more the head of an estate, over more still a statesman or royal ruler, as if there were no difference between a large household and a small city.)

55 *Filmer, Patriarcha*, p. 3. Astell in *An Impartial Enquiry*, pp. 24–28, undertook to supply chapter and verse, drawing on Henry Foulis, *The History of Romish Treasons ...* 1681 edn. (Book 2, ch. 3, pp. 75ff.) who had analyzed the specific indebtedness of Presbyterian advocates of popular sovereignty to the Scholastics and Jesuits, a claim which Astell repeated, to target Locke and the Whigs.

56 See William Nicholls (1664–1712), *The Duty of Inferiors towards their Superiors, in Five Practical Discourses*, 1701, London (Folger Library, 178–610q), Discourse IV, "The Duty of Wives to their Husbands," which Astell attacks in the opening pages of the Preface to the 1706 edition of *Reflections upon Marriage*.

57 Astell, *An Impartial Enquiry*, p. 16: "Since a Dr. *Binks*, a Mr. *Sherlock*, a Bishop of St. *Asaph*, and some few more, take occasion to Preach upon this Day such antiquated Truths as might have past upon the Nation in the Reign of K. *Charles* II. or in *Monmouth's* Rebellion."

58 *Ibid.*, p. 34.

59 William Sherlock, *A Vindication of the Case of Allegiance*, 1691, p. 11, cited in Goldie, "Tory Political Thought," p. 93.

60 Sherlock, *The Case of Allegiance due to Sovereign Powers*, 1691, p. 2, cited in *ibid.*

61 Sherlock, *ibid.*, pp. 21, 14, 45, 42, cited in Goldie, *ibid.*, p. 94.

62 Sherlock, *ibid.*, p. 15, cited in Goldie, *ibid.*, p. 95.

63 Oxford, The Bodleian Library, Locke MSS c.28, fo. 91v, cited in Goldie, *ibid.*, p. 103.

64 Bodl. Locke MSS c.28, fo. 96r, cited in Goldie, *ibid.*, p. 104.

65 Sherlock, *Vindication of the Case of Allegiance*, pp. 18, 13, cited in Goldie, *ibid.*, p. 104.

66 John Locke, *Two Treatises of Government*, ed. Peter Laslett (Cambridge: Cambridge University Press, 1988), Book 2, paragraphs 23, 24, p. 284.

67 Astell, *An Impartial Enquiry*, p. 34.

68 *Ibid.*

69 *Ibid.*, p. 7.

70 *Ibid.*, p. 5.

71 *Ibid.*, p. 8. See Thomas Hobbes, *Leviathan*, ed. Richard Tuck (Cambridge: Cambridge University Press, 1991), pp. 29–30, for Hobbes's famous account of words as counters. Hobbes attributes "insignificant" speech to an ignorance of the relation between sign and signifier:

Nature it selfe cannot erre: and as men abound in copiousnesse of language; so they become more wise, or more mad than ordinary. Nor is it possible without Letters for any man to become either excellently wise, or ... excellently foolish. For words are wise mens counters, they do but reckon by them: but they are the mony of fooles, that value them by the authority of an *Aristotle*, a *Cicero*, or a *Thomas*, or any other Doctor whatsoever, if but a man.

Hobbes's marvelous images for "insignificant" speech often involve the entrapment of birds, as in *Leviathan*, p. 28. If '*truth* consisteth in the right ordering of names in our affirmations," he says, then "a man that seeketh precise *truth*, had need to remember what every name he uses stands for; and to place it accordingly, or else he will find himselfe entangled in words, as a bird in limetwigges; the more he struggles, the more belimed." And, again, *Leviathan*, p. 28:

> For the errours of Definitions multiply themselves, according as the reckoning proceeds; and lead men into absurdities, which at last they see, but cannot avoyd, without reckoning anew from the beginning, in which lyes the foundation of their errours. From whence it happens, that they which trust to books, do as they that cast up many little summs into a greater, without considering whether those little summes were rightly cast up or not; and at last finding the errour visible, and not mistrusting their first grounds, know not which way to cleere themselves; but spend time in fluttering over their bookes; as birds that entring by the chimney, and finding themselves inclosed in a chamber, flutter at the false light of a glasse window, for want of wit to consider which way they came in.

72 Hobbes frequently invokes the scarecrows and straw men created by Catholic casuistry, that, "built on the Vain Philosophy of Aristotle, would fright [men] from Obeying the Laws of their Country, with empty names; as men fright Birds from the Corn with an empty doublet, a hat, and a crooked stick." *Leviathan*, p. 465.

73 Astell, *An Impartial Enquiry*, p. 22.

74 *Ibid.*, p. 9.

75 *Ibid.*, p. 8.

76 *Ibid.*, p. 48.

77 *Ibid.*, p. 32.

78 *Ibid.*, p. 29.

79 Bodleian MS Locke e.18, reprinted in James Farr and Clayton Roberts, "John Locke on the Glorious Revolution: A Rediscovered Document," *The Historical Journal*, 28 (1985), pp. 385–98, esp. pp. 395–98.

80 *Ibid.*, p. 292.

81 See Mark Goldie, "John Locke's Circle and James II," *The Historical Journal*, 35, 3 (1992), pp. 557–86.

82 Locke, *Two Treatises*, book 2, section 198, p. 398.

83 *Ibid.*, book 2, section 122, p. 349.

84 Bodleian MS Locke e.18, fo. 5, reprinted in Farr and Roberts, "John Locke," pp. 395–98.

85 *Ibid.*
86 See Quentin Skinner, "Conquest and Consent"; and Mark Goldie, "Tory Political Thought," p. 98.

FURTHER READING

Ashcraft, Richard, *Revolutionary Politics and Locke's Two Treatises of Government* (Princeton: Princeton University Press, 1986).

"The Radical Dimensions of Locke's Political Thought: A Dialogic Essay on Some Problems of Interpretation," *History of Political Thought*, 13, 4 (1992), pp. 703–72.

"Simple Objections and Complex Reality: Theorizing Political Radicalism in Seventeenth-century England," *Political Studies*, 40 (1992), pp. 99–117.

Astell, Mary, *Letters Concerning the Love of God, between the Author of the Proposal to the Ladies and Mr. John Norris*, Published by J. Norris, Rector of Bemerton nr. Sarum. London, Printed for Samuel Manship, 1695 (Wing 1254).

Ballard, George (1752), *Memoirs of Several Ladies of Great Britain Who have been Celebrated for their Writings or Skill in the Learned Languages, Arts and Sciences*, ed. Ruth Perry (Detroit: Wayne State University Press, 1985).

Blanchard, Rae, "Richard Steele and the Status of Women," *Studies in Philology*, 26, 3 (1929), pp. 325–55.

Brown, Irene Q., "Domesticity, Feminism, and Friendship: Female Aristocratic Culture and Marriage in England, 1660–1761," *Journal of Family History*, 7 (1982), pp. 406–24.

Butler, Melissa, "Early Liberal Roots of Feminism: John Locke and the Attack on Patriarchy," *American Political Science Review*, 72, 1 (1978), pp. 135–50.

Defoe, Daniel (1697), "An Academy for Women," in *An Essay upon Projects*. London, Printed by R.R. for Theo. Cockerill at the Corner of Warwick-Lane, near Paternoster Row (Folger Library, 145226).

(1702), *The Shortest Way with the Dissenters: Or Proposals for the Establishment of the Church*, London (Folger Library, 134–622q).

(1704), *More Short-Ways with the Dissenters*, London (Library of Congress, BX5202.D36).

George, Margaret, "From 'Goodwife' to 'Mistress': The Transformation of the Female in Bourgeois Culture," *Science and Society*, 37 (1973), pp. 152–77.

Goldie, Mark, "Tory Political Thought 1689–1714," Ph.D. dissertation, University of Cambridge (1978).

"The Roots of True Whiggism, 1688–1694," *History of Political Thought*, 1 (1980), pp. 195–236.

"The Revolution of 1689 and the Structure of Political Argument," *Bulletin of Research in the Humanities*, 83 (1980), pp. 473–564.

"Danby, the Bishops and the Whigs," in T. Harris, Paul Seaward, and M. A. Goldie (eds.), *The Politics of Religion in Restoration England* (Oxford: Blackwell, 1990).

"The Theory of Religious Intolerance in Restoration England," in O. P. Grell, J. I. Israel, and N. Tyacke (eds.), *From Persecution to Toleration* (Oxford: Oxford University Press, 1991).

"John Locke's Circle and James II," *The Historical Journal*, 35, 3 (1992), pp. 557–86.

Harrison, John and Laslett, Peter, *The Library of John Locke*, 2nd edn. (Oxford: Clarendon Press, 1971).

Higgins, Patricia, "The Reactions of Women, with Special Reference to Women Petitioners," in Brian Manning (ed.), *Politics, Religion and the English Civil War* (London: Edward Arnold, 1973).

Hill, Bridget, *The First English Feminist: "Reflections Upon Marriage" and Other Writings by Mary Astell* (Aldershot: Gower Publishing, 1986).

"A Refuge from Men: The Idea of a Protestant Nunnery," *Past and Present*, 117 (1987), pp. 107–30.

Hinton, R. W. K., "Husbands, Fathers and Conquerors," *Political Studies*, 15, 3 (1967), pp. 291–300; 16, 1 (1968), pp. 55–67.

Hutton, Sarah, "Damaris Cudworth, Lady Masham: Between Platonism and Enlightenment," *British Journal for the History of Philosophy*, 1, 1 (1993), pp. 29–54.

James, Regina, "Mary, Mary, Quite Contrary, Or, Mary Astell and Mary Wollstonecraft Compared," *Studies in Eighteenth Century Culture*, 5 (1976), pp. 121–39.

Kennett, White (1704), *A Compassionate Enquiry into the Causes of the Civil War: In a Sermon Preached in the Church of St. Botolph Aldgate, On January 31, 1704. the Day of the Fast of the Martyrdom of King Charles the First*, London, Printed for A. and J. Churchil in Pater-Noster Row.

Laslett, Peter, *John Locke's Two Treatises of Government* (Cambridge: Cambridge University Press, 1988).

Locke, John (1693) 1823, "Remarks upon some of Mr. Norris's Books, wherein he asserts P. Malebranche's Opinion of seeing all Things in God," in *The Works of John Locke*, London, printed for Thomas Tegg, W. Sharpe and son, et al., vol. IX, pp. 247–59.

(1695) 1823, "The Reasonableness of Christianity, as Delivered in the Scriptures," in *The Works of John Locke*, London, printed for Thomas Tegg, W. Sharpe and son, et al., vol. VII, pp. 1–158.

McCrystal, John Williams, "An Inadvertant Feminist: Mary Astell (1666–1731)," MA thesis, Auckland University, New Zealand (1992).

"A Lady's Calling: Mary Astell's Notion of Women," *Political Theory Newsletter*, 4 (1992), pp. 156–70.

Mack, Phyllis, "Women as Prophets during the English Civil War," in Margaret Jacob and James Jacob (eds.), *The Origins of Anglo-American Radicalism* (London: George Allen and Unwin, 1984), pp. 214–31.

Masham, Damaris (1696), *Discourse Concerning the Love of God*, London, Printed for Awnsham and John Churchill.

(1705), *Occasional Thoughts In Reference to a Vertuous or Christian Life*, London, Printed for A. and J. Churchil at the Black Swann in Paternoster-Row.

Myers, Mitzi, "Domesticating Minerva: Bathusa Makin's 'Curious' Argument for Women's Education," *Studies in Eighteenth Century Culture*, 14 (1985), pp. 173–92.

Needham, Gwendolyn B., "Mary Delarivier Manley, Tory Defender," *Huntington Library Quarterly*, 12, 3 (1949), pp. 253–88.

Norton, J. E., "Some Uncollected Authors XXVII; Mary Astell, 1666–1731," *The Book Collector*, 10, 1 (1961), pp. 58–60.

O'Donnell, Sheryl, "Mr. Locke and the Ladies: The Indelible Words on the Tabula Rasa," *Studies in Eighteenth Century Culture*, 8 (1978), pp. 151–64.

" 'My Idea in Your Mind': John Locke and Damaris Cudworth Masham," in Ruth Perry and Martine Brownley (eds.), *Mothering the Mind* (New York: Homes & Meier, 1984), pp. 26–46.

Pateman, Carole, *The Sexual Contract* (Cambridge: Polity Press, 1988).

"God Hath Ordained to Man a Helper: Hobbes, Patriarchy and Conjugal Right," *British Journal of Political Science*, 19 (1989), pp. 445–64.

Perry, Ruth, "Mary Astell's Response to the Enlightenment," *Women in History*, 9 (1984), pp. 13–40.

The Celebrated Mary Astell: An Early English Feminist (Chicago: University of Chicago Press, 1986).

Scaltas, Patricia Ward, "Women as Ends – Women as Means in the Enlightenment," in A. J. Arnaud and E. Kingdom (eds.), *Women's Rights and the Rights of Man* (Aberdeen: Aberdeen University Press, 1990), pp. 138–48.

Schwoerer, Lois G., "Propaganda in the Revolution of 1688–89," *American Historical Review*, 82 (1977), pp. 843–74.

"Locke, Lockean Ideas and the Glorious Revolution," *Journal of the History of Ideas*, 51, 4 (1990), pp. 531–48.

"The Right to Resist: Whig Resistance Theory, 1688 to 1694," in Nicholas Phillipson and Quentin Skinner (eds.), *Political Discourse in Early Modern Britain* (Cambridge: Cambridge University Press, 1993), pp. 232–52.

Shanley, Mary Lyndon, "Marriage Contract and Social Contract in Seventeenth-Century English Political Thought," *Western Political Quarterly*, 32 (1979), pp. 79–91.

Smith, Florence M., *Mary Astell* (New York: Columbia University Press, 1916).

Smith, Hilda, *Reason's Disciples* (Urbana: University of Illinois Press, 1982).

Sommerville, Margaret, *Sex and Subjection: Attitudes to Women in Early Modern Society* (London: Matthew Arnold, 1995).

Springborg, Patricia, "Mary Astell (1666–1731), Critic of Locke," *American Political Science Review*, 89, 3 (1995), pp. 621–33.

ed., *Mary Astell (1666–1731), Political Writings* (Cambridge: Cambridge University Press, 1996).

ed., *Mary Astell, A Serious Proposal to the Ladies, Parts I and II* (London: Pickering & Chatto, 1997).

Spurr, John, " 'Latitudinarianism' and the Restoration Church," *The Historical Journal*, 31, 1 (1988), pp. 61–82.

" 'Rational Religion' in Restoration England," *Journal of the History of Ideas*, 49, 4 (1988), pp. 563–85.

"The Church of England, Comprehension and the Toleration Act of 1689," *English Historical Review*, 104, 413 (1989), pp. 927–46.

Squadrito, K. M., "Mary Astell's Critique of Locke's View of Thinking Matter," *Journal of the History of Philosophy*, 25 (1987), pp. 433–40.

Thomas, Keith, "Women and the Civil War Sects," *Past and Present*, 13 (1958), pp. 42–62.

Thompson, Martyn P., "The Reception of Locke's *Two Treatises of Government*, 1690–1705," *Political Studies*, 24 (1976), pp. 184–91.

"The Idea of Conquest in Controversies over the 1688 Revolution," *Journal of the History of Ideas*, 38 (1977), pp. 33–46.

"Revolution and Influence: A Reply to Nelson on Locke's *Two Treatises of Government*," *Political Studies*, 28 (1980), pp. 100–08.

"Significant Silences in Locke's *Two Treatises of Government*: Constitutional History, Contract and Law," *The Historical Journal*, 31 (1987), pp. 275–94.

Yolton, Jean S., and Yolton, John W., *John Locke: A Reference Guide* (Boston, MA: G. K. Hall & Co., 1985).

14

DONNA LANDRY

Alexander Pope, Lady Mary Wortley Montagu, and the literature of social comment

Alexander Pope and Lady Mary Wortley Montagu were both born in the year of the Glorious Revolution, 1688–89. Divided by family circumstance and political allegiance, they have been coupled by literary history. Pope was a Catholic linen merchant's son, born in the City of London, who had to make his own fortune in the literary marketplace by means of such ventures as translating Homer's *Iliad* and *Odyssey* into English for a distinguished list of wealthy subscribers, who paid in installments to receive their multi-volumed sets over several years. Pope earned about £5000 each from these translations, or, at a "conservative estimate," the equivalent in today's money of about £100,000 from each.[1] Lady Mary Pierrepont, daughter of the Earl (later Duke) of Kingston, married in 1712 a fellow Whig, Edward Wortley Montagu, who would soon become ambassador to Constantinople. "A strong sense of propriety led her, as a woman and an aristocrat, not to publish any of her writings under her own name."[2] Pope was a Tory with Jacobite leanings; Montagu supported Sir Robert Walpole.

Pope never traveled to Turkey, while Montagu's journey there as the wife of the British ambassador from 1716 to 1718 secured her literary fame. Her posthumously published letters of 1763, *Written, during her Travels in Europe, Asia and Africa, To Persons of Distinction, Men of Letters, &c. in different Parts of Europe. Which Contain, Among other Curious Relations, Accounts of the Policy and Manners of the Turks*, established her reputation as a woman of letters, since people from Samuel Johnson to Lord Byron read and praised them.[3] Johnson is supposed to have said that Montagu's letters were the only book he ever read for pure pleasure, while Byron claimed to have practically memorized them by the age of ten. Eventually Montagu would leave England and her husband for a wandering life in Italy and France.[4]

If Pope, master of five rented acres at Twickenham, figures the suburban intellectual, Montagu epitomizes the expatriate adventurer, whose aristocratic rank enabled her independence but also meant she could only really practice it abroad. As an adventurer-writer, with a strong influence on Lord Byron, she comes to signify a gender-bending kind of English expatriate eccentricity often named "Byronic," but nearly a century before Byron first left the British Isles. Both Pope and Montagu represent two forms of Englishness that came into being during British imperial expansion. Despite their differences, their lives and writings tell us much about the forging of a national and imperial identity that would become disseminated around the globe.

Such fundamentally differing social views as theirs could well have proved an unbridgeable gap, but once upon a time Pope and Mary Wortley Montagu became friends and neighbors in Twickenham after she returned from Turkey. Then they quarreled – about what, exactly, no one is certain – and ended up celebrated enemies. Horace Walpole delighted in airing their dirty linen in public: "Their quarrel is said to have sprung from a pair of sheets, which, coming down suddenly to her house at Twickenham, she borrowed; and not returning, he sent for, and she sent them back unwashed. Her dirt, and their mutual economy, make the story not quite incredible."[5] Now about those unwashed sheets: dirt, filth, blood, the state of unwashed gameiness, is always attaching itself to Montagu in the anecdotal record. How much of this attributed filth is empirically verifiable, and how much might constitute the revenge of certain men of letters on a witty writing woman who flouted public opinion and condescended to them? Ironically, when Pope satirizes Montagu, he often represents her as wallowing in dirt of the dirtiest sort, namely country filth: he strips her of her aristocratic taste and metropolitan sophistication and portrays her as that lowest form of life, from a suburban point of view, the backward hunting gentry:

> *Avidien* or his Wife (no Matter which,
> For him you'll call a dog, and her a bitch)
> Sell their presented Partridges, and Fruits,
> And humbly live on rabbits and on roots.

(*Second Satire of the Second Book of Horace Paraphrased*, lines 49–52)[6]

Montagu herself was much more infuriated by the double-barreled slur that could always be claimed to be a double-edged compliment in Pope's *First Satire of the Second Book of Horace Imitated*: "From furious *Sappho* scarce a milder Fate, / P-x'd by her Love, or libell'd by her Hate" (lines 83–84). In other words, expect no less from intimacy with Montagu than slander, poison, or hanging. "P-x'd" here quickly glances off syphilis, the obvious general referent for "pox," to light upon the disease of smallpox with which she was widely associated. Having suffered from smallpox as a young woman, she still bore the scars, but by writing "P-x'd by her love," Pope assures us that only Montagu – the woman who had popularized the Ottoman practice of inoculation against smallpox in England by inoculating her own children – could be meant. Pope deviously covers himself by disguising his attack as a potential compliment.

Such passionate disavowal intimates the heat that had gone before. Byron believed that after Lady Mary's return from Turkey, Pope declared his amorous designs upon her person, and she laughed in his face, a story supported by Montagu's own granddaughter, Lady Louisa Stuart.[7] Reading Pope's poem to Gay of 1720, it is tempting to agree he might well have declared a passion for "WORTLEY," hoping to attract her "eyes" to his "structures" – his perfect grounds at Twickenham, and his verse:

> Ah friend, 'tis true – this truth you lovers know –
> In vain my structures rise, my gardens grow,
> In vain fair Thames reflects the double scenes
> Of hanging mountains, and of sloping greens:
> Joy lives not here; to happier seats it flies,
> And only dwells where WORTLEY casts her eyes.
>
> What are the gay parterre, the chequer'd shade,
> The morning bower, the ev'ning colonade,
> But soft recesses of uneasy minds,
> To sigh unheard in, to the passing winds?
>
> So the struck deer in some sequester'd part
> Lies down to die, the arrow at his heart;
> There, stretch'd unseen in coverts hid from day,
> Bleeds drop by drop, and pants his life away.

("To Mr. Gay, who wrote him a congratulatory letter on the finishing his house")

Stimulated by his desire for (Mary Wortley) Montagu, Pope constructs an erotic landscape in which to fantasize about her. The "hanging mountains" and "sloping greens" owe their inspiration to an image of a female body. As so often in landscape poetry, the topography becomes eroticized and feminized, and the male poet is held hostage by the projections of his own imagination. As in Marvell's "The Garden" and Rochester's "A Ramble in Saint James's Parke," such erotic encounters are doomed to incompletion. We notice that only the poet's image of Wortley, projected as the topography of his garden, and not her body itself, is reflected in the Thames.

His imagination is feverishly dominated by her absence, her absent presence.

Having failed to draw Wortley into his grounds, his designs, his private world, Pope represents himself as a wounded deer, the victim of blood sports. She is the huntress, and he the hunted, she the predator, and he the prey. In her absence he is, like the deer, driven to seclusion, where, "stretch'd" out "unseen," he "bleeds" away his life "drop by drop," and "pants" "his life away," while thinking of her. These lines are a little orgy of onanistic imagery. But the wounded deer also figures as more than a merely conventional erotic metaphor, as we shall see. This matter of blood sports will prove a further marker of difference between Pope and Montagu, a point to which we shall return.

The literature of social comment during this period, whether in prose or verse, was very much the currency of polite culture, an important commodity in its own right. And increasingly, in the course of the eighteenth century, the authoritative polite voice came to be associated not so much with London itself as with the environs of London, the suburbs, and a metropolitan culture that claimed to know – and to seek to regulate – the countryside as well as the urban scene. Regulation, or good stewardship as Pope would have it, often meant removing blood from the landscape, tidying away the effluvia of game- and livestock-rearing and killing, of field sports and agriculture, in order that the sanctity of picturesque greenness, of English verdure, might be perceived undisturbed.

Coupled as friends, coupled as enemies: Pope and Montagu have been biographically linked, but they have not been ranked equally within early eighteenth-century literary culture. Pope has long been regarded as the supremely canonical poet of the early eighteenth century; he succeeded in making himself into a monument, the very icon of the major poet, in his own time and has never disappeared from view since. For most twentieth-century critics, Montagu has merely figured as a woman writer and epistolary stylist, as remarkable for her appearances in Pope's satire as for her learning. That Montagu's works are now available in authoritative scholarly editions owes something to feminist interest in recovering neglected women writers during the past twenty-five years. While scholars working in feminist literary history, colonial discourse, and postcolonial theory have recently latched onto Montagu, some Pope scholars have re-evaluated his works in ways influenced by these new fields.

For Laura Brown, Pope is a master tropologist of the discourse of imperialism and the fetishism of commodities. Building on the work of Reuben A. Brower and Louis A. Landa,[8] Brown represents Belinda in *The*

Rape of the Lock, arming herself at her dressing-table for combat in the marketplace of sexuality, as a touchstone at the very heart of eighteenth-century literary culture: "The image of female dressing and adornment has a very specific, consistent historical referent in the early eighteenth century – the products of mercantile capitalism ... Women wear the products of accumulation, and thus by metonymy they are made to bear responsibility for the system by which they are adorned."[9] Brown is particularly interested in discovering how the very structures, conventions, and syntax of literary works bear the marks of the psychic and social anxieties generated by capitalism and empire-building. Thus Brown reworks earlier formalist studies of Pope to achieve a new level of engagement with history and political ideology.

Ellen Pollak's *Poetics of Sexual Myth* and Brean S. Hammond's *Pope* similarly attend to questions of ideology and history as they figure in poetic forms.[10] For Pollak, ideology means the ideology of gender and sexual difference. Her feminist study finds Pope an upholder of ideas of sexual difference and women's inferiority, while Swift emerges as an iconoclastic naysayer to gender ideology, despite the misogyny of some of his poems. Applying a form of Marxist ideology critique – derived from Pierre Macherey – to the contradictions of Pope's writing, Hammond gives us a sense of Pope's simultaneous wielding of cultural authority and exclusion from social power.[11]

This line of inquiry presents a Pope positioned at the center of elite literary culture. Yet his social position was in many ways marginal rather than typical, as Hammond indicates, and his satires directed at the Walpole administration and the Hanoverian dynasty shimmer with the peculiar energy of disaffection. Yet how politically disaffected was Pope? Had he any utopian longings for a radical subversion of contemporary society? It is tempting to read the very furtiveness and political risks involved in Jacobite discourse as a sign of a form of utopian social critique.

For some years there has been a growing interest in the possibility of Pope's Jacobitism, his continuing loyalty to the house of Stuart, over and above his openly Oppositional stance toward the Hanoverian succession and Walpole. If Pope were a Jacobite, he would have been committed to seeing the German Protestant house of Hanover replaced by the English but Catholic house of Stuart. Being Catholic, Pope was an obvious target of suspicion of treasonable Jacobite sympathies, so it would have been only prudent for him to keep any involvement in Jacobite activities secret. Besides, like his close, and most notoriously disaffected friend, Henry St. John, Lord Bolingbroke, Pope also seems to have been keen to advance the cause of Frederick, Prince of Wales, the hero of the so-called "Patriot

Opposition," as Christine Gerrard has most recently shown.[12] The Patriot Opposition consisted of Whigs loyal to the Hanoverian succession, hence "patriotic," and opposed to the leadership of Sir Robert Walpole, therefore in "opposition" to the current government. So there is considerable evidence for Pope having played both sides against the middle in his hope for some dramatic change in English politics.

Yet there remains to be explained that violent energy in much of Pope's social and political commentary, an energy which we might associate with political subversion, even radicalism, in spite of the conservatism of many of his ideas – such as his belief, shared with Bolingbroke, who wrote a treatise on the subject, that a "Patriot" king, such as the Prince of Wales, or more riskily, a Stuart returned to the throne, could transform English culture. It is tempting to attach to Pope something of the romance of adherence to lost causes, at least to what Douglas Brooks-Davies calls an "emotional Jacobitism," rather than a commitment to a program of political action.[13] Two very persuasive articles by Howard Erskine-Hill offer readings of Pope's poetry according to a Jacobite code, in which knowing readers would have delighted.[14] Once the case for such a code has been made, images of conquest, rape, or violent seizure, whether by scissors or swords, and mentions of William I, "the Conqueror," in Pope's poetry, offer themselves as charged with a furtive allusiveness to the Revolution of 1688–89 and William III.[15]

A debate in the *Times Literary Supplement* in 1973 between the literary critic Pat Rogers and the social historian E. P. Thompson raised the issue of whether or not Pope's helping his half-sister, Magdalen Racketts, and her husband and son, who were prosecuted for deer-stealing and Jacobite agitation in the early 1720s, might help document that he was a Jacobite sympathizer. Rogers didn't and still doesn't think so, and he has recently published an incisive review of the evidence,[16] but in *Whigs and Hunters: The Origin of the Black Act*, Thompson makes a persuasive case for Pope's alignment with the Windsor and Waltham "Blacks," those deer-stealers who blackened their faces for better cover by night and were so harshly prosecuted by Walpole on the grounds of Jacobite conspiracy.[17]

According to Thompson, Pope might have been a bit more radical in his sympathies than most literary critics have seen fit to observe. Thompson finds Pope's poem *Windsor-Forest* of 1713 a premonition of things to come under the Hanoverian dispensation (George I accedes in 1714), in which forest law would soon come back into force and the new Black Act would make deer-stealing and associated suspicious activities capital crimes. Within crown forests, the protection of deer was the overriding consideration, and forest inhabitants could expect to have their crops eaten by deer.

Forest law, if strictly enforced, assured the deer free passage at the inhabitants' expense and could also prevent the cutting of timber or peat or turf without a special license. "At least, this was so in theory," as Thompson puts it. "Claim and counter-claim had been the condition of forest life for centuries."[18] As Thompson explains, a forest may appear to be simply woodland and heath, uncultivated land, but in fact it has its own complex economy, providing for royal sport through deer-keeping but also traditionally allowing extensive compensatory common rights to forest inhabitants, including rights to pasturage of livestock, timber and firewood, the cutting of peat, turf, heath, fern, and furze, and the digging of sand and gravel.[19]

According to Thompson, Pope's vindication of Queen Anne's relaxed attitude toward forest law and commoners' cultivation and use of the forest aligns him with poachers and resisters of the repressive Walpole machine. Thompson's Pope does not emerge exactly as a poet of the people – *Windsor-Forest* may endorse Blacking, but in order to celebrate Queen Anne as legitimate, and congenial, monarch: "And Peace and Plenty tell, a STUART reigns" (line 42). But having once read Thompson's presentation of the documentary evidence of Pope's involvement with the Racketts alongside his analysis of *Windsor-Forest*, few readers will remain unswayed in the direction of a Pope whose social comment on the Hanoverians and the Walpole regime should be read as an arrow "expertly flighted and with a shaft of solid information."[20]

Pope was a master of self-promotion, as well as of self-preservation. He perfected turning political disenfranchisement into satirical literary triumphs. This technique made him appealing to some women writers of the time, for who better could serve as a model of the disenfranchised still succeeding in the literary marketplace?[21] As a London linen merchant's son, a Catholic, a Jacobite sympathizer, if not an active conspirator, and a sufferer from Pott's disease, or tuberculosis of the spine, Pope had many disadvantages to overcome to enter into polite society. He stood only four feet six inches high, and was very hunchbacked, requiring in middle age a stiff set of linen stays to hold himself upright. The disease also brought him severe headaches, fevers, sensitivity to cold, and respiratory difficulties as his spine collapsed. His biographer Maynard Mack observes that by the time Pope had become a successful poet, "he was already established in his own mind and in the minds of others as a dwarf and a cripple."[22] According to Kristina Straub, anti-Catholic bigotry often combined with homophobia, so that Pope was also at particular pains to distance himself from homoerotic associations and sexual ambiguity.[23] Yet Pope counted among his friends some of the wealthiest and most influential members of the aristocracy and gentry. How did he manage it?

Pope's ideas about the proper conduct of the country gentleman as a landowner and shaper of the countryside were crucial for his social rise, overriding his sometimes unpopular political sympathies. Fashioning the English countryside and becoming an exponent of fashionable aesthetics became for Pope a ticket to dining at some of the most admired country houses in the land.[24] And he had the nerve to advise lords and great landowners about the landscaping design of their estates from the perspective of his leased five acres at Twickenham, even then a suburb of London.[25] And so we have a paradoxical figure, Pope as the influential gardening advisor and embodiment of polite literary culture, stamping more than one generation of landowning toffs with his own peculiarly London-merchant-middle-class, Catholic, politically disaffected, physically disabled, image and aesthetic preferences. Thus does the Twickenhamization of the English countryside come into being, a movement largely attributable to the influence of suburban intellectuals like Pope.

Beyond having been meticulously edited by Robert Halsband and Isobel Grundy, Montagu's work has not received the same kind of scholarly attention as Pope's. There is no Montagu industry – as yet. Indeed such scholarly finds as Montagu's marginalia in a set of the fourth edition of Robert Dodsley's *A Collection of Poems in four volumes by Several Hands* (1755) that belonged to the British Consul at Venice, Joseph Smith, have only recently come to light.[26] In "The Politics of Female Authorship," Isobel Grundy examines these marginal notes, enabling us to observe closely the tension Montagu felt regarding her poetic gifts – on the one hand, the desire to claim her own poems when they appeared in print ("mine," she writes, or "wrote 2 months after my marriage"); on the other, indignation at appearing in print without either knowledge of it or permission for it, and even greater indignation at misattribution ("I renounce & never saw till this year 1758"). Discovering that without either her permission or her knowledge, a number of her poems had been in print for ten years in the century's most popular anthology, made her furious. By 1758, when Montagu wrote her marginalia, she was, according to Grundy, "an old woman" "unhappily" involved in too many battles and thus "too insecure to accept willingly the role of *published* poet."[27]

What Robert Halsband labels the "Turkish Embassy Letters" in his complete edition of Montagu's correspondence have become once again, as she wished, her chief bid for literary fame. Three books and a cluster of recent essays[28] testify to a resurgence of interest in Montagu under the rubric of colonial discourse and Orientalism, within the terms described by Edward Said.[29] Analyzing the various portraits of herself in Turkish dress that Montagu commissioned, Marcia Pointon constructs a complex model of aesthetic agency for Montagu: "The spectacle of Ottoman culture – of feminized Ottoman culture – enabled Montagu to be both viewer and viewed, to bridge the gap between self as object of another's pleasure and self as narcissistic, a gap that was a powerful ingredient of eighteenth-century social discourse and social function."[30] Pointon answers the question of what Montagu was seeking in Turkey, and in having herself figured in Turkish dress, in terms of pleasure and compensation for losses suffered elsewhere, through smallpox and aging.

Questions such as these will always return us to the imperial observer, not the colonized, or more subtly, the unheard or repressed Oriental other within the texts of western imperialism.[31] In an abstruse but provocative essay, Srinivas Aravamudan has coined the term "Levantinization" for the mechanism by which Montagu attempts to escape from pure Englishness into Turkishness, but fails. "To run or throw a levant was to make a bet with the intention of absconding if it was lost," Aravamudan observes. He attributes to Montagu a form of "intellectual wagering without account-ability."[32] Montagu must abandon her fantasy of assimilation to Ottoman culture, her fantasy of going Levantine. The letters of ambassadorial travel close with a definite return home to Englishness. Aravamudan proposes that we attempt to read Montagu from the position of occluded postcolonial others, that we "tropicalize" her imperial text as we read it.

No scholarly consensus is likely to be reached regarding the critical force of Montagu's celebration of cultural difference during her stay in the Ottoman empire. I am inclined to agree with Meyda Yegenoglu that we should not underestimate the effect of Montagu's positioning within a system of Orientalist representations, however much she might have wished to celebrate the differences between Turkish and English culture. In typically imperial fashion, Montagu regards the purpose of travel to foreign parts as escape from domestic conventions, from scandal and the social demands of home. In "Constantinople, To [William Feilding]," Montagu writes first of her delight in finding a very English form of rural retirement in Turkey, the picturesque little farm that is like a suburban garden:

> Give me, Great God (said I) a Little Farm
> In summer shady and in Winter warm,
> Where a clear Spring gives birth to a cool brook
> By nature sliding down a Mossy rock,
> Not artfully in Leaden Pipes convey'd
> Nor greatly falling in a forc'd Cascade,
> Pure and unsulli'd winding through the Shade.

All-Bounteous Heaven has added to my Prayer
A softer Climat and a Purer air.   (lines 1–9)[33]

Then, having established herself comfortably in an English-style retreat, but with a warmer climate and less damp and sooty air than England could offer, she sets her sights on the Ottoman splendor of Constantinople, only to return quickly to the pleasures of retirement:

Yet not these prospects, all profusely Gay,
The gilded Navy that adorns the Sea,
The rising City in Confusion fair,
Magnificently form'd irregular,
Where Woods and Palaces at once surprise,
Gardens on Gardens, Domes on Domes arise,
And endless Beauties tire the wandring Eyes,
So sooths my wishes or so charms my Mind
As this retreat, secure from Human kind,
No Knave's successfull craft does Spleen excite,
No Coxcomb's Tawdry Splendour shocks my sight,
No Mob Alarm awakes my Female Fears,
No unrewarded Merit asks my Tears,
Nor Praise my Mind, nor Envy hurts my Ear,
Even Fame it selfe can hardly reach me here,
Impertinence with all her tattling train,
Fair sounding Flattery's delicious bane,
Censorious Folly, noisy Party rage,
The thousand Tongues with which she must engage
Who dare have Virtue in a vicious Age.   (lines 92–111)

The pleasures of Turkey are largely its absences, its differences from home. Obviously, Montagu has sought a foreign field that is forever not England, thank God, and where the weather's better, because the sun shines much more often. Montagu glories in her ideal Turkish retreat precisely because it is so far removed from English social demands. She imagines from a pleasing distance exactly what she is escaping from in London, where her rank and marriage would always assure a certain stark publicity.

When the letters from the Turkish embassy were published, Montagu was posthumously subjected to intense public scrutiny. Reception of her letters in the later eighteenth century and early nineteenth century tended to focus on whether or not readers agreed with her reports of Turkish places and customs. Following most immediately in Montagu's footsteps, Elizabeth, Lady Craven, who traveled to Constantinople in 1786 and published her own journal in letters in 1789, so disliked Lady Mary's letters that she dismissed them as forgeries, observing "that whoever wrote L.

M——'s Letters (for she never wrote a line of them) misrepresents things most terribly – I do really believe, in most things they wished to impose upon the credulity of their readers, and laugh at them."[34]

In 1813, Byron's friend and traveling companion, John Cam Hobhouse, annotated his copy of Montagu's letters so contentiously that he seems to have delighted in attempting to refute her point by point, especially with regard to Turkish manners, proclaiming that:

> her representations are not to be depended upon – Some of her assertions none but a *female* traveller can contradict, but what a *man* who has seen Turkey can controvert, I am myself capable of proving to be unfounded – From what I have seen of the country, and from what I have read of her book, I am sure that her ladyship would not stick at a little fibbing; and as I know part of her accounts to be altogether false I have a right to suppose she has exaggerated other particulars –[35]

Hobhouse's disputes with Montagu revolve around issues of taste, in which he figures as a traditional anti-Turkish Englishman. On page 149 of the letters, for instance, when Montagu praises the Turks for having "a right notion of life" because "They consume it in music, gardens, wine, and delicate eating, while we are tormenting our brains with some scheme of politics, or studying some science to which we can never attain," Hobhouse adds a penciled note: "– vile music, bad wine & in such eating as would disgust any but a Turk." If Montagu relished her experiences of Ottoman culture to the point of near Levantinization, Hobhouse, by contrast, seems to have had such a miserable time in Constantinople that he merely confirmed his anti-Turkish prejudices at every turn. His is the more typical experience of English travelers in the period, in itself evidence of the unusually culturally relativist nature of Montagu's vision.

Today Montagu is read primarily as an aristocratic foremother of feminist inquiry, with all the problems this entails. As a woman with an inherited title, she spurned the vulgarity of the commercial marketplace, yet her desire for applause and fame made her continuously seek it in devious ways. Her satiric impulse was as strong as Pope's, and although it was more respectable than his in coming from an aristocrat, such an impulse was simultaneously much less acceptable coming from a woman. Lady Mary Wortley Montagu's cultural heirs include such twentieth-century English women travelers to Turkey as Freya Stark and Christina Dodwell.

Pope's legacy can be seen today in the National Trust taste for stately homes and gardens, the Tory garden festivals of the 1980s and 1990s,[36] the "Heritage Industry" generally, and less obviously, much of the propaganda against hunting. Because along with the industries of countryside-worship and tourism,[37] Pope helped to create a suburban attitude toward the ecology of rural life, from game laws and field sports to the proper attitude toward animals as sentient beings and the desirability of vegetarianism.[38] If we take Thompson's case seriously, then Pope's criticism of aristocratic and moneyed excess, his squeamishness at blood sports, his interest in vegetarianism, and his hoping to make all estates, even the countryside at large, as tame and picturesque as a suburban garden, point in the direction, however covert or tenuous, of what today would take the form of an alignment with class struggle from below.

Notice Pope's ambivalent representation in *Windsor-Forest* of the seasonal round as one bloody field sport after another, with vigorous young Englishmen, their own blood "fermented" by youthful spirits, forever seeking something or someone to kill:

> Ye vig'rous Swains! while Youth ferments your Blood,
> And purer Spirits swell the sprightly Flood,
> Now range the Hills, the gameful Woods beset,
> Wind the shrill Horn, or spread the waving Net.   (lines 93–96)

After the harvest at summer's end, autumnal partridge-netting (lines 97–104) and pheasant-shooting (lines 111–18) give way to wintry hare-hunting and woodcock- and songbird-shooting (lapwings and larks) (lines 119–34), while spring brings fishing (lines 135–46), and summer returns with the pursuit of the hart, the royal chase (lines 147–64):

> See! the bold Youth strain up the threatning Steep,
> Rush thro' the Thickets, down the Vallies sweep,
> Hang o'er their Coursers Heads with eager Speed,
> And Earth rolls back beneath the flying Steed.
> Let old *Arcadia* boast her ample Plain,
> Th'Immortal Huntress, and her Virgin Train;
> Nor envy *Windsor*! since thy Shades have seen
> As bright a Goddess, and as chast a Queen;
> Whose Care, like hers, protects the Sylvan Reign,
> The Earth's fair Light, and Empress of the Main.   (lines 155–64)

That seasonal round of blood sport is how we know all's right with England, the empire, and the world. The shot larks may "fall, and leave their little Lives in Air" (line 134), the glorious plumage of the pheasant may make his death peculiarly poignant, and the human desire to kill something may even corrupt other species: "Beasts, urg'd by us, their Fellow Beasts pursue, / And learn of Man each other to undo" (lines 123–24). But however philosophically ambivalent Pope may sound, his criticism of the bloodiness of field sports functions both literally, as in these two lines, and more metaphorically elsewhere, as a parenthetical intrusion. The ultimate argument of the poem is that these sports are preferable to war. Father Thames is succinctly explicit in his prophecy regarding a future Pax Britannica: "The shady Empire shall retain no Trace / Of War or Blood, but in the Sylvan Chace" (lines 371–72). Imperial Britain demands that "Arms" be employed on somebody, so let them be "employ'd on Birds and Beasts alone" (line 374).

Blood sports *may* just be preferable to war, and the unfolding of hunting seasons for game *may* assure social harmony in the realm at a regrettable price, but one thing is unambiguously clear: the ideology of governance as good stewardship. This preoccupation recurs throughout Pope's writing, including his praise of Anne as lax enforcer of forest law in *Windsor-Forest*. In previous reigns – William I's, and by coded insinuation, William III's – the tyranny of forest law laid waste to vast tracts of land for royal pleasure in the chase, and subjects were as expendable as, though less well fed than, his majesty's deer:

> What wonder then, a Beast or Subject slain
> Were equal Crimes in a Despotick Reign;
> Both doom'd alike for sportive Tyrants bled,
> But while the Subject starv'd, the Beast was fed.   (lines 57–60)

The return of a Stuart to the throne has not only restored hunting to its proper place in the cycle of things, but allowed commoners to repossess their rights in the forest. Because Anne has not been "displeas'd" to see "the peaceful Cottage rise" or "gath'ring Flocks on unknown Mountains fed," or "yellow Harvests spread" "O'er sandy Wilds":

> The Forests wonder'd at th'unusual Grain,
> And secret Transport touch'd the conscious Swain.
> Fair *Liberty*, *Britannia*'s Goddess, rears
> Her chearful Head, and leads the golden Years.   (lines 86–92)

Pope's praise of Anne as a good steward, summarized in the punning line "And Peace and Plenty tell, a STUART reigns" (line 42), parallels his self-praise as generous host in *The Second Satire of the Second Book of Horace Paraphrased* twenty years later:

> Content with little, I can piddle here
> On Broccoli and mutton, round the year;
> But ancient friends, (tho' poor, or out of play)
> That touch my Bell, I cannot turn away.
> 'Tis true, no Turbots dignify my boards,

But gudgeons, flounders, what my Thames affords.
To Hounslow-heath I point, and Bansted-down,
Thence comes your mutton, and these chicks my own. (lines 137–44)

Pope's poetic support for this principle of stewardship was most crucial, I think, in making his work appeal to his aristocratic patrons and friends – the Bathursts, Burlingtons, Bolingbrokes, Cobhams, etc.:

> Who then shall grace, or who improve the Soil?
> Who plants like BATHURST, or who builds like BOYLE.
> 'Tis Use alone that sanctifies Expence,
> And Splendour borrows all her rays from Sense.
> His Father's Acres who enjoys in peace,
> Or makes his Neighbours glad, if he encrease;
> Whose chearful Tenants bless their yearly toil,
> Yet to their Lord owe more than to the soil;
> Whose ample Lawns are not asham'd to feed
> The milky heifer and deserving steed;
> Whose rising Forests, not for pride or show,
> But future Buildings, future Navies grow:
> Let his plantations stretch from down to down,
> First shade a Country, and then raise a Town.
>
> (*Epistle to Burlington*, lines 177–90)

And this ideology of the proper good stewardship of land involves a managerial relation to the rural and the natural world. So does the suburban desire to tidy up the countryside as if it were one's own garden.

A suburban consumer's attitude like Pope's often proffers a sensitivity toward animal sensibilities that makes one peculiarly likely to find things in the country – still the scene of food production and animal excretion as well as extermination – less than lovely. The suburbanite itches to manage and regulate such things, such flows, that the country might be generally picturesque and pleasant to walk in. Visiting the countryside even today is second only to watching television as Britain's favorite pastime: "On a summer Sunday afternoon, the Countryside Commission estimate that eighteen million people, two fifths of the population, like to get away from it all and go to the country."[39] The historical triumph of walking in the countryside over hunting, riding, and field sports is bound up with the Twickenhamization of the countryside, and in Pope and Montagu we can see some of this conflict being played out, as it is still being played out, however residually, in social antagonisms and debates in Britain today.

So let us keep in mind Pope as a figure of exclusion mainstreamed, as a Jacobite canonized, and as a suburban intellectual. For the land-improving classes, Pope served as a legitimating arbiter of taste. Thanks to his influence, the standards applied to country estates were increasingly suburban. As a poet of social criticism and satire, as a promoter of the industry of domestic tourism, particularly of the stately home and country park variety, and as a critic of blood sports and a would-be vegetarian pronouncer upon the proper management of the English countryside, Pope often sounds oddly like our contemporary, despite some obvious differences. He insinuates Montagu into his satires as filthy Sappho or a rustic, if not plebeian, poacher, living off rabbits and roots; and she ventriloquizes him incriminating himself as a toady, a snob, and a seditious fool.

When Montagu takes her revenge on Pope, she does so by ventriloquizing his own verse, with its mannerisms and pretensions made absurdly self-revealing. She so closely shares a certain metropolitan social space around Twickenham that she can twist Pope's own texts inside out. He is for her the chief symptom of the very commercialization and vulgar cheapening of the culture he himself affects to deplore. Her satirical strategy exposes Pope's self-proclaimed superior taste as a cloak for the envy felt by members of the middle-class like himself toward social superiors. Through her ventriloquization of his voice in a poetic epistle to Bolingbroke, we observe how Pope's greed and his perpetual financial cramp drive him to write splenetic attacks on other people's feasts. According to Montagu, his sycophantic relation to Bolingbroke is based on snobbery as well as bad politics – Opposition to the Hanoverians, Whigs (such as Edward Wortley Montagu and Lady Mary), and Sir Robert Walpole; possibly Jacobite treason. Far from being content to "piddle here / On Broccoli and mutton, round the year," Pope envies the rich their elaborate repasts:

> When I see smoaking on a Booby's board
> Fat Ortalans, and Pies of Perigord,
> My self am mov'd to high poetick rage
> (The Homer, and the Horace of the Age).
> Puppies! who have the insolence to dine
> With smiling beauties, and with sparkling wine,
> While I retire, plagu'd with an Empty Purse,
> Eat Brocoli, and kiss my antient Nurse.
> But had we flourish'd when stern Henry reign'[d]
> Our good Designs had been but ill explain'd;
> The Ax had cut your solid Reasoning short,
> I, in the Porter's Lodge, been scourg'd at Court,
> To better Times kind heaven reserv'd our Bir[th,]
> Happy for us that Coxcombs are on Earth.

Mean spirits seek their Villany to hide,
We shew our venom'd Souls with noble Pride,
And, in bold strokes, have all Mankind defy'd;
Past o'er the bounds that keep Mankind in aw[e,]
And laugh'd at Justice, Gratitude and Law:
While our Admirers stare with dumb surprize
Treason, and Scandal, we monopolize.
Yet this remains our more peculiar boast,
You scape the Block, and I the Whipping-Post.

(P[ope] *to Bolingbroke*, lines 76–98)

From Montagu's point of view, it is evidence of the absurdity of the times that Pope and Bolingbroke can command the attention of the reading public with a seeming monopoly on the literature of impolite comment – treason and scandal – while denouncing the current government so openly. Once upon a time, during the reign of Henry VIII, Bolingbroke would have been beheaded for such treason, and Pope merely horse-whipped, as appropriate for one from the meaner, servile classes.

I think we have to admit that Lady Mary gives as good as she gets. It is hard not to credit much of her portrait of Pope, though the picture might be abhorrent to some Pope fans. Now where is she positioning herself, exactly, in order to ventriloquize Pope's self-incrimination? I think that much of her identity is staked on a certain kind of upper-class female identification with the culture of hunting and blood sports. Precisely what antagonizes Pope and gives him profound ambivalence about hunting culture is what gives her a sense of superiority, in spite of the official gender-ban on women speaking their minds in this period. The semiotics of riding the country, or surveying the nation from a position of dominance and horse-mastery, seems crucial to her identity – even to her bodily integrity and her health, as she reiterates over the years:

You'l wonder to hear that short silence is occasion'd by not having a moment unemploy'd at Twictnam, but I pass many hours on Horseback, and I'll assure you ride stag hunting, which I know you stare to hear of. I have arriv'd to vast courrage and skill that way, and am as well pleas'd with it as with the Acquisition of a new sense. His Royal Highness hunts in Richmond Park, and I make one of the Beau monde in his Train. I desire you after this Account not to name the Word old Woman to me any more; I approach to 15 nearer than I did 10 year ago, and am in hopes to improve ev'ry year in Health and Vivacity.

(letter to Lady Mar, August 1725)[40]

Proficiency at riding to stag-hounds gives Montagu the pleasure of "the Acquisition of a new sense." She is happier making "one of the Beau monde" in the Prince's train out hunting than in more urban or domestic settings. She is the English type of hunter-gatherer, not the settled agricultural type. The stewardship of land, dynastic preservation of the large estate, don't really come into it. She writes of riding and hunting sounding more like a pleased insider within English culture than she does almost anywhere else in her writing.

What is striking in this picture is the absence – are they an excluded middle? – of the rural lower classes, some of whom do participate in hunting and country sports, and some of whom do still hunt-and-gather, if not poach, and eat rabbits and root vegetables. They are the modern representatives of the use-rights-seeking, poaching, hunting-without-property-qualification Blacks, with whom Pope may have sympathized more than he was prepared to say openly. A gardener who could identify, to a certain extent, with gatherers and hunters of the lower classes, he was at least ambivalent about the importance of field or blood sports within English culture. And about hunting as a rural lower-class activity he had something, however covert or brief, to say.

The compensations which a Pope and a Montagu sought through literary production differed. Pope's writing must be connected with a desire to acquire symbolic as well as commercial capital, with upward mobility, in short, while Montagu's writing seems often to have served her as a compensation for failed romance and thwarted desires – political, sexual, and touristic.[41] In spite of being a woman and resenting gender restrictions, Montagu has more scope for acting than Pope; she can see the point in physical dash, and riding and hunting as sport and exercise; and, as a consequence, she seems to resent other people's pleasures less than he does. Pope becomes much more fanatical as he is more restricted in his outlets, and more dependent upon the generosity, if not charity, of others, for his pleasures than is Montagu. By my definition, he is more thoroughly "suburban" than she is, much more likely to seem like our contemporary, unless we make a habit of nomadic tourism or take up the life of expatriate exile.

Yet both Pope and Montagu seek to aestheticize and immortalize the minutiae of their very existences in writing, to compose an aesthetics of the everyday. This desire for control over one's own landscape, one's own small patch, is a profoundly domestic and self-righteous way of viewing the world. And the more one seeks to make one's life and its terrain one's own, each consumer purchase reflective of one's tastes and politics, the more vegetarianism and animal rights seem to come into play, and the more the notion of field sports and hunting as part of a national identity comes to seem abhorrent. Some protesters may advocate the rights of foxes over the rights of farmers or riders to hounds, but is there not also a desire to be forever rid of the symbolic privilege of toffs on horseback? To be a plain Alexander Pope getting his own back at a Lady Mary Wortley Montagu? The literature of social comment has usually been dependent upon such breaches.

NOTES

1 See David Foxon and James McLaverty, *Pope and the Early Eighteenth-Century Book Trade* (Oxford: Clarendon Press, 1991), pp. 51–101; this passage p. 101.

2 Elizabeth A. Bohls, *Women Travel Writers and the Language of Aesthetics, 1716–1818* (Cambridge: Cambridge University Press, 1995), p. 24.

3 *LETTERS of the Right Honourable Lady M – – y W – – – y M – – – – e: Written, during her Travels in Europe, Asia and Africa, To Persons of Distinction, Men of Letters, &c. in different Parts of Europe. Which Contain, Among other Curious Relations, Accounts of the Policy and Manners of the Turks; Drawn from Sources that have been inaccessible to other Travellers*, 3 vols. (London: Printed for T. Becket and P. A. De Hondt, 1763). The modern scholarly edition, which labels these the "Turkish Embassy Letters," is *The Complete Letters of Lady Mary Wortley Montagu*, ed. Robert Halsband, 3 vols. (Oxford: Clarendon Press, 1965–67).

4 The recent publication of Montagu's *Romance Writings*, ed. Isobel Grundy (Oxford: Clarendon Press, 1996), provides new autobiographical evidence of this period of Montagu's life, in the "Italian Memoir," pp. 81–105.

5 *The Yale Edition of Horace Walpole's Correspondence*, ed. W. S. Lewis and A. Dayle Wallace with the assistance of Edwine M. Martz (London and New Haven: Oxford University Press and Yale University Press, 1965), vol. XXXIV, p. 255.

6 All quotations from Pope's verse are taken from *The Poems of Alexander Pope: A One-Volume Edition of the Twickenham Text With Selected Annotations*, ed. John Butt (London: Methuen, 1963). See also *The Twickenham Edition of the Poems of Alexander Pope*, gen. ed. John Butt, 11 vols. (London: Methuen, and New Haven: Yale University Press, 1939–69).

7 "Her own statement ... was this; that at some ill-chosen time, when she least expected what romances call a *declaration*, he made such passionate love to her, as, in spite of her utmost endeavours to be angry and look grave, provoked an immoderate fit of laughter; from which moment he became her implacable enemy," "Biographical Anecdotes of Lady M. W. Montagu," in *Essays and Poems and Simplicity, A Comedy*, ed. Robert Halsband and Isobel Grundy (Oxford: Clarendon Press, 1977), p. 37.

8 See Reuben A. Brower, *Alexander Pope: The Poetry of Allusion* (Oxford: Clarendon Press, 1959) and Louis A. Landa, "Pope's Belinda, the General Emporie of the World, and the Wondrous Worm," in *Essays in Eighteenth-Century English Literature* (Princeton: Princeton University Press, 1980), pp. 178–98.

9 Laura Brown, *Ends of Empire: Women and Ideology in Early Eighteenth-*

Century English Literature (Ithaca, NY, and London: Cornell University Press, 1993), pp. 112, 118. See also Brown, *Alexander Pope* (Oxford: Blackwell, 1985).

10 Ellen Pollak, *The Poetics of Sexual Myth: Gender and Ideology in the Verse of Swift and Pope* (Chicago and London: University of Chicago Press, 1985) and Brean S. Hammond, *Pope* (Brighton: Harvester Press, 1986).

11 Three studies illustrate the value of bringing explicitly politicized forms of literary inquiry to bear on eighteenth-century texts, a movement that began in the mid-1980s. See Felicity Nussbaum and Laura Brown's introductory essay in *The New Eighteenth Century: Theory, Politics, English Literature* (London and New York: Methuen, 1987), pp. 1–22, and the essay in that volume by John Barrell and Harriet Guest, "On the Use of Contradiction: Economics and Morality in the Eighteenth-Century Long Poem," pp. 121–43. Most recently, Colin Nicholson has investigated Pope's own financial investments in relation to his satires in *Writing & the Rise of Finance: Capital Satires of the Early Eighteenth Century* (Cambridge: Cambridge University Press, 1994).

12 Christine Gerrard, *The Patriot Opposition to Walpole: Politics, Poetry, and National Myth, 1725–1742* (Oxford: Clarendon Press, 1994).

13 See Douglas Brooks-Davies, *Pope's Dunciad and the Queen of Night: A Study in Emotional Jacobitism* (Manchester: Manchester University Press, 1985) and *The Mercurian Monarch: Magical Politics from Spenser to Pope* (Manchester: Manchester University Press, 1983).

14 Howard Erskine-Hill, "Alexander Pope: The Political Poet in His Time," *Eighteenth-Century Studies*, 15, 2 (1981–82), pp. 123–48, and "Literature and the Jacobite Cause: Was There a Rhetoric of Jacobitism?," in Eveline Cruickshanks (ed.), *Ideology and Conspiracy: Aspects of Jacobitism, 1689–1759* (Edinburgh: John Donald, 1982), pp. 49–69.

15 The most recent study in this vein is Murray G. H. Pittock's *Poetry and Jacobite Politics in Eighteenth-Century Britain and Ireland* (Cambridge: Cambridge University Press, 1994).

16 See Pat Rogers, *Essays on Pope* (Cambridge: Cambridge University Press, 1993), pp. 168–83.

17 E. P. Thompson, *Whigs and Hunters: The Origin of the Black Act* (New York: Pantheon, 1975).

18 *Ibid.*, p. 31.

19 *Ibid.*, pp. 29–32.

20 *Ibid.*, p. 294.

21 See Claudia N. Thomas, *Alexander Pope and His Eighteenth-Century Women Readers* (Carbondale and Edwardsville: Southern Illinois University Press, 1994), and my *The Muses of Resistance: Laboring-Class Women's Poetry in Britain* (Cambridge: Cambridge University Press, 1990), pp. 43–55.

22 Maynard Mack, *Alexander Pope: A Life* (New Haven and London: Yale University Press; New York and London: W. W. Norton, 1985), p. 153. See also Marjorie Hope Nicolson and G. S. Rousseau, *"This long Disease, my Life": Alexander Pope and the Sciences* (Princeton: Princeton University Press, 1968), pp. 7–82.

23 See Kristina Straub, *Sexual Suspects: Eighteenth-Century Players and Sexual Ideology* (Princeton: Princeton University Press, 1992), pp. 69–88.

24 See Peter Martin, *Pursuing Innocent Pleasures: The Gardening World of Alexander Pope* (Hamden, CT: Archon, 1984); John Dixon Hunt, *The Figure in the Landscape: Poetry, Painting, and Gardening during the Eighteenth Century* (Baltimore and London: Johns Hopkins University Press, 1976), and *Gardens and the Picturesque: Studies in the History of Landscape Architecture* (Cambridge, MA and London: MIT Press, 1992); and Morris R. Brownell, *Alexander Pope and the Arts of Georgian England* (Oxford: Clarendon Press, 1978).

25 Malcolm Kelsall, *The Great Good Place: The Country House and English Literature* (New York: Columbia University Press, 1993), pp. 59, 78.

26 Robert Dodsley, *A Collection of Poems in four volumes by Several Hands*, 4th edn. (London: Printed by J. Hughs for R. and R. Dodsley, 1755). In 1982 the set was held by the Pforzheimer Library, New York, but it has since moved to the British Library (shelfmark C.107.dg.28).

27 Isobel Grundy, "The Politics of Female Authorship: Lady Mary Wortley Montagu's Reaction to the Printing of her Poems," *The Book Collector*, 31, 1 (1982), pp. 19–37; this passage on p. 37. The set contains six volumes in all, though Montagu seems to have annotated only the original four from 1755. Volumes v and vi were published in March 1758, the year in which Montagu made her notes, but Grundy opines that, given the slowness of the mails between London and Venice, she probably never saw them (pp. 22–23).

28 See Lisa Lowe, *Critical Terrains: French and British Orientalisms* (Ithaca, NY, and London: Cornell University Press, 1991); Cynthia Lowenthal, *Lady Mary Wortley Montagu and the Eighteenth-Century Familiar Letter* (Athens: University of Georgia Press, 1994); Elizabeth A. Bohls, *Women Travel Writers*; and Meyda Yegenoglu, "Supplementing the Orientalist Lack: European Ladies in the Harem," in Mahmut Mutman and Meyda Yegenoglu (eds.), *Inscriptions 6: Orientalism and Cultural Differences* (Santa Cruz: Center for Cultural Studies, University of California, Santa Cruz, 1993), pp. 45–80. Lowe gives us a Montagu whose feminist identification with Turkish women in the *hamam* disrupts the monolithic othering of Orientalism (*Critical Terrains*, pp. 40–52). Yegenoglu counters with a sharp critique that reveals how inescapable certain Orientalist assumptions remain, even for so unconventional an Englishwoman as Montagu. In order to position herself in the women's baths, Montagu has to assume a masculine, Orientalizing, voyeuristic gaze. Any possible homoeroticism is overcome by Montagu's assuming the position of a colonial male observer ("Supplementing the Orientalist Lack," pp. 67–70).

29 See Edward W. Said, *Orientalism: Western Conceptions of the Orient* (New York: Pantheon Books, 1978; London and New York: Penguin, 1995).

30 Marcia Pointon, "Killing Pictures," in John Barrell (ed.), *Painting and the Politics of Culture: New Essays on British Art 1700–1850* (Oxford and New York: Oxford University Press, 1992), pp. 39–72; this passage p. 63.

31 Yegenoglu is the best and most incisive critic on this question, in "Supplementing the Orientalist Lack."

32 Srinivas Aravamudan, "Lady Mary Wortley Montagu in the *Hammam*: Masquerade, Womanliness, and Levantinization," *ELH*, 62, 1 (1995), pp. 69–104; this passage p. 70.

33 All quotations from Montagu's poetry are taken from *Essays and Poems*, ed. Halsband and Grundy.

34 *A JOURNEY through The Crimea to Constantinople. In A Series Of Letters from the right honourable Elizabeth Lady Craven, to his serene highness The Margrave Of Brandenbourg, Anspach, and Bareith. Written In the Year M DCC LXXXVI* (London: Printed for G. G. J. and J. Robinson, 1789), p. 105.

35 *Letters of the Right Honourable Lady M – – y W – – – y M – – – e: Written, during her Travels in Europe, Asia and Africa, To Persons of Distinction, Men of Letters, &c. in different Parts of Europe. Which Contain, among other curious Relations, Accounts of the Policy and Manners of the Turks. Drawn from Sources that have been inaccessible to other Travellers,* A New Edition, Complete in One Volume (London: Printed for John Taylor, 1790), MS. notes by John C. Hobhouse, AM, 1813. British Library shelfmark: 1477.b.29.

36 See John Roberts, "The Greening of Capitalism: The Political Economy of the Tory Garden Festivals," in Simon Pugh (ed.), *Reading Landscape: Country– City–Capital* (Manchester and New York: Manchester University Press, 1990), pp. 231–45.

37 See Carole Fabricant, "The Literature of Domestic Tourism and the Public Consumption of Private Property," in Nussbaum and Brown (eds.), *The New Eighteenth Century*, pp. 254–75.

38 See Pope's contribution to *The Guardian*, no. 61, "Against Barbarity to Animals" (21 May 1713) in *The Prose Works of Alexander Pope, Vol. I. The Earlier Works, 1711–1720*, ed. Norman Ault (Oxford: Shakespeare Head Press and Basil Blackwell, 1936; rpt. New York: Barnes & Noble, 1968); and Epistle III of the *Essay on Man* (lines 152–68 and 241–68).

39 Nigel Duckers and Huw Davies, *A Place in the Country: Social Change in Rural England* (London: Michael Joseph, 1990), p. 155.

40 *The Complete Letters of Lady Mary Wortley Montagu*, ed. Halsband, vol. II, pp. 54–55.

41 Here I agree with Elizabeth Bohls: "The most painful, deeply repressed, inarticulate and virtually inarticulable longings of eighteenth-century British women were, I suspect, not sexual but finally political," *Women Travel Writers*, p. 45.

FURTHER READING

Aravamudan, Srinivas, "Lady Mary Wortley Montagu in the *Hammam*: Masquerade, Womanliness, and Levantinization," *ELH*, 62, 1 (1995), pp. 69–104.

Barrell, John, and Guest, Harriet, "On the Use of Contradiction: Economics and Morality in the Eighteenth-Century Long Poem," in Felicity Nussbaum and Laura Brown (eds.), *The New Eighteenth Century: Theory, Politics, English Literature* (New York and London: Methuen, 1987), pp. 121–43.

Brower, Reuben A., *Alexander Pope: The Poetry of Allusion* (Oxford: Clarendon Press, 1959).

Brown, Laura, *Alexander Pope* (Oxford: Blackwell, 1985).

Ends of Empire: Women and Ideology in Early Eighteenth-Century English Literature (Ithaca and London: Cornell University Press, 1993).

Erskine-Hill, Howard, "Alexander Pope: The Political Poet in His Time," *Eighteenth-Century Studies*, 15, 2 (1981–82), pp. 123–48.

"Literature and the Jacobite Cause: Was There a Rhetoric of Jacobitism?," in

Eveline Cruickshanks (ed.), *Ideology and Conspiracy: Aspects of Jacobitism, 1689–1759* (Edinburgh: John Donald, 1982), pp. 49–69.

The Social Milieu of Alexander Pope: Lives, Example and the Poetic Response (New Haven: Yale University Press, 1975).

Fabricant, Carole, "The Literature of Domestic Tourism and the Consumption of Private Property," in Felicity Nussbaum and Laura Brown (eds.), *The New Eighteenth Century: Theory, Politics, English Literature* (New York and London: Methuen, 1987), pp. 254–75.

Foxon, David, and McLaverty, James, *Pope and the Early Eighteenth-Century Book Trade* (Oxford: Clarendon Press, 1991).

Gerrard, Christine, *The Patriot Opposition to Walpole: Politics, Poetry, and National Myth, 1725–1742* (Oxford: Clarendon Press, 1994).

Grundy, Isobel, "The Politics of Female Authorship: Lady Mary Wortley Montagu's Reaction to the Printing of her Poems," *The Book Collector*, 31, 1 (1982), pp. 19–37.

Grundy, Isobel, ed., *Romance Writings* (Oxford: Clarendon Press, 1996).

Halsband, Robert, *The Life of Lady Mary Wortley Montagu* (Oxford: Clarendon Press, 1956).

Hammond, Brean S., *Pope* (Brighton: Harvester Press, 1986).

Hunt, John Dixon, *The Figure in the Landscape: Poetry, Painting, and Gardening during the Eighteenth Century* (Baltimore and London: Johns Hopkins University Press, 1976).

Gardens and the Picturesque: Studies in the History of Landscape Architecture (Cambridge, MA and London: MIT Press, 1992).

Kelsall, Malcolm, *The Great Good Place: The Country House and English Literature* (New York: Columbia University Press, 1993).

Landa, Louis A., "Pope's Belinda, the General Emporie of the World, and the Wondrous Worm," in *Essays in Eighteenth-Century English Literature* (Princeton: Princeton University Press, 1980), pp. 178–98.

Lowe, Lisa, *Critical Terrains: French and British Orientalisms* (Ithaca, NY, and London: Cornell University Press, 1991).

Lowenthal, Cynthia, *Lady Mary Wortley Montagu and the Eighteenth-Century Familiar Letter* (Athens: University of Georgia Press, 1994).

Mack, Maynard, *The Garden and the City: Retirement and Politics in the Later Poetry of Pope, 1731–1743* (Toronto: University of Toronto Press, 1969).

Alexander Pope: A Life (New Haven and London: Yale University Press; New York and London: W. W. Norton, 1985).

Martin, Peter, *Pursuing Innocent Pleasures: The Gardening World of Alexander Pope* (Hamden, CT: Archon, 1984).

Pointon, Marcia, "Killing Pictures," in John Barrell (ed.), *Painting and the Politics of Culture: New Essays on British Art 1700–1850* (Oxford and New York: Oxford University Press, 1992), pp. 39–72.

Pollak, Ellen, *The Poetics of Sexual Myth: Gender and Ideology in the Verse of Swift and Pope* (Chicago and London: University of Chicago Press, 1985).

Rogers, Pat, *Essays on Pope* (Cambridge: Cambridge University Press, 1993).

Rumbold, Valerie, *Women's Place in Pope's World* (Cambridge: Cambridge University Press, 1989).

Sherburn, George (ed.), *The Correspondence of Alexander Pope* (Oxford: Clarendon Press, 1956).

The Early Career of Alexander Pope (Oxford: Clarendon Press, 1934).

Straub, Kristina, *Sexual Suspects: Eighteenth-Century Players and Sexual Ideology* (Princeton: Princeton University Press, 1992).

Thomas, Claudia N., *Alexander Pope and His Eighteenth-Century Women Readers* (Carbondale and Edwardsville: Southern Illinois University Press, 1994).

Thompson, E. P., *Whigs and Hunters: The Origin of the Black Act* (New York: Pantheon, 1975).

Yegenoglu, Meyda, "Supplementing the Orientalist Lack: European Ladies in the Harem," in Mahmut Mutman and Meyda Yegenoglu (eds.), *Inscriptions 6: Orientalism and Cultural Differences* (Santa Cruz: Center for Cultural Studies, University of California, Santa Cruz, 1993), pp. 45–80.

INDEX

Act Against Unlicensed and Scandalous
   Books 14, 17, 24, 42
Act of Allegiance 285
Act of Indemnity and Oblivion 189
Act of Settlement 13, 195
Act of Union 3
Addison, Joseph 28, 98, 137
Anacreon 128, 129, 217
Anne, Queen 13, 20, 96, 276, 282, 313, 319
Arbuthnot, John 35, 50, 153, 264
Astell, Mary xii, 27, 276–306; *Bart'lemy
   Fair* 277; *The Christian Religion as
   Profess'd* 276, 281; *A Fair Way with
   Dissenters* 297; *The Ladies' Library*
   278–79; *Letters Concerning the Love of
   God* 276, 277; *Impartial Enquiry into
   the Causes of Rebellion* 283, 284, 286,
   288; *Moderation Truly Stated* 286;
   Reflections Upon Marriage 276, 279,
   283–84; *A Serious Proposal to the Ladies*,
   278
Atterbury, Francis 15
Aubrey, John 58

Barker, Jane 71–72, 127
Barry, Elizabeth 204, 205
Behn, Aphra xii, 27, 90, 130–31, 225–49;
   Abdelazar 94; *Amorous Prince* 243;
   Epilogue to Sir Patient Fancy 238; *The
   Forc'd Marriage* 231; *The History of
   Bacon in Virginia* 234; *Love Arm'd*
   130; *Love-Letters* 232, 233, 239, 241;
   The Lucky Chance 241; *Oroonoko*
   225, 229–31, 234, 243; *The Roundheads*
   96; *The Rover* 91, 234–36; "A Satyr on
   Doctor Dryden" 236; *Sir Patient Fancy*
   69–70, 238; "To the Unknown Daphnis"
   64–65; *The Widow Ranter* 234, 239;
   The Younger Brother 232

Betterton, Thomas 96–97, 111–12
Blackmore, Sir Richard 173
Blow, John 111, 117n30
Boileau, Nicholas 216–17
Bolingbroke, Henry St. John, Viscount 13,
   14, 153, 311–12, 322
Brome, Alexander 129
Buckingham, George Villiers, Duke of 108,
   169, 205, 214
Bunyan, John 268
Burnet, Gilbert 14, 236
Butler, Samuel: *Hudibras* 19, 26–27,
   41–42, 70, 75–76

Catherine of Braganza, Queen 192
Centlivre, Susannah 97
Charles I 5, 7, 58, 60, 63, 104, 105, 121,
   144–45, 187, 204, 234, 288
Charles II 7, 8, 11, 23, 24, 59, 60, 63,
   82–83, 92, 104, 107, 121–22, 128, 130,
   146, 154, 187, 205, 207, 211, 220
Chudleigh, Mary, Lady 136
Churchill, Charles 66
Churchill, John, Duke of Marlborough 10,
   13
Cibber, Colley 87, 92, 155
Civil Wars 3, 39, 40, 41, 48, 58, 61, 63, 82,
   146, 277, 292
Clarendon, Edward Hyde, Earl of 8, 18,
   90, 170–71, 186, 197, 285, 287, 288,
   291
coffee-houses xiii, 6, 26
Collier, Jeremy 97, 189
Collins, William 267
Congreve, William 76, 80n12, 97
Cotton, Charles 40, 129, 133
Cowley, Abraham 40, 122–24, 127, 133,
   138–49, 150
Creech, Thomas 65, 240–41

Cromwell, Oliver 7, 60, 82, 104, 121, 144–45, 146, 168, 185, 193
Crowne, John 96, 110

Dampier, William 253
Danby, Thomas Osborne, Earl of 8, 18, 44
Davenant, Sir William 82, 104–05, 106, 187
Declaration of Indulgence 8, 10, 169
Defoe, Daniel 199, 250–75, 283; *Compleat English Gentleman* 257; *Essay upon Projects* 265; *Journal of the Plague Year* 255, 257, 268, 269; *Jure Divino* 49; *Memoirs of a Cavalier* 255, 257; *Moll Flanders* 12, 254, 257, 268, 269; *Robinson Crusoe* 55, 225, 250–52, 263; *Roxana* 255, 268; *The Storm* 255; *True-Born Englishman* 48–49
Dissenters 4, 7, 9–10, 25
Donne, John 126–27, 135
Dorset, Charles Sackville, Earl of 128, 200, 205
Dorset Garden 85, 95, 109
Downes, John 87–88
Drury Lane 84
Dryden, John xi, xii, 39, 185–203, 220, 227, 236–37; *Absalom and Achitophel* 34, 37, 40, 42, 47–48, 68–69, 70, 192–94; *Aeneis* 150–51, 190, 200; *Albion and Albanius* 111, 152; *Alexander's Feast* 125; *All for Love* 95, 191; *Annus Mirabilis* 147–48, 150, 188; *Astraea Redux* 146, 186, 187; *Aureng-Zebe* 94, 110; *The Conquest of Granada* 93, 106; *Discourse Concerning the Original and Progress of Satire* 36, 38, 40, 48, 209; *Don Sebastian* 196–97; *Essay of Dramatic Poesy* 188, 190; *Essay on Translated Verse* 158; *Essay Upon Satire* 33; *Fables Ancient and Modern* 148, 175–78, 198, 201; *First Book of the Iliad* 157–58; *Heroique Stanza's* 146, 185, 187; *Horace Epode 2* 149–50; *Horace Ode 3.29* 133; *The Hind and the Panther* 70, 75, 194–96, 236; *His Majesties Declaration Defended* 34; *The Indian Emperour* 108; *The Indian Queen* 107, 108, 112; *King Arthur* 112; *Mac Flecknoe* 38, 40, 45–47, 191; *Marriage à la Mode* 91; *The Medal* 38, 70, 194; *Miscellany Poems* 148; "Of Heroick Plays" 106; *Ovid's Epistles* 148; *Religio Laici* 74–75, 194–95;

Secular Masque 185; *State of Innocence* 109, 191; *The Tempest* 109; "To My Honor'd Kinsman" 201; "To Sir Godfrey Kneller" 37; "To the Memory of Mr. Oldham" 137–38; "To the Pious Memory of Mrs. Anne Killigrew" xi, 124–25; *Tyrannick Love* 87, 95, 108
Duke's Company 83, 84, 95, 109, 110, 231
D'Urfey, Thomas 130
Dyer, John 134–35

Eikon Basilike 186, 288
Etherege, George 196; *Love in a Tub* 89; *The Man of Mode* 90; *She Wou'd if She Cou'd* 90
Evelyn, John 105
Exclusion Crisis 9, 17–18, 20, 22, 23, 45, 96, 192, 194, 197, 282

Farquhar, George 89, 92
Fielding, Henry 100; *Essay on Conversation* 27; *The Grub-Street Opera* 99; *Jonathan Wild* 40, 50, 51; *Joseph Andrews* 40; *Tom Jones* 40, 257
Filmer, Sir Robert 173, 193, 234, 235, 288, 289
Finch, Anne, Countess of Winchilsea 72, 126, 134, 241, 228

Garth, Samuel: *Dispensary* 48–49, 50
Gay, John 4, 16, 114, 309; *The Beggar's Opera* 16, 40, 50, 99–100, 113–14; *Polly* 100
George I 14–16
George II 3, 15, 16, 28, 38, 154–55
George III 16
Glorious Revolution 10, 14, 17, 20, 61, 167, 196, 280, 281, 307
Granville, George 112
Grub Street 6, 267
Gwynne, Nell 44, 87, 205, 238

Handel, George Frederick 113, 114
Harley, Robert, Earl of Oxford 153
Haymarket (theatre) 99–100
Henrietta Maria 84, 176
Hervey, John, Lord xi, 35
Hobbes, Thomas 27, 123, 127, 146, 197, 206, 262, 279, 280, 283, 288, 291, 294
Hogarth, William 4
Homer 156–58

Horace 65, 121–22, 131, 143–44, 150, 153–55, 220
Howard, Sir Robert 107, 190

Interregnum 61, 63, 104, 129, 197–98

Jacobites and Jacobitism 5, 14, 15, 21, 197, 307, 311–13
James II 9, 14, 17, 21, 24, 83, 124, 151–52, 167, 193, 195, 197, 210, 234, 283, 285
Johnson, Samuel 33, 199, 307
Jonson, Ben 104–05, 138, 143, 148, 149, 241, 243
Juvenal xii, 36–37, 148

Kennet, Bishop White 277, 285, 291
Killigrew, Anne 72–73, 124–25
Killigrew, Thomas 82–84, 107, 230
King's Company 83, 84, 109–11

Lee, Nathaniel 91, 94, 95, 96, 112
L'Estrange, Sir Roger 43
Licensing Act (1662) 42, 43, 48 (of 1737) 100
Lillo, George 99
Locke, John 10, 206, 276–306; Essay Concerning Human Understanding 280; Reasonableness of Christianity 277, 281; Two Treatises of Government 23, 173, 193, 281, 283, 284–85
Locke, Matthew 104, 109
Louis XIV 12, 13, 24, 211, 284
Lucian 222n, 258, 269
Lucretius 148, 150–51, 240–41

Mandeville, Bernard xi, 27
Manley, Delariver xii, 97
Martial 131
Marvell, Andrew 132, 165–86; An Account of the Growth of Popery, and Arbitrary Government 166–67, 176; "The Garden" 132, 309; "Flecknoe, An English Priest at Rome" 169; "An Horatian Ode" 120–21, 139, 143–46, 158, 170, 192; "Last Instructions to a Painter" xii, 42–43, 170–71; "The Loyal Scott" 171; "On Mr. Milton's Paradise Lost" 173–74; Miscellaneous Poems 167–68; Mr. Smirke 167; "The Nymph's Complaining" 169; A Poem on the Death of O.C. 187; The Rehearsal Transpros'd 171–72; Short Historical Essay 167; "Upon Appleton House" 170

Mary of Modena, Queen 125, 110, 210
May, Thomas 145
Milton, John 28, 58, 143, 165–84, 185, 240; Areopagitica 63–64, 172; De Doctrina Christiana 173; Eikonoklastes 172, 176; "Nativity Ode" 177; Of True Religion 165, 180; Paradise Lost 59, 65, 151, 173–75, 189, 190–91; Paradise Regained 70, 176–77; Samson Agonistes 59, 165, 176, 177–79, 189; Sonnets 129
Monmouth, James Scott, Duke of 9, 23, 111
Montagu, Edward Wortley 307, 321
Montagu, Lady Mary Wortley xi, 139–40, 276, 307–29; "Constantinople" 315–16; Embassy Letters 276, 314–17; Letters 322; P[ope] to Bolingbroke 321–22; "To Mr. Gay" 309
More, Thomas 259–61
Mulgrave, John Sheffield, Earl of 33, 205, 209

Needham, Marchamont 60
Newcastle, Margaret Cavendish, Duchess of 70, 77–78, 240
Newton, Sir Isaac 133, 264
Nine Years War 12

Oldham, John 33, 45, 128, 149
Orrery, Roger Boyle, Earl of 92–93, 133, 190
Otway, Thomas 94; Alcibiades 94; Don Carlos 94, 95; The Poet's Complaint of His Muse 44; The Souldiers Fortune 90; Venice Preserv'd 85, 96, 194
Ovid 68, 127, 147–48

Palmer, Barbara, Duchess of Cleveland 214
Parnell, Thomas 134
Pepys, Samuel 83, 108
Petronius 147
Philips, Katherine 71, 107, 123–24, 126–27, 132, 237, 241
Pindar 121–28, 148–49
Pix, Mary 97
Pope, Alexander 4, 16, 19, 20, 36, 138, 149, 152–58, 307–29; The Dunciad 41, 51–53, 64, 151, 152–53, 189, 262; "Elegy to the Memory of an Unforunate Lady" 138–39; Epistle to Arbuthnot 153; Epistle to Augustus 28, 38–39, 154–56; Epistle to Burlington 320; Epistle to Cobham 156, 320; Essay on Criticism

156, 188; *First Satire of the Second Book of Horace* 308–09; *Iliad* 40, 156–57, 307; *Imitations of Horace* 153; *Odyssey* 307; *Rape of the Lock* 40–41, 58, 60, 61, 77, 78, 151, 310–11; *Second Satire of the Second Book of Horace* 308, 319–20; *Windsor-Forest* 318–20

Popish Plot 4, 8, 95, 169, 281

Prior, Matthew 131–32

Purcell, Henry xi, 112, 113

Rabelais, François 262, 263

Restoration 4, 39, 42, 44, 58, 64, 68, 120, 122

Richardson, Samuel 62, 78, 233, 258, 278

Rochester, John Wilmot, Earl of 66–68, 130, 204–24, 235–37; "The Advice" 127–28, 206; *An Allusion to Horace* 149, 220; "A Dialogue" 206; "The Disabled Debauchee" 209; "Fair Chloris in a pigsty lay" 214; "How happy Cloris" 217; "The Imperfect Enjoyment" 208–09, 211; "To a Lady in a Letter" 67; "Letter from Artemiza in the Towne" 215; "Love a Woman! y'are an Ass" 212, 235; "Platonick Lady" 214; "A Ramble in Saint James's Parke" 206, 212–14, 215, 309; "Satire on Charles II" 210; "Satyr Against Reason and Mankind" 35, 40, 209; "Signior Dildo" 214; *Sodom* 211; "Song" 127, 217; "To longe the Wise Commons" 206; 'Upon His Drinking a Bowl" 130, 218; "Upon Nothing" 218–19; *Valentinian* 220

Roscommon, Wentworth Dillon, Earl of 122, 133, 158

Rowe, Elizabeth 127, 139–40

Rowe, Nicholas 99

Rye House Plot 23

Sacheverell, Dr. Henry 14, 21, 287

Scroope, Sir Carr 204, 205

Sedley, Sir Charles 95

Settle, Elkanah 85, 94, 96, 109

Shadwell, Thomas 47, 89, 97, 109, 110, 111, 191

Shaftesbury, Anthony Ashley Cooper, 1st Earl of 34, 70, 169

Shaftesbury, Anthony Ashley Cooper, 3rd Earl of 28, 277

Shakespeare, William 93, 95–96, 108, 155, 158, 191, 228, 241, 243, 278

Sheridan, Richard 91

Sherlock, Bishop William 289–90

Shirley, James 104

Sidney, Algernon xi, 23, 173

Sidney, Sir Philip 188, 240

South Sea Company 12, 15

Southerne, Thomas 92, 196, 232

Spectator 13, 28

Spenser, Edmund 63, 199, 278

Stanley, Thomas 129

Steele, Richard 28, 98, 278

Sterne, Laurence 261

Stuart, James Francis Edward, "the Old Pretender" 14, 197

Swift, Jonathan 13, 16, 19, 153, 250–75; *Argument Against Abolishing Christianity* 267; *Battle of the Books* 263; *Bickerstaff Papers* 37, 55; *Drapier Letters* 55; "An Epistle to a Lady" 70; *Examiner* 13; *Gulliver's Travels* 40, 50, 53–55, 225, 250–56, 259–61; *The Mechanical Operation of the Spirit* 263; *Meditation Upon a Broomstick* 55; *Memoirs of Martin Scriblerus* 50; *Modest Proposal* xii, 53, 55, 266–67; *A Proposal for the English Tongue* 265; *Tale of A Tub* 34–35, 37, 39, 40, 53, 55, 189, 198, 261, 264, 277

Tate, Nahum 96

Tonson, Jacob 148, 199, 216, 236

Tories xii, 14, 17, 20–23, 130, 153, 193, 277, 279

Traherne, Thomas 135

Trotter, Catherine 97

Tuke, Samuel 96

Tyrrell, James 173

United Company 111

Vanbrugh, Sir John 89, 92, 112

Vaughan, Henry 135

Virgil xii, 40, 138, 146–47, 150, 156, 188, 199, 200

Waller, Edmund 145–46, 148

Walpole, Sir Robert 5, 15–16, 51, 100, 114, 307, 312, 321

Watts, Isaac 136

Wesley, John 4

Wharton, Anne 68, 79n6, 247n38

Whigs and Whiggery 9–24, 120, 135, 167, 258, 283, 307

William III   xiii, 10, 12, 20–23, 48, 96, 125–26, 197, 200, 283, 293, 312, 319
Winchilsea: *see* Finch, Anne, Countess of Winchilsea
Wycherly, William   40, 91; *The Country Wife*   69, 91, 92; *The Gentleman Dancing-Master*   91–92; *The Plain Dealer*   69

York, James, Duke of: *see* James II
Young, Edward   125